J.D. Roth

Handbook of Lutheranism

First Edition

J.D. Roth

Handbook of Lutheranism
First Edition

ISBN/EAN: 9783337042974

Printed in Europe, USA, Canada, Australia, Japan

Cover: Foto ©Lupo / pixelio.de

More available books at **www.hansebooks.com**

HAND-BOOK

OF

LUTHERANISM

BY

J. D. ROTH,

Associate Editor of The Young Lutheran, and Pastor of the Lutheran Church of the Holy Trinity, Catasauqua, Pennsylvania.

FIRST EDITION.

Utica, N. Y.
The Young Lutheran Company.
1891.

PREFACE.

TO walk about Zion and go round about her, to tell the towers thereof and mark well her bulwarks, to consider her palaces, and to tell it to the generations following, is the purpose of this volume. The obstacles to the attainment of such purpose regarding a Church having worldwide organization, more than a half hundred million membership, and polyglot utterance, are known to those only who have experience of them. In such a volume whose almost every sentence is a statement of fact, or of figures, absolute accuracy is not attainable. Substantial accuracy and a sincere purpose are the Author's claim.

In now committing his labor of love to the tender mercy of his patrons, due consideration is asked of the fact that his is pioneer work; to the Author's knowledge, nothing of its kind hitherto having been attempted.

With due acknowledgments to all who have aided him, and particularly to Rev. Theo. B. Roth and his good wife, Amalie, who have read the proofs and seen the work through the press, with devout prayer that through it God's name may be honored and the cause of our dear Church advanced, this book is now sent forth, in the interest of Truth, by

THE AUTHOR.

ADVENT, 1891.

ERRATA.

In addition to a few typographical inaccuracies, and discrepancies in figures, occasioned by fuller reports, in the process of condensing matter into shorter space, several annoying errors have crept in. On page 18, for now Prussian, read non-Prussian; page 178, opposite Germany, for 5,550, read 15,550; page 290, for William I., read Frederick William IV. page 355, fourteenth line from top, the sentence should read The Norwegians have one convert on Mission stations for every 125 members in the home church; page 388, opposite Templeton, being established, strike out the figures; [these figures run through a portion of the edition only;] page 470, the author's table of Lutherans in the world should have appeared at close of Chapter VII.

INDEX.

Aalborg..................................... 80
Aarhus...................................... 80
Abo...161
Abyssinia...................................309
Academies.................. 378, 387, 440-1
Addison, Ill.............399, 400, 440, 443
Adrian......................................440
Africa............179, 180, 408, 471. (See F. M.)
" East................................. 173
" West..................................292
Afton......................406, 412, 438, 440
Aged, Homes for...378, 383, 384, 388, 390, 399, 403, 413, 432, 446. (See under In. Missions.)
Ahlberg, Miss'n School.....................276
Aid Soc. for Ev. Churches.......243, 268, 285
Albert Lea............................412, 440
Albert, Prince.............................. 65
Alabama....................................454
Alexandria.............................291, 292
Allegheny Synod................382, 453, 454
Allentown.............................387, 430
Alpha Synod................................401
Algiers...............................175, 350
Alsace Lorraine.............9, 74, 176, 470
Altdorf, O. H..............................289
Altona...........................41, 251, 306
Ambulatory Schools.........................131
American Religion Suspected................ 16
America, N......................179, 374, 471
America, S............................179, 471
Andersen, Hans............................. 82
Andover, O. H.........................388, 443
Andrew, O. H..........................388, 443
Anhalt................................176, 470
Antananarivo...............................355
Apprentices' Homes. (See In. Missions.)
Arabs, Deaconesses Among..............290-1
Archbishops, Lutheran...........115, 143, 164
Argentine Republic.............174, 179, 471
Arkansas...................................455
Arizona....................................454
Armen-Pflege............................... 28
Arnheim....................................306
Ashanti....................................332
Ashland Academy......................412, 440
Asia, Lutherans in..............177, 179, 471
Asia Minor.................................174
Assiniboia.................................468
Atchison, College.................... 383, 439
Augsburg.........................46, 47, 306
" College........................ 412, 439
" Synod............. 411, 442, 453
Augustana College..............387, 438, 439
" Synod.........385 ff, 387, 442, 453
Australia. (See F. M.)........171, 179, 471
Austria...................168-9, 177, 299, 470
Austro-Hungary, Lutherans in.....168 f, 255
(See under In. Missions.)
Baden, Lutherans in.............177, 180, 470
Baltic Islands..............................156
Baltic Provinces.145, 149, 152, 155, 177, 280, 308
Character of settlers...................153
Integrity of...........................154 f.

Baltimore........................378, 399, 444
Baptists in Sweden......................119 f.
Bavaria............9, 46, 176-7, 180, 470
Missions in..........................285, 339
Basel F. M. Soc.....254, 318, 320, 331, 349. (See For. Missions.)
Batus. (See For. Missions)................ 338
Beneficence...29, 32, 36, 38, 39, 41, 43, 44, 47, 63, 65, 74, 148, 149, 170, 231, 235, 384. (See Contributions, In. Miss's, Deaconesses, Homes for Aged, Funds, Women's Societies, Pensions, Orphan's Homes.)
In U. S..377-8, 383, 388, 390, 403, 413, 427, 429, 430, 433, 443-6, 453.
Beirut, Deaconesses in......................291
Beloit................................413, 444
Bergen, City...............................137
Berlin, City.........................31, 235
Art and Science........................ 32
City Mission Societies..............235, 244
Bookstore............................211-2
Boy Choirs.............................240
Chapel Societies.......................243
Children's Fresh Air Society...........247
Christian Inns.........................246
Churches...............................236
Deacons in.............................246
Deaconesses in..............32, 245, 306, 294
Ev. Soc. for Church Work...............243
Fund for Beneficence................... 248
Girls, Helping.........................240
Helping Societies................ 239, 243
Homes for Poor.......................241-2
Hospices..........................240-2-4-6
Income of..............................243
Industrial Schools.....................240
Invalids, Aiding.......................247
Literature...........................241-2-4
Local Press Used.......................242
Periodicals and Sermons................241
Provincial Aid Societies.............240-7
Prisons, Work in................. 240, 246
Sewing Societies.......................243
Soc. for Young Men................239, 244
" for Ev. Education..................239
" vs. Immorality.....................246
" for Magdalens.....................243-7
Women's Societies............240, 243, 247
Young Men's............................238
Young Women's..........................239
Women, Dependent......................245
Education................ 14, 31, 235
For. Miss. Soc 239, 317. (See For. Miss.) 370.
Jerusalem Society..................174, 387
Jewish Miss. Soc.......................272
Libraries.............................. 32
and London.............................237
New Churches...........................236
People (90 per cent.) Baptized.........237
Population.............................235
Schools................................236
University.............................207
Bern, Deaconesses..........................306
Beth Eden, Col. Inst.................403, 440

Bethany College. 387, 439
Bethlehem, Mission in............. 174
Bielefeld 261, 262, 297, 306
Bible Soc., First Prot..............264
Others..................281, 282, 285
Bible Translations. (See Foreign Missions.)
Bishops, Lutheran.... 87, 115, 140, 143, 164, 169
Bithynia............................ 175
Black Sea, Lutherans on......145, 178, 470
Blair, Neb., Seminary.......412, 438, 440
Blomstrand............................318
Bodelschwing, Pastor von............261
Bode, Luther Acad'y...........412, 441
Bombay, Deaconesses..............292
Books, New, Germany..........211, 264
Other lands.................... 211
In Foreign Tongues........270, 313-4
Bookstores, Christian.........241, 285
Book Trade, German 52, 53, 56
Bonn.............................. 215
Borgo............................161
Borneo, Lutherans in........179, 323, 333, 470
Bosphorus, Lutherans on.............175
Boston, Immigrant Mission.....388, 413, 444
Brandenburg..................30-33, 176
In, Missions................225, 258
Brazil, Church in,.............174-9
Brecklum Mission Society......254, 337, 407
Bremen................177, 306, 309, 470
Breslau...............215, 294. 306, 36, 248
Synod .... 22 f.
"Brook Farm"....................460
Brooklyn, Deaconesses in........415, 446
Immigrant Mission........413, 444
St. Luke's Academy.........400, 440
Brothers. (See Deacons.)
Brun, Malte...................... 82
Brunswick........... 9. 62, 63, 176-7, 306, 470
Bucharest, Deaconesses in...........293
Budapest, Deaconesses in..........299
Buffalo, Synod 411, 438, 443, 453
College and Seminary 412
Orphans' Home................ 388, 443
Burkhardt-Grundemann F. M. Lib......339
Cairo, Deaconesses in 292
California, Lutherans........382, 455
Callenberg and the Jews 270
Cameroons .... 292, 332 ff.
Campanius...................... 308
Canada Lutherans........387, 442, 453, 454, 468
Canstein Bible Soc.................264
Canton, S. D., College.........412, 430
Cape Colony........173, 177, 325, 338 f.
Capital University..............438, 439
Carthage College..............383, 439
Catalogues for People's Libraries.264. (See Press, Using.)
Catechising................122, 346
Catharine II.....................145
Caucasus.....................146, 276
Central Illinois Synod......... 453. 382, 454
Central Pennsylvania Synod......453, 382, 454
Cetewayo's Nephew.................350
Chapel Societies...................243
Charity, Practical.219, 226. (See In. Missions, Religion, Practical.)
Charles IX and Missions.............308
Charleston, Hospital, &c..........403
Chicago, Hospitals, &c. 388, 414, 445, 446
Seminaries...................383, 438
Children's Mission Societies......379, 401

Children, Caring for, 219, 250-1, 255-8. 290, (see In. Miss.)..................431
Schools for, 232, 255, 258-9, 285, 289, 290, 294, 303. (See under In. Missions.)
Fresh Air Society, for............247
(See Deaconesses and In. Missions.)
Chili........................114, 179
China, see F. M.)................. 178, 471
China Grove.......................403, 441
Christian IX.........................81
Christiania............. .....136-7, 306
Mission School....................274
Christiansand....................140
Christian Inns.............223-5, 259
In Cities, 224, 225, 240, 252, 256, 257, 259, 285, 303.
For Girls............225, 240, 253, 256, 259
Y. M. C. A. and........................226
Christianity, Practical.....14, 226, 242, 244, 249
Christina, Queen.............308. (See Love.)
Christlieb.....................15, 340
Church and State...........17, 23, 84, 235, 241
Church Buildings, Good or Noted...29. 32, 34, 37-8, 40, 47-8, 57, 63, 66, 71, 74, 79, 103, 105, 106, 108, 139, 149, 150, 151.
Church Extension..............379, 384, 408
Church Government..............24, 29, 84
Church Song, German....................15
City Missions, 235, 239 ff, 248, 251, 269, 255, 257, 278, 280, 283.
City Missionaries' Work............. 238, 252
Clerical Acts, Prussia................ 27
Coburg...........................65, 214
Coffee Houses................256, 260
Coins, Foreign......................373
College, that Log....................395
Colleges, Aim of......... ....386, 389, 393, 405
Course of Study..................392-3
Expenses...............386, 393-4, 406-7
And Universities..................198
Colleges... 378, 387, 400, 403, 407, 412, 438, 441
College Point, O. H...........399, 444
Colorado.. ....383, 382
Columbus, College and Seminary..405, 412, 438
Columbia, Seminary............... 403, 438
Colportage Houses....................285
Colporteurs................253, 264, 270
Corcordia College.............439, 400
Concordia Seminary.....394-7, 400, 438
Concordia, Mo.................400, 439
Congo...........................351-2, 471
Connecticut..........................455
Conover College......................403
Consistories........24, 29, 30, 33, 143, 146-8, 164
Constantinople, Deaconesses..291-2, 401, 402, 403, 404, 405, 407, 408.
Contributions, Church..28, 217, 251, 252, 253-6, 258, 262, 272-6, 280, 284, 285. (See Funds and Pensions,) 290, 378-9, 380-1, 383, 384. 386-7, 388, 389, 390, 391, 392, 393, 399. 400
Copenhagen..........76, 77-9, 208, 213, 280, 306
Women's Miss. Society.......... 278
Cork (Ireland) Deaconesses...............302
Courland.....................9, 151, 176
Cox, S. S., on the Finns..............150
Conover...........................439
Croatia..........................109
Crime and In. Missions.........16, 108, 261, 265
Crimea............................. 145
Crischona Pilgrim Mission.............297
Dahomey..........................333

INDEX.

Dakota..........456
Dallas, Gaston College........403, 439, 441
Dampier Archipelago..........328
Danes..........81
Danish Missions......276-8, 311 ff
Danish Church Association...410, 411, 442, 453
Danish Church in America....409, 411, 442, 458
Danish West Indies..........9, 77
Danzig..........9, 77, 295 306
Darmstadt..........69, 214, 298, 306
Day Nurseries....231-2, 250, 256, 307, 432. (See under In. Missions.)
Deaconesses, Modern..........229, 286 ff, 426
  Beginning..........229, 286, 426
  Christ-like work..........229, 234, 286
  Course of Study..........233, 432
  Convalescent Homes.288, 290, 293, 298, 299, 300
  Family, Connected with..........233
  Fields of Work..........306-7
  Filial Institutions..........289
  Growth..........285-9, 302, 306-7
  Hospital..290, 294. (See under In. Missions)
  Income..........294, 303, 306-7
  Kaiserswerth..........286-9
  Money Value of Work..........234
  Mother-Houses...233, 293, 295-9, 300, 302, 306, 338, 413, 432, 446.
  Number of..........303, 306
  Parish Work......230 ff, 306. (See under In. Missions.)
  Royal Favor.221, 288, 290, 293, 294, 296, 299, 300
  Scriptural Idea of..........286
  Social Equality..........233
  Tables of..........306-7
  War. Service in..........228, 301
  Some Phases of Labor..........232, 306
Africa..........255, 334, 337
Africa, East..........222, 331
Africa, West..........292
Alexandria..........291-2
Altdorf..........289
Altona..........41, 251, 306
Arabs, Among..........291
Arnheim..........306
Augsburg..........47, 298, 306
Austro-Hungary..........255, 290, 302
Berlin..........32, 245, 294, 206
  Wants More..........245
Bern..........306
Bethania House..........245, 296
Bielefeld..........297, 306
Beirout..........291
Bombay..........292
Bremen..........299
Breslau..........294, 306
Brooklyn..........433
Brunswick..........299
Budapest..........293, 299
Bucharest..........293
Cairo..........292
Cameroons..........292
Cassel..........306
Chicago..........430
China..........336
Christiania..........300
Copenhagen..........300
Constantinople..........291-2
Cork, Ireland..........302
Darmstadt..........298
Danzig..........295
Denmark..........300
Dresden..........257, 297

Deaconesses—Dublin, Ireland..........302
Düsseldorf..........289
Egypt..........232, 292
England..........255, 292, 316, 336
Eraschniss..........295
Erefeld..........290
Flensburg..........42, 251, 297
Florence..........293
France..........170, 255, 299
Frankenstein..........295
Frankfort, a. M..........296
Gallneukirche..........299
Greeks, Among..........291
Haarlem..........306
Hague..........306
Halle..........296
Hamburg..........299
Hanover..........296
Hattingen..........290
Helsen..........306
Helsingfors..........302, 306
Hesse..........290
Holland..........290
Hottentots..........255
Italy..........255, 293
Jacksonville..........430
Jerusalem..........174, 290
Kaffirs..........255
Kaiserswerth, (see Kaiserswerth.)
Karlsruhe..........306
Königsberg..........295
Kraschnitz..........306
London..........221-2, 302
Ludwigslust..........316
Madagascar..........301
Madeira..........292
Madras..........282
Mannheim..........306
Mecklenburg..........297
Milwaukee..........427-480
Minneapolis..........433
Mitau..........301
Mohammedans..........290-2, 307
Neuendettelsau..........298
New Torney..........296
New York..........445, 446-7
Norway..........300, 306
Nowawes..........306
Omaha..........433
Palestine..........232, 290 ff
Paris..........306
Pesth..........306
Philadelphia..........306, 431
Pittsburg..........293, 426
Pomerania..........231
Port Said..........292
Posen..........296
Potsdam..........290
Reval..........301
Riga..........301
Rochester..........293, 431
Rome..........298
Russia..........221-2, 255, 292, 301
St. Loup..........306
St. Petersburg..........301
Sarata..........301
Sarepta..........292
Saxony..........297
Schleswig-Holstein..........250-1
Silesia..........295
Smyrna..........291
Sobernheim..........306

INDEX.

Deaconesses—Speyer..................298
Stettin............................295-6
Stockholm..........................300
Stralsund..........................296
Strassburg.........................297
Stuttgart..........................298
Sunderland.........................302
Sweden........................300, 306
Switzerland........................299
Syria..............................291
Tabris.............................292
Turks..............................291
Tyrol..............................299
Utretcht...........................306
Vienna.............................299
Westphalia.........................293
Wilborg............................306
Zanzibar...........................292
Zurich.............................306
Deacons.................220, 228, 286
Fields of Work 170, 221-2, 246, 257, 259
Royal Favor....................221, 246
Training..............227-9, 246, 257, 285
Deaf and Dumb, Caring for. (See under In. Missions.)
Death Rate, Denmark................80
Decorah, Institutions..........412, 439
Deep Sea Fishers...................275
Degrees, Honorary..................201
Delano, O. H..............399, 443, 446
Delaware, Lutherans on......308, 347. 456
Delitzsch, and Jews.............271-2
Denmark, Land and People.....75, 83, 176
  Education and Religion.........82-7
  Lutherans in......9, 83, 87, 176, 180, 470
  Missions in, 87, 278, 290, 309, 310, 311, 313, 358, 360, 364, 374.
  Royal Relations..................81
Des Peres, Mo...................399, 443
Detmold Library....................214
Dioceses 25, 29, 30. 33, 168, 169
Diaspora Missions........266-7, 305, 311, 368
District of Columbia..........383, 456
District Synod of Ohio....387, 442, 453, 454, 464
Dorpat.................148, 150, 207. 215
Dresden...........................50-2
  Missions in,..............297, 306, 318
Dress, Church......................15
Drexel Mother-House...............433
Drink Habit.........104, 108, 250, 259, 260
Drontheim.....................138, 309
Dublin, Lutherans in,..........278, 392
Dubuque, Seminary............387, 438
Düsseldorf.........................289
Easton........................432, 445
East Ohio Synod............382, 453, 454
East Penna. Synod..........382, 453, 454
East Prussia.......................29
Edelweiss Women's Soc.............247
Education, German, 49, 181 ff. (See Schools, Universities, Lutheranism, and Learning.)
  Scandinavian, 192 ff. (See Schools, etc., as in Germany.)
  Lutheran, in U. S., 377-8, 379, 383, 387, 388-9, 392-398, 400, 403, 412. 433 f.
Education and Lutheranism. (See Illiteracy, Lutheranism and Learning, Schools, Universities, Libraries, Religion in Schools, Parochial Schools.)
Edwardsville, Ala..................403
Eisenach...........................66
Egypt, Missions.......174, 177-8, 232, 292, 337

Egede, Hans........................353
Elizabeth, Queen...................294
Elk Horn...............412, 413, 440. 444
England and Lutheran Kings...42, 64. 141, 167
  And Lutheran Missions......316-8, 336
English Synod of Iowa..............382
English Tongue and Germans........392
Enochville....................403, 440
Epileptics, Homes for, 262. (See under In. Missions.)
Episcopacy, Lutheran. (See Bishops.)
Eraschnis..........................295
Erefeld, Deaconesses...............290
Erlangen...........................215
Erfurt.........................37-8
Estates, Large.....................105
Esthonia..............9, 151, 176, 281
Europe. Lutherans in...........177-9, 471
Ev. Aid Society, (See Aid Societies,) 268, 232, 285.
Ev. League....................268, 285
Factory Girls, Homes for......256, 279
Faith and Works. (See Christianity, Practical; Fliedner; Inner Missions; Wichern.)
Falun.........................107, 365
Faroe Islands........9, 76-7, 176, 180, 470
Fatherland Mission Society..275, 285, 351
Fatherland Women's Society........299
Feejee Islands................179, 471
Filial (Deaconess') Homes.........289
Finland, Land and People....157, 163, 176, 361
  Missions.....................281 ff, 361
  School and Church........163 ff, 280, 470
Finnish Church in America.........411
Fishermen, North Sea..............275
Fjellstedt Mission School.........276
Flensburg.............42. 251, 296, 306
Fliedner and Deaconesses, 228, 286. 239, 292, 294, 295, 297, 426.
Fliegende Blätter.................222
Flierl.........................337-8
Florence, Deaconesses in..........293
Florida, Lutherans in.............456
Flower Mission....................280
Foreign Missions, Lutheran....308 ff, 364-373
  Bible in Heathen Tongues 308-9, 312-3, 314, 327-9, 330-4. 351.
  First Societies for.....308-9, 314, 343, 358
  Fostering Spirit of, 34, 45, 192, 340. (See Mission Literature and Press, Using the.)
  Grammars, &c., in Heathen Tongues, 312-14
  Literature. 264, 320, 324-5, 331, 336 339 ff, 351, 355, 360, 372.
  Literature for Heathen, 308-9, 312, 326, 328, 332, 343, 348.
  Not Always Popular..............310
  Offerings for............305, 362-3
  Royal Favor..........308. 314. 343
  Schools in Heathen Lands......320 ff
  Seminaries 308, 314, 317, 324, 325-8, 331, 343 ff, 261.
  Seminaries in Heathen Lands, 318, 320, 322, 325-6-8, 330, 334-5, 355, 370.
  Statistics....................364-370
  Students' Societies......342, 352, 355
  Synods....................326-7, 329 ff
Foreign Mission Fields........308. 370
Abyssinia.........................309
Africa..................173, 322 ff, 350
Alaska............................365
Algiers...........................350

Foreign Mission Fields—Australia, 172, 177, 318, 323, 337, 407
Baltic Sea..351
Bassuto Land.............................330, 337
Betu Land..338
Behring's Sound................................352
Bellore..359
Borneo.....................................327, 333
Cameroons....................................324 ff
Cape Colony.....................173, 325, 328 ff
Caucasus...351
Cayenne..310
China, 303, 328, 330, 333, 335, 336-7, 350, 352, 356-7, 360.
Congo..351-2
Coromandel Coast............................309
Croatia.....................................169, 308
Dampier Archipelago.........................328
Delaware, on the.......................308, 347
Demarara..343
East Africa.....222, 330, 334, 335, 337, 351, 356
Egypt..............................232, 292, 337
Essequibo..310
Farther India....................................337
Ganges, on the.................................325
Georgia..311
Gold Coast......................277, 310, 332
Greenland............................310, 353 ff
Hawaaii..333
Herero Land.....................................326
Hottentots.......................................329
India,...311, 313, 321, 332, 336, 407, 350-1, 359, 360, 362-3.
Indians, N. A......................308, 311, 348
Japan.................................335, 360, 401
Jerusalem..407
Kaffirs, Among................................361
King William's Land...................328, 339
Kohls...324
Lapland, 308-9, 310, 343, 350. (See Lapland.)
Liberia...362
Madagascar..................................354 ff.
Mahrattas..332
Namaqualand...................................326
Natal...............................322, 329, 354, 356
New Guinea.................328, 335, 338, 407
New Zealand....................................328
Nias...327
Orange Free State.....................322, 329
Orient...305
Ovamboland....................................361
Palestine..174, 337. (See Deaconesses, In. Missions.)
Persia......................................309, 351
Polar Sea...351
Red Karens......................................359
Red Sea Coast.................................351
Sangi Islands...................................325
Santalistan..............................352, 359
Siar..328
Slave Coast.....................................333
Sumatra.......................................326-7
Syria..174, 337
Tamils..312 ff
Tartary..............................311, 319, 324
Toba Sea...327
Togoland...334
Transvaal Republic..................322, 329
Tranquebar.................311, 319, 358-9
Turks (See Deaconesses Among.).......308
United States..................................347
Wends, Among...............................308

Foreign Mission Fields—West Africa, 324, 333-4
West Indies.....................................310
Zulu Land............322, 329, 350, 355-6
(See also, Deaconess, Denmark.)
Foreign Mission Societies............308-378
Tables of..................................364-373
Anagar Association..........................352
Basel..318, 331
Bavarian...334
Berlin I.................................173, 328 ff
Berlin, for E. Africa..................337, 365
Brecklum...................................337, 365
China, Inland...................................356
Com. for Red Karens.......................359
Danish Church............................358-9
Ev. Prot. for Orient.........................335
Ev. Fatherland.................................351
Ev., for E. Africa. (See Berlin, for.)
Falun Soc..305
Finnish....................................361, 365
Gen'l Council Com...................363, 384
Gen'l Synod Board....................362, 379
German and Scandinavian................388
Gossner...................................324, 364
Hermansburg........................173, 321-324
Holland, Lutheran............................338
Immanuel Synod.......................335, 338
Jerusalem, Berlin.....................174, 337
Jönkopping Union............................366
Leipsic...320
Missouri Synod........................303, 391
Neuendettelsau.........................334-5-6-7-8
North German.........................370, 383
Norwegian....................................354 ff
Norwegian, U. S..............................363
Norwegian, China....................357, 363
Ohio (Joint) Synod..........................366
Paris Ev..337
Queensland Synod...........................338
Rhenish......................................370, 325, 364
Santal Com.......................352, 355, 360
Schleswig-Holstein. (See Brecklum.)
Soc. for China..................................337
Schreuder Com....................352, 354 ff
Skrefsund..356
Students (See Students' Societies.)
Swedish Church.............................340
"   Mission Union..........................352
United Synod..........................366, 401
Women's. (See Women's Societies.)....363
Women's Soc. for the East................336
"   China.................................336
Some Foreign Missionaries.308, 309, 310, 311, 314, 344, 353.
Fort Wayne, Ind......................400, 430
France.....................170, 177, 299, 470
Francke.................................39, 266, 270
Franckean Synod.................382, 453, 454
Frankenstein............................295, 306
Frankfort "A. M."..........9, 176, 296, 306
Free-Will Nurses.............................228
Frederick, O. B.......................383, 443
Frederick Franz II...........................298
Frederick William IV.................241, 415
Frederickshamm..............................302
Freedmen, Among.....................391, 402
Free Church Party...........................124
French Papers.................................432
Fromman.......................................270
Funds, Beneficent.45, 248, 254-6, 281, 283, 284-5. (See Pensions.) 381.
Gallneukirche.........................299, 306

Garden of the Gods..........................455
Gaston College...................403, 439, 441
Giessen...............................70, 216
General Council............363, 381 ff, 453, 469
General Synod............................24, 362
"   U. S......377 ff, 382-4, 453, 469
George I., England...........................221
Georgia, Lutherans in.....311, 402, 453, 454, 457
German Hospital............................431
Germans and Religion in America..........16
Germans in United States..................375
Germany and Church in.................13-28
Independent Lutherans................22, 176
Learning in, 180-192. (See Schools and Universities.)
Lutherans.......17-20, 21-23, 177, 178, 376, 470
Missions. (See Deaconesses, Diaspora Missions, For. Miss., In. Miss., Jewish Miss., Seamen's Miss.)
Germantown, Institutions........388, 443, 446
Gettysburg, Institutions..............383, 438
Giessen...................................204
Girls, Christian Inns for, 225, 240, 253. (See under Christian Inns, In. Miss.)
Schools and Homes for, 225, 256, 259, 289-291, 293, 302, 432.
Gold Coast Missions.............277, 310, 332
Gossner and Deaconess......................291
Mission Society.....................324, 364
Gotha.................................65, 214
Gothenburg.........................103-4, 214
Gottingen.................................204
Gotteskasten..............................285
Graham, Va............................403, 441
Granite Falls Seminary...............412, 440
Gravelton College.....................412, 439
Great Britain, Lutherans, 177, 470. (See England and Lutheran Kings.)
Greeks, Teaching them.....................291
Greenland, Land and People........352 ff, 471
Church in..................................83
Missions.........................310, 353 ff
Greensburg, Seminary.................387, 441
Greenville, College..................439, 387
Guiana....................................468
Grundemann...............................339
Guilds, Church............................250
Guntur Mission College...............383, 439
Gust. Adolf. College.................387, 439
Gust. Adolf. Union........254, 267, 2:5, 304, 308
Gymnasiums.............................195-6
Haarlem, Deaconesses......................306
Hague, Deaconesses........................306
Hagerstown, College..................353, 441
Halberstadt..............................37, 39
Halle...................87, 89, 206, 260, 270
Bible Society and Press......264, 311, 313, 340
Hamar.....................................140
Hamburg.....................70, 73, 399, 470
Deaconesses.....................297, 299, 206
Lutherans in.......................9, 71, 176-7
Handel.....................................39
Hanover...............................42, 43
Deaconesses......................296, 299, 306
And Kings of England,......................42
Funds.....................................285
Lutherans................9, 42, 44, 176, 180
Missions, 44, 259. (See Hermansburg F. M. Soc.)
Harkey, S. W., Dr., quoted.................397
Harless....................................46
Harms................................321-324

Harper's Monthly, quoted..................397
Hartwick, Institutions............383, 438, 440
Hartwick, Synod..................382, 453, 454
Hattingen.................................290
Hauge, Synod.........................410, 411
Hawaiian Islands.....................179, 471
Hebrew Colony, N. Y......................392
Hebrew, Christian Books in,...........270-273
Heidelberg................................215
Heilbronn..................................55
Heligoland.........................9, 176-7, 470
Helmstadt..................................68
Helsen, Deaconesses.......................306
Helsingfors.....................148, 160, 209
Deaconesses....................301-2, 306
Hermansburg F. M. Soc. (See under For. Missions.)
Hereros, Missions Among...................326
Herschel...................................43
Hesse.........................69, 296, 470
Hesselholm Mission Soc.,..................276
Heyling...................................309
Hickory, Institutions.........406, 412, 438, 440
Hildesheim.................................44
Hindostan, Lutherans in...................178
Historical Society........................381
Holland..................170, 177, 299, 470
Missions...........................334, 365
Holston Synod......................402, 453, 454
Holls, J. C...............................435
Home Missions, 378, 382, 384, 392, 393, 401, 404, 406, 407, 409, 410, 453.
Honest People...................98, 111, 135
Hospices........224, 240, 242, 244, 246, 256, 298
Hospitals, 299 ff, 285. (See under In. Miss.)
In U. S.,..378, 383, 384, 388, 390, 399, 403, 413, 426 ff, 431, 445, 468.
Hottentots, Among.....................255, 329
Hudson Bay, Danes on......................277
Hungary....................255, 299, 302, 470
Hyder Ali.................................315
Iceland.................................89-98
Church in.....................93, 94, 96-7
Education......................91, 93, 98
Lava-Beds..................................89
Lutherans in...........9, 91, 96, 176, 180, 470
No Prisons..................................98
Pure and Guileless.........................98
Icelandic Church Union..........410, 411, 453
Idaho, Lutherans in.......................457
Ilex, Academy........................403, 440
Illinois, Lutherans.................453, 457
Illiteracy............................183-185
Immanuel Synod........................22, 411
Immigrants, Caring for, 266. (See Diaspora Missions.)
Immigrant Missions, 285, 381, 384, 388, 390, 399, 413, 414, 446.
Immigrants in U. S........375 ff, 389, 415, 436
Immorality, Soc's Against.................247
Independent Lutherans.....................176
Independent Pastors and Synods, 404 ff, 410 ff, 460.
Independent Scandinavian Synods......409, 411
India, 177, 309, 311 ff, 277, 314, 329. (See Foreign Missions),........................471
Indiana, Lutherans in.....................458
Indiana Synod.....................387, 453, 454
Indianapolis, O. H...................399, 413
Indian-Mission School................412, 440
Indians. (See Foreign Missions.)..........468
Indies, West, (See Foreign Missions.)

INDEX.

Industrial Education, 138, 196, 240, 252, 255, 257, 296,297, 298, 299, 307.
Ingweiler, Deaconesses...................306
Inhospitable Lands..........76, 89, 90, 127, 135
Inner Missions, (See City Missions, Deacons, Deaconesses, Diaspora Missions, Ev. League, Free-Will Nurses, G. A. Union, Jewish Missions, Seamen's Missions, Gotteskasten, &c.) pp. 213, 307.
  Aim of..............................14, 219
  Beginning..............................218-9
  Children and (See under In. Mission Fields.)
  Crime, and (See Crime.)
  History of..........................249 ff.
  Institutes..........................305, 368
  Instruction Courses............255-6, 258
  Offerings for, 305. (See Contributions,) 306-7
  Summary of work...........285, 305, 306-7
  Wichern (and See Wichern.)
Inner Mission Societies..................285
  Danish.................278, 279, 280, 285
  German................32, 249-265, 285
  Norwegian............273, 274, 275, 285
  Russian.....................222, 281 ff, 285
  Swedish................275, 276, 285, 351
  U. S.................................425 ff, 437.
Inner Missions, Spheres of Labor.
  Bible Soc's. (See Bible Soc's.)
  Blind, Homes for................285, 304
  Book-Stores, Christian..................285
  Book and Tract Soc's.............285,305
  (See Press, Using.)
  Children, Homes for..........251, 298, 301
  Kindergartens..........................257
  Schools for. 47, 232, 251, 255, 250, 293, 295-6-7-8 299, 301, 302, 306.
  Training Homes, 255, 257, 259, 296, 299, 300, 303.
  Sick..............217, 251, 294, 296, 431, 434
  Christian Inns. (See Christian Inns.)
  Coffee Houses....................256, 260
  Day Nurseries, 47, 231, 251, 256, 297, 299, 307
  Deaconesses, Training, (See Deaconess' Mother-Houses.)
  Deacons' Institutes, (See under Deacons.)
  Deaf, Homes for...................285, 304
  Free-Will Nurses.......................228
  Girls, Homes for (See under Girls.)
  Girls, Schools for.............298, 300, 304
  (See Under Girls.)
  Sunday Soc's for..................258, 259
  Training Homes for........225, 298-9, 300
  Homes for Aged............296, 298, 300, 301
    " " Deaf...................285, 304
    " " Epileptics, 262, 295, 297, 298, 302, 304, 307.
  Homes for Factory Girls.............256, 279
    " " Invalids, 251, 295, 296, 297, 298, 299, 300, 301, 306.
  Homes for Magdalens, 258, 279, 280, 290, 294, 297, 300, 304, 306.
  Homes for Mechanics.............256, 259
  (See Christian Inns.)
  Homes for Poor, 242, 258, 259, 293, 300, 802, 304.
  Homes for Servants, 258 260, 279, 289, 293, 297, 300, 307.
  Homes for Wanderers..................259
    " " Women................259, 260
    " " Sick.................260, 299
    " " Week-Minded........302, 304, 307
  Hospices, (See Hospices.)

Inner Missions, Spheres of Labor.
  Bible Soc's. (See Bible Soc's.)
  Hospitals, 29, 32, 36, 39, 41, 44, 47, 63, 79, 251, 255, 293, 295, 296, 297, 300, 301, 307. (See Hospitals.)
  Hospitals for Men, 251, 292, 295, 297, 298, 300, 301, 302.
  Immorality, Soc's against................247
  Industrial Schools, (See Industrial Schools.)
  Labor Colonies, 304. (See Labor Colonies.)
  Libraries and Reading-Rooms...........255
  (See under Libraries, People's.)
  Orphans' Homes. 47, 293, 295, 296, 297, 298, 300, 302, 304, 307, 367.
  (See Orphans' Homes.)
  Parishes, in 47, 245, 251, 293, 295, 296, 297, 298, 299, 300, 301, 302, 307, 432. (See under Deaconesses.)
  Periodicals,264, 278, 279, 280, 285. (See Periodicals, Press Using.)
  Prisoners, Caring for.......220, 300, 304, 306
  Servants' Training Homes.....228, 295, 297, 300-1, 307.
  Sewing Evenings......................279
  Sunday Societies for Servants. (See under Sunday Societies.)
  Temperance Organizations....259, 260. (Sec Drink Habit.)
  Training Institutes. (See Mother Houses, In. Miss. Houses.)
  Working Men's Societies..262. (See Young Men's Societies, Young People's Societies, Young Women's Societies.)
  Young Women, Helping.................255
Invalids, Caring for...........251, 295, 296
Institutum Judaicum...................270, 273
Insurance Leagues........................381
Iowa, Lutherans in.......................458
  English Synod.................382, 453, 454
  (German) Synod..........387, 406 ff, 442 453
Irving College........................383, 441
Ishpeming College (?)...............412, 411
Israelites. (See Jewish Missions.)
Italy.................174, 176, 255, 293, 470
Jacksonville, Institutions..........388, 443, 445
Jamestown, Institutions..............388, 443
Japan, Missions.......................335, 360
Jena...................................60, 263
Jerusalem...................174, 290, 292, 407
Jewish Missions....270, 273, 276, 281, 285, 301, 305, 392, 407.
Johannelund, Sem'y.....................369
Joint Synod of Ohio.....366, 403 ff, 411, 442, 453
Joliet...............................388, 444
Jönkopping...........................106, 366
Journeymen's Homes...............256, 259
Kaiserswerth...........264, 286 ff. (See under Deaconesses.)
Kaiserswerth and the Orient..174, 290, 292-3, 294, 306, 426.
Kalevala.................................158
Kanai....................................175
Kansas......................382, 453, 454, 459
Kant.....................................199
Karens, Red............................359 ff
Karlskrona..............................107
Karlsruhe...............................206
Kee Mar College....................388, 441
Kaffirs..............................255, 361
Kay, on Education.......................60
Kent, quoted............................192
Kentucky................................459

Kindergartens................32, 257, 258
Kimball, Dr., quoted................416
King William and Deacons.........221, 246
Kiel...............................41
Knabenhort.......................187
Kohls............................324
Königsberg............29, 206, 295, 306
Kraschnitz.......................306
Kroustadt........................222
Kropp.......................254, 360
Labor Colonies...253, 257, 259, 260, 261, 285, 304
Lankenau and Deaconesses...........431
Lapland, Land and People........343, 470
Missions......274, 276, 281, 308-9, 310, 344 ff,
350, 366.
Learning and Lutheranism..........183
(See Lutheranism and Learning,Schools,)306
Leesville Institute.............403, 440
Lepers.......................290, 357
Leibnitz..........................43
Leipsic...........53-5, 202, 215, 318-320
Libraries......33, 38, 51, 55, 56, 63, 65, 66, 67, 69,
70, 72, 74, 78, 80, 83, 103, 137, 139, 148, 193,
204, 205, 206, 207, 208, 209, 212, 216-7.
(See School Libraries.)
Libraries, People's.....93, 250, 252, 253, 255, 257,
262, 281.
Lima, Institutions..............412, 439
Lindsborg, College.............387, 439
Linköping..................107, 214, 217
Lippe..................10, 68, 176, 470
Liszt, Abbé........................66
Livonia.....................9, 149, 176
Löhe.........................298, 301
London..................221, 222, 302, 306
Lord's Day..................258, 259, 264
Louise, Princess.................300
Love, Practical......14, 220, 226, 242, 244, 249
(See Christianity.)
Loysville, O. H...............283, 443
Ludwigslust......................306
Luebeck...............9, 74, 176-7, 309, 470
Lund.........................106, 208
Luray, College...................411
Luther and Schools. (See Schools).....416
Luther Stiftung............268, 284, 285, 304
Luther College, etc........400, 412, 438, 439
Luray, College...................403
Lutheran Church......9-12, 13-23, 176 ff, 470-1
(See under each State named on pp. 9-10.)
375 ff.
Government of.............23-28, 143
(See also under States named on pp 9-10.)
Independent, Germany.........22-3, 176
Never Persecuted Others............348
People to Each Church............180
Persecuted......11, 37, 48, 152 ff, 108, 207, 414
Lutheran Church and Missions. (See City
Missions, Deacons, Deaconesses, Diaspora
Missions, For. Missions. Home Missions,
In. Missions, Jewish Missions, Missions,
Seamen's Missions.)
Lutheranism and Learning..181, 183, 210, 212 ff.
(See Education, Libraries, Schools, Universities.)
Lutherans in U. S...............375-459
Lutheran States................9, 470
Luther's Catechism in Schools.......31
Lutherville Seminary..........383, 441
Madagascar..................354 ff, 470
Madeira, Deaconesses...............292
Madison, Institutions..........413, 444

Madras..................177-8, 292, 301, 314
Magdalens...................243, 247
(See under In. Missions, Homes for.)
Magdeburg, Siege of................37
Maine, Lutherans in...............439
Mainz............................69
Malmo...........................104
Manitoba, Lutherans in............468
Manitou, Pastor's Home.......378, 383, 446
Mannheim, Deaconesses.............306
Maplewood, O. H.............413, 443
Maria Gloriosa Bell................38
Mariedahl, O. H.............388, 443
Marion, Seminary............403, 441
Martensen, Bishop...........300, 354
Martin Luther College.............
Maryland.......................439
Maryland Synod............352, 453, 454
Massachusetts....................460
Massowa.........................351
Mechanics, Homes for. (See Under In. Miss.)
Mechanicsburg, College........383, 441
Mecklenburg....0, 62, 176-7, 178-180, 297, 470
Miami Synod..............352, 453, 454
Michigan................411, 442, 460
Middle Tennessee Synod.........382, 453
Middletown, O.H............383, 436, 443
Midland College..............383, 439
Midsummer Day.............109, 121
Mill Point, Institute.........403, 441
Milwaukee, Institutions.....398, 400, 427, 438,
439, 445.
Minnesota...............377, 399, 442, 461
Minneapolis..387, 412 413, 438, 439, 441, 415, 446
Missions. (See Lutheran Church and)
Mission Festivals..............34, 280, 241 ff.
"   First Protestant..........308, 311 ff
"   Houses.................240, 269
"   Instruction Courses......255-6, 258
"   Leagues................363, 384
"   Libraries..................342
"   Periodicals..118, 264, 305, 312, 314, 320,
330 ff. (See Periodicals under "In. Miss;"
Literature under "For. Miss.;" Periodicals
and Press, Using)................395
Mission Seminaries....246, 267, 281, 305, 368 9,
370. 406 (See Seminaries under For. Miss.)
Missioners, Itinerant............34, 355
Missions and Public Schools.....35, 45, 192, 340
Mission Ships................275, 281, 285
Mississippi...................412, 461
Missouri........................461
Missouri Synod.........389 ff, 398, 418, 412, 453
Mitau......................151, 222, 301, 306
Mohammedans..........200, 292, 327, 362, 367
Montana........................462
Moravians, Aided.........352, 354, 358-9
Moorhead, Academy...........387, 440
Morris, Dr., quoted............393, 433
Moscow.........................283
Moshelm, College.............403, 439
Mother Houses. (See under Deaconesses.)
Mt. Airy Seminary...............387
Mt. Pleasant, Institutions.....403, 439
"   N. C..................441
Mt. Vernon, O. H............426, 443
Muhlenburg College..........387, 439
Müllhausen......................37
Murders, One Day's..............265
Museums, Scientific..........205, 209
Music, Conservatories for........55, 56
Mutual Aid Soc..................408

INDEX. xiii.

Natal, Missions. (See under For. Miss.)
Narva, Deacons in..................222
Native Pastors..............314, 354, 364–6
Nias, Missions.....................327
Nebraska....................382, 453, 462
Negroes, Missions among........391, 401
Neinstedt, Deaconesses.............227
Neuendettelsau.................298, 306
Neukirchen........................334
Neumünster........................253
Newberry College..........403, 438, 439
New Guinea.............328, 335, 338, 470
New Hampshire....................462
New Jersey........................463
New Mexico........................463
New Orleans...................309, 443
New South Wales...................177
New Torney, Deaconesses............306
New Ulm......................438, 400
New York.......387, 400, 442, 453, 454, 463
New York City....338, 399, 413, 440, 444, 445, 416
New York and New Jersey Synod.382, 442, 453, 454.
New Testament, Hebrew.............271
New Zealand........... 175, 179, 323, 471
Niebuhr............................82
Nordhausen........................37
Norköping.........................104
Norris, Institute............ ...399, 443
North Carolina............402, 453, 454, 464
"   "   College........ 403, 439
North Dakota......................377
Northern Illinois Synod........382, 453, 454
Northern Indiana Synod.........382, 453
Northfield, College............412, 439
North German Miss. Soc.........333, 365
North Western University..........439
Norway, Land and People........126, 143
  Church Affairs...................140 ff
  Education and Morals............130 ff
  Lutherans..........9, 141, 176–180, 470
  Missions.275, 354. (See under Missions, In. Miss., For. Miss., &c, as for Luth. Church and Missions.)
Norwegian Church in America 409, 411, 442, 452
Norwegians in America......377, 410, 442, 453
Norwegian-Danish Conf............442
Nova Scotia.......................458
Novgorod......................145, 150
Nowawes, Deaconesses..............306
Nuremberg.......................47 ff
Nysted, School................412, 441
Nyassa, Lake......................330
Oberkirchenrath...................24
Oceanica......................179, 471
Odense............................79
Odessa............................149
Oklahoma.........................464
Oldenburg..............67, 176, 470
Olsen, Isaac......................344
Oldenburg.............9, 67, 176, 214
Olive Branch Synod........382, 453, 454
Omaha, Institutions......388, 445, 444, 446
Orange Free State............322, 329
Order of the Red Cross............301
Orebro............................107
Oregon............................464
Orient........................178, 305
Orphanage, Jerusalem..............174
Orphans' Homes.39, 260, 283, 285, 289, 290, 291, 307, 336, 350, 351. (See under Inner Missions.)...378, 384, 388, 390, 399, 401, 403, 413, 434 f, 443–4, 446.

Ovambos..........................361
Palestine..........174, 178, 232, 290 ff, 471
Parishes, Deaconesses in.230, 285–6, 306. (See under In. Missions.)
Parent Education Society..........380
Paris, Deaconesses................306
Parishes, Big.............140, 164, 171
Parochial Schools......386, 307, 407, 414 ff, 442
Passavant, Dr. and Deaconesses.........426 ff
Pastors, Electing............27, 116, 165
Pastors, Funds for..27, 45, 260, 335, 408. (See under Funds.)
  Families Aided.................45, 304
Pennsylvania..................347 ff, 465
Pennsylvania, Ministerium of.387, 442, 453, 454
Pensacola Missions in..........413, 444
Pension Funds.........27, 45, 62, 131, 186
Peterson, Rev quoted..............425
Periodicals, Church and Missionary...241, 235, 263–4, 282, 304, 372 (See Press, Using the.)
  In U. S......380, 386, 391, 309, 401, 408, 446 ff
Persia, Missions in...............351
Pesth, Deaconesses................306
Philadelphia...306, 288, 431–3, 438, 441, 445, 446
Pilgrim Mission...................227
Pillar of Protestantism...........120
Pittsburg, Deaconesses......388, 426, 445
  "   Synods of........3-2, 387, 453, 454
Plutschau.......................311 ff
Poland..............156-7, 177, 261, 470
Polar Sea Mission.................276
Poles.............................35
Polynesia.........................177
Pomerania.............33–4, 176–7, 261
Poor, Helping....28, 238, 242, 258, 259, 261, 279, 294. (See In. Missions.)
Poreiar, Seminary.................318
Portland, Academy............412, 441
Port Said.........................292
Portuguese, Studying..............312
Posen.....................85, 296, 306
Potsdam........................30, 290
Preaching Stations........382, 398, 412
Press, Using the, 241, 244, 251, 253, 256, 259, 262, 263, 264, 270, 272, 278, 279, 281, 285, 304, 313, 342, 446 ff. (See under City Missions, For. Miss, In. Miss. Literature, Missions, Periodicals, Publication Societies.)
Professors in Institutions......199 ff, 438, 442
Protestantism, Pillar of...........120
Professions, Qualifying for........123, 210
Prisoners, Caring for...220-1, 240, 246, 256, 259. (See under In. Miss.)
Publication Soc...........241, 244, 253, 265
Publication Soc's, U.S.380, 394, 396, 300, 404, 408
Prussia, Land and People............29
  Church in..........17 ff, 29–45, 176–7, 470
Quebec......................412, 444, 463
Queens and In. Miss........280, 292, 296, 300
Queensland...................177, 338
Racine, College...................412
Rajahmundry......................363
Rauhe Haus............219 ff, 246, 331, 435
Real Gymnasiums..................196
Red Cross Soc.............228, 255, 257
Red River Valley, College..........439
Red Sea Coasts, Missions..........351
Red Wing, Institutions........412, 438, 440
Red Karens, Missions Among.......359
Reformation Times.................12
Reformation and Schools.........181 ff
Reformed Church....................18
Reine Lehre.......................23

Religion, Practical..226, 242, 244. (See Inner Missions.)..........249
Religion in Schools....180, 194, 260, 236. (See Parochial Schools)........405, 414 ff
Reuss.... ....10, 67, 176
Reval.................151, 222, 284, 301, 306, 361
Reykjavik.................91, 214
Rhenish Prussia.............. 45
Rhode Island.............465
Richmond, Ind.......412, 443, 446
Riga...........140, 222, 284, 301, 306
Roads, Good...........109, 139
Roanoke College.........408, 439
Rochester, N. Y.........387, 388, 439
" Pa.........293, 306, 435, 443, 446
Rock Island, Institutions.......387, 439, 440
Rocky Mountain Synod........382
Rome and Heretics.........11
Rome.........268, 293
Rostock.........215
Royalty and In. Miss......221, 246, 280, 288, 290, 293, 299, 300, 308, 314, 393.
Royalty and Lutheranism, Eng.........167
Rudolstadt.........214
Rumania.........174, 177, 470
Ruperti, Dr., quoted.........395
Russia...144-166, 174, 177, 180, 222, 281-4, 301-2, 470, 471.
Mission Spirit.........282 ff, 361 ff

S.
Saginaw, Seminary.........412, 438, 440
Sailors. (See Seamen.).........259
St Ansgar, (Io.), Seminary.........412, 440
St. Joseph, (Mo.), Seminary.........441
St. Louis, Institutions.........399, 400, 438
(See Missouri Synod).........439, 445
St Loup.........306
St. Olaf College.........412, 439
St. Paul.........388, 441, 445
St. Peter, Minn.........387, 388, 439, 445
St. Petersburg......146-8, 222, 276, 282, 301, 306
Salaries, Pastors'.........26-7, 62, 84, 115, 142
" Teachers'.........185, 193
Salem, Va., Institutions.........403, 439, 444
Salt Lake, Academy.........387, 441
Samoan Islands.........175, 179, 471
Sandwich Islands.........175
San Francisco.........399 413, 444
Santals.........352, 359, 364 f
Sarata.........301, 306
Sarepta.........292, 306
Saxon Duchies.........64, 176, 180
Saxony, Kingdom.........49 ff, 176, 257, 470
Missions.........257 ff, 320 ff, 364 ff
(See Schools.)
Saxony, Province.........36-40
Scandinavia.........73, 143, 192 ff
(See under For.Miss., In.Miss. and Schools.)
Scandinavians.........377, 409
Scenery, Norwegian.........127 ff
Schaumburg-Lippe.........10, 68, 176
Schwarzburgs, The.........10, 68, 176
Schiller.........56
Schools.........181-217, 416
Religion in.........189-194, 414 f
Teachers.........185 ff, 188, 199, 256
In particular places......29, 31, 33, 35, 36, 37, 38, 39, 40, 42-3, 47, 48, 49, 50, 53, 54, 59, 62, 63, 65, 67, 69, 72, 73, 74, 82, 91 ff, 103, 105, 130, 138, 147-149, 150, 151, 154, 160, 163, 168.
Industrial Schools. (See Universities and Gymnasiums.)

Schools for Young Women.........441, 442
Schleswig-Holstein.........10, 40
Missions.........250, 254
Schreuder.........354 ff
Schwartz.........314 ff
Seaside Homes for Sick.........260
Seamen, Churchly.........121
Missions Among....269, 274, 275, 277, 280, 285, 292, 383, 401, 412, 436.
Sebastopol.........175
Self-Denial.........395, 397
Selin's Grove, Institutions.........383, 438, 440
Serbia, Lutherans in.........470
Sermon Distribution.........253, 269
(See Berlin.)
Servants, Homes for..253, 258, 260, 259, 289, 290
Schools for.........289, 290, 295
(See under In. Missions.)
Shultz, Stephen.........271
Siberia.........153, 177
Sick, Deaconesses Among....294, 296, 302, 426 ff
(See under Deaconesses and In. Missions.)
Silesia.........65-6, 295
Sioux Falls.........412, 413, 441, 445
Skana, Missions in.........276
Skrefsund.........356
Slave Trade Stopped.........277
Smyrna, Deaconesses.........291
Sobernheim, " 306
South America.........174, 177-9
South Carolina.........402, 453, 454, 466
South Dakota.........
Southern Illinois Synod.........382
Spain, Missions in.........278
Speyer, Deaconesses.........293, 306
Springfield, Ill..........400, 438, 441
" O.........383, 438, 439
Stanton, Io.........387, 388, 441, 443
Staunton, Va.........403, 441
State Churches.........284
Statistics, Tables of..176-180, 215-217, 285, 306-7, 364-371, 382-3, 387-8, 398-9, 400, 402-3, 411 ff, 438-471.
Stavanger.........139
Stettin.........84, 295-6
Stockholm.........99-102
Missions.........276, 300, 306
Stoecker and City Missions.........269
Storjohan's.........274
Stoughton.........412, 441
Strackholt.........407
Stralsund.........34, 296
Strassburg.........74, 297, 306
Students..197, 201, 379, 383, 385, 389, 401, 403, 407, 412, 438-442.
Mission Socs....272, 276, 285, 342, 352, 355, 367
Stuttgart.........55-6, 282, 255-6, 298, 306
Suffering for Truth.........11
Sulphur Springs, O. H.........443
Sumatra.........179, 180, 326-7
Summus Episcopus.........24, 87, 117
Sunday Schools.........382, 387, 398, 420
Sunday Societies.........258, 259, 264
Sunderland.........302
S. S. Instruction.........279
Suomi Synod.........410, 411
Superintendents, Church.....25, 29, 33, 146, 148
Susquehanna Synod.........382, 438
Sustentation Funds. (See Funds.)
Sweden, Land and People.........98, 126, 470
Church Affairs.........114 ff
Education.........105, 192-197, 208, 212 ff, 215 ff

Sweden, Land and People—Law and Order, 111 ff
Lutherans..................10, 115, 176-7, 180
Missions. (See under different heads as for
Lutheran Church and Missions,).....308 ff
Morals and Piety.......................111 ff
Sects in........................117, 119
Swedes in U. S.................347, 375, 385
Switzerland................170. 173, 299
Synodical Conference..............388 ff, 469
Synods, Foreign 24-5, 117, 164
Synods in General Council ....387 ff
" " General Synod.................383 ff
" " Independent.....................403 ff
" " Synodical Conference,........388 ff
" " United Synod..................399 ff
" " Heathen Lands ....326-7, 329 ff
Syracuse, O. H. 443
Syria, Deaconess 174, 337
Tabris 292
Tacoma, Institutions 412, 413, 439, 444
" Talitha Cumi "............................174
Tamils ....312 ff
Tanjore, famine..........................315
Tartary 175
Taylor, Bayard, quoted 347
Teachers, European. (See Schools.)
Teachers' Seminaries.........406, 421 ff, 440
Temperance. (See under In. Missions and
Drink Habit.)
Templeton, Cala., O. H..............388, 444
Tennessee 402, 453, 466
Texas 442, 466
Thiel College.........................387, 439
Theological Seminaries,..383, 387, 394, 400, 403,
406, 412, 438. 442.
Thirty Years' War,...............11, 37, 54
Thompson, Dr., quoted,....................414
Thuringia........................177, 470
Tilly in Magdeburg...................37-8, 54
Toledo, O. H. 388, 443
Tongues, Many............................314
Tornäns...................................308
Tractatus Adami...........................126
Training Schools, Nurses'................255
(See Under In. Miss's.)
Tiamps' Home.......................258, 261
(See Labor Colonies.)
Tranquebar................311, 318, 358 9
Transvaal Republic..................322, 329
Transylvania........................169, 470
Trichinopoli..............................314
Trinity Seminary......................403, 441
Tromsoe...................................140
Traber, Primus............................308
Tübingen................................205
Tunis, Com. for..........................175
Turks, Deaconesses Among.................291
Tyler, Minn., School.................412, 441
Tyrol, Deaconesses in....................299
Theological Students.........201-2, 205, 383
(See Seminaries.)
Ulm.....................................55, 57
Union Cadettes...........................279
"United" Churches............17, 20 ff, 174
United Norwegian Church......409, 411, 453
United States, Lutherans in...........375-471
United Evangelical Church................410
U. S.,—Lutheran Synodical Bodies in
General Council...........382, 387, 469
Institutions..........................387
Missions..........................363, 384
Publications..........................385

U. S.,—Lutheran Synodical Bodies in
General Council.
Schools........................383, 385, 387
General Synod..................377 ff, 469
Institutions..................373, 383
Missions.........................362, 379
Publications..........................380
Schools.........................377-8, 383
(Other) Societies......................379 ff
Independent Synods............403 ff, 469
Institutions..........................404
Missions.............................404
Publications..........................404
Schools.............................404-5
Synodical Conference...........388 ff, 469
Institutions.......................389 f. 399
Missions.........................390, 392
Publications.......................390-1
Schools.................389, 393 ff, 400
United Church ....399 ff, 469
Institutions 400, 403
Missions 401
Publications 401-2
Schools 401, 403
Universities, 197-211, 215-7, 41, 70, 137, 148, 149
Upsala 105, 208
Uruguay 174, 170
Utah 466
Utrecht, Deaconesses....................306
Vasa.................................388, 443
Venezuela 174
Vermont..................................
Vesteras 108, 214
Viborg...................................160
Victoria 177
Vienna 170, 298, 306
Virginia 402, 453, 466
Volga....................................145
Von Westen 343
Von Bora College.....................403, 441
W.
Wagner College.......................387, 439
Wahoo, Neb., Academy..............387, 440
Waldeck 177, 470
Waldenstrom 119, 124
Walker. Rev., quoted.....................425
Wallenstein's Boast........................34
Walther College....................400, 439
Wangemann...............................340
Warneck...................................339
Warner, Charles Dudley, quoted..........396
Wartburg College....................387, 439
Wartburg Synod................382, 442, 453
Washington...............................467
Washington, D. C............378, 383, 445, 446
Water Falls...............................128
Watertown, Wis....................439, 400
Waverly, Ia....................387, 408, 439
Weimar..............................65-6, 214
Welz. Justinian von......................310
Wends, Missions Among...................308
Wernigerode..............................214
West Denmark......................412. 438
West Indies........77, 176-7, 277, 310, 470, 471
West Pennsylvania Synod...........382, 453
Westphalia....................176, 180, 293
West Roxbury, O. H...............399, 443
West Virginia............................467
Wiborg....................................306
Widows and Orphans..256. (See Funds and
under In. Missions.)
Wichern..218 ff, 227. (See Deacons, In. Miss.)

Wilhelm IV. and In. Miss..............221, 290
Willmar................................412, 440
Winnipeg..............................412, 441
Wisconsin...................398, 442, 453, 467
Wittenberg.......399, 412, 413 ;440, 443. 444, 446
" College....................383, 438 9
" Synod..................382, 453, 454
Wolf, Dr., quoted...................... 11, 61
Wolfenbüttel.............................63, 214
Women's Aid Societies, 42, 239, 243, 247, 265, 285, 299, 305. (See under Berlin.)
Women, Dependent........................245
Women's Mission Societies, 250, 252. 265, 278, 267, 285, 304, 355, 361, 36}, 367, 379, 384, 401, 454. (See under F. M.)
Women's Soc. of the Good Shepherd........243
Women Teachers..........................186
Women, Work Among......................279
(See Girls, In. Missions, Young Women's Soc's.)
Woodville...........................412, 440
Working-Men's Soc's......................262
Wörm, Jacob..............................309
Worms,..................................70

Württemberg.............10, 55-62, 176-7, 470
Education...........................59 ff, 184
Funds...................................254
Missions, 61, 254, 331. (See Heads as under Luth. Church and Missions.)
Wytheville...........................403, 441
Wyoming.................................468
Young Children (See Children.)............231
Y. M. C. A's.—A Hint for..................226
Young Men in Berlin......................288
Young Men's Soc's. 244, 252, 256-7, 258, 263, 279, 295, 304.
Young People's Soc's........252-3. 257, 256, 259
Young Women's Soc's. 252, 257, 258. (See Girls, and under In. Missions.)
Youth, Saving Neglected...218-9, 227. (See Children, Girls, under In. Miss's, and Orphans.)
Zanzibar........................222, 292, 337
Zelienople, O. H..........388, 430, 434. 436, 443
Zenana Missionaries....................362-3
Ziegenbalg............................311-314
Zinzendorf at Copenhagen.................358
Zulus.......................322, 329, 350, 355 6
Zurich, Deaconesses......................306

CHAPTER I.
INTRODUCTORY.

"And Jesus came to them and spake unto them, saying, All authority hath been given unto me in heaven and on earth. Go ye therefore, and make disciples of all the nations, baptizing them into the name of the Father and of the Son and of the Holy Ghost: teaching them to observe all things whatsoever I commanded you: and lo, I am with you alway, even unto the end of the world."—Matt. 28: 18-20. *Revised Version.*

OUR Saviour's commission to the Apostles enjoins the world-wide preaching of the world-saving Truth. Following the divine order of procedure, namely, (1) discipling the nations through Baptism, (2) nurturing them through the Word, the Lutheran Church (3) has realized the promise of the Saviour's presence with her. Having now a membership of more than fifty millions, her claim is nothing less than that she is doing the Master's work in the Master's way, as set forth in the Master's word. Not yet has she succeeded in discipling all the nations, but she has so girt the globe with her net-work of missions that her organization is world-wide, darkness never settles upon the steeples of her temples, and the music of her matins, following the course of the sun and keeping pace with the hours, encircles the earth with an unbroken strain of churchly melody.

While carrying out the great Commission entrusted to her, in the providence of God the Lutheran has become the established or State Church in Alsace-Lorraine, Bavaria, "this side the Rhine," Brunswick, Courland, Danish West Indies, Denmark, Esthonia, Frankfurt-on-the-Maine, Faroe Islands, Finland, Hamburg, Hanover, Heligoland, Iceland, Livonia, Luebeck, Mecklenburg-Schwerin, Mecklenburg-Strelitz, Norway, Oldenburg, Oldenburg Principality of

Luebeck, Reuss Elder Line, Reuss-Younger Line, Saxony, (the Kingdom,) Saxe-Coburg, Saxe-Gotha, Saxe-Meiningen, Saxe-Oldenburg, Saxe-Weimar, Schaumberg-Lippe, Schwarzburg-Rudolstadt, Schwarzburg-Sonderhausen, Schleswig-Holstein, Sweden and Würtemberg.

She also has representation in Abyssinia, Africa—North, South, East coast, West coast, Algiers, Anhalt, Argentine Republic, Asia, Asia Minor, Asiatic Russia, Assiniboia, Austria, Australia, Baden, Baltic Islands, (Oesel, Mohn, Runs, &c.,) Bavaria, Batu Island, Bassutoland, Bessarabia, Black Sea coasts, Bengaloor, Belgium, Bohemia, Borneo, Brandenburg, Brazil, Bremen, Bulgaria, Cameroons, (Africa,) Canada, Cape Colony, Carinthia, Carniala, in the Caucasus, Chili, China, Congoland, Courland, in the Crimea, Croatia, Dampier Archipelago; Darmstadt, Damaraland, Dutch East Indies, England, East Prussia, Egypt, Esthonia, Farther India, Feejee Islands, France, Gold Coast, (Africa.) Greenland, Hawaiin Islands, Hereroland, Hesse-Cassel, Hindostan, Holland, Hungary, Ice Sea Coasts, Italy, India, Indian Archipelago, Ireland, Japan, Java, Kanai, King William's Land, Lapland in Russia, Lapland in Scandinavia, Lippe, Livonia, Madagascar, Madras Presidency, (India,) Manitoba, Moravia, Natal, Namaqualand, New Guinea, New South Wales, New Zealand, Nias, Nova Scotia, Ontario, Oramboland, Palestine, Persia, Poland, Pomerania, Posen, Queensland, Rangoon, Red Sea Coasts, Rhine Provinces, Roumania, Russia, Salermo, Samoan Islands, St. Petersburg, (District,) Scotland, Servia, Siar, Siberia, Slave Coast, (Africa,) Slavonia, Society Islands, Solomon Islands, Servia, Silesia, Spain, Sumatra, Switzerland, Syria, Tanjore, Tartary, Togoland, Thuringia, Transvaal, Trans-Caucasia, Transylvania, Tunis, Turkey, United States, Uruguay, Venezuela, Victoria, on the Volga, Waldeck, Wales, Westphalia, West Prussia, West Indies, Winnipeg, Wituland, Zanzibar and Zululand.

Although the great Church of the Reformation is thus at work among all the nations, she has her greatest strength where she is best known and most dearly loved—in Germany, the land of her emancipation. Here her children have testified, with their blood, that no sacrifice is too great if made in her defence. Ever refusing to employ the civil power at their command, to propagate their faith; to defend that faith against those who by craft or sword would wrest it from them,* German Lutherans have poured out more of both blood and treasure than has been required of all other Protestant peoples.

Of deep, serious nature, sensitive to religious influence, profoundly moved by religious conviction, for long centuries, without a murmur, the German people submitted to the arrogance of alien masters because it wore the garb of religion. At length papal usurpations became intolerable and protest was made. Rome never argues with a heretic, she burns him. Her policy, the growth of the ages; her organization, the most wonderful fabric of human contrivance; the latter always in waiting to enforce the former, she had set up kings, toyed with them, and put them down again. What then will be her reply to German protests? She answered, with fire. Well might history repeat what the pen of Inspiration has recorded of more ancient heroes: "They had trial of cruel mockings and scourgings, yea, moreover, of bonds and imprisonment; they

---

* The Thirty Years' War, 1618-1648, is a case in point. Having resolved to crush Protestantism, the Roman Catholic Princes united their armies to overrun Germany. Lutheran Germany and Scandinavia rose in defence. Thirty years of carnage ensued. Twelve millions of lives were sacrificed; thirty thousand hamlets and villages were devastated; the richest nation of Europe was reduced almost to beggary; forests grew up where before had been fertile fields, and Germany was set back a hundred years in the march of civilization. And but for this sacrifice, Germany, as was France, would have been swept of Protestantism. (See Lord's *Beacon Lights*, iv: 24-56.)

were stoned, they were sawn asunder, they were tempted, were slain with the sword; they wandered about in sheepskins, and in goat-skins; being destitute, afflicted, tormented, (of whom the world was not worthy;) they wandered in deserts, and in mountains, and in dens and caves of the earth."*

But the death of these martyrs was the life of the Church. The spiritual atmosphere seemed charged with influences betokening, to the weary and heavy-laden, the nearness of a mighty convulsion in which the prophetic longings of the long line of martyr-heroes should find fulfillment in the emancipation of the German people, and the restoration to them of the religion of Jesus Christ in the purity and freeness of its apostolic origin. The times and the man met in Martin Luther, and the product evolved was a torch of flame to light the way to God for lost humanity. And that torch, by the orderings of divine Providence, from that time till now, has been borne in the van of Christian civilization by the spiritual sons of Luther, the greatest of Germans.

Fitting it is, therefore, that a sketch of the present condition of that great communion on which her persecutors fastened the name Lutheran, should begin with the German Empire, the school-master of the world. - The chief religious body in that Empire is popularly known as the Lutheran Church: but called by whatever name, "her center is the Gospel; Gospel grace over against Legalism; Gospel sufficiency over against Traditionalism, the abuse of reason and Fanaticism; and Gospel Unity in Faith and Sacraments over against the separatism of sect, and the spurious Unionism of compromise and of ignored truth."†

---
* Heb. xi: 36–40. † Krauth.

CHAPTER II.

I. IN GERMANY.

THE German Empire is made up of thirty-eight states, with a population of 46,900,000. Of this number, 31,000,000 are reported Evangelical in belief; 15,300,000 Roman Catholic; and 600,000 as other Christians and Jews. In North Germany, of the thirty or more millions, the Evangelicals are to the Roman Catholics as three to one; in the South German states, as two to three. Of what are usually reckoned the twenty-six states of the Empire, three have a predominantly Roman Catholic population,—Alsace-Lorraine, Bavaria and Baden; and in four of the Protestant states the Roman Church has from 23 to 33 per cent. of the population,—Prussia, Würtemberg, Hesse and Oldenburg. In Saxony, and in eighteen of the minor states, the Roman Catholics number but from one-tenth of one per cent., to three and three-tenths per cent. of the population.*

The testimony of competent, disinterested men, who for years have made the study of German religious life the subject of thought, who themselves have lived in Germany and know much of the Germans, who are at home in the use of the German tongue and keep step with German theology and German Church life, is against the claim of the Roman Church that German Protestantism is in a decline.† Pages

---

**En. Brit.*, art., Germany.

† Not a few Americans, who have passed through the by-ways of Germany without understanding the tongue or the customs of the people, have come back and declared religion dead there. The facts on the following pages of this book will be sufficient answer to these croakings. Where there are fruits there is life.

enough to leave us room for nothing else might be filled with evidence on this point. Dr. Wolf, author of *The Lutherans in America*, has condensed their substance as follows: "Germany still believes. The land of Luther has not given up the faith of Luther. Despite all discouraging appearances, there exists, undoubtedly, more true faith in the Fatherland to-day than at any time since the opening of the present century. Such is the general conviction of earnest pastors, devout professors, and prominent laymen, who, while their hearts mourn over the desolation of Zion, behold on the face of the sky the dawn of a new day. . . . When the modern doctrine that man is a beast was illustrated by the human tiger displaying his fangs, the common sense of the German mind revolted, and, with the religious instincts once more awakened, men would rather hold on to the rule of the Cross, . . . than bend their necks to the reign of atheism and anarchy."

The rising generations of scholars are believers in a Christianity that is practical; and their thought has penetrated all classes of people in the Church. All these have for decades been engaged in practical Church works. Societies for the better observance of the Lord's Day; for the promotion of temperance, the improvement of prison discipline and the care of dismissed convicts; the establishment of institutions for the laboring classes, colliers, sailors, orphans and the poor; and of asylums, hospitals and deaconess homes; and all the efforts and means for the moral and religious reforms of society, which are comprehended under the name of Inner Mission, are multiplying in every quarter. All these have the heartiest support of men high in authority. The present Emperor and Empress give them whole-souled service. All have their representatives, not only in the leading cities, but also in all parts of the Empire.

The character of these people, and of their religion, is reflected in their Church music and their worship. No other people possess such a treasure of Church song. In it is all that hidden, serious, earnest fervor that lies at the base of ideal heroes, thinkers, and philosophers. Their hymns are used throughout the land; the same ones for centuries; age after age has grown up with them. They have entered into the race with an effect which we cannot calculate. Sung Sunday after Sunday,—on the many Church holy days,—learned for confirmation; yea, more, used as a text-book in the day school; they become part of the people themselves. These sacred poems are taught in all the schools, and there is as perfect familiarity with them as with the Sacred Scriptures. A thousand University students have been seen, cap in hand, without note or book, stand up and sing without falter, from beginning to end, *Ein Feste Burg*. Every man and woman has known both words and music, not only of this, but of many others, or of all, their great hymns, from childhood. " These hymns, laden with the highest hopes and inspirations of past centuries, take hold upon the German heart to-day. In the presence of this great influence, creeds are as nothing. The men who hold them and the men who deny them are alike—their aspirations alike are borne upward on these mighty billows of song. In the Churches, the service of praise comes from the hearts and the voices of the whole congregation. The praise is not delegated to a quartette club. I think the most unbelieving German would feel personally hurt to be thus robbed *more Americano*."*

The earnestness of these people is also manifested in their manner while in the house of God. There is a wonderful contrast between the German Churches in Berlin, and the fashionable City Churches of America. Style in dress for church services is not considered in good taste: and is shunned even by the nobility and the Imperial Family. Only the plainest attire is seen in the house of worship.

*President White, Cornell University.

One who writes from the German capital, says: "What pure, single worship is possible here! You go to any church; the crowd presses in, the people do not seem to know each other; there is one purpose in the heart of each. There is no private conversation; on entering, each stands a moment with bowed head, and then awaits in silence the first note from the organ, when as with one prayerful, praise-overflowing heart, the hymn breaks forth. Nothing distracts. With all the liturgy and ceremony there is still a wonderful simplicity; in some indefinable way the world and its cares are dismissed, and the soul freely rises to heights of blessedness. There is a solemnity and beauty in its worship, an earnestness and reverence within its sacred temples, a richness, depth, satisfaction in its services—a reverence, in all, that fills the soul with a completeness of devotion. How one grows to love the Protestant Church of Germany!"*

Devout, and severely practical in their religious thought, the members of our churches beyond the sea are suspicious of American piety. They base their opinions of its fruits on what the press has to report of our popular life; and conclude that this piety is superficial, hypocritical, Puritanical—a mere Sunday formality. They estimate its real power by the corruption among us in official life, which is something almost unknown there; by our fearful record of crime and the laxity of justice; by the infamous management so often revealed in our larger cities, as reported in our periodicals; by the character of a large part of our press, admitted into families with all its disgusting and polluting details of crime; by the prevailing worldliness which has crept into the Churches, and has given us abroad the reputation of being practical materialists; by our unhealthful types of Evangelism; by the sensational preaching that loses sight of the Gospel if only it can entertain and amuse, and by our readiness to start out the callow youth

---
* Emma L. Parry.

to preach the Gospel without any special training for his work, although we think he ought to stay with his master for three years or more if he would learn to make shoes. They pity the gushing sentimentality that so largely takes the place of obedience to God's commandments and leads honored men to commit themselves for life to the propagation of ideas and doctrines which bear on themselves the stamp of their own absurdity. They think it next to silliness to imagine that our Sunday School training of the young is sufficient to make of them men and women versed in the knowledge of God's Word. They point to our many sects, and sects again divided and sub-divided; and, on the whole, many most pious and zealous souls in our churches across the sea congratulate themselves that their Church is not in this condition.

2. LUTHERAN, REFORMED AND UNITED CHURCHES.

Owing to its connection with the State, the Church in Europe is cut up into as many sections as there are separate governments; but in them all, as everywhere else in the world, the Lutheran Church is everywhere the Church of the Augsburg Confession. Excepting a few cities on the borders of Switzerland and Holland, the Evangelical religion of Germany, orginally, all was of the Lutheran type. In sections this type has been diluted and weakened by Zwinglianism and Calvinistic admixtures; and the resultant churches are now Reformed or United.

The provinces of Prussia, excepting the new territories, (Hanover, Hesse-Nassau, Schleswig-Holstein, and Lauenberg,) are in the United Church, by an act of the King. This, however, did not change the convictions of men, readily as it changed their external Church relations; and under the apparent union, much of the old time tendency toward Lutheranism, or toward the Reformed faith, remains.

In Berlin, for example, the headquarters of the United Church, two foreign mission societies exist, and both are more or less pronouncedly Lutheran. In Hesse-Nassau, Hesse-Cassel, Hohenzollern, and in some of the Rhenish provinces, the Reformed faith is the prevailing element of the United Church; in the other provinces, the Lutheran. In several of these, as Silesia, Pomerania, etc., there is Lutheranism of the strictest type. In the now Prussian states, Anhalt, Baden, Lippe, Bremen and Waldeck are prevailingly Reformed; and the other states prevailingly Lutheran—many of them nearly exclusively so. The greatest mixture of faiths is found in the larger cities.

That we may have some data to guide us in reaching an approximately correct idea of the comparative numerical strength of Lutheranism and of the "Reformed" Church in Germany, let us bear in mind the following facts:

(1.) Those stated in a paragraph just preceding, as to the original type of Evangelical religion in Germany.

(2.) At the time when the King introduced the Union into Prussia, (1817,) by far the greater proportion of the population were in opposition to the Reformed Confession.*

(3.) Lutheranism is the prevailing form of Protestantism in Saxony, Hanover, Würtemberg, and the greater part of North Germany.†

(4.) In 1885, in the election for members of the General Synod, of 150 persons elected, 50 were Confessional Lutherans; 56 were friends of the "Union;" 38 belonged to the Middle Party, and six were liberals.‡

(5.) It has been calculated, however, that of the twenty-five millions of Protestants in the German Empire, twenty millions, at least, are of Lutheran extraction.§

Some years ago, (1884,) a homiletic monthly of New York asked Prof. Christlieb, of Bonn, to give to the Ameri-

---
* Kurtz. † Chambers' En. ‡ Stuckenberg. § *Cyclopedia of Education*, Kiddle & Schem, N. Y.

can public, through its columns, an opinion concerning the character of the preaching done in the "German Protestant Pulpit of To-day." He complied, and the substance of his opinion was as follows: In Würtemberg the preaching is almost entirely of a Scriptural faith, and frequently pietistic; in Bavaria proper, Lutheran and Confessional; in Hesse-Darmstadt, Nassau and Alsace, divided between Rationalism and positive Evangelicalism; in the Rhine Provinces and in Westphalia, the positive Evangelical sermon prevails —in the former of a Reformed, in the latter of a Lutheran coloring; in the Province of Saxony and in Silesia, "liberal" preachers are found side by side with Lutheran Confessional; in Silesia, strict Confessional, or "Independent" Lutherans. This strict Lutheran and Confessional preaching largely prevails in the Kingdom of Saxony; while Rationalism comes to the front in some of the Thuringian dukedoms, as in Gotha, Weimar, and elsewhere. In Northern Germany there predominates, on the whole, an Evangelical Lutheran tendency, from Hanover to the Russian frontier, and even beyond into the Baltic provinces of Russia. The preachers of Hanover are nearly all positively Lutheran; also in Frisia, though mixed with the Reformed. In Oldenburg, Holstein and Hamburg, Rationalism is somewhat more strongly represented in the pulpit; and predominantly in Bremen. In Mecklenburg and Pomerania a strict Lutheran Confessionalism prevails; and in Posen and Brandenburg the sermon is almost exclusively positive and Evangelical, with a Lutheran coloring, save as to Berlin, a majority of whose preachers are Rationalistic. East and West Prussia are divided between the Evangelical Lutheran and Rationalistic tendencies. This brief sketch, therefore, will show that the overwhelming majority of the German ministers of to-day are positively Evangelical;* and at the same time it will show that the overwhelming majority of

---
* Christlieb.

them are more or less positively Lutheran. This is true even of the pastors within the United Church, among whom a spirit of adherence to church confessions has made great growth during the past half century.

The Prussian Union expressly declared that it did not wish a change from one church to another. The King himself said that it was not intended to be a fusion of the two faiths, but an external union for mutual admission to the Eucharist, and for the convenience of using the same liturgy. Opposition was offered by many Lutheran clergymen and their congregations. A Lutheran Church entirely independent of the established one was organized, with its chief seat at Breslau, and received Royal recognition. Many other congregations were kept in the established Church only through special concessions in regard to worship and the liturgy.

In 1834, the King issued a royal decree, declaring the continued validity and authority of the symbolical books of the two confessions—plainly a concession to the Lutherans within the church. Eighteen years later (1852) he so far yielded to the pressure of the powerful party headed by Hengstenberg, Stahl, and others, that, also by a royal order, he allowed a confessional division in the Oberkirchenrath— the highest church tribunal in Prussia. Accordingly, in the July session of that body, in the same year, six of the members declared themselves Lutherans friendly to the Union in the sense of the royal order of 1834, (which maintains the Union without weakening the authority of the old confessions;) one declared himself a pure Lutheran, without any qualifying clause; two professed themselves Reformed, in the sense of the royal order of 1834; and one declared that he belonged to both churches, *i. e.*, he took the consensus of both confessions as his faith. In other words, of these ten members of the Oberkirchenrath, seven upheld the confessions of the Lutheran Church; one was lukewarm concerning them;

and two were upholders of the Reformed confessions: So that we may say that seven-tenths of the members of the Supreme Church Council of the United Church reported themselves Lutherans.

In the United Church of Prussia to-day there are three parties—the Positive Right, the Centre, and the Left.

⤳The Positive.Right holds that the individuality and confessional standing of local Lutheran Churches can be maintained in the Union as before the year 1817. They hold to the governmental union, . . . but, within its limits, maintain the rights of the confessions, especially of the Lutheran symbols. The "Union," by them, is resolved into a confederation, under one ecclesiastical government, presided over by the King, his Minister of Worship, and the Oberkirchenrath. This party, therefore, might properly be styled confederalists. It is very influential in Prussia, and has numbered among its most active supporters the distinguished jurists, Goeschel, Stahl, etc., eminent leaders of the conservative section in the Prussian chambers; who also have acted with von Gerlach, the leader of the high-church, aristrocratic reaction party in the same chambers. This party has been developed almost wholly within the last fifty years; yet it seemed that the "dry bones" were ready, but awaiting the breath from on high to give them fullest life. Among its active and leading divines have been such men as Claus Harms; Hengstenberg, Sartorius; Rudelbach, one of the most learned theologians of his day; Guericke, who was leader in establishing a Journal for Lutheran Theology; von Harless, author of Christian Ethic, Theological Encyclopedia, etc.; Hofling, a co-worker of Harless; Thomasius; and Harnack, of Erlangen. Yet more thoroughly devoted to exclusively Lutheran teachings, have been Vilmar and Krabbe. We may mention, also, men of a third group, like von Hofmann, of Erlangen; Baumgarten, Luthardt, Drechsler, Caspari, Oehler, Keil, etc.

The Left wing is made up of liberal and latitudinarian unionists, who hold to the Bible as the only rule of faith and practice; and resist the binding authority of Symbolical Books as another form of popery, incompatible with the spirit of Protestant freedom. Happily, these have but little power and influence.

The Centre is the third party of the United Church, and is made up of those who nominally accept the consensus of the Lutheran and the Reformed symbols as the doctrinal basis of the Union. The orthodox section of the Schleiermacher-Neander school, and many well known divines, are supposed to belong here; yet the doctrinal coloring of the writings which go forth from this body reveals the unsatisfactory nature of the consensus as a basis of faith. Among the disciples of this school from the Lutheran Church may be named Luecke; Nitzsch; Julius Mueller, author of the unsurpassed work on the Christian Doctrine of Sin; Twesten, Dorner, Rothe, Beck, Umbreit, Meyer, Tischendorf, Stier, Kurtz, Koestlin, Tholuck, Hase, Jacobi, Ebrard and Ullman. One of the principal literary organs of this school has been the "Allgemeine Kirchenzeitung;" while the principal organ of the Right wing has been the "Evangelische Kirchenzeitung."*

In addition to the Lutherans within the "United" Church in Prussia, there are, also, two bodies of Lutherans who will have nothing to do with the Union, although on territory over which it claims to have jurisdiction. One of these is known as the Old Lutheran Church Union; the other, as the Immanuel Synod, usually called the Breslau Synod, and known also as the Independent Lutheran Church of Prussia. The former body reports about 2,950,000 members; the latter, about 45,000. The Old Lutherans have a Supreme Church "Collegium" in Breslau, one director, a Church Council of four members, and a.theological examining

---

*cf: Kurtz's Church History, Vol. II.

committee. Seven dioceses are reported, as follows, each with a superintendent, viz: that of Berlin, Breslau, Elberfeld, Liegnitz, Militsch, Thorn, Trieglaff. The Immanuel Synod reports two senior pastors, one in Strassburg and one in Wallin, 64 parishes, 66 pastors, 87 churches and 25 teachers.

These strictly symbolical Lutherans reject every kind of union and confederation. Their watchword is *Reine Lehre und reines Bekenntniss.* To this everything else is made subordinate. They say that the Union is the work of religious indifferentism, and is downright treason to Lutheranism, tending only to poison and destroy it.

The most learned and worthy champions of the theology of this wing have been Harless, of Munich; Löhe, and the whole theological faculty of Erlangen, (except Herzog,) but especially Thomasius and Delitzsch; Kahnis of Leipsic; Kliefoth and Philippi, of Mecklenburg; Petri, Rudelbach, and Guericke, of Halle. Their principal theological organs have been the "Kirchliche Zeitschrift," "Zeitschrift für Protestantismus und Kirche," and " Zeitschrift für die Gesammte Lutherische Theologie und Kirche." This wing has many adherents in Bavaria, Mecklenburg, Silesia, Saxony and Pomerania. (The Buffalo and the Missouri Synods were originated by men of this wing, who fled from persecution in Germany.)

3. CHURCH GOVERNMENT.

Chiefly because of the exigencies of the times in which the government of our Church took form, the princes became its responsible heads. In the beginning it was unavoidably so. The Lutheran Church, believing in the universal priesthood of all believers, cannot endure the doctrine of an essential distinction between the clergy and the laity. Hierarchical grades among the clergy are considered antagonistic to the spirit of Christianity ; but officers of authority, (such as superintendents, provosts, bishops, etc.,) are deemed not only allowable, but advantageous. And because no others existed for this purpose, church government passed into the hands of the princes, just after the Reformation. As the years passed by, this matter of exigency was regarded as a matter of right. Generally, therefore, where the Lutheran is the established, or State Church, the King is "Summus Episcopus," or its Supreme head. He is represented in the exercise of his ecclesiastical functions by the Minister of Public Worship and Instruction. In Prussia, the Oberkirchenrath, or Chief Court of the State Church, retains the Supreme right of the management of church affairs in the old provinces. It acts through provincial consistories and superintendents appointed by the crown. The Cultus Minister is at its head ; and he is assisted by a secretary and a director, as, also, by an Advisory Council of fourteen members. Next in authority is the Evangelical Supreme Church Council, composed of nine members and an assistant. By the side of this Council stand the Directors of the General Synod—seven in number—with five "associates," and the General Synod Council, composed of eighteen members, and selected from the different provinces of the Kingdom. The Directors have the general oversight of the State Church; and the members of the General Synod Council assemble each year, in Berlin, with the Supreme Church Council, and deliberate on the general affairs of the Church.

The General Synod of the State Church met first in 1879, and again in 1885. It is composed of about two hundred members, appointed as follows :

(1.) The twelve General Superintendents of the nine older provinces.

(2.) Thirty members named by His Majesty.

(3.) Six representatives of the theological faculties.

(4.) One hundred and fifty members from the Provincial Synods. These, along with the Imperial Court of Justice for ecclesiastical affairs, composed of a president and ten members, constitute the official authorities of the State Church.*

The church affairs of the several provinces are directed by provincial consistorial boards. The Provincial Synods watch over the doctrinal and spiritual affairs of the Church for their respective provinces, and are formed of the superintendents, along with deputies from the district synods. These meet once in three years, but their proceedings must be confirmed by the proper state authorities. The district synods are composed of all the ministers, and one deputy from each congregation, in their respective districts. These meet each year, under their own superintendents, who are elected for six years by and from the members of the synod.† (Much in the same way, and for the same ends, district and general synods are held in Würtemberg, Oldenburg, Hesse, Mecklenburg, Baden, etc.) Within the district synods, the parishes are grouped into Dioceses, presided over by superintendents, who are subordinate to the Superintendent General of the province, (or part of a province.) In some of the

---

*An American who attended the convention of the General Synod of the State Church of Prussia, in Berlin, in 1885, speaks of the methods of the members as follows: The opening services of the Synod were held in the Dom, October 11, and daily sessions were held for more than two weeks thereafter. The business of the body was transacted without that rush and hurry which seem to be such pronounced characteristics of similar bodies in America. No one seemed to be in a hurry to catch the next train out of the city. Nearly, if not all, the sessions were presided over by laymen. Often the debates were very spirited. Sometimes, when it seemed probable that an excited speaker was about to say something which he should not say, the president of the meeting would tap his bell, rise and quietly request the speaker to calm himself and take special heed to his words, after which all would go on regularly. During debates the members would often leave their seats and crowd around the speaker, who spoke from his own desk.

† *Amtskalender für Geistliche:* Bielefeld and Leipzig.

provinces, different names are given to these things; the district presided over by the official under the General Superintendent is called an Inspectorate, a Circle, a Synod, a Diaconate, etc.; and the official is styled the Provost, the Metropolitan, or the Dekan, but the significance, in either case, is about as above. The salaries of all officials are paid by the State.

The president of the Supreme Church Council receives 21,000 marks; five advisory members receive from 7,500 to 9,000 marks each; three assistants have from 1,500 to 2,400 marks each; and a lay representative of the president, and a vice president are paid 1,500 marks each. The other officials, of other departments, have salaries ranging from 12,000 marks to less than 1,000 marks each. The directors of the General Synod are paid 9,900 marks each; and six of the general superintendents have each 9,000. (These are in Königsberg, Posen, Breslau, Magdeburg, Munster and Coblentz.) Six assistant general superintendents—three in Berlin, and one each in Königsberg, Stettin and Magdeburg have salaries each varying from 2,400 to 7,500 marks. The total paid yearly to these officials is over 420,000 marks. In Hanover and Schleswig-Holstein, the President of the State Consistory is paid 11,400 marks; two directors receive each 9,900, and the salaries of other officials vary down to 900 marks.* (Some associates have as low as 450.)

Of the lower officials in Prussia some seem to have slender salaries connected with their official work. In the province of Bradenburg there are over 2,300 congregations, with 48 bishops or superintendents to ordain and induct pastors and elders, to conduct parochial elections, to consecrate churches, inspect churches and schools, and generally to carry on a large amount of correspondence. For this work they get nothing except their traveling expenses, which are paid by the congregations. The State gives them their title, but

---
* *Amtskalender für Geistliche.*

adds no pay. The synod of the province a few years ago discussed the question of bishops' incomes, and decided that they might have $25 a year for office expenses, together with a gratuity varying according to parochial income. One of these bishops has an income of $410 a year and seven others have incomes falling below $750.

When a pastorate becomes vacant, the Supreme Council of the Church in the province in which the vacant parish is located, chooses three pastors, each of whom preaches before the people of the congregation, and the final decision as to which of the three shall become pastor rests with them. By a law enacted a few years ago in Prussia, the salaries of regular pastors in the State Church range from 1,800 to 3,600 marks, with parsonage. The lowest salary paid a regular pastor is 1,800 marks and a parsonage. After five years' service he will receive 2,400 marks, and after five other years 2,700 marks, etc., until the salary is 3,600 marks, when the increase will stop, except that older pastors may receive special grants from sustentation funds, which have been increased lately to 6,000,000 marks. The State Church also has special funds for superannuated or disabled clergymen; and has paid out in one year, as much as 1,500,000 marks to these classes, and to the widows of clergymen. The last years have seen the introduction of a new pension law, which deals more liberally with the claimants than the old laws. The clergy in active service are assessed according to their ability for regular contributions towards the pension fund. The Protestant pastors are required by law to pay two or three per cent. of their salary into the Pastors', Widows' and Orphans' fund.

In 1885 the Prussian Churches reported 501,430 baptisims; 250,517 catechumens; 106,200 marriages; 223,229 funerals; and 5,631,957 communicants. Forty-eight churches were consecrated, and 230 candidates for the ministry were ordained. Fourteen new pastorates were reported and eleven of the new churches were in districts where an Evangelical Church had not previously been known. Collections are lifted for Bible Societies, the Gustav Adolf Union, Heathen Missions, Jewish Missions, Inner Missions, City Missions, assisting students of theology, and for various other churchly works. Among the latter were included assistance given needy preachers at home and among the Diaspora, collections to buy sites for churches, etc. For Deaconesses and their work, the collections amounted to 237,350 marks. The total collections amounted to $260,000; the gifts and bequests to $540,000, (2,160,178 marks.)* For Prussian funds, and funds for widows and orphans of deceased pastors, the collections are reported at 2,440,000 marks, in 1890. Church periodicals report the whole sum given to church and charity objects, in the year, by Protestants of Prussia, at $1,255,000. (These figures are for the "United" Church.) In addition to this, through the State, they pay their proportion (say nearly ⅔) of the cost of caring for the poor and infirm— *armen pflege*—which is written at $13,716,000 a year. As to the number of churches and chapels in Germany, there are no recent and reliable published statistics; but the Kingdom of Prussia, it was estimated, (1867) had 12,959.

Amtskalender für Geistliche.

CHAPTER III.

1. PRUSSIAN PROVINCES.

EAST and West Prussia are two of the eastern provinces of the Kingdom of Prussia. Together they have an area a little more than half that of Pennsylvania, and a population of 3,340,000. Of this number 950,000 are Roman Catholics; 50,000 are in other churches, and the rest are Lutherans.

Königsberg is an important town of East Prussia, 400 miles northeast of Berlin. Its cathedral was begun in 1322; and the new university buildings, completed in 1873, are among the finest architectural features of the place. The city has four gymnasiums, two commercial schools of the first rank, an academy of painting with a public picture gallery, a school of music, and other educational establishments. Hospitals and other institutions of beneficence are numerous. Königsberg is one of the important trading centers of Germany; and 1,650 ships and upwards enter its harbor every year. The population (1880) is 140,000, having increased to this number from 83,000 since 1858.

At the head of the church affairs of East Prussia is the Consistory, of which Baron von Dörnberg is, at present (1890) president, with residence at Königsberg. The seat of the General Superintendent, a member of the Consistory, is vacant. Along with these leading officials are seven members, some lay and some clerical. The examining committee is made up of the General Superintendent as president, the clerical members of the Consistory, the members of the theological faculty (of the university,) and deputies appointed by the provincial synod, numbering seven. The churches are divided into two governmental districts, viz : those of Königsberg and Gumbinnen ; the former has 21 dioceses, the latter 16, and each diocese has its superintendent. The preaching of the pulpits was, by Christlieb, characterized as " divided between the evangelical Lutheran and the rationalistic tendencies."

In West Prussia, the Consistory at the head of church affairs consists of eight members, and an examining committee of the same number. The officials of the provincial synod are five, of whom Count von Rittberg is president. The governmental districts in the church are two ; one has its seat at Danzig, and the other at Marienwerder. Each has nine subdivisions, and as many official heads. They are not styled dioceses, or superintendents, etc. The tone of the preaching here is about the same as in East Prussia.

Brandenburg, one of the largest provinces of the Kingdom, has an area of 15,403 square miles, and was once popularly described as "the sandbox of the Holy Roman Empire." The province is a sandy plain with numerous fertile districts and considerable of woodland. It is generally well watered by rivers and their tributaries and has between 600 and 700 lakes. The climate is cold and raw in winter, excessively hot in summer, and violent storms of wind are frequent. The usual agricultural pursuits are carried on, and the manufacturing industries are varied and extensive. Educational institutions are numerous, both in the capital and throughout the province.

Potsdam is the capital of Brandenburg, the summer residence of the Emperor, and is sixteen miles southwest of Berlin. It is handsomely built, contains numerous churches, orphanages, military and other educational establishments, and is surrounded by a fringe of royal palaces, parks and pleasure gardens. It is styled "the German Versailles." The population is about 50,000.

Berlin is not only the chief city of Brandenburg, but of the German Empire. Built on a sandy, marshy district, on both sides of the river Spree, and subject to extremes of heat and cold, there was little in the site to foreshadow the greatness of the German capital. It is so flat that some of its streets have less than a foot of descent in two miles. Only in the last decades has its growth been rapid. In 1861, it covered 14,000 acres ; in 1871, its area was 24,000. Between 1871 and 1874 the value of the household property of the city increased $90,000,000, and about the same rate of increase has been kept up to this time. Since it has become the capital of the German Empire, the increase of population has been much more rapid than before, and has trebled in 34 years. It is reckoned that one-tenth of that population have to live in cellars.

Berlin is rich in all kinds of public buildings. Palaces, academies, museums, castles, &c., abound. The exchange was finished in 1863, at a cost of $900,000, and the Rathhaus, in 1869, at a cost of $2 500,000. It is probable that no city in the world can show so large a number of fine structures so closely huddled together.* The Royal Palace, the Emperor's Palace, the Palace of the Crown Prince, the Royal Library Building—with its 750,000 volumes and 15,-000 manuscripts—the arsenals, the museums, and the guard-house, are among the finest. The most of them are on the "Unter den Linden," one of the finest and most spacious streets of Europe. The city has 520 streets, and 60 squares, with numerous statues of military heroes.

Berlin is as rich in schools as in public buildings. It has 14 gymnasiums (colleges?), 8 real-gymnasiums ; 40 higher girls' schools ; 3 seminaries ; 184 parochial schools, (of which 174 are Protestant, and teach Luther's Catechism, etc.,) with 184 rectors, 3,552 teachers, and over 172,000 pupils. In addition to these are many special schools—for medicine,

---

* *En. Brit.*, art.; Berlin.

mining, military science, architecture, &c.—and there are between fifty and sixty *Kindergartens*. The museums and the gallery of paintings are among the most important in Europe. It has a Royal Academy of Sciences, a Royal Academy of Arts, for the departments of painting, sculpture, architecture, and music; an Academy of Music, and a Royal High School for Music, in all its branches, and other learned bodies and associations of various kinds. It has nine public libraries, at the head of which stands the Royal Library with 750,000 printed volumes (now said to number 1,000,000) and 15,000 manuscripts; and, in addition to these, there are fifteen people's libraries established in various parts of the city. Four of these have 982,000 volumes, or, including the university library, 1,184,000. Most of the libraries are open to all responsible persons. The Egyptian museum has a fine collection of engravings numbering upwards of 500,000; and the picture gallery of the old museum has about 1,500 paintings.

Berlin has 64 churches,* in all, some of them dating back to the thirteenth and fourteenth centuries. Its institutions of mercy are numerous. The Charité Hospital, existing since 1725-1730, and with certain departments in the care of Deaconesses, is an immense institution with accommodations for 1,500 patients. The Bethany, Elizabeth, and Lazarus hospitals, are wholly in charge of Deaconesses, of whom 163 are engaged, and care for over 6,000 sick yearly; and the "Paul Gerhardt Stift," with 70 Sisters and an income of 36,000 marks, exists to care for the sick poor at their own homes. There are four Deaconess Mother-Houses in the city, with over 500 Sisters in all, looking after the sick and the needy. The Augusta Hospital is under the protection and management of the Empress; and is in the hands of women nurses, who attend the sick without assuming the garb and

---

* Others are now being built.

the character of a religious order. The population of Berlin (1890) is written at 1,550,000.

At the head of church affairs in Brandenburg there is a Consistory, with its seat in Berlin, made up of a president, three general superintendents, a dozen other members, and aided by an examining committee of eight members and a special committee of three. The officials, or directors, of the provincial synod number six, of whom two reside in Berlin. The churches of the province are arranged in three general governmental circles, viz.: that of Berlin, of Potsdam, and of Frankfort-on-the-Oder, each with a general superintendent. The Berlin circle comprises eight dioceses and eight superintendents, each of whom is also pastor of a church; the Potsdam circle has 42 dioceses and as many superintendents; and the Frankfort circle has 27 dioceses and the same number of superintendents. There is, also, a French-Reformed inspectorate, with an inspector, who is also pastor of a French church in Berlin. Christlieb characterized the preaching of the pulpits of Brandenburg as "almost exclusively positive and evangelical, with a Lutheran coloring, save as to Berlin, a strong majority of whose preachers are rationalistic."*

Pomerania is one of the larger of the Prussian provinces, touching on the Baltic, with an area of 11,620 square miles. The people, generally, are tall and well built; cautious and persevering in character; they have a strong theological bias, and a turn for dry humor. New ideas have to fight their way into their minds and hearts. In 1883, but 0.32 per cent. of their recruits were illiterate, which fact tells its own story of the educational advantages of the province. The educational system is capped with a university at Griefswald. Of the population, about 24,000 are Roman Catholics, 14,000 are Jews, and there are some " Reformed,' although Prof. Christleib styles the preaching of the Protestant pulpits "strictly Evangelical Lutheran."

---

* *Hom. Magazine*, N. Y.; June, 1884.

Stettin is the chief town of Pomerania, and the leading seaport of Prussia. Its church of Sts. Peter and Paul was originally founded in 1124. It has several churches; an old palace, of which an admirer said, "it does not yield in magnificence to the palaces of Italy;" and statues of Frederick the Great and of Frederick William III. It has important manufactories, has made a reputation for building iron-clad war vessels, has a flourishing commerce, and the schools, benevolent, and scientific institutions, common to German towns of its size. Population, 99,475, (1885.)

Stralsund is also a seaport, on an arm of the Baltic, 115 miles north of Berlin. It has three vast Gothic churches, now four to five hundred years of age. During the Thirty Years' War it was besieged by Wallenstein, who had sworn to take it, "though it were chained to heaven." He besieged it for eleven weeks, and was then forced to retire with the loss of 12,000 men. A yearly festival in the town hall still celebrates this event. The city is well supplied with schools, &c., and its public library has 60,000 volumes. Population (1885) 28,981, of whom about 1,000 are Roman Catholics and 140 Jews.*

The Lutheran Church of Pomerania consists of twenty synodical districts. To waken, and to keep alive a missionary spirit among the people, two pastors are appointed every two years as "itinerant missioners" for each synod, who go from church to church conducting missionary meetings and distributing literature. The results of these journeys are regularly reported at the annual missionary festival in October, on the third day of a week wholly devoted to religious conferences. Similar activities are carried on in

* The church affairs of Pomerania are managed in substantially the same way as those of the provinces already described; and we know of nothing to be gained by repeating the particulars. The same is true, also, of the Prussian provinces yet to pass under our review. We, therefore, dismiss further details of church government, as to these provinces. *Ex uno disce omnes.*

other parts of the Fatherland. The Lutheran Missionary Conference of Pomerania also has arranged a course of instruction in Foreign Missions for the parochial teachers of the province. The latter are taken to and entertained at Berlin free of charge.

Posen is another of the Prussian provinces in which the majority of the population is Roman Catholic. It belongs, physically, to the great north-German plain; and has the characteristics elsewhere noted as belonging to that section. The Protestant population numbers but 532,500; while that of the Roman church is more than double these numbers, and mainly Poles. This province enjoys the unenviable distinction of being the worst educated corner of the German Empire. The relations between German and Polish elements are yet somewhat strained. Posen and Bromberg are the chief cities. The tone of the Protestant pulpits Christlieb characterized as "almost exclusively positive and evangelical, with a Lutheran coloring."*

Silesia has the largest area of any of the Prussian provinces, (15,560 square miles,) and a population of 4,007,925, of whom the majority are Roman Catholics. There is, however, a Protestant population of about 1,900,000, nearly all of whom are in the Lutheran church. Nearly the whole of this province lies in the basin of the Oder, which flows through it from southeast to northwest. Large estates are the rule, properties of from fifty thousand to one hundred thousand acres are common, and over one-third of the whole province is in the hands of men who own at least 250 acres each.

To the east of the Oder, the population is principally of Poles, and, in all the provinces of Germany where they are found, the ratio of illiterates is greatest. Yet, despite the one million Poles in Silesia, the illiterate recruits numbered

* *Hom. Monthly*, N. Y.; June, 1884.

but 1.70 per cent. of the whole. The educational system of the province is headed by the university of Breslau.

Breslau is the capital of the province, with a population (1880) of 272,890, and next to Berlin, is the most populous city of Germany. Educational institutions are numerous, including four gymnasiums, a higher girls' school, a normal school, and a school of arts and manufactures. There are, also, an institute for the deaf and dumb, an asylum for the blind, several orphanages, seventeen hospitals and numerous other institutions of beneficence. Commerce is active, and large fairs are held for the sale of goods each year. More than half the people are Evangelicals. Christlieb characterized the preaching in Silesia as strictly confessional Lutheran, (*i. e.* of "Separatists," or "Independent" Lutherans,) with some "liberals."

While the Kingdom of Saxony is a sovereign state of the German Empire, the province of Saxony is an integral part of Prussia. It lies in the northern part of the kingdom, is very irregular in its form and has a surface that, generally, is flat. It has no natural connection with the kingdom of the same name. The wheat crop of this province is the best in Prussia, and, on the whole, it is one of this kingdom's most fertile provinces. Nearly two-thirds of its surface is under cultivation; about one-fifth is forest, and grain crops are raised to meet home demands, and leave some for export. It produces much beet-root sugar, and the city of Erfurt is widely known because of its market gardens. Of underground productions, the salt and brown-coal mines are important, and three-fourths of the output of copper in all Germany is from the mines of this province. It, also, yields considerable silver. Most of the mines are in the Harz district, including the base of the Harz mountains.

The population is given at 2,428,000, of whom 146,000 are Roman Catholics and 7,000 Jews. The principal towns are Magdeburg, with a population, including its suburbs, of

150,000; Halle, with 81,900; Erfurt, with 58,400; Halberstadt, with 35,000; and Nordhausen, Mülhausen, &c. The illiteracy of the province is 0.17 per cent.

Several of these cities are of much historical interest. Magdeburg, the capital, is one of the strongest fortresses of Germany, and is built on the river Elbe. It has a cathedral dating from the 14th century, handsome and massive in its structure, with two fine towers; two gymnasiums, two "Realschulen," schools of art, medicine, surgery, and mining, and numerous scientific and charitable institutions. The city dates its beginning in the ninth century, and became the seat of an archbishop in 937. Its people embraced the doctrines of the Reformation in 1524, and because of their steadfastness in the faith the place has been besieged time and again during religious wars, sometimes captured, and made the scene of the most horrible cruelties. During the Thirty Years' War, Wallenstein laid siege to it for seven months, and was successfully resisted; but two years later it was stormed and sacked by Tilly. The whole town, excepting the cathedral, the Frauenkirche, and fewer than a hundred and fifty houses, was burned, and 30,000 of its 36,000 inhabitants were put to death, many of them with shocking cruelty. From this seemingly deadly blow, however, it recovered with wonderful rapidity. We here append William Howitt's pen and ink sketch of Tilly and his Magdeburg horrors: " Steam whirled us over the level plains to Magdeburg, that city of vast fortifications and many sieges; where Tilly in the Thirty Years' War glorified himself in one of the bloodiest massacres in history, and in his account of it to the Austrian court, said he thought there had been no such destruction since that of Troy or Jerusalem. In fact, these were some of the most shameful and disgusting brutalities committed on helpless women and children, and were of all things the last to entertain any ladies but those of such a court as that of Ferdinand II. The description of this monster Tilly is itself a horror. He is believed on principle, like Alva, to have studied to render his appearance as terrible as possible. There he sate, watching with delight the ravaging and burning of the city by 40,000 soldiers. The church of St. John, filled with women, was nailed up and burnt. The whole city to 137 poor houses was burnt down before he would listen to entreaties to stop the carnage; 30,000 murdered people lay about or were devoured by the flames. For two days went on this horrible scene, till Magdeburg was a wilderness; and the wives and daughters of the murdered citizens, tied to the horses' girths of the troopers, were dragged after them to the camp. We saw with pleasure the noble cathedral itself, one of the finest in Germany, full of exquisite architecture, exquisite carvings, and monuments, amongst which the large bronze altar-tomb of Archbishop Ernest, with the figures of the Twelve Apostles, by the famous Peter Vischer, of Nuremberg, were alone a treasure to any city." Such were the horrors perpetrated in that city, (A. D. 1631,) in which, somewhat more than a century before, Luther had sung in the streets for bread.

Erfurt is also full of historical interest to us. It is irregularly built, but also has a cathedral erected between 1319 and 1351, which is one of the finest church buildings in Germany. In it are some rich sculptures and bronze castings, and in one of its towers is the famous *St. Maria Gloriosa* bell, weighing 27,000 pounds. The old-time monasteries left buildings for modern uses, the Ursuline being now used for educational purposes and the Augustine, in which Luther lived as a monk, as an orphanage, under the name of the *Martinsstift*.

Many educational institutions exist here. The old-time university was closed in 1816, but the city has an institution known as the Royal Academy of Practical Sciences; a public library of 60,000 volumes and over 1,000 manuscripts; a gymnasium, a normal seminary, a military school, a school of art and of architecture, a midwifery school, and a commercial school. Besides the Martinsstift, there are two orphanages, a hospital, an eye hospital and two infirmaries. The town dates its origin from the fifth century. The cultivation of flowers and vegetables is the most notable industry, and had its origin in the large gardens attached to the monasteries.

In this province, also, is Halle, famous for its university and for the " Francke Orphanage,"—rather, for a series of institutions known as the *Frank'sche Stiftungen.* The place itself was known before the Christian era, and owes its name and its origin to the salt springs which abound in and near the town. It is twenty miles northwest of Leipsic, on the Saale river, at the junction of six railways. It is irregularly built, has narrow streets, and bad pavements, but has been much improved of late by the construction of new and pleasant promenades. Several interesting old churches remain here. Handel, the musician, was born in this city, and a bronze statue, erected in his honor some years ago, stands in the market place.

The Francke Institutions embrace an Orphanage, a laboratory where medicines are prepared and distributed, a Bible press from which Bibles are issued at a cheap rate, and a number of schools of various grades, such as a Latin school, a higher real-school, a citizen school, a higher girls' school, and a free school, attended in all by over 3,000 pupils. (A fuller account of these institutions will be found elsewhere.) An authority terms them "that noble monument of faith in God and charity to man." In addition to these "children of the church," Halle also has its city gymnasium, the provincial trade school, the provincial lunatic asylum, the penitentiary, the town hospital and infirmary, and the deaf and dumb institute.

Halberstadt is a town of 31,250 souls, in a beautiful and fertile country, and about 30 miles southwest of Magdeburg. Among the interesting buildings is a cathedral that dates back to the thirteenth century, and the *Liebfrauenkirche*, dating from the twelfth, and containing noteworthy wall-paintings, &c. It has a gymnasium, new buildings for which were opened in 1875, with a library of 30,000 volumes; a real-school of the first order; a normal school, connected with which is a deaf and dumb institute; and a provincial trade school. In this province, says Christlieb, " liberal preachers are found side by side with Lutheran and confessional, as well as with numerous ministers of a positive Biblical and Evangelical tendency; " which we understand to mean that Lutheranism is the faith of the people, and that the Doctor thought some of the preachers too confessional and the others too " loose" in their preaching.

Schleswig-Holstein, the small province which forms the connecting link between Germany and Denmark, is about 140 miles long from north to south, and from 35 to 90 miles in width. Some of its lands are below the level of the sea, and have to be protected by a system of dykes, or embankments, 25 feet high.

The Lutheran is the established church, and reports 483 church buildings and 440 pastors. This province stands in the front rank as to educational interests generally. In 1883-4, but 0.11 of its recruits were unable to read and write. The proportion of illiterates is among the smallest of any people known. * Within six years 227 new school-buildings were erected. The total expenses for elementary schools were 6.2 marks per capita in the year; and the disbursements for every pupil, 40.62 marks in the cities and 32.31 marks in the country.†

---

* Kolb, *Condition of Nations*.

† About 140,000 of the population of Schleswig-Holstein are Danes, who went to Germany in 1866 through the fate of war. Of the total population nearly all are Lutherans. Of 500 pastorates only thirteen were not Lutheran. Eight of the thirteen belonged to the Roman Catholics, two to the Reformed, and one each to the Mennonites, the Moravians and the Methodists.

Kiel is the chief town of the province, and has a population of 43,600. It is situated at the southern end of the Kiel Fiord, and has picturesque surroundings. It is supposed to be nearly a thousand years old; has a church, the St. Nicholas, that dates from 1240, and a palace built in the 13th century, and enlarged by Catharine of Russia in the 18th. Kiel is the most important naval harbor of Germany, and is strongly fortified. It has a sea-bathing establishment, three public hospitals, an asylum for the blind, an orphanage, an asylum for the weak-minded and idiotic, and a large institution for poor citizens and their widows, and numerous schools. The university of this place was founded in 1665 by Christian Albert, Duke of Schleswig. It was named *Christiana Albertina*, has a library of 200,000 volumes, a teaching staff of 78, and 576 students. New buildings were completed for it in 1876. Connected with it are a hospital, an observatory, a botanical garden, a natural history museum, and a good collection of northern antiquities. The castle has a good sculpture gallery, containing, among many other works of art, some of Thorwaldsen's best productions.

Altona is another important town of the province, separated from Hamburg by "the state line." It is on the Elbe, and is the largest and richest city of Schleswig-Holstein. Commercially, it is one city with Hamburg, and has a population of (1880) 91,047.

In this place our Deaconesses have a Mother-House, built at a cost of 150,000 marks. The institution consists of a Sick-House for women; one for men; an invalid's home; an asylum for neglected children; a children's "waiting school" for little children whose parents are away at work, and a training school for Deaconesses. The number of sisters in the institution is 67. In addition to the work in the Mother-House, they are engaged at twenty outside stations, where they have charge of four waiting schools for children, four hospitals, four other institutions of mercy, and fourteen parishes. They are aided by the Women's Society of Altona, the Fatherland Women's Society of Schleswig, the Society for General Beneficence in Wandsbeck, the Fatherland Women's Society of Hadersleben, and three other societies of women.

Flensburg, with a population (1880) of 31,000, is the most important commercial town of what was the duchy of Schleswig. It has a real-school, and an agricultural school, in addition to all necessary schools of lower grade. Also a celebrated hospital and other institutions of mercy. In this city, also, our Deaconesses have a Mother-House, with 73 sisters, at work in 42 different places.

Hanover is, in area, next to the largest of the provinces of Prussia, and has been a part of this kingdom only since 1866. Up to that time it was an independent kingdom. Like other countries of north Germany, Hanover is amply provided with educational institutions. It has about 3,600 free parish schools, generally dependent on the local churches; eighteen gymnasiums, ten pro-gymnasiums and grammar schools, eleven normal and training schools, twenty-one polytechnic schools, a military academy at Hanover, schools of surgery and midwifery, several good mining and forest schools, and schools for the blind, and the deaf and dumb. Charitable institutions are numerous. Of the population—2,120,168 (1880)—about 276,000 were non-Protestant, mostly Roman Catholics. Of its recruits in 1880, the per cent. of illiterates was 0.53. The Lutheran is the established church; and the preaching is "positively Evangelical Lutheran," with a very few "Reformed" congregations in the province.

During the eighteenth century, three of the rulers of Hanover were also* kings of England, beginning with

* For additional facts concerning Lutherans and the English throne, see chap. vii.

George Louis, elector of Luneberg, who ascended the English throne in 1714 as George I.

Hanover, the capital, is situated on the river Leine, 107 miles south of Hamburg. The town has many handsome buildings and beautiful squares, with statues of King Ernest and Schiller, and a marble bust of Leibnitz. The royal palace contains a fine picture gallery and a collection of natural curiosities; and a notable collection of relics, antiques, "bones of saints," etc., brought from Palestine by Henry the Lion, in 1172. It also is noted for the magnificence of its interior decorations, and for the number and value of the objects of ancient and modern art which it contains. It was built in 1632. The palace of Ernest Augustus, the present king, is remarkable for its historic collections. In the market place is a stately town hall, with an adjacent public library of 40,000 volumes; the royal library, with 170,000 volumes and 2,000 manuscripts, incunabula, archives, and valuable state papers.

Hanover is well provided with educational institutions. Among them are the *Georgianum*, a collegiate school for the sons of noblemen; a gymnasium, a lyceum, polytechnic and medical schools, and free public schools. Several learned societies also have their seat here. Among charitable institutions are an orphanage, school for the blind, infirmaries, hospitals, houses for the poor, etc.

The town has large cotton mills, iron foundries, and machine factories. It was the first German town lighted with gas, (1826.) Its annual fairs for cloths, linen, yarns, etc., are frequented by large numbers of buyers. Almost every industry is represented in it. It is the birth place of Sir William Herschel, the astronomer, and of the brothers Schlegel; and the philosoper Leibnitz died there. The population is, (1880,) including the suburbs, 127,576. Near it are two royal palaces, with large pleasure gardens open to the public.

Hildesheim, 18 miles southeast of Hanover by railway, is the seat of several counts, and of a general superintendency of the church. A church in it belonging to the Roman Catholics, has a rose bush on the wall of the crypt alleged to be a thousand years old. It has several noteworthy church buildings. Among the educational institutions are two gymnasiums, a normal school, a weaving school and an agricultural school. The institutions of beneficence include a lunatic asylum; the *Georgstift*, for daughters of employees of the state; the maternity hospital, two orphanages, and several other hospitals and infirmaries. In 1868, near this place, workmen digging ten feet below the surface unearthed sixty pieces of ancient silver plate, plainly of the Augustan age, and some authorities think it belonged to Drusus himself. Population (1880) 25,887.

In Hanover the "Union" met with no favor, and most of the clergy have been thoroughly penetrated by confessional Lutheranism. More than once have they protested against the incongruity existing between the union theology of the national university, Goettigen, and the legal as well as actual Lutheran confession of the established church. The number of pastors is 1,078; of churches, 1,446; and of souls, 1,910,000—an average of one pastor to about 1,760 men, women and children. There are, also, 23 Independent Lutheran congregations, numbering 4,800 souls, and served by 20 pastors. About 100 of the charges are reported vacant.

The people are active in mission work. The Hermannsburg Society, a "wonder to the world," has always drawn support from Hanover, although the misunderstandings and difficulties of the last few years led the Hanover churches to strengthen their relations with the Leipsic Society. Now, however, the troubles seem removed, and the former amicable relations again exist.

The consistory of Hanover has directed the school authorities and teachers to awaken an interest in inner and foreign missions by making frequent and regular mention of these branches of church work during the hours assigned for religious instruction and geography. When speaking of India, for example, they direct that care shall be taken to speak not only of the pearls and corals of that country, but also of the misery of heathenism, and the labors and trials of missionaries.

Rhenish Prussia, though peopled chiefly by Roman Catholics, etc., has a number of Lutheran churches. The celebrated works of Krupp, the cannon king, are at Essen, in this province.

The churches throughout Germany generally have Pension Funds, from which aged and feeble pastors are aided. In the eastern provinces of Prussia, last year, 2,024,000 marks were paid into this fund, and 500,000 marks remained for the permanent fund after all beneficiaries were paid. At the close of 1890 the Fund had a reserve of six million marks. In the Rhine provinces each beneficiary receives 750 marks yearly. The total yearly pension funds in Prussia are 627,000 marks.

Regular collections are also made for the aid of widows and children of deceased pastors. These amounted, in all, in the past year, to 418,500 marks. The largest amounts were given by Brandenburg, with Berlin, and by Saxony. The contributions from the former were 180,000 marks; from the latter, 93,000. A total of 5,380 pastors are enrolled as entitled to aid from these funds. The total of church taxes in the nine old provinces is, yearly, 51,350,000 marks.

CHAPTER IV.

NON-PRUSSIAN STATES.

Bavaria is largely a Roman Catholic country, yet about the third part of the population are members of the Lutheran church. The Lutheran population is reported at 1,668,000. The preaching is Lutheran and confessional.* Bavaria has the honor of having given the world a *Harless*, who long stood at the head of the church of his native country, although he abandoned the position of court preacher in Dresden to accept that work.

Augsburg is one of the celebrated cities of Germany. It is situated in the angle between two rivers, in Bavaria, has rather an antique air, and a population of over 61,000, (1880.) It dates its origin in the old Roman days. It has had great importance as a commercial and manufacturing town, and its merchant princes, the Welsers and the Fuggers, had their ships in all seas. It is pleasantly situated, and the country round about is very fertile.

The Fugger house, with a front painted in fresco, is one of the interesting buildings. The palace of the bishops, where the memorable Confession of Faith was presented, is now used for public offices. William Howitt wrote of the place as follows : " It is, indeed, one of the handsomest, most substantial, and wealthy looking cities of Germany. The Maximilian Strasse is justly celebrated for its extent, breadth, and imposing character, with its three bronze fountains, large and tasteful, and its lofty, clean, bright, and palace-like houses. It is, in fact, one of the finest streets in Europe.

---
* Christlieb.

You feel that these abodes must be those of wealthy people; and indeed Augsburg is now as famous for its millionaire bankers and brokers, as it formerly was for its diets and weavers. On all sides are old churches and chapels, towers and bastions, orphan-houses, convents and monasteries, Bürgher hospitals, and many other institutions of support and instruction, the Protestant college, the evangelical orphan house, the evangelical poor children's house, the general sick-house, the religious institution, endowed for the education of English young ladies by a certain Boinz de Acton Ireton, of the princely family of the Earls of Torky, probably Torkay, still ably maintained, and furnishing excellent lady teachers for the higher as well as for the female Folks' schools; the Incurable, or sick-place of St. Gervatius, etc., etc.

"Surely never was a city of the same extent so nobly endowed with institutions for the protection of the young and old, of the deserted and infirm."*

The Deaconesses have a Mother-House here, with 75 sisters. Eleven are engaged in a hospital, ten in private nursing, five in parishes among the poor and the sick, and one in a school for little children. Outside of Augsburg 19 of them are engaged in four hospitals, four are busy in two parishes, three are in an orphanage, and the rest in other institutions —schools for little children, day nurseries, training schools, etc. The income of the institution is 34,000 marks.

Nuremberg is second in size of the towns of Bavaria, and first in commercial importance. It is situated in the midst of a sandy but well cultivated plain, and is still surrounded by its ancient walls, although of the 365 towers which formerly strengthened them, only about 100 remain. It has a population of 103,000, (1883;) and the houses of its citizens generally stand with their gables to the streets. The notorious "Iron Virgin" of the dark days before the Reforma-

---
* Rural Life in Germany, p. 118.

tion, is still preserved in the castle. Several of its churches date from the thirteenth and fourteenth centuries, and are notable for their finely carved doorways and their treasures of art. Other interesting buildings are the town hall, with frescoes by Dürer; the law courts, the hospitals, and the houses of the patrician families. Of special interest are the houses, yet standing, of Albert Dürer; Hans Sachs, the cobbler-poet; and of Johann Palm, the patriotic bookseller, who was shot by order of Napoleon.

The educational, scientific, artistic, and charitable institutions of the place are worthy of its ancient renown. The Germanic National Museum has one of the most important historical collections in Germany, stored away in an old Carthusian monastery. It includes a picture gallery, with works by Holbein, Dürer and others. The city library has 50,000 printed books and 800 manuscripts.

Much of its old-time importance clings to Nuremberg as a place of commerce and manufactures. Its manufactures once were so important that it was said: "Nuremberg's hand goes through every land." Pope Pius III. left it on record that a simple burgher of Nuremburg was better lodged than the king of Scotland, (ca. 1450 A. D.) While the place is not so well in the front to-day, its "Nuremberg Wares"—lead-pencils, gold and silver wire, toys and fancy articles—are known throughout christendom. It was the home of the inventors of watches, (at first called "Nuremberg eggs,") the air-gun, gun-locks, the terrestrial and celestial globes, the composition now called brass, and the art of wire-drawing; as also of Faber's lead pencils.

Nuremberg was among the first of the great imperial cities to cast in its lot with the fortunes of the Reformation. In it, Charles V. concluded a peace with the Protestants in 1532. In it, too, Gustavus Adolphus was besieged by Wallenstein, during the Thirty Years' War, for eight or ten weeks, and 10,000 of its citizens died of want or disease. Of the population to-day, about 20,000 are Roman Catholics and 3,000 are Jews.

Saxony, in population, ranks third among the States of the German Empire. In 1885, its people numbered 3,180,-000. The soil is among the most fertile in the German Empire. In 1883, there were 192,000 persons who owned land; but over the five-sixths of this number had less than 25 acres each. The people, therefore, are not rich. Ninety-four of every 100 assessed for taxes report incomes of less than $500 each per year; and 83 of every 100 have less than $125 each. Yet taxpayers, generally, are heads of families, and German families are not small. How a family of six or eight can be supported on an income of from $75 to $125 a year is a mystery to the majority of people in our country. Yet many people in Germany have solved the mystery.*

Saxony is one of the most highly educated countries of the world. In 1883-4, of nearly nine thousand recruits, but 13 were unable to both read and write, (or 0.15 per cent.) The schools are of all grades, from the primary State school to one of the greatest of universities, and may be classified about as follows: Universities, 1; school of mines, of woods and forests, 1 each; schools of art, 2; gymnasium, (colleges,) 13; high class grammar schools, 11; second class grammar schools, 21; seminaries, 18; business schools, 11; high-class national schools, 19; national schools, 2,205; adult schools, 1,953; children at school number 654,700.

When the population was nearly half a million less than it is to-day, there were in all, in Saxony, 4,014 establishments for education, about seven thousand teachers, and over 530 pupils. The total expenditure was £853,090, of which sum £616,694 were for salaries. (The U. S. Commissioner of Education not long ago reported the number of schools at

---

* In one of our own States, six years ago, the average wages of a working man were over $550 a year; but the cost of supporting his family was over $750 for the same time.

2,205; but he evidently lost sight of the large number of "adult schools," (about 1,800,) which continue the work of the primaries, and encourage youth to continue study after confirmation.)

A system of Evening Continuation Classes has been developed for primary pupils. It carries on their educational work for two or three years after they are dismissed from the regular schools. The boys who leave the primary school, if they do not go to the higher schools, must attend for three years longer—say, until they are seventeen—continuation classes for at least five hours per week. But teaching is provided for them, and they are encouraged to attend twelve hours per week. So complete is this system that even the waiters at the hotels up to the age of seventeen attend afternoon classes and are taught one or two foreign languages. The law is much the same in Würtemburg and Baden, and the system is found to work so well that it is in contemplation to extend it to all the states in the German Empire.

In Saxony we have the anomaly of a Lutheran people governed by a Roman Catholic king. And it has been thus since 1697. Less than 75,000 people are Roman Catholics; about 10,000 are Reformed, etc., and over 3,000,000 are reported Lutherans. The Roman Catholic Church has the patronage of the Royal Family, and perhaps it is because of this that there is a Roman Catholic Church in the capital.

Yet the Lutheran is the State Church, and strict Lutheran and Confessional preaching largely prevails throughout the Kingdom.*

Dresden, the capital, had a population of over 245,000 in A. D. 1885, and is the fourth in point of population of all German cities. It is nearly seven hundred years since history first made mention of it. This city is often called "The German Florence." It has also been styled "The Fine Lady of Germany." William Howitt says, "there is a feeling of

---

* Christlieb.

solid, undisputed respectability about it; a quiet and refined manner, and the intelligence of a well-educated and tasteful people." There is not much that is gaudily showy externally; the houses are not kept painted as in some other cities of Germany; and the general use of coal for fuel has diffused over all a marked dingy blackness, while soot falls on visitors much as it does in London or in Pittsburgh.

The Royal Court is at home in Dresden; the city has some fine specimens of architecture, and most magnificent collections in art; artists and literary personages are numerous, and the excellent society of the place soon makes its somewhat common-place external appearance to be forgotten. In the Royal Public Library there are about 350,000 volumes, among them many curiosities, and most valuable works on the history of Germany, as also on the history of more ancient times. In addition to the books the library has 200,000 pamphlets, 20,000 maps, 3,000 manuscripts, and 2,000 incunabula. It contains the most complete collection of historical works in existence. Each hall is devoted to the history of a separate country. Among the rare manuscripts are old Greek works of the seventh and eighth centuries. There are also Mexican manuscripts, written on the Cloe leaf, and many illuminated monkish volumes of the middle ages.* But Dresden's picture gallery is its great pride, and the thing of greatest interest to visitors. It has upwards of 2,500 paintings, mainly by the "Old Masters"— Raphael, Titian, Correggio, Leonardo da Vinci, Rubens, Vandyck, Rembrandt, &c.—and many of them are known over the civilized world. Artists from all quarters go there to see them, to study them, and not a few, to copy them. Indeed, we read of those who make the copying of these paintings their life-work.

William Howitt, who is generally recognized as an authority on anything pertaining to Germany, wrote that if "Dres-

* Bayard Taylor: *Views A-Foot.*

den had only its gallery, that were enough to make it a most desirable place of residence. It affords one of the most delightful luxuries a city can possess." Appleton's encyclopedia says that these art collections are among the finest in Europe, . . and the gallery contains some of the most valuable of the existing works of art. Yet it is free to the public, and is open every day from nine to four o'clock. In addition to this, Dresden has many most excellent educational and charitable institutions; celebrated museums of natural history, cabinets of coins and engravings, and very noted collections of precious stones, pearls, and articles wrought in gold, silver and ivory. One of its churches, the Frauenkirche, is grand in its style, and has a tower 335 feet in height. This capital has many pleasure-gardens in its suburbs where music and popular enjoyment are as rife as anywhere in Germany.

In the Green Vault of the Royal Palace there is an unequalled collection of precious stones, pearls, and works of art in gold, silver, amber and ivory—some of the most costly treasures in the world. The number of objects in it is about 3,000. It is impossible to estimate the treasure these royal halls contain. That of the gold and jewels alone must be many millions of dollars. Gems are there by the hundred, and every gem is a fortune.* The Royal Palace also has a noted "Gallery of Arms," consisting of over 2,000 weapons.

In one of the museums of the city there is a collection of drawings and engravings, numbering 350,000 specimens. A number of hospitals, asylums and other charitable institutions exist here. The city hospital has 400 beds.

Dresden has an extensive trade in books and other objects of art. Its chief industries are the manufacture of machinery, of mathematical instruments, musical instruments, gold and silver ware, china and porcelain, &c. It is the center of a

---

* Bayard Taylor: *Views A-Foot.*

brisk trade, and multitudes of strangers are constantly visiting the place.

Dresden is famous even in Germany for its excellent public schools. There are more than 500 teachers in the employ of the city, which spends $300,000 yearly on its schools. Among these institutions are a technical college with 50 professors and teachers, three gymnasiums, two real-schools of the first class, and two seminaries for the education of teachers. The city is also the seat of a number of well-known scientific associations, of the Royal Academy of Arts; of the Art Union; and of a number of private art societies more or less distinguished. There are numerous important hospitals, asylums, and other charitable institutions, of which further mention is made in our chapters on Deaconesses and Inner Missions.

Leipsic, the "home of the lime tree," is a city of Saxony, situated in a large and fertile plain, sixty-five miles northwest of Dresden. It has a population of 170,000, the vast majority of whom are Lutherans. It now stands, in importance, among the first cities of Europe. The men of eight centuries ago saw it in its youth, and it has gradually increased in prosperity and importance. Next to Hamburg, it is the greatest seat of trade in Germany.

It is especially noted for its university and its book trade. Its publishing establishments are the largest in the world. It has three annual fairs—one at Easter, another at Michaelmas, (29th of September,) and a third at New Year. At the Easter fair, goods to the amount of 70,000,000 Prussian thalers are sold or exchanged, of which sum about one-eighth is for books. On these occasions, strangers from all parts of the Old World are present, and not infrequently outnumber the population. Turks, Greeks, Persians, Armenians, Jews, Hungarians, Chinese, &c., walk the streets in their picturesque oriental costumes. A thousand dealers are represented by their commissioners at these fairs, and the ci itself has over three hundred houses engaged in the book trade, and fifty printing establishments. Among them are the renowned houses of Brockhaus and Tauchnitz.

The place also has great historical importance. In and around it, in October, 1813, was fought the memorable Volkerschlacht (battle of Nations) in which 86,000 men were lost in three days, and Europe was delivered from French domination. Nearly half a million men were engaged; the battle was most decisive and bloody, and the victory of the allies was complete.

Almost two hundred years prior to this, the same fields witnessed the victory of Gustavus Adolphus over Tilly and Pappenheim. In the language of Schiller, the result of that battle was to decide the fate of Germany and of the Protestant religion. Gustavus himself said that the stake was nothing less than a crown and two electorates; while Schiller writes that "the whole age awaited with deep anxiety the issue of the battle, and posterity was either to bless or deplore it forever." The numbers engaged were not over seventy thousand, of whom nearly one of every seven were left dead on the field; but while the forces were very equally divided, the "Snow King" gained a complete victory over the "elite of the imperial army, and the most experienced troops in Europe." Germany and the Protestant religion were safe. The city was besieged six times during the Thirty Years' War.

The famous *Leipsic Conference* between Luther, Eck and Carlstadt; and the *Leipsic Colloquy* between Lutherans and Calvinists, also lend historical importance to the place and are familiar to all readers of Reformation history.

In addition to the most extensive book trade of Europe, and one of the Continent's most famous universities, Leipsic has many educational institutions, including two gymnasiums, several benevolent foundations, numerous scientific associations and various institutions for the cultivation of the fine arts. Its Conservatory of Music is reckoned one of the finest in Europe. The university has a library of 350,000 volumes, and the city library consists of 100,000, while the university and the city together have 4,500 valuable MSS.

Thus have our Lutheran fathers, in times that tried men's souls, girded them for the fray, and decided the fate of nations and religions at the point of the sword or the mouth of the cannon ; thus have they, when these dark days were passed, laid aside their swords and other implements of war, to become leaders in the world of thought and teachers of the race. A faith that has produced such heroes as these is certainly a faith worth living for as well as a faith worth dying for.*

Würtemburg is the third in area, and the fourth in population among the different states of the Empire. The widely-known Black Forest is partly in this kingdom. The manufacture of wooden clocks ("Dutch clocks") has been carried on here for generations, and $10,000,000 worth of them are exported each year. Yet despite all the industrial resources, and the money introduced each year by tourists, the population of the district cannot find support at home. Large numbers of the people go abroad as merchants, teachers, agents, &c. The Lutheran is the established church. The preaching is almost exclusively Scriptural and often Pietistic.

Würtemberg has fifteen towns of more than 10,000 population each. Stuttgart stands first, with a population of 126,000; Ulm has 34,000; Heilbronn has 28,000, &c. Stuttgart is charmingly situated among vine-clad and wooded hills. Clustered around the Schloss-Platz are the old palace,

---

* "A few years ago charges were made that Leipzig, in Germany, was in a state of religious indifference. It appears from reports for the past year that in the four large Lutheran parishes there has been an unusually large growth. The communicants number 25,334, an increase of 3,467. There were 4,447 baptisms and 1,957 confirmations."—*Independent, N. Y.*

of the 16th century ; the new palace, an imposing structure of the present century ; the Königsbau, a huge modern building, the *Acadamic*, where Schiller received part of his education, and now occupied by the King's private library ; the palaces of the crown prince and of Prince William ; the *Stiftskirche*, or collegiate church ; the extensive royal stables ; the central railway station, one of the handsomest structures of its kind in Germany. Near by is Thorwaldsen's statue of Schiller, who was a native of Würtemberg. To the northeast of the new palace lies the beautiful palace park, embellished with statuary and artificial sheets of water, and extending nearly all the way to Cannstatt, a distance of over two miles. In the environs of Stuttgart and Canstatt, are the royal chateaus, Rosenstein, the Solitude, Hohenheim and the Wilhelma.

The art collections of Stuttgart are numerous and valuable. The museum of art comprises a picture gallery, an almost unique collection of casts of Thorwaldsen's works, and a cabinet of engravings. The royal library contains 350,000 printed volumes, including what is said to be the largest collection of Bibles in the world, and, also, 4,000 manuscripts, many of them of great rarity. The city has numerous educational institutions, and two of its most prominent buildings are for the polytechnic and the architectural schools. The Conservatorium of Music has long been renowned. Stuttgart is the centre of the publishing trade of South Germany, and has a busy industry in everything connected with books. It also takes a high place in various other departments of industry.

Stuttgart, not only has been, but is to-day, a comparatively religious city. It may be doubted whether any other city of its age and size has remained so true to the old faith, and to the old usages. Perhaps the churches are a little more liberal in their views ; perhaps they are more ready to work for things outside of denominational lines than some may think consistent with sound churchliness. Perhaps the same things may be said of the churches of the Kingdom, as a rule. Yet the fact remains, that their faith is a power that drives their members to action, leads them to prize the church and her works; and has won for them the respect of the world. The Lutheran is the established church, with which there is one Reformed and several Waldensian congregations.

Ulm is an important commercial town, forty-five miles southeast of Stuttgart, and noted also for its agricultural and mechanical industries. It is the boundary town of Würtemberg, and overlooks the great plain of Bavaria. Its glory is its cathedral, perhaps the finest and largest of Lutheran churches, with capacity to seat 28,000 worshippers. The building was 130 years in construction. Its extreme dimensions are 485 feet in length, and 200 in width.

The history of the origin and progress of this building is very interesting. The citizens of the place (population now about 34,000) determined to build it entirely of their own resources, and not only did not ask for, but rejected all offers of state aid, and of gifts from cities. When the Burgermeister, Ludwig Krafft, had laid the first stone, A. D. 1377, accompanied by the nobles and the gentry of the city, by a procession of youths and maidens, and a band of music, he drew out his purse, and laid on the stone 100 gold gulden. His example was eagerly followed by other nobles and gentlemen; all, great and small, rushed down, one after another, to the foundation to deposit their offerings, and thus provided so much that work on the building went on for a long time. A hut was erected near by, to which all who wished to contribute daily carried money, jewels, bracelets, rings, gold and silver articles, etc.; and as the walls arose, vessels were set in the church, into which offerings were thrown. Workmen came from far and near to Ulm, offering to labor for certain periods gratis; farmers and peasants came pouring in with their wagons to convey materials; and this and that guild, rich family, or rich person, undertook to complete a certain part at his or their own expense. Thus, for near a century and a half, was kept alive this patriotic fire; and besides all the gratuitous labor and material, were expended on it 900,000 florins, a vast sum for those days.

The light and graceful architecture is most beautiful. The whole is one of the most perfect and glorious things of the kind in the world, and the whole tower is of correspondent proportion and perfection. Its great windows, pillars, bands, tracery, buttresses, and all its ornaments, are most exquisite.

Before the Reformation, this great minster was most gorgeously and wealthily fitted up internally. It had no less than fifty-one altars ranging round the main body of the church, with all their rich accompaniments. These are now all cleared away; but the pulpit and its lofty carved canopy; the stalls of the choir, ornamented with heads of almost all the celebrated characters of antiquity, Greek, Roman or Hebrew; the tabernacle in the choir; the chapels of the Von Besserers, the Neithardts, etc., with all their carving, images, paintings, and emblazoned windows, and still splendid testimonies of the zeal and talent with which the native artists attracted hither by the fame of the work, emulated each other in this great temple of the city. The sculptors and carvers, Jörg Syrlin, father and son; the glass-painters, Hans Wild and Crämer; the organ-builders, Schot and Schneider, and Konrad Rottenburgher, a barefooted monk; Wassermann, the image-founder, with the painters, Moosbruker, Schaffner, and other artists, have yet evidences of their genius here remaining, perhaps unsurpassed by any in Germany. In the sacristy, too, may still be seen a figure of Christ, the size of life, seated on an ass on wheels, as it used to go round the city in the procession on Palm Sunday.

The cathedral yard is shaded with venerable lime trees, planted, it is said, in 1699.*

The work of the restoration of this old pile was begun in 1844; and the long time half-finished tower now stands completed at a height of 534 feet, one of the highest, if not the highest, known. (The spire of the cathedral at Cologne is only intended to reach a height of 511 feet.†)

The population of Würtemberg is 1,995,000. Of these souls, about 590,000 are Roman Catholics; 13,000 are Jews; and 4,200 are "other Christians," with 229 who are "holding no creed." The rest are Lutherans. About 800,000, (of the 885,000 males) are occupied on lands, in forests, and fisheries; 370,000 are employed in manufactures and mining; and 75,000 are engaged in trade and commerce. The Kingdom has about 60,000 acres in vineyards, yielding average yearly returns of about £265,000. The cultivation of other fruits is, also, an important industry. The State has nearly 900 miles of railroad, nearly all of which is the property of the State, and yields a net return over all working expenses of £180,000. The telegraph lines send, on the average, 460 telegrams for every 1,000 souls in Würtemberg, each year.

Education is compulsory, universal and most satisfactory. About 99 per cent. (98.9 per cent.) of all children of school age attend school. Every community of thirty families, or more, is compelled by law to have a public school. There is one university with 93 professors and 1,400 students. Besides this, there is a polytechnic school at Stuttgart with 600 students; an academy for the study of agriculture and forestry at Hohenheim; a school of art, also, at Stuttgart; a conservatory of music; four colleges for evangelical theology; and two Roman Catholic training schools. The total number of schools, of all classes, is about 2,500; and the total of pupils is 350,000. Included in these numbers are

---

* Howitt, Rural Life in Germany, p. 117. † *En. Brit.:* Art., Hamburg.

many industrial schools, specially for teaching women's work.

In Würtemberg . . perhaps even more has been done to promote the intelligence, morality, and civilization of the lower orders of society, than in Prussia. . . Every village has a good school house, and at least one learned and practically efficient teacher, one who has been educated for several years at a college.

In none of these . . . is there any class of children analagous to that which swarms in the back streets, alleys and gutters of our great cities and towns and from which our paupers, our disaffected, and our criminals grow up. All the children are intelligent, polite, clean and neatly dressed, and grow up from their sixth to their fourteenth year under the teaching and influence of educated men. *

The power of the religious training afforded by the schools, brought to bear on the children through the formative years of life tells its story in these results. The schools of Würtemberg are grounded and conducted on this Lutheran conception of child nurture; and the results as sketched above are only what are to be expected whenever this training is had.

William Howitt, who visited this kingdom some years ago, when leaving it, wrote as follows : In leaving the little Kingdom of Würtemberg we could not avoid paying it the tribute of our regret. A more pleasant, flourishing, contented country we never saw. The King is popular; the people active, cheerful, healthy and good-hearted.

It would be difficult to find a country which, in proportion to its size and the number of its inhabitants, has given birth to a greater number of distinguished scholars and literary men. The poets Schiller, Wieland, Schubert, Uhland, Schwab, Kerner, Pfizer, Morike, Knapp, Bahrdt, Eyth ; the philosophers Schelling and Hegel ; the Protestant theologians

---

* Kay's Social Condition, &c., of the People . . in Europe.

Brentius, Oecolampadius, Andreä, Osiander, Pfaff, Bengel, Oetinger, Planck, Storr, Schmid, Baur, Beck, Dorner, Hoffman; are natives of Würtemberg, and most of them—Schiller excepted—graduates of Tübingen, although the most celebrated of them (Wieland, Schiller, Hegel, Schelling, etc.) spent much of their public life in other parts of Germany. The country is so small that not a few of its able sons are obliged to seek their fortune elsewhere.

Würtemberg contributes annually more men and means for the promotion of the kingdom of God, than many a Christian country of double its size and ten times its wealth. . . . The people crowd the churches of those who proclaim the whole counsel of God.

On this question, Dr. Wolf, of Gettysburg, says: The most blooming condition of the church (in Germany) is at present found in Würtemberg. This is surprising, especially when one remembers that here was the center of the Tübingen School; that here was the home of Strauss; and that, since the death of Palmer, Oehler, and more recently Beck, the ancient University of Tübingen is by no means counted a bulwark of orthodoxy. Rationalism is comparatively unknown in the churches. The people, you are informed, would not suffer it in the pulpit. They love the Evangelical doctrines, and if their pastors will not preach these, they shall not preach at all. A very good means, no doubt, of keeping some men within the limits of Orthodoxy. Such is the crowded attendance at the churches of Stuttgart, that it has become a maxim: "If you want a seat in any church, you have to be there half an hour before the time of service."

To account for this flourishing religious life, which distinguishes Würtemberg from some other countries of the empire, would require a very extensive acquaintance with facts and circumstances. It may be in a measure attributed to the development, freedom, and activity of the lay element, which have always characterized the Würtemberg Church. The spirit of pietism impressed itself so deeply upon this land, that its hallowed influence has never vanished from it. There are said to be in this little kingdom to-day one hundred thousand Christians that habitually attend the weekly meetings for prayer and the study of the Bible.

The church in this kingdom bears the name Evangelical, although Lutheran in doctrine. Nearly three hundred young men are in the university studying for the ministry, and nearly as many (284) graduates, candidates of theology, are at work as assistants or instructors. Salaries of pastors are smaller than in the provinces of Prussia. In the latter, after twenty-five years' service, the salary of a pastor is $900; in Würtemberg it is $550. In cases of sickness or disability, pastors are entitled to aid from the Sustentation Fund of the kingdom ; and after their death, their widows and children are fairly assisted from it.

In the two Mecklenburgs the educational institutions partake of the high character common to those of the German empire. The two duchies contain nine gymnasiums, seven "Realschulen," three normal schools, and an adequate number of schools of a lower grade. In 1880-81, only 0.56 per cent. of the recruits in Mecklenburg-Schwerin were unable to read and write their names, while all those of the other duchy were able to do both. The educational system is capped by the university at Rostock. The Lutheran is the established, or state, church ; and the preaching, according to Christlieb, is that of "a strict Lutheran Confessionalism."

Brunswick is a duchy of North Germany, and has a population of 370,000, of whom 7,000 are Roman Catholics, 3,000 are Reformed, and the rest are Lutheran. Its educational status is high. The educational institutions comprise three seminaries for training teachers, an anatomical and surgical college, an architectural school, five gymnasiums,

25 "Burger" schools, and upwards of 400 village schools, besides the important institutions in the capital.

Brunswick, the capital, has a population of over 75,000, is a very old place, supposed to have been founded in the ninth century. Among the ten or twelve churches in the city, one is said to date from 1031; the cathedral dates from 1173, and another from the thirteenth century. St. Andrew's has a spire 318 feet high. The educational and charitable institutions are numerous. Among the former are the "Collegium Carolinum," founded in 1745; the Consolidated Gymnasiums, formed by the union of three different institutions; the Medico-Chirurgical College, and the Academy of Forestry. Of institutions of charity we may mention one for the deaf and dumb; an asylum for the blind, an orphanage, and various hospitals and infirmaries. There are two public libraries, and several scientific societies. The museum has interesting antiquities, and works of art by Durer, Holbein, Rembrandt, Raphael, Guido, Michael Angelo, and others.

Wolfenbuettel, including the suburbs, has a population (1880) of 13,500. The library contains 300,000 printed volumes and 7,000 manuscripts, and is especially rich in copies of the Bible and in books of the early Reformation period. There are three Evangelical churches in the place and one Roman. The "Wolfenbüttel Fragments," which created great stir in German theological circles a hundred or more years ago, were given to the public from this place.

Helmstaedt, or Helmstedt, is another town of this duchy, and has a population of 8,700. Its library numbers 40,000 volumes. The Church of St. Stephen dates from the twelfth century. An institution for girls and young women has connected with it a beautiful church "in the Roman style." Among the educational institutions are a gymnasium, two city schools, an agricultural school, and two female schools of the higher grade.

Saxe-Altenburg, Saxe-Coburg-Gotha, Saxe-Meiningen, and Saxe-Weimar-Eisenach, are small Saxon States, together occupying an area equal to but a small county, yet having a population greater than that of half a dozen of the new states and territories of the West, more than twice that of Vermont, and more than one and a third times that of West Virginia. In each, the Lutheran is the established church. Saxe-Coburg-Gotha ranks as a grand duchy; the other three, as duchies. In their government all are limited (and all but one, hereditary) monarchies. The people, generally, are engaged in agriculture and manufactures. In Altenburg, the farmers are very prosperous; but, as a rule, the youngest son inherits the property, or, should there be only daughters, the eldest acquires it. An estate is seldom divided, and the children thus passed over often find themselves in distressing circumstances.

The people, almost exclusively, are members of the Lutheran church. For example, Saxe-Coburg-Gotha reports 198,000 Lutherans and 2,701 of other faiths; Saxe-Meiningen has 214,500 of the former, and 4,105 of the latter.

The Grand Duke of Saxe-Weimar-Eisenach is the next heir to the throne of Saxony, should the present "Albertine" line become extinct. Among his ancestors have been men of great gifts, patrons of literature and art, who attracted to their court the leading scholars and authors of Germany. Goethe, Schiller and Herder were members of the illustrious society of this capital, and the university of Jena became a focus of light and learning, that attracted the eyes of Europe. The ducal family of Saxe-Coburg-Gotha is distinguished for its mental and physical gifts. The present Duke is a brother of the late Prince Albert, of England; and the heir apparent to the Duchy is Alfred, Duke of Edinburgh, second son of Victoria.

Of the principal towns, there may be mentioned Weimar, Eisenach, Gotha, Coburg, Altenburg, and Jena. Altenburg, the capital of Saxe-Altenburg, has a cathedral, a gymnasium, a library, a gallery of pictures, a school of art, an infirmary, various learned societies, and several "elementary" (higher) schools. The population is 26,241.

Coburg is the capital of Saxe-Coburg-Gotha. Originally, it was a convent of the Barefooted friars. The city has several beautiful churches, a gymnasium, a Realschule, a normal college, a school of architecture, a deaf and dumb asylum, and a public library, in addition to government buildings. On a height near the town is the old castle, perhaps eight hundred years of age, in which Luther remained for three months in 1530, and which thus became the birthplace of the famous hymn, " Ein feste Burg ist unser Gott." The bed on which he slept, and the pulpit from which he preached, are still shown to visitors. In the vicinity, is the ducal palace in which Prince Albert of England, was born.

Gotha has a ducal library of 245,000 volumes—some of them very rare, 6,900 manuscripts, and a ducal coin cabinet. There are, also, a picture gallery ; a cabinet of engravings ; a natural history museum ; a Chinese museum ; a cabinet of art, which includes a collection of Egyptian, Etruscan, Roman and German antiquities, etc. The house of the painter, Lucas Cranach, is now used as a girls' school. Other educational institutions, are a gymnasium—founded in 1524, and one of the most famous in Germany, the land of schools, —a woman's school of the first rank, a training school for teachers and another for women teachers, a trade school, a commercial school, and excellent city schools. Among institutions of mercy are a lying-in hospital, a surgical and eye hospital, a private lunatic asylum, an orphanage, a reformatory, a Magdalen institute, and a school for the board and education of destitute girls. The population is about 28,100.

Weimar is the capital of the grand duchy of Saxe-Weimar-Eisenach. It is an unpretending, quiet place ; but there is an air of elegance in its clean streets, and an indescribable atmosphere of refinement, dating from its golden age, when it won the titles of the " Poet's City," and the " German Athens." It abounds in excellent educational, literary, artistic and benevolent institutions. Here is the extensive palace of the Duke, erected under Goethe's superintendence, and with its " poet's room," dedicated to Goethe, Schiller, Herder and Wieland ; here is the grand-ducal burial vault, where the remains of Goethe and Schiller are at rest; here is the church, built about A. D. 1400, where Herder preached ; close by is his statue, while his house is still the parsonage; and within the church is an altar-piece, the crucifixion, the master-piece of Lucas Cranach, whose house stands in the market place. Among the prominent buildings in Weimar are the library, containing 200,000 volumes and a valuable collection of busts, portraits, literary and other curiosities ; a museum, the ancient church of St. James, and the town-hall. The muses have never left Weimar. Since 1860 it has been the seat of a good school of painting; and here, also, Abbé Liszt frequently found residence from 1848 to 1886, and preserved for Weimar an important place in the musical world. Population (1885) 21,565.

Eisenach is located in a romantic district at the northwest end of the Thuringian Forest. It was the birth-place of Sebastian Bach, and he and Martin Luther were educated at its gymnasium, then a Latin school. Near by is the Wartburg, where Luther, on his return from Worms, was imprisoned, and where, from May, 1521, to March, 1522, he devoted himself to the translation of the Bible. Its population is (1880) 18,624.

Jena is best known because of its celebrated university. The church of St. Michael is an interesting relic of the 15th century, with a bronze statue of Luther, and a tower 318 feet high. In this town, also, is the Black Bear tavern, where Luther spent the night after his flight from the Wartburg; and the castle where, in 1620, Goethe wrote his "Hermann and Dorothea."

Oldenburg is a Grand Duchy of Germany. The Protestant population is 260,416; Roman Catholic, 74,254; and Jews, 1,654.

The educational status of Oldenburg is on a footing similar to that of North Germany, generally. In 1882, the proportion of recruits unable to read or write was 0.27 per cent. There is an ample supply of primary, secondary and special schools, and several universities within easy reach. The Constitution of the State is one of the most liberal in Germany, and all citizens are alike in the eye of the law. The religion of the Protestants is Lutheran almost wholly; the Lutheran is the established church, and the law demands that the Grand Duke shall be a member of it.

Oldenburg is the capital, with a population of 24,700. Here are the gymnasium, the commercial school, and three hospitals, the buildings all new and prominent. Here, also, the grand-ducal picture gallery, with works by Veronese, Velazquez, Murillo and Rubens; here are collections of modern paintings and sculptures, arranged in the two palaces; and here is a museum with a collection of antiquities and a cabinet of natural history. Here, too, is the public library with 150,000 volumes,—and the Duke's private library with 50,000 more.

Reuss-Greiz, ("Alterer Linie,") and Reuss-Schleiz, ("Jungerer Linie,") are two principalities of the German empire with a joint population of over 152,000, and in both of which the Lutheran is the established church. Greiz, with a population of 13,000, is the principal town of the principality first named, located in a beautiful valley on the White Elster. It is well built and surrounded by walls. It has the prince's palace, surrounded by a fine park; the summer palace with rich gardens; the old residence castle on a rock overlooking the town; an old church dating from A. D.

1225, with a beautiful tower; the city school buildings, and the normal seminary for the principality.

Gera is the chief town of the other principality. Several times in its history it has been almost destroyed in wars, or by fires. Its educational establishments include a gymnasium, a real-school of the first order, a higher female school, a commercial school, a normal school, a weaving school, three citizens' schools, and the general town schools. Population, 20,810.

In "Germany, Present and Past," Baring-Gould has few good things to say of Protestantism in Germany. He seems to make an exception in behalf of the family of Reuss, and quotes an authority as writing : " Perhaps no country house in Germany has, for a long period of years, produced such good, wise, excellent rulers; perhaps no other house rests on such firm, well considered, and lasting bases of internal family settlements ; few houses have produced such a number of sons who have distinguished themselves in war or political life in, or outside, Germany ; few German territories of like extent have reared more brave and learned men, among the subjects ; there are few which have been such Canaans of happiness and content."

Schwarzburg-Rudolstadt and Schwarzburg-Sonderhausen are two little principalities, together having a population of over 151,000, of whom not quite twelve hundred are outside the Protestant church. Here, also, the Lutheran is the established religion.

Schaumburg Lippe is a small, independent principality, whose people nearly all are Lutherans, and which has the Lutheran as the established church; while its nearest neighbor, Lippe-Detwald, is 95 per cent. Calvinistic. The Prince governs under a constitution, yet the whole government is said to be quite patriarchal.*

---
*Kolb ; Condition of Nations.

Hesse-Darmstadt, the Hesse of the present day, has a Protestant population of about 690,000, and a Roman Catholic population of nearly 270,000. Of the Protestants of this Grand Duchy, about two-thirds are Lutheran. In what were known as Hesse-Cassel and Hesse-Homburg, while the Protestant population is largely of the Calvinistic faith, there yet is a Lutheran population of about 150,000. We may include all under the one general head, and unite the Lutheran population of Hesse at 675,000 ; the churches are given at 753, and the pastors at 464. The ruler of Hesse-Darmstadt bears the title of Royal Highness, and ranks as Grand Duke. He must be a Lutheran. The people are well educated, the proportion of illiterates among the recruits being but 0.21 per cent. Besides its numerous national schools, the Grand Duchy has six gymnasiums, eleven real-schools, various theological, technical, industrial and agricultural schools; while the higher educational wants are supplied by the University of Giessen, with its noble library and numerous scientific institutions connected. The chief towns support scientific and literary societies, and the duchy is generally distinguished for diffusion of knowledge.

Mainz, with a population of over 61,300, is on the Rhine, and one of the strongest fortresses of Germany. Two thirds of the population are Roman Catholics, yet there is a palace of the Grand Duke here; and the old electoral palace contains a valuable collection of Roman and Germanic antiquities, a picture gallery, and a library of 130,000 volumes. It has a celebrated cathedral.

Darmstadt is the Grand Duchy's capital, with a population of about 50,000. It is the residence of the Grand Duke, and the seat of the Consistory of the Lutheran Church. It has four churches. The Grand Ducal Museum includes a library of 500,000 volumes, 4,000 manuscripts, a gallery of 700 paintings, coins, drawings, engravings, and collections in natural history. In the Cabinet Museum there are 60,000 volumes. The city has a gymnasium, two real-schools, a technical school, an Agricultural Society, an Historical Society, the Middle Rhine Geological Society, and the Society of Architects.

Worms is one of the oldest, and, historically considered, one of the most interesting cities of Germany. It has eight churches. The old Bischofshof, in which the Diet of Worms was held, is replaced by a handsome modern residence ; and an imposing Luther monument was unveiled in 1886 in the Luther-Platz. It consists of a series of twelve statues on a platform 16 feet square; and the colossal statue of Luther rises in the center, with a pedestal at the base of which are Waldus, Wycliffe, Huss and Savonarola, the heralds of the Reformation. At the corners of the platform, on lower pedestals, are statues of Melancthon, Reuchlin, Philip of Hesse, and Frederick the Wise of Saxony; between which are allegorical figures of Magdeburg (mourning), of Spires (protesting), and of Augsburg (confessing.) The population of the place (1885) is about 22,000, one-third of whom are Roman Catholics.

Giessen is a town of over 16,800 people, (1880.) It has various endowed schools, among which are a gymnasium and a real-schcol. The university is the principal object of interest. It was founded in 1607, and now has a teaching force of 59, while the students number 616, (1889.) The library has 160,000 volumes, and is specially valuable. Connected with it are a botanical garden, an observatory, an anatomical theatre, an infirmary, a maternity hospital, a museum of natural history, and a chemical laboratory which was directed by Professor Liebig. The university is well endowed.

Hamburg, formerly a free city, now is a state of the German Empire, and consists of the city of Hamburg, with the incorporated suburbs of St. George's and St. Paul's, the surrounding districts with sixteen suburban hamlets, several small islands in the Elbe, etc. The whole territory has a population of 519,000 in 1885, which, in the preceding decade, had been increasing at the rate of about 11,000 souls a year, and now is written at 584,000. From the Reformation to the beginning of this century Hamburg was a purely Lutheran State, members of other confessions not being allowed to reside in it. Full religious liberty has been enjoyed by its citizens for years. The Lutheran is the established church, and the preaching, generally, is soundly Lutheran. In 1880 the returns showed about 23,000 persons of other faiths. Forty-three pastors and nine city missionaries are at work, and a City Mission Society has existed for over forty years.

Hamburg suffered much at the hands of the French from A. D. 1806–1814. Over 1,200 houses were destroyed in 1813 by Davout. In 1842 the great fire destroyed 4,220 buildings on 75 streets, valued at $67,500,000.

The St. Nicholas Church, one of the five that give names to the five parishes of the old city, is remarkable for its tower, which rises to a height of 483 feet. The building now standing was erected from 1845 to 1874, (the former St. Nicholas having perished in the great fire,) and cost over $1,000,000, which was mostly paid by weekly shilling subscriptions. The tower of St. Michaels is 428 feet high, and the church itself ranks ninth in the list of loftiest buildings in the world.

The church authorities of Hamburg are the Supreme Church Overseers, composed of the "Patronat"—the Evangelical Lutheran Senators; the Synod—which consists of two senators, sixteen clerics and thirty-five laymen; and the Church Council—made up of two senators, three pastors and four laymen. There is, also, the usual Theological Examining Committee.

From the report of the Board of Education for the year 1882-83 we take the following figures: In that year Hamburg had 61 public elementary schools, with 34,847 scholars, and 540 male and 247 female teachers. Of the 34,847 children 33,819 were Lutherans, 352 Reformed, 143 Catholic and 29 Jews. The teachers' seminary for men had 102 and the teachers' seminary for women 66 students; there were 2 preparatory schools for teachers, with 111 male and 94 female students: giving a total of 373 individuals studying the profession of teaching. The Wilhelm Gymnasium had 203 students, the Realschule 531, the higher burgher school 388, and the Johanneum school 633 students. Preparatory schools for these higher institutions had a total attendance of 534 scholars. The poorhouse school had an attendance of 95; the orphan asylum school, 462; the institute for the deaf and dumb, 65; and 47 other public schools had an attendance of 6,623 in all. The total public school attendance was 44,381 persons. There were 27 church, foundation and association schools, with 7,780 children in attendance. There were 129 private schools of all kinds, with an attendance of 14,453. The total of all persons receiving instr ction was 66,614.

The list of Hamburg's public institutions is one of which any city might be proud. It has an Exchange where, from from 1 to 3 o'clock each business day, as many as from 3,000 to 5,000 merchants and brokers congregate. Connected with it is a commercial library of 40,000 volumes. The Natural History Museum was founded in 1843, and in 1875—1,200,000 marks were assigned to supply it with better quarters for its valuable collections. The library of the Society for the Encouragement of Science and Art contains 5,000 volumes dealing with Hamburg affairs. The College of Surgeons has a library of 12,000 volumes. Here are extensive botanical gardens, a notable observatory, a chemical laboratory, ethnographical collections under special curators, a medical union, a mathematical society, a society for natural science, an anthropological society, a geographical society, etc., etc., with zoölogical gardens and an aquarium.

Hamburg is one of the most remarkable cities of Europe. It ranks first of all the seats of commerce on the Continent. As a commercial centre it is surpassed only by London, Liverpool, Glasgow and New York. Several of its banks have capitals each ranging from $5,000,000 to $11,250,000. In 1880 its citizens owned over 480 vessels, of which 111 were large steamers and 147 were built of iron. These maintained direct communication with North and South America, the West Indies, and the "ends of the earth." In one year, ships and cargoes to the amount of $500,000,000 have been insured in this city. Its trade with Great Britain, until 1861, exceeded that carried on by the whole of France with Great Britain by half: it was often even double, although the trade with England occupied by far the foremost place in the "French Commercial List." More goods are sent even now from England to Hamburg than the same country sends to the whole of France.* Over a quarter of a million persons sailed from its port for the United States in the six years from 1874 to 1880.

Luebeck was founded about 750 years ago. Although subject to many changes during these centuries, it yet preserved its republican form of government. For six centuries it has been entered by the same gates and traversed by the same streets. It is remarkably well supplied with schools, and has a celebrated gymnasium in what formerly was the home of the Franciscans, and now is known as the *Catharineum*. At the close of 1882 it had 76 other schools, 374 teachers, and 11,478 children in the schools—an average of about one for every five of the population. Among the 76 schools, in addition to the *Catharineum*, are a higher burgher school, a business school, a school of navigation, an industrial

---
*Kolb: Condition of Nations.

art school, church and charity schools, private schools of all kinds, and the public elementary, or primary schools. The churches are an honor to the place, magnificent in structure, and all Lutheran. Of the total population, 67,700, fewer than two thousand, belong to any other denominations. The charitable institutions enjoy a large, well administered property. The pastors number twenty-two and the churches fifteen.

The funded property of the public charitable institutions is worth over £182,000, and the revenues are large. The numerous private institutions of a like nature have still larger funds, and their revenues are correspondingly increased.* St. Mary's Church is one of the most beautiful specimens of Gothic architecture in Northern Europe. It was finished in 1304, and has two towers each 382 feet high. The public library has 100,000 volumes. Including the suburbs, the educational institutions number 91.

Alsace Lorraine was acquired in 1871, and the United Church has never been set up there. Not more than one-fifth of the population belongs to the Protestant Church, and of these 254,000 are Lutherans. Our church here is known as the Church of the Augsburg Confession, and is the established church of the Province. The people are divided into 199 pastorates, have 223 congregations and 222 pastors. Five religious journals are published, and eleven mission societies are at work at home and abroad. Half of the population of Strassburg is Lutheran.

* Kolb; Condition of Nations.

CHAPTER V.

SCANDINAVIAN COUNTRIES.

Denmark has known days in which its king had a stronger voice in the councils of nations than he has to-day. "Hamlet" is supposed to have had his original within its boundaries. Its history is one of interest as thrilling as that of Norway and Sweden, and this is saying much of it.

The area of Denmark proper is but about 14,550 square miles—not a third that of Pennsylvania; or, including its dependencies, 79,000; and the population 2,172,000. The surface is uniformly low; the coasts, low and sandy; yet the landscape of the islands and of the southern part of Jutland is rich in beech-woods, corn-fields and meadows. Danish forests are almost exclusively beech, although oak was the characteristic tree up to within the last two centuries. Wheat, rye, barley, buckwheat, oats and potatoes are freely grown; the usual fruits of northern Europe flourish, and, in proportion to its size, excepting Belgium and England, there is not a country in Europe that can compete with this as a corn (*i. e*, edible grain) producer. About sixty-five per cent. of the whole area of the country is under some sort of crop or in grass. A remarkable feature in Danish husbandry is that greater value is attached to the produce of the dairy than to that of the soil; and that much of the horse power is withdrawn from the fields and employed in dairy work. The greater part of the land is in the hands of small land owners, and much of it is divided into very small tracts. This is owing, mainly, to the State law, which interdicts the union of small farms, and in various ways encourages the parceling out of landed property.

Manufactures are not carried on to any great extent. The most noticeable of any is the manufacture of porcelain, begun over a hundred years ago by the making of china out of the clay found on the island of Bornholm. The Copenhagen potters now are famous for their very graceful designs, and their porcelain has a distinct value of its own. The Royal China Factory of the capital is celebrated for its models of Thorwaldsen's works in " biscuit china." There are woolen, cotton and linen manufactures, chiefly for home use; as is true, also, of sugar refineries, etc. Iron works are making considerable progress; and iron foundries exist in Copenhagen, in which city, also, are manufactories of locomotives and of machinery of various kinds.

The Faroe Islands form a dependency of Denmark, and are situated in the North Sea. They number twenty-two, with an area of 510 square miles. Seventeen of them are inhabited, with a population of 11,220. The islands consist throughout of rocks and hills, and everywhere present to the sea perpendicular cliffs, broken into a thousand fantastic forms, and presenting to those sailing around the coast the most picturesque and varied scenery. Fogs are common; severe storms are frequent at all seasons, and July and August are the only true summer months. Yet the winters are not severe; it seldom freezes for more than a month, and the harbors are rarely ice-bound. The cultivated land is to the uncultivated as one to sixty. Plows cannot be used because of the rugged surface, and the ground cultivated is usually turned up with the spade. Sheep form the chief riches of the islanders, some individuals having flocks of from three to five hundred, which are never housed. Houses are built of wood, roofed with birch bark and covered with turf, which usually is so green that it is difficult, at a short distance, to distinguish the place from the surrounding fields. The islanders are skillful in climbing the high and dangerous cliffs, and are experts in fishing for seals and whales. They are of Norwegian origin, a vigorous, laborious, loyal and religious race, belong to the Lutheran Church, and now are under the ecclesiastical dominion of the Bishop of Zealand.

The inhabitants of the Danish West Indies number over 33,000; but only 4,800 are Lutherans. There are three parishes, each supplied with a pastor from Denmark. The Lutheran churches of these islands are not self-supporting. The ministers and clerks receive by far the largest part of their salary from the public funds, and the churches have a few privileged incomes. They use a hymn book printed in Copenhagen, Denmark, and the catechism from Philadelphia. All of them have voluntary choirs, Bible-women, sick-nurses, benevolent societies, and Sunday schools.

Mr. Lose, a resident of St. Croix, writes thus of the churchly habits of the people: " Better behaved congregations are nowhere found. Late comers are few, and they glide in during a hymn, but never during the scripture reading nor during the sermon; everybody is quiet and attentive, and wherever the minister turns his eye he meets the eyes of his flock. Everybody joins in hymns and responses; nobody thinks of leaving before the service is out, no matter how long it lasts. At our four or five yearly communions there is no elbowing one's way up to the altar, but every one waits till the clerk or one of the helpers gives him a sign. And at the altar no one is found whose life is an offense to the brethren. The Lutheran is the established church. Services are held in the Danish and in the English tongues each Sunday."

Denmark's capital is Copenhagen, a city of 286,900 souls (in 1880 they numbered 235,254), and situated at the southern extremity of the Sound, 180 miles northeast of Hamburg. It is built on low ground, with the sea to the front and a series of fresh water lakes to the rear. There are numerous pretty parks within the city, and it has an excellent harbor.

The royal palace of Christiansborg is one of the principal buildings, adorned within and without by numerous works of Thorwaldsen. Its "Knight's Hall" (Riddersal) is a magnificent apartment, 120 feet long, 44 high, and 50 wide. In it, also, is the Royal Gallery of Paintings, enriched by many valuable specimens of the Flemish, Dutch and Italian schools. Both houses of the Danish Parliament have apartments in this palace in which they hold their sittings. Connected with it is the Royal Library, with about 500,000 volumes and 30,000 manuscripts. Another palace, dating from 1604, contains a most valuable coin and medal cabinet, a fine collection of Venetian glass, a famous silver drinking-horn, the regalia and other objects of interest as illustrating the history of Denmark. In one end of the Knight's Hall there is a silver throne. The palace of Charlottenborg, named from Charlotte, wife of Christian V., is now used as a place for the exhibition of paintings and sculpture. Of four palaces on the Amalienborg, built by four nobles as residences for their families in the long-ago, one is inhabited by the king, another by the crown-prince, a third by the queen-dowager, (when there is such an one,) and the fourth is the seat of the principal court of justice.

Another old-time palace is now used to contain the Royal Museum of Art, the Ethnographical Museum, and the Royal Museum of Northern Antiquities—the richest collection of Scandinavian antiquities in the world. The Thorwaldsen Museum, erected to contain his works, is a two story building, 230 feet long, 125 wide, and 46 high. About 300 of the great sculptor's works are gathered into it; and in one apartment is his sitting-room furniture, arranged as it was found at the time of his death in 1844.

The Cathedral is one of the principal church buildings in the city, and is ornamented by numerous works of Thorwaldsen. In the ornamental front there is a terra-cotta group of sixteen figures, representing John the Baptist preaching in the wilderness; and Christ's entrance into Jerusalem adorns the portico. St. Peter's Church has a fine spire 260 feet high; Trinity Church, a round tower 115 feet high; and the Church of Our Saviour, a curious steeple 300 feet high, ascended by an outside spiral staircase.

Numerous institutions of beneficence exist. Among them are Frederick's Hospital, with accommodations for 600 patients; the Communal Hospital, with accommodations for 850; and Barton Hospital, with accommodations for 508. In addition there are the General Hospital, the Garrison Hospital, a children's hospital, a maternity hospital, an asylum for lunatics, Abel Kathrine's building for poor women, an orphan asylum, a blind asylum, a deaf and dumb asylum, and an asylum for imbeciles.

Copenhagen is an important trade centre. Over five hundred merchant vessels are owned by its residents. By the aid of canals, large vessels can approach almost to the centre of the town. It has, also, extensive cloth and calico factories, foundries and iron works, tanneries, sugar refineries, tobacco factories, etc. Its National Bank has a capital of about $11,000,000; and other banks have proportionate capitals. Its population is about wholly Lutheran, there being but few "Reformed," Catholics and Jews,—perhaps six thousand in all.

Of educational buildings and institutions, this capital has a generous supply. In addition to the schools of lower grade, it has a polytechnic school, a veterinary and agricultural school, a military school, and a school of navigation. At the head of all stands the University.

Odense, the birth-place of Hans Christian Andersen, is an important place of over 20,000 inhabitants, and the chief town of a province of that name. A ship-canal, ten feet deep, affords an outlet to the sea. It contains glove factories, match works, mineral water works, chemical works, tobacco works, etc. In it is St. Canute's Church, one of the largest and finest edifices of the kind in Denmark, built of brick, and dating back to 1081. Under the altar lie the remains of Canute, once the patron-saint of Denmark; and Kings John and Christian II. are buried within its walls. Other buildings of note are "Our Lady's" Church, of the 13th century; Odense Castle, the Provincial Infirmary, the new post-office, and the (old Franciscan) hospital. We may also mention Karen Brahe's library, and the Episcopal library of 25,000 volumes.

Aarhuus is a seaport town of Denmark, on the Cattegat, and a city of about 25,000, (1880.) Its cathedral is a gothic structure, and the largest in Denmark. The town has, also, a lyceum, museum, and library. The harbor is good, and Aarhuus has an extensive trade, with regular steam communication to Copenhagen, and railway connection with the interior. It is the residence of a bishop, whose salary is £600.

Aalborg is another Danish seaport, and the capital of the district of the same name in Jutland. It is a place of considerable commercial importance, and of manufacturing industries. It contains a cathedral, and a school of navigation; and is the residence of a bishop whose salary is £400.

In 1877, the death rate in Denmark was the lowest of the European States. Next to Norway, it is reputed the healthiest country in Europe. The criminal classes have diminished during the last decades.

"There are upwards of 200,000 estates, and of these 170,000 are independent freeholds. There are about 280,000 families in the country districts, of whom 170,000 own the above freeholds; 30,000 families farm hired lands, and 26,000 familes are without land; but living with farmers, and taking part in farm labour. Denmark has but few native industries, and depends chiefly for subsistence upon the produce of the land and cattle stocks." The Danes dispose of much of their farm produce and live stock to the English markets. There are about 2,693,566 acres of land under cultivation. The children of Christian IX. have made the most brilliant matrimonial alliances of any dynasty in Europe. The heir apparent is married to a daughter of King Charles XV. of Sweden and Norway. The oldest daughter, Princess Alexandra, is wedded to the Prince of Wales. Prince Wilhelm, now Georgios I., of Greece, selected as his queen a Grand Duchess of Russia, daughter of one of the late Czar's brothers. Princess Dagmar was espoused by Grand Duke Alexander, now Emperor of Russia; and another daughter became the bride of the Duke of Cumberland. But one child—a prince—remains.*

In general the Danes are tall and robust, with regular features, florid complexions, and hair inclined to yellow or red. The people are divided into five classes: first, the nobility, who hold privileged estates under the king; secondly, the titular nobility, which embraces the two orders of knighthood, all counts and barons possessed of privileged estates, and all the higher officers of State, civil, military and ecclesiastical, who hold their nobility by virtue of their offices; the latter are frequently purchased for the sole purpose of acquiring rank, without the holders discharging the duties they nominally involve, or acquiring emolument from them. Thirdly, the inferior clergy, lawyers, and students. Fourthly, merchants and citizens. Fifthly, farmers and seamen.

The houses of the Danes are generally of timber; and it is only in cities that any considerable portion of brick houses is to be met with. Each house has a kind of piazza before it, where the family often sit in summer, and the landlord smokes his pipe.

---
*Lapp, Norsk and Finn.

The tables of the rich abound in every luxury common to Europeans; and even those of the middle classes frequently exhibit a variety of foreign delicacies. But the food of the lower orders consists of oat cakes, rye bread, fish, cheese, and other ordinary products of the country. It has been charged that excess in the use of wines and other strong liquors is a bad characteristic of these people: and "a drunken Dane" has become proverbial; yet the reports for late years show that the number of public drinking places, (saloons,) has decreased from 1,350 some years ago to 300 at the present time. The French fashions are generally adopted by both sexes in summer; but in winter, they have recourse to furs and woolen garments. The common people are neat, priding themselves in different changes of linen; and even the peasants exhibit a neatness in their dress which seems to surpass their condition. They enjoy dancing to the music of a violin; and bands of itinerant Germans supply them with nearly all kinds of harmony. Two other diversions are so common that they may, perhaps, be styled national; these are "running at the goose" on Shrove-Tuesday, and being drawn over the ice in sledges in winter.

Education in Denmark is compulsory, but it is all afforded by parochial schools and higher institutions working to the same end. The schools number over 3,000; half a dozen training colleges qualify teachers for them, and the whole educational system is crowned with the University of Copenhagen. The professional and tutorial staff of the University (of about fifty teachers) is remarkable for the high order of instruction imparted. It is rarely you meet a person who cannot read and write. Science and literature have long been cherished; and this smallest among the States of Europe has produced celebrated philosophers, mathematicians, astronomers, painters, sculptors, physicians, philologists and theologians. It was the birth-place of Hans Andersen, the children's story-teller; of Niebuhr, the traveler; of Malte-

Brun, the geographer; of Martensen, the theologian. Copenhagen, the capital, has three public libraries, of which the royal library, with 500,000 volumes, is especially rich in Oriental and Icelandic MSS.

"Denmark has, till within a few years, been an exclusively Lutheran country. No other church was tolerated, and apostasy from the Lutheran creed was punishable with exile and confiscation of property. Dissenters (mostly Baptists and Methodists) are called and treated as mere "sects." The church service is of a more highly ritualistic type than in the Lutheran churches of Germany. The prayers, the Gospels and Epistles, the benediction and the responses are intoned. The candles are kept burning on the altar, the communion is called mass, and even the elevation of the host (without the adoration) is retained. I attended two Danish services in Copenhagen, and never heard better singing at the altar and in the choir."*

A clergyman of the Danish Church writes as follows concerning our church in Denmark: "As to the body of the clergy, we have two degrees, priests and bishops. The country is divided in parishes, every one (or two) parishes having its rector; most of the parishes of the greater cities, and a very few of the country have, besides, one or more perpetual curates; the older rectors have curates besides. Every diocese has its dean, who is rector of the Cathedral, and the dioceses are divided into *Provstier*, (rural deaneries,) the rural dean having also some of the duties of the Archdeacons of the English Church. The Bishop has every fourth year to visit every parish of the diocese, inspect the schools, catechize the youth, (the priest performing the Confirmation service twice a year;) he alone ordains pastors and consecrates the new churches. The rural dean institutes the rector of every parish, and has to visit all the schools of the rural deanery every second year; he inspects the church

Ev. Alliance Report.

fabric and the parsonages. All bishops, rectors, and perpetual curates are nominated by the King; till 1849, the rector of a living, where the tithes of the Church fabric were in the hands of a nobleman, was nominated by him.

At the Reformation, the Church was robbed of the greatest part of her property. One-third of the tithes the rectors retained; one-third (the Bishop's tithes) was taken by the Crown, and the greatest part of it given to colleges and hospitals, to poor livings, or to the salary of the Bishops; one-third, (the tithes of the Church fabric,) was afterwards sold to laymen, whose duty it is to keep the Church fabric in good repair. Since 1849 the Bishops are paid by a fixed salary from the Government, which has retained their above-named title. The rector's salary is: 1. The Tithe, (now converted into a fixed number of bushels of corn, paid by the land-owner;) 2. Parsonage, with glebe; 3. Fees. The salaries vary greatly,—from under £100 to £700*; and it, therefore, often seems necessary for the priests to seek translation, as they always begin with the smallest livings, and, as a rule, have no property of their own.

In the Constitution of 1849 it is said: "The government of the church shall be organized by law;" but the radical political party has hindered this promise from being fulfilled; therefore no constitution of our church has been framed. Theoretically, we are under the sway of the Parliament and the government; practically, we have very great freedom, and this freedom has been very beneficial to the church. Many of the clergy having again remonstrated against the anomalous government of the church, the government has decreed that every year the bishops shall meet at Copenhagen, and before them shall be laid all the bills on church matters which the Government is about to propose to Parliament.

*The Bishop of Zealand has £1,000.

The ritual of our church has also retained much of what is old, and I think we feel as the members of the Anglican Church do—we think it the best possible, because in it we have found nourishment for our spiritual life. It is not strictly enforced, some of its regulations having fallen into abeyance. Our churches are all consecrated, and in the country they are surrounded by a churchyard, where everybody who lives in the parish has a right to be buried. At the eastern end of the church is the altar, as a rule formed by masonry, and with an interval between it and the eastern wall of the church. Above it is a picture or carved figure, and lights stand upon the altar, and are to be lighted at the Holy Communion. Round it is a rail, where the communicants kneel. The baptismal font is generally in the choir. The priest is robed in a black cassock, with a white, round cravat: at the Holy Communion he puts a white surplice on, and then a red velvet cope with a cross on the back. The eastward position is observed, as the rule.

The service begins with a fixed prayer and the Lord's Prayer, at the door of the choir, by the clerk. Then one or two hymns are sung. Then the priest, standing at the altar, turns his face to the people and sings, "The Lord with you;" and the congregation answers, "And with Thy spirit." Then, turned to the altar, he sings the Collect of the day, and, (addressed to the congregation,) the Epistle of the day, and, on the greater festivals, the Gospel. Then follows a hymn; then from the pulpit, an unwritten prayer; then the sermon on the Gospel of the day; then an extempore prayer for the church, the king and his house, the sick and afflicted, and others; then the blessing. A hymn having been sung, the priest, from the altar, sings, "The Lord be with you," answered by, "And with Thy spirit." Then comes a fixed prayer, (the priest being turned to the altar,) then the blessing, (the priest turning to the people,) then a hymn, and the service is ended by a fixed prayer and the Lord's Prayer by the clerk.

Baptism is, in the country generally, celebrated during the service—after the first hymn following the sermon. It is always celebrated by affusion (not aspersion, not immersion) of water; this is on the head of the infant. The ritual is strictly observed, and we lay great stress on our having retained the old question, " Do you renounce the devil, and all his essence, and all his works?" Certificates of baptism and confirmation are indispensable to entering service, apprenticeship, or matrimony.

The Holy Communion is to be observed every Sunday, at the forenoon service, if anybody wishes to commune. The ritual is strictly observed. During the reception of the holy elements the priest says to all present, "This is the true Body of Jesus." "This the true blood of Jesus." The priest himself does not commune. The sick and infirm are allowed to partake of the Holy Communion at home.

For marriage our appointed ritual is observed, the priest giving besides a free address. At the churching of women the priest gives an address. At burials the priest gives an address, and earth is thrice cast upon the coffin in the grave, with the words, " From earth art thou taken ; to earth thou shalt go ; from earth thou shalt rise."

As to the doctrine of the Danish Church, she accepts as her Symbols, besides the three Œcumenical Symbols, *Confessio Augustana invariata* and Luther's Lesser Catechism. The other symbolical books of the Lutheran churches do not concern us at all.

Rationalism is almost unknown with the Danish clergy. I never remember to have heard a Rationalistic sermon. A strong Sacramental belief in Holy Baptism as the means to convey regeneration to the baptized, and the real presence of the Body and Blood of our Holy Saviour in the Holy Communion, is characteristic of the Danish Church. But we try with all our might to weaken the belief that the Sacraments work *opus operatum*, and to enforce the necessity of giving the whole soul to the Saviour in a heartfelt faith.

Of the population of Denmark perhaps from 15,000 to 25,000 are outside the Lutheran Church. Dr. Kalkar, before the Evangelical Alliance in New York, said: "Up to the present time we know very little of denominational disputes, as all are Lutheran. Methodism, despite its elegant church in Copenhagen, built with American money, has no adherents. The Baptists have lost their popularity since the law enforcing baptism has been abolished, and comprise a few members, who convene in a little church in the suburbs."

The King of Denmark must be a member of the Lutheran Church, and he exercises ecclesiastical jurisdiction through the bishops. These church officials are all equal in rank although the Bishop of Zealand is considered *primus inter pares*, as he has the most extensive diocese, and the prerogative of crowning the king.

The bishops of the Church in Denmark number eight, including one for Iceland. Each bishop has under him several provosts, each of whom superintends a district which he visits once a year. Of these there are in Denmark proper, 160; in Iceland, 19. Two thousand parishes are reported, with many affiliated churches; nearly seventeen hundred parish ministers, and over sixty rectors. The ministers are ordained by the bishops. The theological faculty is located at Copenhagen, and is composed of five professors.

Dr. Kalker said, further:

"The growing societies for promoting Christian life and work are laboring hard. Missions to the heathen, which have reoccupied the East Indies, their old field of activity; the Society of Deaconesses, the Society of Released Convicts, the societies for prisons, the different societies for schools for infants, the Mission for Sailors, (which has established preachers in London, Hull, and Newcastle, who take care of northern seamen,) the society for sending preachers to Danish emigrants in America, different charitable societies for taking care of the sick, the blind, idiots, and still others—these are all laboriously working. The income from the societies is considerable, and speaks in favor of private charity, although in Denmark, as in other countries, one must confess that liberality shown toward Christian objects does not bear quite the right proportion to the great prosperity of the population, more especially the agricultural portion. The sign of activity is in the present system of preaching, which has great advantages over that formerly in vogue. As a rule, the sermons are lively, intellectual, and taken from the vital truths of Christianity. Martensen, Fog, Bladel, Frimart, Anderson, P. Nordam, Monrad, (who for many years was Prime Minister,) deserve mention, and many others whom we cannot name here, however deserving they may be to be mentioned.

"A good step has also been taken in placing the Church of Greenland on a better footing. For many years the desire has been expressed that the preachers of that country should be natives. The candidates who were sent thither from Denmark seldom learn the very difficult language thoroughly, and regard their position in a barren land only as a passage to a better one at home; there are also good prospects for only a few candidates. A commission appointed by the Government has studied the whole condition of Denmark and made a report as to the education of native pastors and the elevation of the people generally. A beginning has also been made, as F. Moe, a native of the northernmost colony, has been called to Copenhagen in order, after sufficient preparation, to be ordained by the Bishop of Zealand. (Other natives have been ordained since the doctor made his report.) Thus in Denmark the kingdom of God is being assisted in many ways, although dark shadows may sometimes pass over the church, since on one side Socialism, and on the other lukewarmness and want of resolution are undermining its foundations, but it cannot be denied that the powers contained in the Gospel are showing activity, and with the assistance of the Holy Ghost create an active life in the different districts of the little country."

Iceland is about four-fifths the size of Pennsylvania; but is a land of volcanoes, ice-hills, lava-beds, and hot springs. The inhabited parts are but as little fringes of territory bordering the coasts. No kind of corn is grown. Agriculture is almost unknown, and the kitchen garden generally produces but potatoes, turnips, carrots, &c. The pastures and the fisheries are the chief sources of wealth, if we are allowed to use this word in connection with a people among whom the richest man has a property income of but $1,500 a year.

Despite all these things, there are few countries in which it is so easy to live with little labor as in Iceland. If there are but few there who are very rich, there are none who are abjectly poor; and the people, in many parishes, pay more for the aid of their needy fellows than for all other taxes put together.

In addition to its location just under the polar circle, and a consequent harsh climate, Iceland has been plagued with lava streams, ice drifts, famine, pestilence, and pirates. Hecla is the most noted of volcanoes, and has been known to send columns of ashes 16,000 feet into the air, which afterwards were drifted by the winds as far as Norway and Scotland, 500 to 600 miles distant. In a volcanic eruption in 1783, one of the principal streams of lava was 50 miles long, 12 to 15 miles wide and 100 feet deep. Another stream was 40 miles in length. Together, the two covered nearly the one-ninth of the surface of the island, and in the eruption which produced them one-sixth of all the people, and one-half of all the live stock, perished. Three-quarters of a century before that, 18,000 people died of small pox. A hundred years before that, pirates from Algiers ravaged one settlement after another, and carried many of the captives into slavery.

Patriotic natives have styled Iceland "the best country on which the sun shines;" but by impartial strangers it must be regarded as one of the worst that has ever been inhabited by civilized human beings. It is a country of snow and glaciers, without trees and coal, where peat is of bad quality, and can be dried only with great difficulty. There are no trees growing now except dwarf birches and willows. Outside the little town of Reykjavik there are no roads—merely tracks worn deeply by the feet of ponies in soft peat or in hard lava. Along these the little ponies pick their way with singular intelligence. Fords across glacier torrents full of rocky boulders are often disagreeable, sometimes dangerous; and bridges are rare. The main difficulty in Icelandic traveling is to find ground firm enough to bear a horse and his rider. Water is everywhere, and the traveler constantly crosses fords, either in the river whose course he is constantly following, or through torrents rushing down from the fjeld on either side.

Roughing it in every possible way; facing all the hardships of a colonial pioneer without his prospects and hopes; in a land which seems to have been left unfinished by the hand of nature, and under a most inclement sky, the Icelander still has a healthy and vigorous constitution, and lives in peace and content. Perhaps in no country is social equality more complete than in Iceland. The priest, indeed, enjoys a certain rank and distinction, along with the title, "Sira;" but even the governor himself, whose office is one of power as well as of dignity, is liable to have his hand grasped by farmer or fisherman, with the familiar inquiry, "How are you, Finsen?"*

---
*Nineteenth Century, Aug., 1880.

Educational interests have firm friends among the Icelanders. The people are very poor; yet they can say with Sydney Smith and his friends: "We cultivate literature upon a little oatmeal." Only that sometimes, alas, even the oatmeal is lacking.

The last biennial budget appropriated 228,788 *kronen* for educational purposes, or more than one-fourth of all the expenditures of the government. A school-law of 1880 makes it the duty of parents, under the supervision of the pastors, to see that their children are instructed in the catechism, in writing and in arithmetic. Whenever the parents neglect this duty, the pastor is to see that the children receive such instruction, and the parents must pay for it. A school commission appointed in 1881, in its report, declared that it was the duty of the smaller political sections of the people to see to the elementary education of the young; but that the high schools, of which there are sixteen on the island, should be supported by the Government. As the population in the island is very much scattered, most of the rudimentary teaching is done in the houses by the parents; and a systematic inspection of schools and of education in general is, naturally, a somewhat difficult matter. Recently five schools for girls have been established, and several agricultural and technical schools are in operation. The one "learned school" (gymnasium) is found at Reykjavik, and is in a flourishing condition, numbering now 120 students. Its course is six years. The Althing decided to unite the different high schools in the capital, and create a university with three faculties; but the King of Denmark has refused to sanction this law, probably on account of the growth of radical ideas among the Icelanders. The only theological school is that at Reykjavik, which is in the hands of three professors. The Lutheran is the confession of the whole Icelandic Church.

Where the population is too sparse for a church-school, the education of the young is in the hands of the mother. No one is admitted to confirmation who cannot read the word of God. Education in the ancient languages is more general than in any other country of the world, and the English language and literature are studied by many of the peasantry. A striking instance of this is narrated by the late Bayard Taylor, who was asked by an humble hostler boy with a relay of horses for him, concerning the comparative merit of the writings of a leading English poet! Indeed, knowledge is universal and ignorance is a disgrace.

It is no exaggeration to say that in no other country is such an amount of information found among the classes in a similar position. A child of ten unable to read is not to be found from one end of the island to another. A peasant understanding several languages is no rarity.

Time for teaching is afforded by the long, dark winters, when out-of-door work is impossible; and teachers for children are abundant, where all in childhood have been instructed. Even in the remotest habitations, a knowledge of the humane arts has produced softness of manners. In Reykjavik, and among the clergy generally, are to be found men of high literary culture,—scholars who would do credit to any seat of learning in Europe. The people are intelligent, cultivated, kindly; they can boast of many learned men, and several poets are now living. In this respect no community of equal numbers can rival them; and they deserve all praise for their gallant struggle with nature, under a hostile sky, and on an ungrateful soil.*

During their long winter evenings, when high winds toss the falling snow from the cliffs, and almost bury with a white mantle the humble dwelling of the Icelander; parents, children and domestics are seated on their lockers, or beds, in their principal apartment, under the light of the single

———————
* Nineteenth Century, Aug., 1880.

lamp suspended from the ceiling. A member of the group designated takes from the shelf an Ancient Saga, or Shakespeare or Milton, in their native language, and reads aloud, while the rest listen with hands busy in various work. Sometimes recitations from some favorite historical poem will be the entertainment.

Such domestic scenes have been common for centuries in Iceland. Very young children will read excellently, and write with elegance.

Four physicians have the island in charge, some of them having circuits a hundred miles or more in diameter. Law givers have never been wanting. No visitor to a metropolis of our day listens to keener retorts, more artful evasions, or sharper chicanery, than were heard in the Althing, long before a parliament sat in London. They have no "members of the bar," all acting as their own attorneys, and from boyhood studying the laws by which they are governed.

Everybody must have an education in Iceland. Here is a marvel of history,—in such a country, in mere huts, amid loneliest, barrenest solitudes, is a culture that would shine in the most brilliant circles of our best society. Such triumphs of mind and heart as this nation presents have no parallel in all the wide world's arena of knowledge and virtue.

The school-year is from October to the end of May. After mastering Latin, and making some progress in Hebrew and Greek, with the rules of interpretation of the Old and New Testaments; the student leaves school to study at home. He then reads ecclesiastical history, homiletics, etc. Some, in addition, visit Copenhagen or Stockholm, or both, to complete their general culture. Most of the churches and families have libraries, in which light literature, beyond the romances of the old Sagas, have no place. The women receive exactly the same education as the men.

The Icelander's religious faith has for centuries been very simple. Infidelity, in its multiplying forms, is unknown.

If no other volumes are in his home, the Icelander is sure to have the Bible and books for church-service.

Before setting out on a journey, it has been the custom to invoke God's blessing. When the fishing boat is ready, the crew, reverently placing their hats before their faces, pray for success and safety, repeating the same ceremony on reaching their destination. The moral and religious habits of the people at large may be spoken of in terms of the most exalted commendation.

The Sunday scene at an Icelandic church is one of the most singular and interesting kind. The little edifice, constructed of wood and turf, is situated, perhaps, amid the rugged ruins of a stream of lava, or under the shadow of mountains covered with never-melting snows. Here the Icelanders assemble for worship. A group may be seen around the door of the church, waiting the arrival of the pastor; all habited in their best attire, their children with them, and the horses, which brought them from their respective homes, grazing quietly around the little assembly. The arrival of a new-comer is welcomed by every one with the kiss of salutation. The priest makes his appearance among them as a friend; he salutes individually each member of his flock, and stoops down to give his almost parental kiss to the little ones who are to grow up under his pastoral charge, after which they go together into the house of prayer. The pastoral care is next to the parental in watching over the family, without, however, interfering with the proper authority of the father and the mother. The presence of the preacher is not dreaded as an interference with domestic order or social freedom and innocent pleasures.*

All candidates for the ministerial office in Iceland, must assume the following obligations before being ordained, viz:

I, N. N———, swear, and, in the sight of God, solemnly attest:

---
*Headley; Island of Fire.

First. That I am sure in my heart and conscience, that I have been lawfully called to this sacred service, so as to have used no means divinely prohibited, whether privately or publicly, to be advanced to this office.

Second. I promise that I will labor with the utmost diligence that the heavenly doctrine, contained in the Prophetic and Apostolic Scriptures, and in the Symbolical Books of the Danish Churches, be faithfully instilled into my hearers; the sacraments be decently and devoutly administered according to the form prescribed by Christ; Church discipline be diligently practiced; catechetical instruction be inculcated; the ceremonies received in the Church be observed, and nothing be done contrary to the ecclesiastical regulations.

Third. I earnestly and solemnly vow that I not only wish to flee and detest doctrine contrary to the divine word, but desire also, according to my ability, to fight for the same, and would rather shed my blood than approve false and fanatical dogmas.

Fourth. I will most earnestly read the sacred records, and will study the articles of faith with such diligence as is proper; nor will I allow any day to pass without devoting time to sacred reading, unless prevented by sickness or unavoidable hindrances.

Fifth. I will live a life worthy a minister of the divine word, zealously endeavoring to afford my hearers a laudable example of godliness, honesty, and holiness, and never by any act disgrace this holy and revered order.

Sixth, and last, I undertake and religiously promise that, besides the obedience due the secular magistrate, I am willing to render my bishop, as well as my provost, all lawful obedience, to do what is enjoined most promptly, and so to conduct myself towards my brethren in Christ, that no one can or ought justly complain of me.

These things, one and all, I promise to observe as truly, as I truly and sincerely desire God to aid me with his holy gospel.*

From olden times it has been the prevailing custom to engage in devotional exercises every day, especially during the winter. For this purpose are used on the week-days various short devotional chapters from older, and from more modern, times; while on Sundays, and on other sacred days, sermons are read from house-postils on the Gospels for the Church Year. The home devotion of Iceland consists in reading and singing. Both before and after the reading, quite long hymns are sung. Family devotion is considered specially important during Lent; and for this season they have a special set of devotional books, treating exclusively of the sufferings of Christ.†

The official confession of Iceland is the Lutheran, but in 1874 liberty of confession was established. The recent attempt of French missionaries to win the Icelanders over to Catholicism failed entirely. According to the statistics of 1880, the Non Conformists on the island are 1 Methodist, 1 Roman Catholic, 4 Unitarians, 3 Mormons, and 3 without any religious profession. In regard to ecclesiastical affairs, the island is divided into 20 districts, with 141 parishes, 180 pastors and 299 congregations. Each congregation is governed by a congregational committee, and each larger district by a number of selectmen. Positions with an income of 1,800 *kronen* or more, are filled by the appointment of the king of Denmark; others are under the control of the bishop. These are all recent arrangements, the last mentioned being established by the law of October 3d, 1884. Since 1801 Iceland has but a single bishop; before that there were two, one at Holar and the other at Skalholt. The bishop resides at Reykjavik, where the theological

---
* Handbook (Liturgy) of the Icelandic Church, Reykjavik, 1879.
† Headley; Island of Fire.

seminary and other higher schools are situated. Of the 299 churches in Iceland, 217 are built of wood, 75 of peat, and 7 of stone. On October 1st, 1880, the total number of inhabitants were 72,445—namely, 34,150 males and 38,295 females, belonging to 9,796 families. Of late there has been considerable agitation in Iceland, but chiefly of a political nature. The Icelanders want absolute self-government, and nothing but a formal connection with the government at Copenhagen. As yet the King of Denmark has an absolute veto over the transactions of the Althing in Iceland.

Sometimes complaint is made that some of the clergy are too much devoted to secular pursuits. It is widely known that the people of Iceland are poor. What they do not have they cannot give. Many Icelandic pastors, therefore, find it an absolute necessity to give some attention to business or to toil with their hands, to keep "the wolf from the door." They have little time for miscellaneous study. They have no morning papers to read with their breakfasts. They have no surfeit of religious periodicals or reviews. They are not in touch with the outside religious world on many of the topics which stir the churches to their centre in many parts of Europe and America. Sam Jones and the Boy preacher do not interest them.

But, while in occasional instances there may be justice in the complaint, the great body of the clergy are true to their mission.

Some of the Church customs in the country are peculiar. At the end of the Sunday service the whole congregation come up and salute their good pastor with a kiss, and he each one of them in return, and then they kiss one another, and this without regard to sex or station, the daughters of the pastor, if he have any, coming in for their full share. Such simplicity is certainly very charming. It is the relic of an age long since gone by.

Iceland, the region of intense natural cold, is full of religious warmth. The Word of God is the text book of the people. Every home has its Bible, not as an ornament, not as the well-kept, cherished marriage gift, nor because of some undefined superstitious feeling of reverence, but for daily use. In Iceland the Bible is constantly read. As a consequence, Iceland is without a theatre or prison. There is no such office as sheriff. They own no cannon, and military drill is an unknown science. Dishonesty, theft, and other crimes rarely occur. Some time ago, in the *New York Observer*, the Rev. T. B. G. Peck, who had spent a summer among these people, and who wrote of "Summer Days in Iceland," said: "I hesitate not to say that they are the purest and most guileless people in the world."

Sweden, in area the largest Lutheran country of the world, extends from 55 degrees to 69 degrees north latitude. Its greatest length is 986 miles, and its total area 170,713. It has 1,600 miles of coast line; and its boundary line towards Norway is over 1,000 miles in length. The population (1885) was numbered 4,770,000. In one of the southern counties the population averages 193 to the square mile; while in Norrbotten, farthest to the north, and by far the largest county, the average was but 2.4. This country, with the sister kingdom of Norway, is rapidly becoming a favorite of summer travelers; and Du Chaillu has made the "Land of the Midnight Sun" known to thousands of Americans.

The frontier towards Norway consists of a continuous mountain range, the source of very many streams and rivers, which generally flow south-east to the Gulf of Bothnia. In the districts nearest the mountains many lakes are formed, and about one twelfth of the whole surface of Sweden is covered with water. The kingdom is divided into three chief parts: Götaland in the south; Svealand or Sweden proper, in the centre; and Norrland in the north. Norrland, again, in its north-west parts is called Lapland. In Svealand there is a system of lakes, of which some are so near the level of the Baltic that, under certain conditions, water flows from the sea into the lakes. The greatest part of the country consists of low hills, clothed with forests of pine and fir. The valleys are generally filled with water, although there is, also, some arable soil. In Skane, in the extreme south, the surface is low and fertile, as may also be said of several other low-lying tracts.

The rivers and lakes of Sweden are well stocked with fish, which are not only an important article of food, but also an important item in commerce. One hundred and forty different kinds of them are found in Sweden and along its coasts. The salmon, the herring, the cod, and the "stromming" are the most important. As many as 1,500 millions of herrings have been taken in one year. The average annual value of the Swedish fisheries is from two to three millions of dollars. The forests also are an important factor of the kingdom's prosperity. In minerals, Sweden is rich, especially in iron ores; and Swedish iron is celebrated for its good quality. In 1884, 526 iron mines were worked, the joint produce of which was nearly a million tons. The mileage of railroads (1884) was 4,194; of telegraph wires, 12,969. The messages forwarded numbered nearly 1,180,000.

Not far south of 60 degrees North latitude, and nearly as far north as the northern parts of Labrador, is Stockholm, ("the isle of the log," "an island on piles,") the most beautiful capital of Europe. Built, partly upon eight islands, intersected by many canals, surrounded on the land side by rocks, forests and hills; and on the water side by Lake Maelar and the Salt Sjo, (salt lake,) an arm of the Baltic, its site is universally recognized as extremely picturesque, and as presenting one of the most remarkable panoramas in the world.

Its massive palace, its open squares, the museums, gardens, libraries, scientific institutions, schools, churches, statues, bridges; its splendid quays, which form the finest feature of the city, and at which vessels are continually loading and unloading; the numerous miniature steamboats, which fill the office of omnibuses, carrying passengers to and fro; and the abundant evidences of good government and prosperity, all combine to make it one of the most attractive cities of Europe.*

This northern capital is of no mushroom growth. A settlement has existed at that spot since 1187, the days which succeeded the Viking era, and when pirates preyed on the towns of the Maelar coast; although the renowned Birger Jarl is the reputed founder of the city. Those were the

<blockquote>
Days of old,
When Knights were bold,
And barons held their sway,
</blockquote>

and the fortress city was frequently obliged to undergo most desperate sieges by pirates.

But the times are changed. The spirit of the nineteenth Christian century has a home in Stockholm. Over two dozen churches exist in it: it has about three hundred manufacturing establishments; an export trade of $30,000,000, and an import of about $50,000,000 a year. In shipping, over 1,600 foreign vessels land at the quays, and nearly ten thousand others are engaged in coasting trade.

The city is well built, although many of the streets and of the sidewalks are narrow. The islands are connected by stone or wooden bridges, and many handsome residences adorn the city and the suburbs. Over-topping all others is the Royal Palace, completed in 1754, a quadrangle of solid granite, remarkable for its grand and admirable proportions, and its chaste yet massive style of architecture. It is built

---
* Du Chaillu.

on the highest of the three islands of the original town. Next in beauty to the Palace is the National Museum. This fronts the home of royalty, overlooks the harbor, is 260 feet long, 170 feet broad, and 90 feet high.

Stockholm is the seat of government, the centre of the literary and social activity of the country, and has many scientific, artistic, educational and benevolent institutions. In Stockholm royalty makes itself felt, and increases the formality and politeness which is natural and universal among the Swedes. It has palaces and public buildings suited to a capital, and whatever of display the nation makes, is made there.

But the suburbs of the city are its greatest charm. Here you find the parks,—among them Deer Park, (Djur-garden,) of which a recent traveler says, "There is nothing equal to it (elsewhere?) in Europe." It occupies an island about 18 miles in circumference, and is adorned with villas, romantic drives, lovely walks, paths through glades, forests of magnificent trees, lakes and masses of rock.

Summer is the best season to visit the city. The month of June—especially the last two weeks—is the pleasantest time of the year, as many of the people have not yet gone into the country, and the inhabitants then make most of the fine weather. Rich and poor pass their leisure hours in the open air, and in the afternoons and evenings the pleasure gardens and parks are thronged; and good bands of music play. Whole families—father, mother, children, uncles, aunts, cousins, friends—spend many of their evenings there. Every one is neatly dressed; there is no roughness, no vulgarity.*

In 1888 the population of Stockholm was written at 235,000. Its manufacturing industries have increased with the growth of population. It has 275 factories, employing about 10,000 persons, and producing to the value of about

---
* Du Chaillu.

$9,000,000 yearly; over 3,800 merchants, who have 6,550 assistants; over 11,000 mechanics, of whom 8,700 belong to the wage-earning class. Sixty-three small steamers are used to carry passengers from one part of the city to another, in addition to the tramways used on land.

Seven "academies" have their seat in it. The Swedish Academy deals with the language and literature of Sweden; the Academy of Sciences has charge of the Royal Museum of Natural History, the botanical institute, and the physical, astronomical and meteorological institutes; the Academy of Belles Lettres occupies itself with history and antiquities; the Academy of Agriculture sees to affairs of agriculture and of the fisheries; the Academy of Fine Arts has charge of the official school of art; the Academy of Music has the care of the State Conservatory of Music; and the Academy of Military Sciences has a sphere well defined by its name. Membership in each of these academies is limited, and is generally made up of regular, honorary, and foreign members. Only such as have proved themselves experts in the studies pursued by the different respective academies are eligible to membership. Each is a distinct body, and has its own library.

There are, also, several private societies of a very like nature. Such are the Society for the Publication of Historical Documents, the Historical Society, the Society of Anthropology and Geography, the Society of National Antiquities, the Geological Society, the Entomological Society, etc. Stockholm also has a high school of medicine, a technical school, a high technical school, a military school, a high military school, a veterinary school, a school of pharmacy, seven secondary schools, two seminaries for women teachers, besides its private schools.

Among the interesting public collections are the Royal Historical Museum; the Royal Numismatic Collection, with 90,000 coins and medals; the royal collection of armor and dresses; the Royal Museum of Fine and Industrial Arts; the Royal Museum of Natural History; the Northern Museum; the Royal Library; the Royal Archives, etc. This capital is rich, also, in statues, those of Birger Jarl, the founder of the city; of three Gustavs, I., II., III.; of three Charleses, XII., XIII., and XIV., and of the uncrowned kings of science, Berzelius, of chemistry, and Linnæus, of botany, adorning its different sections.

Gothenburg (Göteborg) is the second city, and the chief commercial town of Sweden, but a few miles from the Cattegat. It is well and regularly built, mostly of stone or brick, with wide and well paved streets. It is the seat of a bishop and of a provincial governor. It has 34 schools of different kinds, including two Latin schools; a teacher's seminary; an extensive elementary school, founded in 1630, with a library of 15,000 volumes; a trade institute, two technical schools, a "real-gymnasium," and a navigation school. The museum contains collections for natural history, entomology, anatomy, botany, archæology, ethnography, a picture and sculpture gallery, and a collection of 6,000 coins and medals.

Gothenburg has numerous fine buildings and pleasant promenades. Several of the churches are worthy of note, of which the finest is the the cathedral, (the *Gustavii Domkyrka*,) founded in 1633, twice burned down and rebuilt, and now stands a cruciform structure, 173 feet high, 194 feet long, and 75 feet broad. The city has numerous benevolent and charitable institutions, mainly supported by private beneficence.

Gothenburg has its own method of dealing with the drink question, initiated in 1865. Under it, the authorities contract for a term of three years with a limited company, which takes all the licenses for selling strong drinks, and hands over to the town treasury the net proceeds of its trade. All "bars" are closed from 6 P. M. on Saturday until 8 A. M. on Monday. Under this system the licenses issued have decreased from 119 in 1865, to 56 in 1876, (of later times we have no report concerning this.) In the same time, the apprehensions for drunkenness decreased 22 per cent.

Malmö is a seaport town of Sweden, on the southern coast, and the eastern shore of the sound, opposite Copenhagen and 16 miles from it. In importance, it ranks next to Stockholm and Gothenburg. It is built on a plain: has considerable trade and a number of manufactures, that of gloves being the specialty. It has a population of about 40,000. The Church of St. Peter, founded in 1319, is well worth a visit, its transepts being extremely beautiful and light in form. In it, the Lutheran faith was first promulgated in Sweden. The City Hall was built in 1546; is remarkable for its handsome exterior, and its magnificent festival hall, 100 feet long, 19 wide, and 12 high. In it the St. Knut Guild held its meetings. (This Guild was a powerful organization, every member of which was equal to six witnesses before a court of justice). Here, also, is Malmö Castle, in which the third husband of Mary Stuart was kept a prisoner, but which now serves as barracks and as a prison.

Norrköping is "the Manchester of Scandinavia," 113 miles by rail south-west of Stockholm, and built on both banks of the Motala, a tributary of Lake Wetter. Among the conspicuous buildings are St. Olaf's Church, erected by Gustavus Adolphus in 1616; the Gustavus orphanage, and the palatial high school. Woolen cloth is the staple in manufacturing industry, 33 factories being engaged; and steamers, gun-boats, and iron-clads are built in its shipyards. The population is about 30,000. Some of the woolen mills employ from 500 to 700 or 800 hands. The power, generally, is supplied by the rapids of the river. The manufacturers are awake to the importance of using the almost unlimited water-power at their doors, and of adopting the latest improvements in machinery devised in England, France, Germany and America. The working population is thrifty, and their houses exceedingly neat. Eighteen miles west of this place is the magnificent estate of Finspong, with iron-works and a cannon-foundry. It has a fine castle, with a chapel and a valuable library, and beautiful parks. It belongs to Louis de Geer, and his heirs or assigns, and covers an area of 96,000 acres.

The high school building in Norrköping is an ornament and a credit to the town, and would compare favorably with any in the United States. One of the rooms is 80 feet long, 40 wide and 25 feet high : there is plenty of light and the the ventilation is good. It has a small museum furnished with zoölogical and mineralogical specimens, skeletons and skulls, shells, eggs, corals, fishes, turtles, etc. : and a library stored with scientific works and books of reference. French, English and German literature are well represented. The school also possesses a good laboratory for the study of chemistry. The number of teachers is between twenty and twenty-four. The schools of the place are among the finest in Sweden, and this is saying much.*

Upsala is a town dear to Sweden, not only because of its age but because for centuries it has been a seat of learning. Here is Sweden's oldest university and the residence of its arch-bishop. The place is situated on the small river, Fryis, 42 miles north of Stockholm, in a vast and fertile plain. Not far from the town is old Upsala, and the old church where, in heathen times, was a great temple for the worship of Thor, Adin and Freya. Then a sacred wood covered the country, and human sacrifices were made to the gods. In Upsala of to-day, perhaps the most remarkable of its buildings is the cathedral, founded in the thirteenth century, but not completed until 1435. It is of brick, and the propor-

---
*Du Chaillu.

G

tions are uncommonly noble and harmonious. The length is 390 feet, and the inside height 88.

Ten miles north-east of Malmö, on the line of railway to Stockholm, is Lund, said once to have had 200,000 inhabitants. There is an old saying that,
> When Christ was born,
> Stood Lund and Skanör in the corn.

When acquired by Sweden in 1652 it was little more than a village. In sixteen years after that date a university was begun there, and the city advanced thereafter. It has the hospitals of Skane, many school buildings, an institute for the deaf and dumb, and the Cathedral of St. Lars. This building is in the shape of a cross, is 271 feet long, 72 feet high, and was begun in 1145. The inner parts of the church are very fine. Perhaps more remarkable than the church is the crypt, extending under the entire chancel, with a length of 126 feet, and a width of 36—one of the largest in the world.

At the southern end of Wettern Lake is the city of Jönköping, with a population of over 16,000, in a beautiful valley, and with an excellent harbor. It has a noted church dating from 1649, supreme court buildings, a town house, artillery barracks, a high-school building, &c., worthy of note. It is the centre of a net-work of railroads, which give it easy communication with all parts of the country. Water communication also is had with Stockholm and with Göteborg and ports on the lake. The industrial establishments are numerous, embracing paper and linen mills; steam dyeing works; manufactories of cigars, wall-papers, and chemicals; a machine-shop, iron foundry and match factory. This latter, thirty years ago, manufactured 35,000,000 boxes of safety matches, valued at about $60,000. Fifteen years later the yearly product was worth $750,000. Ten miles out of the city is Taberg, a mountain of iron ore, 1,129 feet above the level of the sea.

A couple miles from the west end of Lake Hjelmar stands Oxebro, a town in which have been transacted some of the important affairs of Swedish history. The principal church dates from the beginning of the fifteenth century. An old castle, built on one of several islands formed by the river on which the city is built, was erected by Birger Jarl six hundred years ago. Not fewer than twenty diets or important assemblies of representatives of the people have been held in it; and there Bernadotte was elected crown prince in 1810.

Karlskrona is a Swedish naval station, and the most important of all belonging to the kingdom. The town is built on several islands, connected by floating and other bridges. The streets are broad and regular; dwelling houses are large; there are many squares, and a shaded "garden" or park. Barracks, fortifications, men-of-war, cannon-balls, etc., give a warlike appearance to the place. The sailors live in clean, well-ventilated barracks; and a good library is open to all.

Falun is a little town of but about 7,000 population, but widely known because of its copper-mines. These are known to have been worked for over six hundred years, and extend miles under ground. Gustavus Adolphus styled them "the treasury of Sweden;" and Bernadotte gave splendid banquets in their vast chambers, when the mines were brilliantly illuminated for the occasion. In former days, some mine-masters were very rich, and are said to have attended weddings on horseback, their horses shod with silver. Years ago, the mines yielded 3,000 tons annually; but the out-put is much smaller now. The fumes from the smelting houses destroy all vegetation near them; and the houses of the place, all of wood, are blackened by them. Falun is the chief town of Dalecarlia; and different kings have manifested much interest in the mines.

Linköping is an old, inland town, with a population of about 8,000, a cathedral that was begun A. D. 1150, a castle that was built four hundred years ago, and an elementary school that has a library of 30,000 volumes, together with coins, portraits, and antiquities, &c.

Vesteras, a small town of 6,000 people, has a cathedral 306 feet in length, with a steeple 320 feet high. The elementary school has a library of 12,000 volumes, including that of the Electoral Prince of Mayence.

About 2,400 families of Sweden, belong to the nobility, and it is estimated that these own about the one-eighth of the lands of the kingdom. The burdens of state taxations, &c., belong to the landed estates; and when a member of the peasant class buys a nobleman's estate, he enjoys the nobleman's freedom and assumes his responsibilities in the way of maintaining the provincial army and bearing other state burdens. The number of grave crimes, and of convictions, lately decreased 30 to 40 per cent.*

The Swedes are of the middle size, and few of them are corpulent. They have light flaxen hair, and a ruddy countenance. The women are distinguished for their beauty. Their general resemblance would indicate that they belong to the same family, rather than that they are natives of a large country. In their manners, such is their vivacity that they have been styled the "French of the North."

The national character of the Swedes is highly respectable and interesting. They are remarkable for great simplicity in manner, in dress, and in feeling. They are eminently hospitable, honest, contented, industrious, brave. The population being thinly settled, and communication with strangers not being very frequent, they, like the Scotch Highlanders and the Welsh, are attached to ancient usages, and traditionary legends; and their tendency in this respect is found to be considerably inveterate, not being easily changed or modified by recent improvement.

---

* In seven years the production of alcoholic drinks decreased 44 per cent.—*Kolb: Cond. of Nations.*

Sweden is not more celebrated for any thing, than for the state of its roads. The high roads wind agreeably through the country, are made with stone or gravel, and are as good as the turnpike in England; and yet not a single toll is exacted from the traveler. Each landlord is obliged to keep in repair a certain part of the road, in proportion to his property; and for the purpose of ascertaining their respective portions, small pieces of wood or stone, marked with numbers and capital letters, are placed at different distances on each side of the way. Such, indeed, is their goodness throughout the whole country, that during several thousand miles, which I traveled in this, and in my former tour, I scarcely met with fifty miles that deserved the name of indifferent. They are also as pleasant as they are good, and in many places look like gravel walks, carried through gentlemen's grounds and plantations, as they wind through the fields and extensive forests, the lofty trees casting a gloomy shade with their overhanging foliage.* These observations have been confirmed by more recent travelers. Sweden, in truth, has been gradually making improvements in the departments in question, especially in the eastern and southern divisions of the kingdom.

The first of May and Midsummer-day, are consecrated to mirth and festivity, during which the Swedes display all their gayety by dances and songs; the greater part of which are national. On Monday, large fires are lighted in the fields, as emblematical of the natural warmth which is about to succeed the severity of a long winter; and around these the people assemble to enjoy good cheer, and amuse themselves with sports. On the eve of Midsummer day, a season still more calculated to inspire hilarity and joy, the houses are ornamented with boughs, and the young men and women dance round a pole till the morning. They then take a few hours' repose; after which they repair to the church to im-

---
* Goodrich: Manners and Customs of Principal Nations.

plore the divine protection, and then give themselves up to fresh amusements.

Considerable attention has been paid by the Swedes to agriculture, but owing to the poverty of the soil, they scarcely raise enough for home consumption. In respect to summer agricultural operations, the Swedish farmer is obliged to observe the greatest despatch, or the season will be gone. Summer bursts suddenly from winter, and vegetation is quick, the valleys are green in a few days, which were before covered with snow : this verdant prospect lasts about three months, during which short period they sow and plant. The people are, in general, healthy, complaisant, and courageous; both sexes can endure hunger, cold, and poverty. Their animals are similar to those of Norway. To their horses a decided preference is given over those of Germany, for purposes of war. Sweden abounds in venison and fish, and the Gulf of Finland furnishes them with innumerable seals, from which they produce train-oil in sufficient quantity to render it an article of commerce, which they export. There is excellent pasturage, but not much corn.

Many of the quaint old houses from their walls speak to the entering stranger of the spirit which rules within. Entering them, he sees shelves on which the Bible and other sacred books are kept, and here and there sacred inscriptions on the walls. In the lower story he may see here and there, cut in wood, the date of finishing the structure, and, above or below it, the words, " Soli Deo Gloria." At another place he may see the inscription, " May God send seed to all sweet creatures ; " at another, " Houses and goods are inherited from parents, but a sensible women comes from the Lord ; " at another, the exhortation, " Trust in God."

Passing along their highways after the lamps are lit, the farmers may be seen with the big Bible on the table, and reading it to the family. They are generally content with their lot, and their belief is that whatever God does for them is best, even though they live on coarse flat bread and sour milk, with cheese, and sometimes butter, but rarely tasting meat. They do not care for the allurements of the world. "There is another world," they say: "let us be good, and love God with all our hearts."

Mothers sit by the cradles of their babes and lull them to sleep with hymns and psalms. They say, "We want our children from their birth to hear us sing praises to God; we want them to fear and love God when they grow up, for He is good to us all." *

Men are rich and learned, and able to trace their genealogy for centuries; and yet so treat their dependents as to keep up a most friendly feeling between servants and masters.

Next to agriculture, mining constitutes the most important branch of national industry, and, in some provinces, is the principal employment; yet strikes have been but rare, and there are no threats of intimidation, no arson, no carrying of arms, no murder, no lying in ambush and beating of those who will not join the strike; no armed bands parading streets and districts with looks of anger and hate.*

"I think it may be safely averred that Sweden is the most remarkable of all the European nations. On account of this virtue doors are constantly left upon the latch. Horse-stealing and sheep-stealing are unknown. Of sacrilege there is no example on record; indeed, excepting at Stockholm and where a taint of foreign manners obtains, every description of property may be considered as safe from dishonesty."†

"They are an honest people. We see no beggary, no poor-houses, no jails, and we hear of very few crimes or violence. No locks are needed on the doors. Drunkenness is rare. They love music and flowers, and are devoted to their church and their families. I have had full opportunity

---
* Du Chaillu.   † Conway.

to observe the characteristics of this people from one end of the land to the other; and never lived upon the earth a more simple-hearted and pious people than these fair-haired descendants of the old Northern Vikings. Above all, there is not a public scandal in the whole country.*

Of the fishermen, Du Chaillu wrote: The steadiness and good behavior of these sturdy sons of the sea I have never seen equaled in any other country. During my sojourn among them there was never any fighting or quarreling, and the (lendsmandan) under naval officer was the only man there to enforce law and order. At all the fishing stations everything is as safe as on shore; the doors are left open, chests are never locked, and no one would think of stealing fish that were drying.

In Scandinavia, the laws, even in the more northern provinces, are rigidly enforced; disorderly conduct, shouting in the streets, and disturbances at night, fighting, mutilation of trees, violation of game laws, disobedience on shipboard, disrespect to the police, and many other offences, are promptly punished; and, above all, theft of any article, however small, subjects the offender to a heavy penalty.

The public peace is kept by a very few policemen, for they are a law-abiding people, and ruffianism and rowdyism are unknown.

The peasantry have many primitive ways, and some of them seem rather shocking to people accustomed to the artificial modes of English and American society. *But statistics show no more moral a people in Europe.* Even the peasant women are very particular in their deportment, and no debased woman would be tolerated in any hamlet in that part of the country.

In an important and standard law book, lately from the press of T. H. Flood & Co., of Chicago, the author, who is

---
* Hon. S. S. Cox.

a learned LL. D., dedicates his work to a law official of Stockholm, Sweden, and says:

"Sir: I beg leave to dedicate this work to you, in recognition of the efforts you have made, through various published writings, . . . especially to inculcate the obligation of speaking the truth in forensic controversies. One who has traveled in your country, and who has everywhere observed the pride of honesty which animates the Swedish people, can scarcely understand how it is that you need courts of justice at all. Several hundred thousand of your countrymen have made homes in America. They are among our most honest, industrious, peaceful, and law abiding citizens. Would that we had more of them."

Nearly everybody of average intelligence has heard or read the same testimony, again and again, from distinguished travelers in Scandinavian lands. And yet some American sects, turning away from Asia, Africa, and the islands of the sea, away from the negroes, the Chinese, and the native Americans, many of whom can give points in every sort of deviltry to the average heathen, send missionaries to Lutheran Sweden, of the honesty of whose people the eminent jurist writes the words quoted above.

Every Swede, male or female, leaving his village or city for some other part of the country, is obliged by law to have a certificate of character, called prestbetyg, (Clergyman's Certificate.) This document states the name of the person as numbered on the register of the parish church, whether married or single, and gives his qualifications in reading and writing.

There are three degrees or classes in education, and the class to which each belongs is indicated in his certificate, as is also his rank in Christian knowledge, *i. e.*, it is stated whether the individual has attended the meeting where all the people are examined in Scripture once a year by the pastor, whether confirmed or not, whether he has attended communion, and his general moral character. If one has been in prison, . . . it is so stated.

Probably in no country of Europe did the doctrines of the Reformation leave a deeper impress upon the minds, hearts, and character of the people than in Sweden. To inculcate a true worship of God was the end and aim of all the laws which regulate the affairs of Church and State. The government took the position that as there was only one true religion, so it was the duty of all members of the State to confess that religion. Under severe penalties, therefore, it was forbidden to spread or teach any doctrine which was contrary to the teachings and confessions of the Church of the Reformation. United with the State by the most intimate ties, not of bondage, but of mutual love, entering thoroughly into every part of the national life, exercising, through its control of the schools, the mightiest and holiest influence in the training of the young, the Church of Sweden, under the providence of God, has a history of which she need not be ashamed. In no country, and under no system, including even the well known parochial system of the Roman Catholic Church, is the religious instruction of youth so thorough and systematic, being a part of the daily instruction during the course of public education. And nowhere have the Church and State worked together more harmoniously and with more blessed results. The government professes to have established a system of religious instruction which best promotes the piety, welfare, and usefulness of its citizens, and the experience of centuries does not guarantee any change of system; and even to this day it allows of no dismissal from the State Church under the age of eighteen. Neither are nunneries or convents tolerated, and if parents belonging to a denomination other than the Swedish Lutheran Church neglect the religious instruction of their children, the government insists that these children must receive religious instruction in the schools of the State, for it tolerates no form of religious ignorance.

It was not until 1860 that permission was granted to other denominations to organize congregations; but now any member over eighteen years of age can withdraw from the State Church and connect himself with any other denomination, if he definitely state to what individual congregation he wishes to be dismissed. But Sweden knows of no Christian at-large. Every member of the State is regarded as a religious being, and if he wishes to remain a citizen of Sweden, he must at least outwardly belong to some religious congregation. The government here assumes parental authority. The unbeliever may refuse to go to the house of God, he may deny the truths of the revealed religion, but the government treats him as a disobedient child of the family, which has not yet come to a better understanding.*

The Episcopal system of church government prevails in Sweden, with the distinct understanding that it is not a scriptural or necessary arrangement, but only that of prudential policy. There are twelve bishoprics and one archbishopric—that of Upsala. The Bishop of Upsala is Archbishop of Sweden. The bishopric of Lund embraces 716,791 souls; that of Upsala, 602,936; of Göteborg, 496,667; and the others in proportion. The salary of a pastor, in addition to the parsonage, and probably a little land, is from 2,500 to 4,500 kronen, 1 kronen=26 cents. The bishops draw from 10,000 to 18,000 kronen, and have free rent. Those, too, who sever their connection with the State Church are compelled to pay the tenth of all their property tax to the maintenance of the State Church; for in Sweden all property, without exception, is taxed for the benefit of the Church as well as of the State.

---
*Dr. Weidner.

Every bishop is assisted in the discharge of his duties by a consistory. A bishop in Sweden ordains ministers and supervises the work of the church. Confirming children is not his exclusive right as with the Episcopalians. The confirmation is entrusted to the pastors. Although the Church of Sweden has the so-called apostolical succession, ministers, ordained by other Lutheran churches, are recognized as true pastors and not reordained, if admitted into the ministry of the Church of Sweden. There are different ranks in the Swedish ministry, but no orders except Episcopacy and the regular clergy. Episcopacy is looked upon as a good institution, but not as an essential of the church. Every pastor is a bishop, and the diocesan Episcopacy is considered useful for the welfare of the church. The different ministerial ranks in the Swedish State Church are: Archbishop, bishop, dean, provost, rectors or pastors, comministers and assistant ministers. The pastor of the diocesan church or cathedral is called a dean. Provosts are pastors of a church, but at the same time assistants to the bishop as superintendents of a certain part of the diocese. There are about 180 provosts in Sweden. The rectors or regular pastors number about 2,300. The church buildings number at least 2,500. Comministers are settled assistant pastors. Sometimes there are two comministers in a pastorate and an assistant minister to the regular pastor besides. Among the pastorates some are regal, *i. e.*, the king has the appointing power. When a charge is vacant, three candidates of the applicants are nominated by the government or the consistory, and the parishioners have the privilege to nominate a fourth. The candidate who receives the majority of votes is elected. As a rule the king, through his ecclesiastical secretary, appoints the candidate for a regal pastorate whom the people prefer. At elections the only drawback for the common people is the law that the votes are determined by the voters' property. A rich man has then more votes than a poor parishioner.

The repeal of certain church laws at various times during the last half century has opened the door to isms of various kinds, and some sects have shown themselves anxious to propagate their interpretations of Scripture among this "most honest people on the globe." Among these, the Baptists have had the greatest success, numbering 331 congregations and 22,691* members, and 18,463 Sunday school scholars. The Methodist Episcopal Church reports 7,572 members in sixty four congregations, served by ninety-six local preachers. About 2,000 Jews are in the country, while the Roman Catholics number only 600 adherents, and the Irvingites have one congregation with about one hundred members. Others, such as the Mormons, the Adventists, the Unitarians, etc., are also taking advantage of the religious freedom of the country. Besides these there are also about 40,000 Lutheran separatists who adhere to Socinian and Donatistic errors.

For over a quarter of a century, now, the Synod of the Swedish Church has had a part in the management of religious affairs in Sweden. Concerning it, the following is translated from the Allgemeine Evangelisch-Lutherische Kirchenzeitung: The Swedish Synod, which was called into existence by a royal order in 1863, shares with the king and the Reichstag the right of ecclesiastical legislation. It meets every five years, and consists of sixty in part clerical and partly secular members, who are elected, with the exception of the bishops and the Pastor primarius of Stockholm. From September 4th to October 10th of a year lately past, the Synod was in session for the fourth time in the capital city of the kingdom.

At the audience with the king which followed the opening of the Synod, the archbishop in an address to the Summus Episcopus, considered the Church of Sweden fortunate

---

* In 1890, the Baptists claim a membership of 32,305. Boston sends $6,000 a year to their aid.

in the king's sincere devotion to her welfare, and expressed the wish that the bond which unites Church and State might remain vital enough to render impotent and unavailing all efforts at dissolution, for there were no grounds for desiring the success of such efforts. The reply of the king was worthy of a successor of Gustavus Adolphus. In few and striking words he lamented the absorbing increase of material interests and the excessive claims made upon rich and poor in this earthly life, and then added: "But in the midst of this rapid whirl appears our Divine Master with the Gospel of peace, warning and exhorting us not to permit our thoughts and attention to be given exclusively to the temporal and fleeting, but to elevate them to that which is eternal and imperishable."

PARTIES IN THE CHURCH.

There seem to be three parties in the Lutheran Church of Sweden, if we acknowledge Waldenström to belong there as the law allows him. Each party is headed by its own leader. The point of controversy seems to be the repeatedly referred to Fourteenth article of the Augsburg Confession. It is more especially the word "*called*," referring to the ministry—over which the different leaders fight.

First of all we have the Right Wing of the State Church led by Bishop Billing. It is the bishop's idea that a layman should be allowed to preach only in extreme necessity. It is the exclusive privilege of those ordained to preach the gospel, as those are legally ordained and called for that purpose. If the layman be authorized to preach he will soon assume the right of administering the sacraments.

The Middle Wing is led by Archbishop Sundberg, who is at the head of the Fatherland Alliance. This party says that lay-preaching organized under the supervision of the church, is the most powerful defence against separatism. Many facts are adduced to prove this statement. The

Fatherland Alliance is a society of pious pastors and laymen who try to find out, educate and to send out good men to assist the pastors in their work. Every one of these preachers must go to the pastor and show testimonials of deportment and doctrinal position. They are generally orthodox and enthusiastic Lutherans. These are in brief the two divisions among the Lutherans proper. On the Extreme Left we find Doctor P. Waldenström and his friend, O. J. Ekman, whose business it is to hurry the procession that it may reach the scene in time to witness the funeral of the State Church.

The spirit of the clergy in our church in Northern Europe may be inferred from some of the doings at the third General Conference of the clergy of Sweden, held in Stockholm. It was attended by several hundred ministers. Among other things, the speakers considered what could be done to awaken among the people greater love for the Church. They deprecated all attempts at sensationalism, or compliance with the worldly spirit of the age. They suggested that churches be opened during the entire week, so that they may be regarded by the people not merely as a place where they can go to hear a sermon preached, but also as a place for private devotions; that more attention be paid to church music, and the people be taught to sing rythmic psalms and hymns; that services be held more frequently, and finally, that the churches be kept cleaner, warmer, and made more agreeable by artistic decoration.

Among non-Lutheran bodies in Sweden, the Baptists have been the boldest in abusing the privileges granted them by the laws of the State. Although permitted by law to form separate Church communities, these non-conformists have hitherto refused to avail themselves of this permission, but continue to remain legally and nominally members of the State Church, though they violently condemn its dogmas, refuse to avail themselves of its sacraments, and have pastors and teachers of their own. These non-conformists decline to recognize the right of the State to interfere in any way with their organization, and hence will not register their secession from the State Church. Hence they remain legally members of that church, and have the legal right of instructing in religion the children of members of the National Church, while they often attack that church in the bitterest terms, and refuse to recognize it as a church of Christ. Such conduct is not unnaturally vehemently denounced by the clergy of the State Church as immoral and dishonest; and while many of the latter are perfectly willing to recognize avowed Baptist communities as Christian Churches, they refuse to meet in conference men who remain in a church which they denounce, and remain in it only for the purpose of working its ruin.

As to the regular worship of the Church, the interested reader may turn to what is said concerning worship, ritual, etc., in the Danish Church, which is also substantially true of the Church in Sweden. In this connection, also, we may present the views of an outsider in regard to these things. He says: "Perhaps among our English race it is hard to conciliate a stately ecclesiasticism and a gorgeous worship with salvation by faith alone; but it is perfectly possible among Lutherans. Sweden has a ritual which appears to be, at least at certain times and places, hardly inferior to that of Rome in splendor, and, of course, greatly superior to it in depth. On great occasions, especially at a coronation, the Archbishop of Upsala and his suffragans appear in all the magnificence of the ancient vestments, with cope and mitre. But the land of Gustavus Adolphus, 'the stainless hero of the north,' is for all this an unswerving pillar of Protestantism, and has been so ever since Protestantism was."*

Churches are built everywhere, and pastors sent even to the fishing-stations,—occupied, perhaps, but three months in-

---
*The Independent, N. Y.

a year. Fishermen quit work on Saturday, prepare for the services, and attend church by the thousand on the Lord's Day.

"It was really beautiful to see so many men, bred among the rocks of the North, amidst storms and privations, come to pay homage to the Creator. I doubt very much if such a sight could be seen in any other Christian country. There was not a fisherman at Hennigsvaer in his cabin all that day, unless detained by sickness."*

Not only are churches built, but they are used. People attend the services in them. A traveler says:

My journey was made on a Sunday, and judging from the concourse of people who thronged the road, and particularly from the multitude assembled in the church yards which lay close to it, I had every reason to conclude that the Swedes are a church-going people. I was exceedingly pleased with the respectable appearance of the peasantry. I know that they are poor, but they had neither forgotten the way to the house of God, nor omitted in their poverty to provide decent apparel for their appearance there. From a height over which the road passed, in the course of this day's journey, I counted no fewer than eleven churches in sight at the same time. From other specimens than that which I have mentioned, I have no reason to doubt of their being well filled.†

The fervid religious nature of the Scandinavian rural population, leads them to celebrate all festivals by first going to church. Midsummer (24th June) is, after Christmas, Sweden's most merry festival; but the first duty of all the people is to attend the church before they enter on the festivities of the day. By five o'clock in the morning they are on the way, from grandfather to great-grandchildren, the babies being carried in the arms. They go by land and by water. Each girl carries in one hand a little boquet of wild flowers, and in the other her prayer-book, carefully wrapped

---
* Du Chaillu.   † Conway.

in an embroidered handkerchief. Soon the church-yard is crowded with people waiting for the services to begin; the children play, and the more aged are busy reading their prayer-books. As many as five thousand people assemble in a church which has a seating capacity for four thousand. During the singing of the hymns the whole congregation accompanies the organ with a fervor which cannot be surpassed. The sermon is listened to with attention, and the communion is administered on feast days as on every Sunday. During its administration the whole congregation joins in chanting the old tunes used at the time of the Reformation.

At the Swedish "spas," at eight o'clock P. M., the festivities cease, and the pastor of the place offers thanks to God for his goodness, and beseeches Him to bless those who have come there in quest of health. No one thinks of leaving the spring before this act of devotion.*

On ordinary occasions, the sermon sometimes occupies an hour to an hour-and-a-half. If children are baptized, this adds about twenty minutes, and makes a lengthy service. During the altar service, the clergyman is clothed with a white surplice; but when he ascends the pulpit he divests himself of this, and appears in a black cassock, with ruffles around the neck.

In the churches, the men and women generally sit apart. The rich meet with the poor, and their pews are in no way distinguished from those of the less wealthy. Most of the old churches contain portraits of former pastors and their families as memorials. All the members of the family attend the church service, and it sometimes occurs that as many as two hundred infants are in the church when the congregation is large.

At stated seasons, after the service, the young are arranged in the aisles, and examined as to their knowledge

---
* Du Chaillu.

of the Bible and the Catechism, preparatory to their confirmation.

It is one of the characteristics of the Swedish clergy that they mingle in the pleasures of the people among whom their lot is cast, witnessing their simple dances, and enjoying their social gatherings. The clergyman is often seen looking on with a smiling face, happy at the sight of his merry, contented flock ; and he is often considered an integral part of this family. A good moral influence is thus exerted over both the clergy and the people; producing in the latter a restraining effect, and giving to the pastor an understanding of his people which no man can have who is unacquainted with human nature.

To become a pastor in Sweden, the candidate must pass through the common school, be admitted to High School and Gymnasium, and there take a course of study which requires from eight to ten years. Then he is ready for the University course, which at present is six years for theological students. Hence, if a student is ready to enter the college or high school when he is ten years of age, and is a successful student, he is ready for ordination at the age of twenty-six. After his ordination, the candidate must pass another examination, before he can become a pastor, and to which he is not admitted until he has reached the age of twenty-eight. They want no callow religious teachers, just as they want no conceited upstarts as teachers in their common schools, or as practitioners in medicine.

Graduation at the University of Upsala or Lund is necessary to all who would be lawyers, physicians or preachers.

For either of the three "learned professions"—law, medicine and divinity—therefore, the laws demand from thirteen to eighteen years of study after the candidate has proved himself a studious youth, and has finished the course of the common schools. In Sweden, too, the teachers' profession should be added to the learned ones, inasmuch as the rule expect of him nearly the same amount of study, and many teachers are graduates of a university. Learned in other realms, this people have no faith in ignorant pretenders in the things that are spiritual.

The movement in favor of a Free Church has many adherents among members of the State church who yet remain faithful to it. They see the difficulties in the way of enforcing strict discipline so long as the Church and the State are so closely united. The pastor can, indeed, refuse the sacrament to an open sinner, but there can be no excommunication of the offender. As a citizen of the State, every man belongs to a certain parish. There are, therefore, many earnest believers in the State Church, both ministers and laymen, who are hoping, that at God's appointed time, a peaceable separation between the State and the Church will take place, and who are patiently seeking to bring this about, but who, nevertheless, are opposed to all revolutionary acts. This party, however, has no sympathy with the movement headed by Waldenström.

Waldenström has promulgated views concerning the doctrines of the atonement and of justification by faith, which are contrary to the distinctive tenets of Protestantism. His views, however, in many respects, may still be regarded as conservative, in comparison with those of some of his colaborers, and of many of his followers. This tendency, known as the Separatistic Free-Church movement, has organized some four hundred so-called mission churches, and, refusing to withdraw from the State Church, seeks, by all possible means, to destroy the work of reform within the Church herself. Among them extreme views have been taught, and still are promulgated, concerning the doctrines of the atonement, of the Church, of Church discipline, of baptism, of sin ; and, in fact, to describe the fanaticism shown by many of the adherents of this movement, in their spirit, in their doctrines, and in their revolutionary tendencies, would be a most painful task.*

What many term a true spiritual revival has done a blessed work for the Swedish Church, and at no time in the history of Sweden has it showed more fruit, more activity, more true godliness, and more fervent zeal than at present. The labors and writings of men like Schartau, Sellengren, Rosenius and scores of others, have had the greatest influence, and the work is still being carried on by other faithful men. The twenty-five hundred ordained clergymen of the Church of Sweden, in character, ability, learning, earnestness, piety and zeal, compare favorably with an equal number of clergy of any other denomination, or of any other country, and among them are to be found hundreds of most earnest Christian men, who in their devotion to the cause of Christ, and in their zeal for promoting true reform within the Church, stand second to none. There are tens of thousands of laymen, members of the State Church, earnest Christians, who are seeking to promote the cause of Christ in a manner and with a devotion which we of another temperament and country can scarcely comprehend.*

The pietists of Sweden are generally known as "The Readers."

Sunday is observed as a Christian holy-day in all places. The word of God is preached in every parish. Wherever you go, you will find people going to church or other places where the Word is preached, and some walk a good distance and do not remain at home on account of disagreeable weather. The stores and public places are closed, and the Sunday laws are kept strictly during the time of divine services.

In some of the large cities, the observance is not as good as it ought to be. Sunday excursions are permitted and passenger trains run. Human nature is not better in Swe-

---
* Dr. Weidner.

den than in any other country. Sunday in Sweden is not kept so well as to deserve a special commendation, but we believe that Sweden compares favorably in this respect with any other country.

We must mention one peculiarity of the Swedish Sunday, although we will not recommend its adoption. A good many people in Sweden look upon Sunday as virtually at an end at 6 o'clock P. M. The evening service is generally held before that time. Of course no *work* is done, but at 6 o'clock P. M. the people turn out, more especially in summer. On this account a foreigner may get the impression that Sunday is not kept properly.

That the Swedish people respect the Lord's Day, is proved by their way of keeping it in this country, where they are free from the coercion of the state church.*

The "Tractatus Adami" was written A. D. 1080. It makes everything wonderful because unknown. In it, it is said that "Norway and Sweden are two widely extended kingdoms of the North, hitherto almost unknown. There are vast deserts and mountains of snow, where are herds of monstrous men, which shut out all approach; also Amazons, baboons, Cyclops, having but one eye in the middle of their foreheads; hemantopeds, skipping or leaping with one foot only; man eaters, without speech," etc.

A. D. 1080 is somewhat in the past now for the majority of men. Travelers and geographers go about describing these kingdoms in the ordinary ways. They tell you that Norway is situated principally between 60 degrees and 70 degrees north latitude, and has an area of over 122,800 square miles (English.) Its whole western coast is washed by the sea. Speaking in general terms we may say that the nine-tenths of its surface is high plateau, much of it barren and dreary; one thirty-eighth of it is continually covered with snow; four-fifths of it is forest of birch, pine and fir;

---
*Augustana Observer.

not over one-fifth of it is inhabited, and but about 140 square miles of it are under the plough; and the arable land of the whole country amounts to but 740 square miles.* There are but two comparatively level tracts in it: one at Drontheim, (Trondjhem,) the other at Christiania. These are extremely fertile. The remainder of the surface consists, chiefly, of rock and snow. The people, generally, live in the narrow valleys along the sea, or along the fiords. One settlement may be cut off from its nearest neighbor by many miles of rough, mountain masses, over which it is impo sible to cut a road.

Here is the home of avalanches, glaciers, waterfalls, fiords, and the Maelström, and of scenery so weird, ruggedly majestic and beautiful that it, perhaps, has not elsewhere its equal. The surface, generally, is barren, and the yield of grains far from sufficient for home consumption. The rough territory is scantily endowed by nature, thinly populated, and has few high-ways. Manufacturing industries are few; and the people, generally, are confined principally to navigation or fishing. Yet in twenty years the land-owners of the country were more than doubled in numbers, and the wealth of the country increased more than two hundred and fifty per cent. In simplicity of manner and solid practical tendency, the people of Norway are closely allied to those of Switzerland.

If the Icelander thinks his the best land on which the sun shines, the Norwegian sings:

<blockquote>
Yes, glorious is my Fatherland,
The ancient, rock-ribbed Norraway;
With flowery dales, crags old and gray,
That, spite of time, eternal stand!
</blockquote>

---

*Cox, in *Arctic Sunbeams*, puts it somewhat differently, and says of Norway: Her land can give but twelve hundred of its square miles to grain, four-fifths of it is forest, and the rest is given to fish piles and warehouses, to timber and duck.

"In the natural scenery of Norway there is a peculiar blending of the grand, the picturesque, the gigantic, that is bewildering and majestic. There is in it something that leaves you in bewildering amazement, when you have seen it, and makes you ask yourself, " Was it real, or was it only a dream ?"

Norway is, in fact, one huge, imposing rock, and its valleys are but great clefts in it. Through these clefts, the rivers, fed by vast glaciers upon the mountains, find their way to the sea. They come from the distance, now musically and chattingly meandering their way beneath the willows, now tumbling down the slopes, reeking and distorted by the rocks that oppose them, until they reach some awful precipice and tumble down eight hundred to a thousand feet in a single leap into the depths below, where no human being ever yet set his foot.

You can not get to the foot of such falls as the Voring Force or the Rjukan Force, but you may look over the precipice from above and see the waters pouring like fine and fleecy wool into the seething caldron, where you can discern through the vapory mists shoots of foam at the bottom, like rockets of water, radiating in every direction.

Make a journey by steamer on some of those magnificent fiords on the west coast of Norseland. The dark mountains rise almost perpendicularly from the water's edge to an enormous height; their summits, crowned with ice and snow, stand out sharp and clear against the bright blue sky ; and the ravines on the mountain-tops are filled with huge glaciers, that clasp their frosty arms around the valley, and send down, like streams of tears along the weather-beaten cheeks of the mountains, numerous waterfalls and cascades, falling in an endless variety of graceful shapes from various altitudes into the fiord below. Sometimes a solitary peak lifts its lordly head a thousand feet clear above the surrounding mountains, and, towering like a monarch over all, it defiantly refuses to hold communion with any living thing save the eagle. Here and there a Force appears, like a strip of silvery, fleecy cloud, suspended from the brow of the mountain, and dashing down more than two thousand feet in one leap; and all this marvelously grand scenery, from base to peak, stands reflected, as deep as it is lofty, in the calm, clear, sea-green water of the fiord, perfect as in a mirror.

There is no storm; the deep water of the fiord is silent and at rest. Not even the flight of a single bird ruffles its glassy surface. As the steamer glides gently along between the rocky walls, you hear no sound save the monotonous throbbing of the screw and the consequent splashing of the water. All else is still as death. . . . Sunshine reaches the water only when the sun's rays fall nearly vertically, in consequence of the immense height of the mountain sides, whose enormous shadows almost perpetually overshadow the narrow fiord. . . . It is awe-inspiring. It is solemnly grand. You can but fancy yourself in a fairy land, with elves and sprites and neckens and trolls dancing in sportive glee all around you."*

We cannot resist the temptation to give here, yet, a few lines from Cox's *Arctic Sunbeams*.

"The marvel is, and is ever repeated here, that a whole land, running so far toward and into the frozen zone, bending like a monstrous bow, should be so crowded with these giants (the mountains) of earth and yet so easily reached and seen by the sons of earth. I have seen the Sierras of Spain and California, and the Atlas and Alpine ranges, with their gorges and glories; and yet it would seem as if these visions were as nothing compared with these thousands of miles of majesty, with their waters and isles, glaciers and peaks, all canopied with blue skies and fleecy clouds, and all reproduced in lakes more magical than Maggiore or

---

* Andersen, *Norse Mythology*, 68.

Como. They seem skeleton ribs of the earth, in its desolation and sublimity."

The population of Norway is (1886) 2,004,000, of which not half a million live in cities or towns. The average population is but eighteen to the square mile, it being the most sparsely settled country in Europe. Emigration to America and to Australia has been great for many years, yet the population of the country shows a steady increase. At the beginning of the present century it was but 800,000 ; less than two-and-a-half centuries ago it was 300,000.

Agricultural productions are scant, amounting to an annual value of from fifteen to twenty million dollars. The fisheries form one of the most important sources of national wealth. Over 120,000 men are employed in them, and the aggregate profits are five-and-a-half million dollars a year. The cod-fisheries among the Lofoden islands employ over six thousand boats, and, in one year reported a catch of 28,-400,000 fish, valued at over one-and-a-half million dollars. In the same year the cod-fisheries of Finmark yielded 13,-000,000 fish valued at over six hundred and fifty thousand dollars. The herring and mackerel fisheries are next in importance, and yield returns of one-and-a-half to two million dollars a year. Manufactures are a source of considerable wealth, consisting of saw-mills, cotton-mills, shipbuilding yards, etc. Mines of silver, copper, nickel, are worked with fair returns; and iron-works are operated to advantage.

Norway has about 1,000 miles of railway. Because of the mountainous nature of the country it is impracticable to greatly extend it. At the close of 1882, there were over 47,000 miles of telegraph lines with about 86,000 miles of wire. In education, as elsewhere noted, Norway takes a leading place among the nations of Europe. The whole number of schools is about 6,750; the pupils in attendance, 275,550. About one ninth of the total of pupils are instructed in "Ambulatory" schools; *i. e*, schools kept by regular teachers in districts where they go from place to place and instruct the children, because the population is too sparse to establish a stationary school. These ambulatory schools number over 1,900, with about half that number of teachers, and 30,000 pupils. The teachers' pay is secured by an individual tax here as in Sweden, and in both countries, after thirty years' service teachers receive a pension. What has been said of the schools of Sweden, as to course of study, management, etc., applies also to the schools of Norway, except that the average length of the school term is not so long as in Sweden. But here, also, there are sewing and other industrial schools for girls, and for children under legal school-age; state high-schools, seminaries for the training of teachers, and free evening-classes (400) for the continuation of school-work for those beyond legal school-age, and some private high-schools, mostly for girls. It does not appear that women are here so much employed as teachers as in Sweden. A writer in the *Century* says: In Norway, the aristocracy of birth has long been abolished, and its place is occupied by an aristocracy of culture. The diploma of academical citizenship amounts almost to the same as a letter of nobility. It makes its possessor eligible to any civil office under the government, and gives him access to the best society. In politics, no amount of influence or wire-pulling can secure a man an office to which his age and ability do not entitle him.

All Norwegians are equal in the eyes of the law: since, constitutionally, there is no longer any nobility in existence. The owners of real estate in the rural districts number over 173,000; although the yield of grains is far from sufficient for home consumption. The value of the lands of the country, however, more than doubled in forty years.

Norway, in its constitution and methods of government, has always been more democratic than its neighbor, being assimilated in feeling to our Republic, while the government of Sweden is more of the English type. The laws are faithfully administered. Serious crimes are rare. Murders are almost unknown, and the murderer's punishment is decapitation with a sword. A writer in Scribner's Magazine some time ago said: A man's chances of getting killed are, I believe, smaller in Norway than almost anywhere else on the globe. Du Chaillu says Norway is (with Sweden) the safest country (for life and property) in the world.

The Norwegian houses, mostly built of wood save in the large towns, often are very attractive in their interiors. As a rule, they are furnished quite plainly; and the floors are either bare or covered with oil-cloth. Before the pretty lace curtains of many sitting-room windows one often sees, from the street, banks of beautiful flowers neatly arranged in porcelain pots. The ceilings, generally, are the floors of the rooms overhead; and the walls often are made of canvas. Like the Danes, the Norwegians are extremely polite to each other on the streets, continuously removing and replacing their hats.*

In general, the Norwegians are above the middle stature, well-shaped, with fair complexions, blooming countenances, and light hair. The men have an engaging appearance; and the women, who are also tall, remarkably fair, and obliging, are frequently handsome, notwithstanding their exposure to an ungenial and boisterous climate. The mountaineers acquire surprising strength and dexterity, by temperance, endurance of cold, laborious exercise, climbing rocks, skating on the snow, and defending themselves against wild beasts of the forest. Those in the maritime parts, pursue fishing and navigation, whence they become very expert mariners. The peasants have much spirit in their manner, yet are not inso-

---
* Vincent; Lapp, Norsk and Finn.

lent; never fawning, yet always paying due respect to their superiors. Their principal mode of salutation is, by offering the hand; and when anything is paid or given to them, instead of returning thanks by words, or bowing, they shake the hands of the donor with great cordiality.

Goodrich, in his Customs and Manners of the Principal Nations of the World, says of them: The character of the Norwegians, as a people, is more interesting and estimable than that of most other nations. Their expressions are clear and energetic, their answers distinct and correct, their questions pertinent and judicious, their reflections often profound and intelligent. There is a generosity of heart and elevation of mind about them, which gives to their manners a very frank and decided stamp. They speak and act in the full spirit of freemen, open and undaunted, yet never insolent in the presence of their superiors. They are reproached with being slow in reconciliations, but are obliging, hospitable, and liberal, even to display, when they possess the means. In some of the cities, there is a cultivated style of conversation, and polish of manners, mixed with the high and independent spirit of the nation, which form altogether an accomplished character, not to be expected in the remote latitudes and limited advantages of Scandinavia; and in some of the inland districts, where the corrupting influence of commerce has not reached, there prevails a pure and primitive spirit of religion, united with a quiet industry, and domestic retirement, which are peculiarly suited to cheer the state of poverty and privation in which their days are spent. They are generally animated by an ardent spirit of patriotism.

The cleanliness, even of many unpretending cottages, is remarkable. The ceilings, windows and walls frequently are painted with showy colors. There are many elegant country-seats, which are oblong buildings, consisting of one floor, the outsides painted red and the frames of the windows green. The dwelling houses in the country, generally situated in the most pleasing and picturesque spots that can be found, are usually spacious and well arranged.

The diet of the inhabitants of the towns resembles nearly that of the other countries in the north of Europe; but in the country districts, peculiar modes of living prevail. At an entertainment given by the better class, the guests place themselves at table without etiquette, and every one sits as he chooses. They continue long at their meals, but converse with much liveliness. They do not remain at table after dinner; and the constant presence of the ladies, who often take the lead in conversation, renders their social meetings cheerful and agreeable. Their fare is of a very substantial nature, yet not without elegance; and even at supper, three or four courses of soup, fowls, ham, fish, etc., follow one after another, while, perhaps, a quarter of veal appears at last as the concluding delicacy. After dinner, the company all bow to the hostess, drink her health, and then suddenly rising, push back their chairs with a tremendous noise to the sides of the room. Then they stand for a short time as if they were saying a grace; after which, bowing to the master of the house, and to each other, they shake hands with the host, kiss the hand of the hostess, and conduct the ladies out of the room. Coffee is then served, while some gentlemen retire to smoke tobacco in another room. Tea is then brought in, after which the card tables are set out, and punch served up. A solid supper finally appears, as before mentioned.

While the nobility and merchants of Norway fare thus sumptuously, the peasantry live with the utmost frugality and temperance. Their common bread is oatmeal cakes, about the size and thickness of pancakes; and this is made only twice a year. In times of scarcity, to which such a country is much exposed, they boil, dry, and grind the bark of the fir tree into a kind of flour, which they mix with their oatmeal; and sometimes the bark of the elm is used in a similar manner. In places where a fishery is carried on, the roes of cod are kneaded with the oatmeal; or, mixed with the barley meal, they are made into a kind of hasty-pudding and soup, which is enriched with a pickled herring, or a salted mackerel. The flesh of the shark is considered a dainty; as are also thin slices of meat sprinkled with salt and dried in the wind. Fresh fish are had in abundance on the sea-coast, but, for want of means of quick conveyance, they are unknown in the interior. Here, however, grouse, partridges, hares, red deer, and reindeer, are hunted and eaten. Cows, sheep, and goats, are slain for winter stock; the flesh being preserved by pickling, smoking, or dry-salting.

The people are so honest that, when they leave their houses, they hang up the key on the outside. "We left our umbrella in the cars (reaching Copenhagen); and as an illustration of the regard to the *meum et tuum* which obtains among these people, we afterwards found it at our hotel in Norway, forwarded as if it were actual property, and at a cost too small to record!"

At the Gaards, or farm centres, we found, suspended on the walls, maxims expressing the simple faith of this Norman blood. There is one motto common in Norway, and carved around this room of Ole Bolkesæ, (whom the author was visiting,) and which he pointed at, as his rule of conduct:

"Naar vi guaar rind; naar vi gaar ud;
Da taenk paa as, O milde Gut,"

which, being translated, is

"When we go in; when we go out;
Then think of us, O merciful God."

Another motto we see. It is worthy of a Trappist cloister: "Go to bed and slumber! Reflect now (Betenk du nu!) that it may be thy last sleep."*

---

* Cox; Arctic Sunbeams, 173.

In latitude 60 degrees N., and 250 miles N. W. of Stockholm, is Christiania, the capital of Norway, at the head of Christiania fiord, and eighty miles distant from the sea. It is almost surrounded by wooded hills. In 1885 the population was given at 128,000, and the city is constantly growing in importance. As far back as 1030, when the spirit of the Viking was not yet dead, King Harold Haardrada, ("Harold the Severe,") commenced the town of Apslo, now one of the suburbs of the capital. But the open sea seemed to lead the wild spirits of those days towards the Skager Rack and the Cattegat; these, in turn, pointed toward the Christiania fiord, and at its head was Apslo, in the way of the untamed neighbors of Harold Haardrada, who sought for booty even through fire and blood. Three times was the city burned ; twice did the plague carry off half its inhabitants.

The more modern town proper, of which we write, dates from about 1624, when it was laid out by Christian IV. in the form of a parallelogram, 1,000 paces in length and in breadth. The streets, therefore, are at right angles, generally broad, and lighted with gas. The houses, except in the suburbs, are generally of brick or stone, many of them stuccoed, and mostly two stories in height and roofed with tiles.

Among the public buildings is Oscar's Hall, the summer residence of the King, a short distance from the city. (The constitution requires that the King shall spend at least three months in the year in Norway.) In this city, the Storthing (Parliament) of Norway has its seat; and the King of Sweden and Norway, his residence, when in this kingdom. The Royal Palace is one of the noticeable buildings; so, also, is the cathedral, built of brick, and in the shape of a Greek cross. Yet other structures worthy of attention are the free museums; the observatory; the military, naval, and art schools; two orphan asylums; the railway-station, and the Athenæum.

The university was founded in 1811, and has a staff of 50 professors and several "docentes," and the students number about 1,000. The library has 230,000 volumes. Connected with the university are various scientific collections, a botanical garden, and an observatory. Christiania also has good schools, and several learned societies, among which that for Northern antiquities is famous. The industrial establishments include weaving and cotton spinning factories, paper and saw-mills, soap and oil-works, tobacco factories, etc. In commerce, this city has become the first port of Norway. As the stranger wanders through its broad streets he is struck by the steady, thoughtful demeanor of the inhabitants. . . . Within a few years a large number of villas have been built, and in the new parts of the city are beautiful gardens surrounding many of the houses, and some of the private residences are very fine. There is an appearance of thrift and comfort; order and good behavior prevail everywhere. Along its quays vessels are continually loading or discharging their cargoes; and steamers leave at all hours of the day for the cities, the commercial marts along the coast, or for distant European seaports.

"I often love to think of Christiania, and of its kindly and hospitable inhabitants. The well-to-do people are simple in their tastes, live comfortably, and are fond of home life. Society is agreeable. The ladies, like their Swedish kinswomen, are well educated, proficient in the use of foreign languages, very attractive, amiable, and cultivate simplicity of dress—in a word they are charming. The gentlemen are warm-hearted, polite, obliging; and there is a freedom and manliness in their bearing which always pleased me."*

Olaf, the Peaceful, laid the foundations of Bergen in the eleventh century. It is now the second town in size and importance in Norway, is located at the head of a deep bay, and surrounded by hills, some of which reach a height of

* Land of the Midnight Sun, I; 298.

2,000 feet. The port, especially in the spring of the year, is very animated, when several hundreds of small craft return from the fisheries. Great quantities of dry cod, cod-liver oil, and several hundred thousand barrels of pickled herring, are exported yearly. Bergen is in latitude 60 degrees north, and has a population of over 40,000 souls. It is situated in the most rainy spot in all the coast of Norway—which is saying a great deal, but it is well deserved. The average number of rainy days in the year is 134, and of snowy days, 26. The climate is mild; the mean temperature for January being but little above the freezing point. It has a (domkirke) cathedral, several churches, hospitals, a national museum, a diocesan college, a naval academy, a school of design, public libraries, various charitable institutions, and a theatre. It is the seat of a bishopric, and possesses one of the three public treasuries of Norway.

One of the most valuable institutions in this city is the free industrial school, where poor girls are taught the arts of female industry. The ages of the pupils generally range from seven to sixteen years. They are grouped together in classes according to their proficiency, and taught hemming, stitching, mending, knitting, darning, making shirts and dresses, etc., under the care of faithful and competent teachers. Some of the girls become wonderfully expert and able to darn a rent so that one can only with difficulty distinguish the place that has been mended. It has over 500 pupils. The day sessions are of six hours—nine to twelve and two to five; and three of these are given to study, while the other three are for lessons in the use of the needle, etc.

Drontheim (or Trondhjem) is nearly nine hundred years old, having been founded by Olaf Tryggveson in 997. It is in latitude nearly $63\frac{1}{2}$ degrees, away from the sea-coast, but on the shores of the Drontheim fiord. It is honored as the place where the King of Norway and Sweden is crowned as king of Norway, and in summer-time is filled with tourists, most of them English. It is the residence of a bishop, the seat of a high court, and has a large hospital. The cathedral in it ranks as the finest ecclesiastical building in Norway, and is 324 feet long by 124 wide. In it, the King is crowned. In addition to the buildings already named, Drontheim has a grammar school, a real-school, a deaf and dumb institute, a hospital, etc. It is the seat of the Royal Norwegian Scientific Society, in connection with which are an excellent library of 50,000 volumes, and a good zoölogical and antiquarian museum. It carries on an extensive trade in copper, oil, timber, and dried and salted fish. Its industries are shipbuilding, saw-milling, tanning, rope-making and ribbon making. The population (1885) is 24,000.

Drontheim is about 350 miles by rail north of Christiania. Leaving the northern city by the magnificent highway which connects it with the Capital, much of the scenery is beautiful and grand. In places, the road is cut out of the solid rock, along the brink of precipices, with the river seven hundred feet below. Norway has produced some of the finest road engineers in the world, and their skill has triumphed over difficulties apparently insurmountable in locating roads in their own land; and, excepting Switzerland, there is no country known where their skill is more heavily taxed.

Stavanger dates from the eighth or ninth century, and is the centre of a governmental district of, perhaps, 120,000 souls. It is built on the south side of a beautiful fiord; and signs of its wealth are seen in the well built stone houses which have been erected in the last half century. The life of the town is in its shipping trade and herring fishery. The old cathedral, though the town has had no resident bishop for over two hundred years, remains, next to that of Drontheim, the most interesting piece of Gothic architecture in Norway. The town has an important Latin School, and large communal hospital. The population is about 25,000.

Christiansand is a fortified seaport of Norway, capital of a "stift" (county) of the same name, and situated on a fiord of the Skager-Rack. It is surrounded on three sides by water and is defended by the fort of Fredericksholm. The streets are wide, houses regularly built, and well painted. The principal industries are tanning, ship building, dyeing, brewing, and the exportation of timber, pitch, copper and iron, fish and lobsters. The place has a fine cathedral and cathedral school, a naval station, is the residence of a bishop and of the governor of the province.

Tromsö is another little seaport of Norway, yet a busy and charming town of over 5,000 inhabitants. The houses are well painted and cheerful in appearance, there are some very pretty villas, and the situation of the place is delightful. It sends yearly expeditions to Spitzbergen and other places North for seals, and has some wealthy and enterprising merchants. Many bears' skins and other furs find a market here, and the herring fishery is very productive. The town is the residence of the governor, and of a bishop. It has the cathedral, several other notable buildings, a museum, wh'ch contains a good zoölogical collection, a high school, and a normal seminary.

Hamar is the sixth in order of the towns of Norway which each afford a residence to a bishop. Formerly it was a town of great importance, but was destroyed over three hundred years ago. Not far from it are interesting ruins,—all that remain of its cathedral. The regions round about are among the finest agricultural districts of Norway; and the lake on whose shores Hamar stands is 60 miles long, and, in places, 240 fathoms deep.

In Norway, church matters resemble greatly affairs in Denmark, with which country it was allied for 400 years. Here the bishops have been retained, who are, however, only superintendents of the ecclesiastical revenues. In Norway there are no elections. Clergymen are directly named by the King. In the University of Christiania they have capable professors, who hold fast to the tenets of Lutheranism. They have, however, not been able to prevent "Grundwigism" from gaining ground, especially among the younger portion of the clergy, which has caused many literary feuds. The Church is not represented in the Diet (Storthing). The earnestness of the people is shown in the moral support which they give to every Christian mission. The mission to the Jews began at a time when it was not permitted a Jew to live in the country. Other mission works are the missions among the heathen, among sailors at home and in foreign ports, and like organizations.*

Norway embraced the Lutheran Reformation in the sixteenth century, and has ever remained true to it. Till within a few years every other Church was rigidly excluded from the rights of public worship in Scandinavia; but now religious liberty, with a few restrictions, is granted to all sects. Lutheranism is still the national church, supported and ruled by the civil government, which appoints the bishops, ministers and theological professors in the universities. All the other churches have to support themselves, and, in turn, enjoy the advantage of governing themselves. The Scandinavian countries differ from all other Lutheran countries, in having the Episcopal form of government. Norway has six bishops, each of whom receives 13,000 crowns—*i. e.*, about $3,500—salary. But the Scandinavian episcopate is merely a superintendency, and claims no apostolic succession. Yet the Episcopal Church in the United States was near getting its Episcopal ordination from Denmark, and Bishop White, of Pennsylvania, would have proceeded to Copenhagen for that purpose, if the English Parliament had not, in the meantime, passed a law enabling

* Dr. Kalkar.

the Archbishop of Canterbury to ordain bishops for foreign countries.

"Inferior" clergy are provosts or archdeacons, parish priests and chaplains. Each diocese is divided into districts, under care of provosts; each district, into parishes. A large parish, besides the principal church, has one or more chapels of ease, under the care of chaplains. The livings vary from £60 to £200 sterling. A clergyman's widow is entitled to his salary for a year after his decease, and to a pension from his successor of ⅓ of the annual income.

In many of the Norwegian districts the office of the pastor is no sinecure, either inland or by sea. Some of the parishes are very extensive, and occupy an almost uninhabited country; the hamlets being far apart, of course they cannot have a pastor for each church. Chapels, therefore, are built, often at a great distance from the parish church, and can be reached only by bridle-paths, narrow mountain roads, etc. A schedule of time for the year designates the date of service in each place, and in sunshine, rain, or snow, the clergyman, on horseback or in his cariole, must reach the church, —often wet, overcome by the heat, or half frozen. It is no unusual thing for a pastor to have under his care three or four churches, and services are held in each of them only once every three or four weeks. When the churches are in the neighborhood of a fiord, he has to go in a boat, and the weather often is stormy.

The clergy are hospitable and kind-hearted. As a rule, the Scandinavian clergy are loved and respected. Not a few of them are ministers of mercy to their parishes, and not only spend all their income on and among the people under their care, but also draw on their paternal estates for means to relieve the necessities of the poor. The work is generally done in a quiet way, in harmony with the principles of the religion they profess; and when a poor widow, or an over-grateful man with a large family cannot refrain from telling what the good pastor has done, they are chided for having told of the good deeds done in secret.*

Here and there through the country, and occasionally on the steamers during the summer months one meets with people called Läsare, (a kind of pietistic-religious folk,) who sing their hymns as they go to and return from their meetings.

---

* Du Chaillu.

† The Lutheran Church has a hierarchial form of government only in the Scandinavian lands. Sweden has 1 archbishop and 11 bishops; Norway has 6 bishops; Denmark, including Iceland, 8, and Finland 1 archbishop and 2 bishops. In Germany the Lutheran Churches are governed by consistory, there being one for every country or province, thus making about fifty in all. In France, Hungary, Austria, Holland and elsewhere, a similar organization exists. In North America and Austria synods have been organized and the congregational system prevails, the synods having no legislative or judicial, but only advisory powers.— *Zöckler's Statistics of Christianity.*

CHAPTER VI.

IN RUSSIA.

In all parts of Russia, from the Baltic to the Pacific, from the peninsula of Kola to Tiflis, there are Lutheran churches and associations. But the members belong to very diverse nationalities, speaking different languages. The circumstances of the congregations are very different, also. There are great stretches of country, inhabited entirely by Lutherans. Then there are immense parishes with but a meagre Lutheran population.

Ivan IV. was the first Russian sovereign who gave legal recognition to the Lutheran Church. In 1575, Duke Magnus of Holstein was permitted to erect a church at Semljanoi Gorod for the use of himself, his Livonian attendants and other Lutherans. From this seed, planted 300 years ago, a stately tree has sprung. Under Peter the Great, Catharine II. and Alexander I., the Lutheran emigration increased. The seizure of the Baltic Provinces and Finland brought entire Lutheran countries into the empire. At present the Lutheran Church of Russia numbers more than five million souls, and ranks third among the churches of the empire. No small proportion of its membership is found among the most educated and well to do classes.

On the shores of the Baltic begins the great arch of Lutheran congregations, which encloses with its semi-circle European Russia. In Finland, the Lutheran is the State Church. The Baltic Provinces (Esthonia, Livonia and Courland) are preponderatingly Lutheran. The churches in Lithuania and Poland are joined on the east by the German colonies of Volhymnia and Podolia. Then come the colonies in the Steppe, which are very numerous in Bessarabia, and stretch across Kherson and Ekaterinoslav into the Crimea. A number of German Lutheran settlements are found in the Caucasus, but along the Volga, from its mouth clear to the Ural Mountains, are found the prosperous colonies founded by Catharine II. The rest of Russia is covered with associations of Lutherans, whose members are naturally more numerous in the cities. But such congregations take in a wide sweep of territory and embrace many nationalities.

The Lutheran Church in Russia, exclusive of Finland and Poland, may be divided into three general groups: 1. The Baltic Sea Provinces; 2. The colonies on the Volga and in the South; 3. Settlements scattered through inner Russia.

The Baltic Sea Provinces were opened to settlement by Lutherans through Peter the Great, who adopted the saying of Frederic the Great, that in his kingdom every one could be happy after his own fashion. Both rulers, in so saying, had special reference to religious motives. Religious freedom was laid down as a condition of migration to the kingdom. Catharine II. knew the worth of German settlers, and knew that they would not go to Russia uncalled. Under her reign, the settlements on the Volga were begun, and now 300,000 Evangelical Germans have homes there. About 1817, Alexander I. gathered Germans,—mostly Würtembergers,—into settlements along the Black Sea, where they have prosperous colonies and well-organized congregations.

The scattered settlements of the interior, however, are not so well located or so prosperous. Some of them, indeed, live under difficulties of which we have little conception. The Novgorod pastor must be able to preach in six different tongues, and averages four regular sermons each week. In the *Wolhynien* pastorate in 1859, the settlers numbered 4,800; in 1883, 74,000, scattered over a territory of 63,000 square kilometers, with three churches. In the Crimea, the parish of Neusalz has 203 filials, which the pastor must attend. In the Caucasus, one pastor must travel 6,000 miles a year. In Siberia is perhaps the largest Lutheran pastorate in the world. It includes a territory larger than that of all Europe. In four years time the pastor traveled 35,000 miles. To attend a wedding in a settlement at the mouth of the Amoor river, he left home in February and returned in September. Such journeys, naturally, are attended with great fatigue and many privations. They lead through real wildernesses, and nothing can be bought, in places, even for gold.

The pastors in Pskoff, Novgorod and many other places often have to travel 100 or more versts (a verst is two-thirds of a mile) in the discharge of official duties. And the pastor of Irkutsk, in Siberia, though he has but 1,086 members, must travel 14,000 versts a year (or 30 miles every day) ministering to them.

In 1832, the Church which had hitherto been divided into 10 districts became united under the General Consistory at St. Petersburg, to which there are eight under consistories subordinated. The Vice Presidents of these consistories are the general superintendents. The decisions of the consistories are transmitted to the pastors through the provosts. In 1867 there were 31 of the latter and 452 pastors in Russia, not including Finland and Poland.*

The Consistorium in St. Petersburg is composed of six members, viz., a lay president and a clerical vice president, both directly appointed by the Czar, and two clerical and two lay members selected from a number of candidates named by provincial bodies. It is the final court with respect to matrimonial questions and the discipline and removal of ministers; and is occupied also with all complaints touching variations from the doctrine and worship of the Church, which it refers, after examination, to the Min-

---

* Friedensbote, of Elsass and Lothringen.

ister of Internal Affairs. Under it are eight district consistorinms, each of them presided over by a clerical president, who in the five larger districts has the title of General Superintendent, and in the three smaller, of Superintendent. The provincial synods have no legislative or administrative power, but are purely advisory.

All pastors, professors and teachers of the young, are required to subscribe to the Book of Concord. Yet all are obliged to strictly observe the boundaries of the other churches tolerated in Russia, and especially to abstain from all official acts with respect to members of the Greek Orthodox Church, which, on the other hand has no limits placed to its authority, and claims as its members even those who receive communion at the hands of its priests, in cases where death seems imminent. In 1881, the following statistics were given:

Baptisms... 90,347
Confirmations... 51,727
Marriages... 20,067
Funerals.. 62,963

The Lutheran population of St. Petersburg is between 60,000 and 70,000. Among the churches of the capital are a Finnish, a Swedish, an Esthonian-German, a Letonian-German, and a German Russian. In 1881, there were in the city over 2,000 Lutheran baptisms; and the number of those who communed was over 33,802. The best evidence both of the fidelity of the people to their confession and of their Christian earnestness, is seen in their schools and their institutions of mercy. Eight of the congregations had twenty church schools, (three of them classical,) attended by 3,471 scholars.*

The 42,000 Evangelical Germans in St. Petersburg have fourteen congregations and thirty preachers. All contributions for Church purposes are free-will gifts. Yet these are

* Herzog-Plitt Encyclopedia.

by no means scant. One of the congregations numbers 3,000 souls; and for the last thirty years its contributions have averaged 25 marks for every one. It has a church building for which it paid 900,000 marks; and it supports a gymnasium; a home for the poor, and for boys and girls; a retreat for the aged; etc. Another congregation, for the last twenty-five years, has given 80,000 marks yearly for the support of its schools. In addition, they support City Mission works, Deaconess works, people's libraries, etc.*

The City Mission work in St. Petersburg is carried on vigorously. For some time past, its friends have desired earnestly to secure it a home. Late last year a prominent member of a Lutheran church in that city gave the Society 100,000 rubles more for this purpose; and now the Association has bought the elegant church occupied for one hundred and twenty-five years by the Moravian Brethren, presented to them in 1765 by Catharine II., but in which services were indefinitely discontinued last May, " under the pressure of circumstances." The building was bought for 130,000 rubles.

Our congregations in Russia generally support church schools, of which 2,100 were reported in 1885, with 3,050 teachers. Some higher schools exist. The educational system of the Germans in Russia is crowned with the University of Dorpat with over seventy professors and 1,751 students; while that of the Finns has the University of Helsingfors, with 100 professors, from 1,300 to 1,400 students, and a library of 300,000 volumes. The Lutherans on the Volga, reporting a population of 300,000, seem to be most needy, although they are provided with church privileges.

Outside of Finland and Poland, in 1886, the Lutheran parishioners of Russia were given at 2,670,000. The church had nine consistorial districts, 39 superintendents and

---
*Fliegende Blatter : Rauhe Haus, 1890.

provosts, 427 pastorates and 564 pastors, 1,138 church edifices, church property whose cash value was written at $1,075,000.00, and over 178,000 children in her congregational schools. Returns published recently in church periodicals give the number of pastoral charges at 457, and the number of members at 2,678,000.

Something of the influence and spirit of these people may be inferred from such facts as follow: In Odessa, a metropolis of 184,000 people, the German Lutherans own a church edifice which cost $50,000. Its communicant membership is considerably over a thousand and is served by two very able pastors. In the pastorate there is a Lutheran gymnasium; also a "real-school" for boys and a high school for girls, and two elementary schools. Near the parsonage stands a hospital for the aged and the sick, an orphan home for boys and one for girls. All these institutions are flourishing. In the suburbs of the city there are three other German Lutheran congregations which have their own houses of worship, besides a number of preaching places. A new hospital lately was built in this place, and began its work with an endowment fund of $65,000.00. In Riga, as church periodicals inform us, $40,000.00 were contributed in one day to build a Lutheran church in a town near by.*

South of the Gulf of Finland, and adjoining the Baltic Sea, are the three provinces of Livonia, Esthonia and Courland, generally known as the Baltic provinces, and often styled "the German provinces of the Baltic." Together, they have an area of 36,000 square miles, equal to about three times that of the state of Maryland. Livonia is the largest of these provinces, and, with its island possessions in the Gulf of Riga, has an area of 18,160 square miles, and a

* The General Consistory of the Lutheran Church in Russia for 1891 -93 consists of the following members, besides the officials of the crown : Pastor K. Freifeldt of St. Petersburg ; Pastor Everth of Moscow; Privy Counsellor Count Sievers, and Privy Counsellor Baron Schwanebach.

population (1882) of 1,121,000. The prevailing religion is Lutheran, although the Russian residents, (85,000,) together with 50,000 Lithanians and 80,000 Ehsts in Livonia and Esthonia, belong to the Greek church.

Riga is the capital of Livonia, and the seat of the Governor General of the Baltic provinces. It is a city of 168,700 inhabitants, (1881,) a seaport of Russia, situated at the southern extremity of the Gulf of Riga, 375 miles southwest of St. Petersburg. About half the population is German; the other half is composed of Russians, Esthonians, Letts and foreigners. Among its educational institutions are a polytechnic institute, a Greek seminary, four gymnasiums, ten private schools for higher education of boys and girls, in addition to a large number of primary schools. There is a municipal library which contains very interesting material relating to the history of the Baltic provinces; and the city has a rapidly extending book trade. The old *Domkirche*, founded in 1204, was burned down once, but again rebuilt. In it there is a great organ, containing 6,826 pipes, with a gas engine of four horse power, and said to be the largest in the world. It has been in the church for nearly sixty years. St. Peter's church is nearly five hundred years old, and has a tower 440 feet high. In this city, also, is an old castle, built by the master of the Knights of the Sword, but now the seat of the Governor General; "the house of the black heads," founded in 1232, and more recently the meeting-place of some of the wealthier youth of the place; the municipal picture gallery, and the gymnasiums of Alexander I. There are, also, sea bathing resorts, with many summer visitors.

Dorpat is an important city of Livonia, with a population of about 30,000, (1880,) situated on the Embach, nearly 160 miles northeast of Riga. Its streets are straight and clean; its houses handsome and often showily painted. In the winter it is the residence of the Livonian nobles and gentry.

It is well supplied with churches has a hospital, an orphanage, a medico-physical society, an economical society, and a veterinary institute. Its glory, however, is its famous university.

Courland is next in size of the Baltic provinces, having a population of 682,000, mostly Lutherans.

Mitau, the capital, was founded 1266, and has often changed masters. It is well provided with educational institutions. A former palace of the Dukes of Courland is now used as a gymnasium, and has a rich library; and there are about forty other schools. The town is also the seat of a society of art and literature; of a natural history society, which has a good museum; and of the Lettish Literary Society. The population is 22,000, about half of whom are Germans.

Esthonia has a population of 350,000 (1880.) The higher education, under the influence of the clergy and the nobility, is true to German tradition. The National Church is Lutheran, and the province is divided into eight dioceses. One-thirteenth of the population is Germanic; the rest are principally Esthonians, who belong properly to the Finnish family. The province may be briefly characterized as a country fundamentally Esthonian, with a German aristocracy and a Russian government.

Reval is a seaport of Russia, capital of Esthonia, with a population of over 50,000 (1881.) Several of its churches date their origin back several centuries. The St. Nicholas was built about 1317, and contains many antiquities of Roman Catholic times and old German paintings. In it, also, is the grave of the Duc de Croy, who was denied burial because of his debts, and whose mummy, dressed in velvet and fine lace, was exposed until 1862. The church of St. Olai was first erected in 1240, has since been restored, and has a bell tower 429 feet high. The "Domkirche" contains many interesting shields, and the graves of several circumnavigators. Reval is the seat of the provincial church consistory.

Because of Russia's cruel policy toward our church folk of the Baltic provinces, it has been thought well to present an account of how our people became subjects of the Czar, and of what has stirred up the trouble between them and the officials of the Empire. As full and fair an account as we have seen of these things was prepared by Dr. Wells, and first published in the *Northern Christian Advocate*. Because of its source, we give it here rather than write out an account of our own. The Doctor's words are as follows:

On the eastern shores of the Baltic, extending from the German boundary to the Bay of Finland, lie the Provinces of Courland, Livonia, and Esthonia, usually known as the Baltic provinces. They belong politically to Russia, though largely settled by Germans. These latter migrated thither a century ago, when they were little more than barren and waste lands, and they went at the invitation of Russia under the promise that their language and religion should be unmolested. It was for a long time the policy of Russia to invite the neighboring Germans to settle on their lands, with a view to obtain European culture as a training for their people.

The Germans who went to the Baltic provinces were treated fairly well for a while, but of late years the Russians throughout the country have instituted systematic persecutions of the Germans in all their land; they have learned from them largely the arts and industries of civilization, and would now fain drive out the people who have done much towards giving them European culture. But the Germans of the Baltic provinces have all their interests so closely allied to their present homes, that to leave them would be to make themselves beggars and outcasts, so they are obliged to stay and fight it out with their oppressors. They have had much sympathy and aid from their fellow countrymen and co-religionists in Germany, but this seems only to make the persecution more keen on the part of the Russian rulers.

The Russians make the complaint that they remain Germans in spirit, customs, and especially in religion, instead of identifying themselves with Russian aspirations and faith,--but this they never promised to do and never will do, except so far as they are forced to do so by the right of might. The German "*Balts*," as they are called, have always been a source of profit and advantage to Russia, and in many ways have exerted a wholesome influence in all the surrounding land. They have been at the least expense for administration, and have given comparatively the largest revenues. They more than support their own schools, and these are the best in all Russia; the only respectable modern university in Russia is that of Dorpat, in these provinces, and that is now continually annoyed by the government because it would remain German in language and system of thought and teaching. It has been greatly crippled in its labors for the last few years because of the efforts of the government to force it to use the Russian tongue in the lecture rooms. This matter has now gone so far that no one may be a member of the faculty unless he is able to teach in the Russian idiom, and in certain departments the language is already used by command, so that Dorpat is in a fair way of being transformed into a Russian school.

These Germans of the Baltic have always been loyal to the government in time of trouble and have willingly fought on many battle fields, sometimes by their skill and valor turning the tide of fortune. There is scarcely a Baltic family that does not count the grave of some dear one fallen in the distant Orient.

The importance of these provinces to Russia in the line of culture and industrial progress is indisputable, and their influence is felt in this line in all the surrounding region. The Baltic courts and magistracy and the whole civil corps of officials are noted for their efficiency, and here alone in all the land can justice be obtained without bribery;—at least this is the reputation of the administration of the laws. In the schools of these provinces the teaching methods are modern and effective, founded as they are naturally on the German system. Their contrast with the Russian schools is most marked; the one aims at the conscience, the heart and the character, while the other seems only to cultivate ambition and personal vanity. The Baltic teachers are loyal to their calling and live exemplary lives; the Russian teachers are loose and inexact in their ways, careless in the fulfillment of duty and thoughtless about the moral influence exerted on their pupils. The Nihilism of Russia is largely cultivated in the higher schools.

In social life and customs the difference between the two races is very patent. In the provinces the mothers of the better classes take care of their own children in infancy, and in childhood are zealous in their religious instruction, training their hearts to the love of Christian practices and the study of the elements of the Christian religion. The Russian women of the upper classes know little about domestic duties and leave their children to the care of servants, with no opportunity for religious training in childhood; the accomplishments of their daughters consist mainly in fluency in French and readiness in music. The comparison may be drawn in nearly every sphere of life with no disparagement to the Baltic provinces; here one finds order and cultivation—good roads, well-cultivated fields, rational methods in agriculture and the arts, and increasing prosperity. But cross the Russian line and the scene suddenly changes; miserable roads which for a portion of the year are impassable, forests exposed to depredators, and country and people a picture of poverty and misery. The peasantry of Russia is with few exceptions in a very low state of culture.

In the line of literary development the Baltic provinces are far in advance of anything in Russia; the teachers and preachers are men of thought and study and receive the best productions of Germany in scientific as in popular literature, while in Russia proper a literature for the people and the children is scarcely known. But the sharpest thorn for the Russian government is the fact that these people of the Baltic provinces desire to retain not only their language and their schools, but also their Lutheran religion. For the last few years the greatest efforts have been made to bring them over to the Russo-Greek Church. The annual appropriations to the native churches have either been greatly decreased or entirely withheld, and it is being daily made more difficult for the Lutheran peasants to live in their own Church, for in that they must pay increased tithes because of the delinquency on the part of the government; while they are invited to the Russo-Greek altars free of all expense and with certain local privileges. In short, the most systematic means are being adopted in every sphere where the government can interfere to stamp out all that is German and introduce all that is Russian. The natural result is a very bitter state of feeling, that threatens at the first opportunity to break out into open rebellion.

Recent estimates give the population considerably greater than our figures show it. The Lutheran population in these provinces, and in other parts of Russia outside of Finland and Poland, is put at 2,710,000.

In Siberia there are two Lutheran pastors, under control of a General Superintendent at Moscow. The pastor at Wladiwostok (Kamtchatka) must be able to converse in German, Swedish, Finnish, Danish, Estish and Lettish. A pastor is located near Archangel, on the White Sea, and has members living near the North Cape. He carries religious works in five different tongues to suit the needs of his parishioners. In Novgorod alone services are held in six different languages.

In the Baltic Sea are the Islands Oesel, Mohn, Runo, etc., subject to all the winds and storms that make this great sea dangerous to navigation. Oesel is the largest and most important of the three named, and has an area of 1,010 square miles. With other islands it forms a district of the government of Livonia. It is the home of the Oesel ponies, greatly prized because of their smallness. The majority of the inhabitants are of the Esthonian race, and 30,000 Lutherans are found here and on the smaller neighboring islands.

The Lutheran Church, in what formerly was known as the Kingdom of Poland, and now is a province of Russia, numbers 300,000 members, in 62 charges and 53 under parochial churches. It calls itself the Evangelical Augsburg Church in the Kingdom of Poland. It is controlled by a consistory located in Warsaw. Its ministers are held to perform their office conscientiously; to strengthen their parishioners in the truth of the Christian doctrine, and especially to abstain from preaching any opinions which do not agree with the Evangelical Church. The Polish Lutheran Church once had 505 religious schools wherein the instruction was given by means of the German language. But most of these schools have been made secular schools, and the Russian language has superseded the German. The pators are supported by the congregations, the consistory by the State.

Only in a few of the congregations is the Polish the prevalent element. Only in five is the Lithuanian the language; in the great majority, German is the language of both church and school. The schools are not under church control, except in so far as two hours per day are devoted to religious instruction, and one hour to instruction in the mother tongue, the rest being devoted to Russian. The emigration of Germans in Poland to other parts of Russia, has been a great hindrance to the Church. Considerable influence is manifested in Foreign Missions, contributions having been sent to Leipsig, to Barmen, Basle and Hermannsburg.

Missouri literature is widely read in Poland, and in the recent revision of the Church Book, the Missouri Synod's hymn book was freely used. The new book bears the seal of the Evangelical Augsburg Consistory of Warsaw, Vice-President General Superintendent Everth. Their aim was "a hymn book above all things loyal to the Confessions" of our church.*

Finland is a Grand Duchy in the northwestern part of the Russian Empire, bordering on Archangel, Sweden, Norway and the Baltic Sea. It is a land of marshes and mountains, lakes and rivers, seas, gulfs, islands and inlets. The climate is more severe than that of Sweden; the mean yearly temperature in the north being about 27 degrees F., and about 38 degrees F. at Helsingfors, the capital. In the southern districts the winter is seven months long; and in the northern provinces the sun disappears entirely during the months of December and January.

The inhabitants are strong and hardy, with bright, intelligent faces, high cheek bones, hair yellow in early life, brown in mature age. As to their social habits, morals and manners, all travelers agree in speaking well of them. Their temper is mild; they are slow to anger, and when angry they keep silent. They are happy-hearted, affectionate, and honorable and honest in their dealings with strangers. They are a cleanly people, being much given to the use of vapor baths. They are not over-easy of access, yet are not inhospitable; and are not friends of new fashions. They are steady, laborious, careful, valuable in the mine, in the field, on ship-board; and, withal, good soldiers on land. They are a very ancient people; and it is claimed that they began

---

* *Lutheraner*, St. Louis.

earlier than any other European nation to collect and preserve their ancient folk-lore.*

One of the most celebrated poems of Finnish literature, the *Kalevala*, has recently been translated into English and published (1888) in New York. It is supposed to date its origin back to a period at least a thousand years before Christ; and language-masters and critics give it a front rank among the literary gems of the world. Topelius and Lönnrot, Finnish scholars of renown, were at great pains to gather together the fragments of the poem and give the whole to the world in a finished form, over fifty years ago. The leading scholars of Europe were attracted to it. Men like the Grimms, Steinthal, and Max Müller, hastened to acknowledge its intrinsic value and beauty. Longfellow caught its inspiration, and modeled the metre of Hiawatha by it. Max Müller says, "it equals the Iliad in length and completeness; nay, if we can forget for a moment all that *we* in our youth learned to call beautiful, it is not less beautiful. . . It will claim its place as the fifth national epic of the world." Steinthal ranks it as one of four great national epics; the other three being the *Iliad*, *Nibelunge*, and *the Roland Songs*.

Finland has an area of 144,200 square miles, or over three times that of Pennsylvania. The population is 2,111,-240, (1882,) of whom 2,069,720 are Lutherans. Strangely enough, the Emperor of Russia is Grand Duke of Finland. This Grand Duchy is ruled by a Governor General, assisted by the imperial Senate, over which a representative of the Emperor regularly presides. It is, in a manner, independent. It pays no tribute to Russia, and the consent of the Diet must be obtained for the introduction of new laws and taxes. The interior is for the most part a vast plateau, and its entire area is abundantly supplied with lakes and swamps. Hence its name, Fen land, or swampland. Fully

* Preface to *Kalevala*.

one half of the surface is covered with forests. Excellent post roads lead in every direction. The greater part of the population are peasants who make their own clothes and furniture. They are affectionate, honest, hospitable, and peaceable; though in ancient times they were, according to Pritchard, savage as the Lapps, and divided into tribes generally at war with each other.

Cox introduces us to Finland with these words: " Finland was once a political part of Sweden, but the union was dissolved by force in 1809. The Finns like the Swedes better than they do the Russians, though they are not discontented with Russian rule. They are a brave and frugal people. They fear no danger; they court the perils of the sea and the Northern climate. Along the Gulf, they are so immersed in the races about them that they partake of, if they do not surpass, the civilization of their neighbors. They are farmers, cattle raisers, and butter makers.

"Their country is more than half water. Its lakes, as the maps show, are as plentiful as those of Sweden. The latter country has the credit for a good deal of what Finland has accomplished. In science and navigation these Finns are not to be passed by. It is enough to say that Nordenskiold, the Polar explorer, was born at Helsingfors. He is a sample of the best Finnish blood, which, before the Goths conquered it, controlled all Sweden.

"Whatever may be said of Russian rule elsewhere, she has let Finland have her autonomy, with independence in church and state. The Finns have a legislature of their own. It consists of one body, the Senate. It has a peculiar coinage, with a mark (a franc) and its one hundred pennies. The Governor is appointed by the Czar, but in local matters the ancient order and manners of the country are respected and protected. Other parts of Russia complain of this liberality and leniency, but the fact remains, and it is owing to the orderly good sense of the Finns themselves.

"The Finns are not Norse, Dane, or Swede; and they are not Lapps. The Finns we have seen have light hair—yellow or red, and when not too much mixed, are shorter than the Norwegian or Swede. They are rather chunky, but stalwart and hardy like the Norse people. Nor must the Finns of Swedish history and association be confounded with the Finns of Russia proper. The Russian Finns spoken of by Wallace . . . are entirely dissociated with these Finns of the peninsula immediately north of the gulf of that name."

Helsingfors is the chief city of this grand-duchy, situated on the Gulf of Finland, 274 miles by rail west of St. Petersburg, in latitude 60 degrees north. It is the seat of the Governor General of Finland, the imperial Senate, and all the central officers of the government. It has scientific, literary, and other learned societies; a normal lyceum, polytechnic institute, school for the blind, school of navigation, asylum for the insane, hospitals and other educational and charitable institutions. It has several machinery manufactories, one of which employs 850 hands; and has sugar, porcelain, and tobacco factories, etc. A series of formidable batteries command its harbor and are of such strength that competent authorities have termed the place the Gibraltar of the North. The united fortresses mount 1,000 guns. The town is a favorite bathing place and attracts many visitors.

Viborg, or Wiborg, a city of 15,800, (1884,) is the capital of the province of the same name, and is situated at the head of the Bay of Viborg. It is also at the mouth of a canal, and on the railroad that connects Helsingfors with St. Petersburg. The town is picturesquely situated, has an old castle dating from 1293, court house, town house, museum, gymnasium, an excellent library, a school of navigation, a literary and an agricultural society, several benevolent institutions, several private schools, and the necessary public schools. In industrial establishments, there are sawmills, match factories, iron works, steam engine works, etc. Great quantities of timber are exported. Much of the scenery around Viborg is very picturesque, and attracts many tourists.

Borga, or Borgo, 25 miles northwest of Helsingfors, was at one time a wealthy and handsome city, but has somewhat decayed. It has a beautiful cathedral, a gymnasium, and is the seat of a bishopric which extends over a great part of Finland.

Abo is a seaport of Finland, and, up to 1819, was its capital, but was nearly wholly destroyed by fire. Up to that time it was the seat of the university. It now has a cathedral, a custom house, etc.; and is the seat of the archbishopric of Finland. Population about 20,000.

The houses in Finland, and frequently even the churches and other public edifices, are constructed of wood, generally painted red; but they are warm, and sometimes too much so for those unaccustomed to a close atmosphere. The habitations of the peasants are well built, and afford complete protection from the severity of the winter cold; and, notwithstanding the long duration of that season, and the seeming sterility of the soil, the people are in many respects better provided than the same class in more southern regions. They can generally set before the traveler fresh and curdled milk, salt herrings, or a little salt meat; and they are rich in all that they consider as constituting the enjoyments of life. If at any time they have more money than their immediate wants require, they lay it up for future emergencies, or convert it into some domestic utensil; and it is not uncommon in a small wooden dwelling, to see the water presented in a silver vessel of the value of fifty or sixty rix-dollars. The peasantry are remarkably dexterous both in the use of the bow, and of the fowling-piece, loading the latter always with ball, and rarely missing the smallest bird.

They employ for this purpose a kind of rifle-gun, with a narrow bore, which requires but a very small charge, and yet carries to a considerable distance. The winter is the principal season of traffic; and all the great fairs are held in that time of the year, in consequence of the facility of carrying goods over the ice, and traveling in sledges on the snow. The peasants on these occasions frequently undertake journeys of three or four hundred English miles, carrying along with them whatever articles they have for sale. In Finland, the sledges are very narrow, containing only one person, and drawn by a single horse; and the roads are deep ruts formed by the successive passage of these vehicles, thus admitting none of a larger size than those generally used in the country. The circumstance of being overturned is rarely productive of any serious consequences; and the dangers attending the traveler arise chiefly from those parts of the rivers or lakes where the ice is insufficient to support the weight.*

Most of the peasants have a small house built expressly to afford bathing privileges. Their bath is peculiar. A number of stones in the innermost part of the chamber are heated by fire till they become red. Water being thrown upon them in this state, the bathers are involved in a cloud of thick hot vapor air; they remain naked for the space of half an hour, or even a whole hour, rubbing their bodies, or lashing them with bunches of twigs; and frequently go out, without any covering, into the open air, or even roll themselves in the snow, thus making an instantaneous transition of perhaps 100 degrees, which is almost equivalent to a passage from boiling to freezing water. This practice, they affirm, has a most invigorating effect upon their frames, and recruits their strength as much as rest or sleep.

In earlier times but little was known of the Finns. In the twelfth century they made their piratical inroads into

---

* Goodrich.

Sweden, and so exasperated the King, Eric the saint, that he undertook a crusade against them, and compelled them, by force of arms, to profess the Christian religion. He set up his banners among them and said, " Choose between the good and evil: Be baptized or die." Since that century they have been a Christian people, and at the Reformation Finnish Reformers, who had been students of Luther at Wittenberg, led the people to Lutheranism, in which faith they have remained to this day.

As in the Scandinavian countries, so in Finland there is much religious activity. Conferences of ministers, previously almost unknown, have been held three times in late years ; and have been found so satisfactory that hereafter they will be held yearly. The pastors of districts meet annually, as required by law ; but latterly the meetings have become more interesting through their giving more attention to the discussion of questions of the times.

A General Council of the whole Finnish Church (Lutheran) is held once in ten years. In all questions of reform, each congregation has to give its opinion before the General Council can take action.

The new church law (1857) puts all power in church affairs into the hands of the people. Two-thirds of the members of the Council are laymen. Congregations have the most to say in calling pastors. Voting is based on property qualifications. The new law has opened the way for disunion efforts. The Baptists went in from Sweden twenty or thirty years ago, but are confined, chiefly, to the coast provinces. There, too, they reap where others have sown. The Methodists, also, have entered Finland. Common schools are found in cities and large towns. In the country, education is mostly attended to by the pastors. The Finns are reputed good public speakers. The 236 gymnasiums or lyceums have 2,445 students, the 66 primary schools 921 scholars, the 69 female schools 734 scholars, and the polytechnic school at Helsingfors has 118 scholars. There are also real-schools, two industrial real-schools, 6 navigation schools, 1 cadet school, 2 agricultural institutes, 31 mechanics' schools and 2 schools for the blind and 4 for the deaf and dumb.*

The Lutheran is the state church. It reports 345 parishes, 800 ministers, 487 churches and 515 chapels. The system of assistant minister prevails here as it does in no other country. It frequently happens that a number of congregations constitute one parish, but are presided over by several ministers. The Finns require all ministerial acts, such as burials and liturgy, to be performed by an ordained minister and not by a schoolmaster or sacristan. Toward the North are living small congregations, frequently scattered over an immense extent of territory. Thus, for instance, the parish of Limingo in the provostship of Ulenborg has 9,248 parishioners upon an area of 1,335 square miles; the parish of Pudasjaereoie 7,133 parishioners upon area of 10,-379 square miles, and the most northerly Utesyoke has only 1,152 parishioners upon an area of 19,250 square miles.

The church officials include one archbishop, two bishops, and 46 superintendents. The administration of the ecclesiastical government is in the hands chiefly of the bishops, while the legislation emanates from a General Synod, composed of two fifths ministers and three-fifths laymen. Measures passed by the Synod must be approved by the parliament of the country, and be confirmed by the Czar, or may be proposed by a so-called clerical Diet. If they refer to church books, the congregations must also agree to their introduction. There are active organizations in connection with the congregations to limit the evils of vagabondage and drunkenness, and to recover those who have been ensnared by them. The clergy are earnest and faithful adherents to

---

* A recent periodical puts the number of Lutherans in Finland at two and a half millions, with 5,547 schools and 111,024 scholars.

the confessions. The pastor is elected by the congregations, and is ex-officio president of all congregational meetings. The pastors elect the bishops and these, together with the clergy of the archbishopric and members of the Cathedral Chapter, elect the archbishops. The chapter (equivalent to a German consistory) consists of the bishop, the pastor loci, two other pastors, a lawyer as secretary, and a notary.

The present law accords to members of the Lutheran Church the right to separate from the same; but in the absence of a dissenter law, no recognized churches of other confessions can exist. Any one leaving the State Church—the Evangelical Lutheran—has no other denomination to unite with. In Finland no one is allowed to marry unless he is a regular communicant, and under the present law only Lutherans are regular. This makes it impossible for Baptists and other denominations to enter into matrimony, unless they commune in the Lutheran Church, and of course non-Lutherans are not admitted to the Lord's Supper. It is very natural that these Lutherans should think their Church good enough, and that no sects are necessary for the happiness and salvation of the Finnish people.

The Finnish Church owes much to the Swedish Government, which in former years extended over this country. The melancholy wars which swept over Finland scattered many congregations, and caused the Lutheran bishop and a hundred of his clergy to take refuge in Stockholm.

Russia succeeded in 1809 in gaining possession of the whole country, and transferred the seat of government and the university from Abo to Helsingfors. The Lutheran Church for a long time fared well at Russia's hands. Now however, the policy adopted towards the Germans is being pursued in regard to the Finns. Finland is not Teutonic, but in Russian eyes it has the same demerits as those which are complained of in the German sections. The Finns are Lutheran; and they have hitherto been allowed to have an administration of their own—an administration in harmony with their ancient traditions and suited to their general habits and modes of living. Finland has long been threatened with absorption ; and the only answer which the people have been able to obtain to vigorous and earnest protests against the proposed policy is the appointment of a commission to inquire into the best way of amalgamating the post, the customs and the mint of Finland with the corresponding services of the empire at large. The clergy of Finland, generally, use the Finnish language ; but an imperial ukase has ordered that all the schools of Finland use the Russian language exclusively.

---

* Dr. Prime, late editor of the *Observer*, of New York, (Presbyterian,) tells that in his travels he visited the University at Helsingfors. He understood no word of Finnish, but was introduced to one of the professors, who addressed him, consecutively, in Latin, German, French, Swedish, Norwegian, and finally in classic English.

CHAPTER VII.

IN OTHER LANDS.

In England, the Royal Family itself has been connected, in one way or another, with the Lutheran Church or its members, since the beginning of the eighteenth century. Anne, second daughter of James II., married Prince George of Denmark in 1684, and ascended the throne in 1702. She outlived her husband and all of her children, and George I., originally, at least, a nominal member of the Lutheran Church, was her successor. From that time on to the accession of Queen Victoria, the sovereigns of England were also kings of Hanover. The first George was not even familiar with the English language. As King of England he had to be a member of the English Church; but he had the English Church service translated into German, and worship was—and still is—conducted in St. James' Chapel in the German tongue.

Not only so, but in the course of these years there has been a new accession of the German Lutheran element to the Royal Family to England.* Under George II. (1727–1760) the Prince of Wales married a princess of Saxe-Gotha, one of the Lutheran duchies of the German Empire. In 1840, Victoria, the young Queen of England, married Prince Albert, second son of the late Duke of Saxe-Coburg-Gotha, the Queen herself being of the House of Hanover. Until A. D. 1837, the King of Hanover was at the same time the sovereign of Great Britain; at the death of William IV., the Duke of Cumberland became King of Han-

---
* Mann; *Halle Reports*, vol. I.: 35; and *En. Brit.*; Art. *Hanover.*

over, because a law of this kingdom prevented any woman from occupying the throne. Hanover is yet more positively Lutheran than Saxe-Gotha; but both these political divisions are represented on the throne of Great Britain. It is not difficult to understand why Lutheran court preachers should officiate in the court chapel of St. James; nor is it difficult to know why the German tongue should be heard there. By act of Parliament, the Royal Family must belong to the Church of England, and in these latter days they do not usually attend the German service; but it is attended by Lutheran members of the German embassies in London. The German language is used, it is said, by Queen Victoria, and those around her, in the privacy of court life. Members of our church are scattered through London, and are found in other parts of the kingdom, to the number of 24,000.

According to the census of 1880, the percentage of persons of the Evangelical (Augsburg) Confession in the Kingdom of Hungary was 8.2 of the total population of the country, which then was written at 13,728,000.* This gives a population of nearly 1,125,000. Of 15,824 denominational schools then in existence, 1,443 were "Augsburg Evangelical." Of 151 gymnasiums, 25 were of the same confession; and of about thirty-five thousand students in these schools, 3,699 were "Augusburg Evangelical."

Later returns through church periodicals write the Lutheran population at one and a half millions; with, at present, five dioceses, 51 senior pastors, 881 pastors, 271 assistant pastors, 1,627 parochial schools, with 2,338 teachers and 147,690 pupils.

The members of our churches here have endured so many persecutions since the days of the Reformation, as to entitle them to be called a martyr church. And to-day they suffer at the hands of the Magyars. Believing Lutheran pastors

---
* Report U. S. Com'r of Education, 1881, ccxliii.

are displaced for men hostile to the confessions, but more agreeable to the Magyars, the latter are bent upon rooting out not only Lutheranism, but the German and the Slovak tongues, and substituting their own language. The Lutheran colleges, founded at great cost, and with amazing sacrifices, have been closed. The Lutherans are expected to send their children to colleges where neither their faith nor their language is tolerated, and to a theological seminary, of whose professor no one knows whether he is baptized or is a Reformed Jew. In this time of conf sion, the Methodists are going through the land reaping where they have not sowed.

"Beyond the Woods" from Hungary is a mountainous, "forest-land" principality, known as Transylvania, with a population of over two millions, of whom over a tenth are Lutherans.* Quite recent statistics are wanting, but the latest reports accessible put the Lutheran population at 211,000, with 270 churches, 448 pastors, and 30,200 children in the parochial schools. The head of the church is a bishop. Surrounded by Magyars, Slavonians and Rumanians, the people still worship in the German language, as their forefathers did six hundred years ago, when the Saxons settled among these "seven mountains."

In the other countries of the Hungarian crown, (Croatia-Slavonia and the Military Frontier,) about 18,000 members of our faith are found; and in the fourteen "Crown Lands" of Austria proper, there are over 252,000,* making a total in Austria-Hungary, outside of Hungary and Transylvania, of over 290,000. This part of the church is divided into six dioceses, with fifteen seniorates, 143 parishes, 92 stations, 150 pastors, 172 schools with 287 teachers. The mother churches number 126, chapels 116, and school-houses used for churches 281,—a total of 523. A teachers' seminary exists in Bielitz, Silesia, self-sustaining and prosperous.

---

* Kolb; Condition of Nations.

K

The Lutheran churches of Vienna report 9,200 communicant members, and a population of 30,000. They have a hospital, and several deaconesses at work in parishes.

It is estimated that there are over 90,000 Lutherans in France, but many of them are not under the direct charge of the church. About 35,000 of them are in Paris, with fourteen places of worship. Fifty-two "deacons" work among the poor, without salary. A Deaconess House exists in the capital, which has fifteen sisters at work among the parishes. A seminary for the training of men for the ministry exists at Dasle. The Alsatians who were Protestants were nearly all Lutherans, but they are now counted among the Germans. The Lutheran pastors of France have two synods, viz.: that of Montbeliard, and that of Paris; and these two are again united in the General Synod.

The strongest Lutheran church in Switzerland is to be found at Geneva. The members are mostly Germans. The pastor reports for last year 447 communicants, 17 baptisms and seven catechumens. The Sunday school, better the "Kinderlehre," is attended by 75 children; the parochial school for infants numbers 50 children. Numerous Lutherans are living in the Rhine-cantons, especially at Basel. The Breslau Lutherans have a missionary near Basel, who is traveling through Switzerland in quest of the dispersed members of the Lutheran Church. The Würtemberg Lutherans at Basel, numbering at least 3,000, go to church with the Swiss Reformed, who, at least in that city, are more Lutheran than Calvinist.

There are two Lutheran bodies in Holland. The one calling itself the Old Lutheran Church, consists of 50 congregations, with 60,000 members; the other, called the Re-established Lutheran Church, has eight congregations, with 12,000 members. Three churches are German, the others Dutch. There are yet two German churches, one at the

Hague, the other at Rotterdam, which are under the jurisdiction of the Prussian high consistory.

In Australia, there are five synods of German churches, made up of 65 parishes, not a few of the latter having, each, from four to eight churches and preaching stations. The first German organization there dates from 1838-40. Lutherans from Prussia, who were not willing to conform to the regulations of the United Church, sought the forests of Australia that they might be able to worship God after the manner of their fathers. The settlements have increased in number from that day to this; and to-day 75,000 German brethren-in-the-faith are under the care of our churches in Australia.

These settlers are devoted to their churches. No one, who is not absolutely prevented, remains away from church service; although their churches are fifteen or twenty miles apart. The churches are filled with worshipers, and the sermons must be as long again as they are in Germany, (say three times as long as with us,) to satisfy the people. The Wittenberg Church liturgy is widely used, and the hymns of Luther and of Reformation times are sung. Nearly all the principal congregations have their own schools, as the public schools will give no religious instruction, and these people think it not safe or right to send their children where this is neglected.

Some of the pastors in Australia have big parishes and hard work. We read of one who has six congregations scattered over a territory that is 58 miles long and 40 miles wide. All his travel, at best, must be done with the horse, and in winter the roads are almost bottomless. He holds three services each Sunday. In Melbourne, our churches have appointed, and support, a city missionary.

At least four church papers are published and circulated there. These are "The Lutheran Church Messenger," "The Australian Christian Messenger," "The World and the Times," and "The Church and Mission Periodical." All are in the German tongue; and nearly every Lutheran family reads one or more of these publications. Taken all in all, considering the difficulties with which the people there have had to contend, the schools and the churches must be regarded as in a very encouraging condition. They not only care for themselves, and strive to gather in the immigrants who yearly add to their numbers, but have, also, for years, carried on mission work among the heathen natives.

The Evangelical Lutheran Synod of Australia, doctrinally considered, is "Missouri" in Australia; the Victoria Synod is mild and charged with unionistic practices; and the Immanuel, is "Iowa" in Australia. The Synod of Queensland is composed of Germans and Danes. The Germans all have substantial churches, parochial school-houses, parsonages with a piece of ground for a garden, Sunday schools and high schools. The Australian Synod has in Hahndorf a college and parochial school teachers' seminary, with an attendance of some 44 students, and at Adelaide, in 1884, a new high school was established.

Missionary work has been done among the natives. The Hermannsburg Society has been engaged in it for years. The Immanuel Synod, also, has reached out a helping hand to the dark brown, curly-headed natives, who are reckoned among the rudest and wildest of heathen tribes. The institution at Neuendettlesau, Germany, has sent men to aid in this work; and the Gossner and the Leipsic Societies also have lent assistance. The Immanuel Synod is reported as having a small congregation of natives.

Once, at least, during the history of our mission work in Australia, the very existence of the mission was threatened. The country is subject to protracted droughts; but one more severe than the rest continued for a year. In this time, both food and water had to be carried hundreds of miles, for the missionaries and the colonists who had settled around there.

Perhaps not fewer than 100,000 Germans have found homes in South Africa. Up to 1845, nearly all such immigrants united with the Reformed churches which the earlier settlers from Holland had established there. About the year named above, however, a German congregation was organized in Cape Town, and connected with the Lutheran Church of Hanover; and this was the beginning of what is now a net-work of Lutheran churches and missions in the Southern States of the Dark Continent. About 180 pastors and missionaries now are at work on that field, apart from all the native helpers. The majority of these European laborers are on mission fields; yet there are a score or more of charges made up of congregations of Germans, and a goodly number of the mission organizations are self sustaining.

In Cape Colony and neighboring districts, congregations of German Lutherans are found in Cape Town, Stutterheim, Paarl, King William's Town, Brunswick, Frankfurt, Panmure, Keishammahock, Kimberly, Bloemfontein, etc.; in Natal, Orange Free State, and the Transvaal, congregations exist in New Germany, Beaconsfield, Johannisburg, Pretoria, Hermansburg, New Hanover, Wichsdorf, Marburg, Helpmakaar, Luneberg, Bergen, Bryheit and Rustenburg. All of the above have their own pastors, and many filial organization are served in connection. A number of the congregations have a membership of from five hundred to eleven hundred each. Cape Town returns a congregation of about 1,200 communicants, who gave in one year £2,450 for church and school purposes, and over £100 additional for missions and beneficence. These German congregations are apart from the missions of the Hermansburg, the Berlin and other Lutheran foreign mission societies in the same

South African States, which number over 50,000 baptized members.

Of those congregations which are more or less on the basis of the United Church, we may mention half a dozen in Palestine and other parts of the Orient; nine in Rumania and Serbia; eleven in Italy; fifteen in England; thirty-four in Brazil; and three in each of the South American States, Venezuela, Chili, Uruguay, and the Argentine Republic. The Jerusalem Society of Berlin has been engaged in mission work in the Holy Land, Egypt, Syria and Asia Minor, for over forty years. Pastor Schneller, now at the head of this society's mission forces in the East, was born in the Holy Land; but studied at Berlin, and was pastor of a Lutheran Church in Pomerania before he returned to Jerusalem, to succeed his lamented father as director of the society's work there. This society there maintains the Syrian Orphan House; and the Managers of the Kaiserswerth Deaconess Institute, their hospitals and schools for girls. The former society also has three churches, one each at Bethlehem, Bet Djala and Hebron. At Bethlehem and Bet Djala, the missions also work through schools and orphanages. In Bethlehem, a beautiful church is being built, for which stones are being contributed from all parts of Evangelical Christendom.

In the Syrian Orphanage, young men are trained in the evangelical spirit, and afterwards sent out among the people of Palestine that they may carry this spirit to them. Twice a year, are evangelists sent out from the Orphanage. A like work is done among the girls in the Talitha Kumi Institute, where eight Deaconesses have charge of 110 girls and young women, and are training them to carry the Gospel spirit into the homes of Palestine, or into the institutions into which these pupils may be called in the future. Both the institutions here named are in Jerusalem. In addition, Deaconesses are at work in an asylum for the blind, in an institute for sick children, and in a home for lepers.

For some years past German and Scandinavian members of our church have been settling on the islands of the seas. In New Zealand, the Germans number about 8,000 ; and we read of seven Lutheran congregations and as many parochial schools among them. About 10,000 Scandinavians are found on the same island, and four-fifths of them are reported true to the faith of their fathers. The Danes there publish "The Evangelical Lutheran Monthly Magazine for New Zealand and the Australian Colonies." Germans also are settling in the Sandwich Islands, and planting church and school there. On the island of Kanai, northwest of the Sandwich Islands, four Lutheran churches have been erected since 1883. Some Germans are found, also, on the Samoan Islands ; but we have not learned that they have a church. The bulk of the trade of the islands is in the hands of the successors of a celebrated Hamburg firm.

For many years there has existed a special commission of the General Pastoral Conference in Alsace-Lorraine, for the affairs of Protestantism in Algiers and Tunis.

A German Lutheran congregation was organized in old Tartary (in Neusats) in 1803. From there they spread over the Steppes, bought land of the Tartars, and are, mostly, wheat-growers. About 10,000 souls belong to the parish of Neusats. Half a dozen other settlements are served from this.

In Sebastopol there are 300 German Lutherans, and 500 Lutheran soldiers.

Beyond the Bosphorus, and among the slopes of snow-capped Olympus, lies the Bythinian city of Brussa. At the foot of this mountain is the Evangelical Orphanage and Training College of Brussa, conducted by a Würtemburger. It is a missionary institution, has 108 pupils now, and has received 400 since it was founded. It is a saying of Armenian officials that "there is no Christianity without schools, and no schools without Christianity."

LUTHERAN STATES.

Name of State.	Ruler.	Title.	Area.	Lutheran Populat'n.
Alsace-Lorraine......	(Imper'l Territory.)	....	3,360	254,000
Bavaria, this side the Rhine...........	Otto I.	King.	29,177	1,668,000
Brandenburg........	Pr. Prov.	....	15,405	3,100,000
Brunswick...........	Albert.	Prince Regt.	1,425	340,000
Courland...	Russ'n Prov.	....	10,535	682,000
Denmark............	Christian IX.	King.	14,550	2,172,000
Esthonia............	Russ'n Prov.	....	7,817	296,000
Faroe Islands........	Christian IX.	King.	510	11,200
Finland.............	Alexander III.	Gr. Duke.	144,222	1,908,000
Frankfurt-on-the-Main.............	United with Prussia	....	?	154,000
Hamburg....,.....	" " "	....	157	584,000
Hanover............	Pr. Prov.	William I.	14,800	1,910,000
Hesse-Darmstadt ...	Ludwig IV.	Gr. Duke.	2,950	676,000
Heligoland..........	(Imper'l Territory.)	....	......	2,000
Iceland...	Christian IX.	King.	38,860	72,000
Livonia.............	Russ'n Prov.	....	18,160	1,120,000
Lubeck.............	United with Prussia	....	116	64,000
Mecklenburg-Schw...	Fr. Franz III.	Gr. Duke.	5,136	575,000
Mecklenburg-Str....	Fred'k William.	Gr. Duke.	1,000	110,000
Norway...	Oscar II.	King.	122,800	2,004,000
Oldenburg..........	Nicholas Fr. Peter.	Gr. Duke.	2,480	260,000
Pomerania..........	Pr. Prov.	....	11,620	1,400,000
Prussia, East and West	" "	....	24,130	2,340,000
Reuss, Elder........	Henry XXII.	Prince.	318	100,000
" Younger.......	Henry XIV.	Prince.	122	50,100
Saxony, Prov.......	Pr. Prov.	....	9,750	2,200,000
Saxony, Kingdom...	Fr. Aug. Albert.	King.	5,789	3,200,000
Saxe-Coburg-Gotha..	Ernst II.	Duke.	760	192,025
Saxe-Meiningen......	George II.	Duke.	935	202,970
Saxe-Weimer-Eish...	Chas. Alexander.	Gr. Duke.	1,387	297,700
Saxe-Altenburg......	Ernst.	Duke.	510	145,000
Schaumburg-Lippe...	Adolf.	Prince.	175	30,000
Schleswig-Holstein...	Pr. Prov.	....	7,280	1,127,000
Schwarzburg-Rudolt.	Victor Gunther.	Prince.	363	78,000
" -Sonderh'n	Gunther.	Prince.	333	65,000
Sweden.............	Oscar II.	King.	170,713	4,770,000
Westphalia.........	Pr. Prov.	....	7,800	1,000,000
West Indies, Danish..	Christian IX.	King.	105	4,800
Würtemberg..... ..	Chas. Fr. Alexander	King.	7,531	1,380,000
Independent Lutherans in Germany........				3,000,000

In the 31 political divisions named above, outside the " Pr. Provinces," the Lutheran is the established, or State Church. In the " Pr. Provinces named, the bulk of the population is Lutheran.

LUTHERANS IN THE WORLD.*

I. AFRICA.

1. Egypt............... 2,000
2. Cape Colony........... 5,000
3. Mission Stations...... 40,000
4. Madagascar.......... 25,000

Total.............. 72,000

II. AMERICA.

Greenland............ 8,000
United States..... 3,955,000
West Indies........ 2,500
Brazil............. 40,000
Other S. A. States... 4,000

Total...........4,009,500

III. ASIA.

Siberia............... 1,000
India................180,000
Other parts............ 5,000

Total.............186,000

IV. AUSTRIA and POLYNESIA.

New South Wales...... 3,000
Victoria............. 15,000
South Australia......25,000
Queensland...........20,000

Total............63,000

V. EUROPE.

1. Denmark............ 2,083,000
   a. Denmark..2,000,000
   b. Iceland.... 72,000
   c. Faroe Ils.. 11,000
2. Germany......... 28,014,000
   a. Anhalt... 205,000*
   Baden.... 450,000*
   Bavaria.. 1,350,000
   Brunsw'k. 365,000
   Bremen*.. 110,000
   Hamburg. 530,000
   Heligol'd. 2,000
   Hesse*... 550,000
   Lippe*... 5,000
   Lubeck.. 64,000
   Meckl'b'g-
   Schw.... 575,000
   Meckl'b'g-
   Str..... 110,000
   Oldenbu'g 278,000
   Prussia*..17,367,000
   Imp.Ter.* 275,000
   Saxony... 3,200,000
   Thuring'a 1,260,000
   Waldeck.. 55,000
   Würt'b'g. 1,375,000
3. France............. 80,000
4. Great Britain...... 50,000
5. Holland........... 75,000
6. Italy.............. 5,000
7. Norway............ 1,825,000
8. Austria........... 1,550,000
   a. Hung. and
      Tr'sylv'a.1,200,000
   b. Oth'r parts 350,000
9. Rumania............ 4,500
10. Russia............ 5,060,000
    a. Finland...2,100,000
    b. Balt. Pr'v's2,700,000
    c. Poland.... 250,000
    d. S. Russia. 10,000
11. Sweden............ 4,600,000

* Exclusive of Reformed.

*This table was prepared by the Rev.J.Nicum, of Rochester, New York. The figures for Germany are taken from the "Statistical Year Book of the German Empire, 1889," as they were admitted up to Dec. 1st, 1885. Including the estimated increase since then, the total of Lutherans now in the world is written at 49,596,000.

LUTHERANS IN ALL LANDS.

EUROPE.	Ministers.	Churches.	Members Bapt'd.
Germany	5,550	20,450	28,369,000
Denmark	1,700	1,900	1,967,000
Sweden	2,418	2,400	4,580,000
Norway	869	960	1,910,000
Iceland	180	300	70,000
Faroe Islands	22	22	9,982
Finland, Russia	800	1,002	2,028,000
Poland, Russia	72	104	300,000
Remaining, Russia	520	1,132	2,289,500
Austria	183	209	292,866
Hungary	425	950	1,123,508
France	124	95	80,000
Holland	67	58	68,070
Great Britain	24	27	24,000
Italy	11	11	3,089
Roumania, Servia	12	12	7,576
Switzerland	8	9	11,095
Total in Europe	22,980	29,644	43,133,696

ASIA.			
Palestine	15	9	700
Hindostan	134	86	67,926
China	24	17	4,679
Asiatic Russia	18	18	12,000
On Black Sea	5	5	3,716
Orient	7	7	1,948
Total in Asia	203	142	90,969

AFRICA.			
North Africa, Egypt	2	2	850
West Africa	40	20	8,612
South Africa	209	158	57,433
South Africa (Colonists)	19	26	22,170
East Africa	8	4	76
Madagascar	36	27	20,660
Total in Africa	314	237	103,821

LUTHERANS IN ALL LANDS, (Continued.)

OCEANICA.	Ministers.	Churches.	Members Bapt'd.
Australia colonists	76	252	100,000
Australian heathen mission	9	6	281
New Zealand	14	14	10,643
Hawaiian Islands	1	4	1,000
Borneo	9	6	1,063
Sumatra	17	15	12,350
New Guinea	5	2	130
Feejee Islands	1	1	100
Samoa Islands			127
Total in Oceanica	132	310	125,794
NORTH AMERICA.			
United States and Canada	4,692	7,948	6,500,000
Greenland	15	12	10,000
West Indies	3	4	1,500
Total in North America	4,710	7,964	6,511,500
SOUTH AMERICA.			
Argentine, Uruguay	4	4	6,500
Brazil	40	54	85,000
Chili	3	3	4,000
Total in South America	47	61	95,500
SUMMARY.			
Europe	22,980	29,644	43,133,696
Asia	203	142	90,969
Africa	314	237	103,821
Oceanica	132	310	125,794
North America	4,710	7,964	6,511,500
South America	47	61	95,500
Jewish Missions	20	23	....
Total in the world	28,406	38,381	50,061,280

This table is prepared by Rev. J. N. Lenker, Grand Island, Nebraska, through whose courtesy it is given to our readers.

LUTHERANS IN ALL LANGUAGES.

The Lutheran is a Church of many languages. The latest statistics show that of her baptized membership throughout the world 32,000,000 speak German, 5,300,000 Swedish, 2,500,000 Norwegian, 2,300,000 Danish, 2,048,000 Finnish, 1,250,000 English, 1,113,000 Hungarian, 624,000 Livonian, 480,000 Courlanish, 272,000 Esthnian. 70,000 French, 70,000 Icelandic, 48,000 Bohemian, and that in every other civilized tongue she is well represented, numbering in the world 28,406 educated ministers, 38,381 church edifices and 50,061,280 baptized members.

TABLE OF PEOPLE* TO EACH LUTHERAN PASTOR AND CHURCH.

NAME OF STATE.	People to one Pastor.	People to one Church.
Prussia, Germany	1,865	1,304
Westphalia, Germany	1,850	?
Hanover	1,400	1,100
Hesse, (Electorate,)	1.450	769
Schleswig Holstein	2,475	?
Bavaria	1,102	848
Würtemberg	1,161	1,010
Baden	1,113	1,054
Saxe-Weimar	869	514
Mecklenburg-Schwerin	1,700	1,180
Mecklenburg-Strelitz	1,580	?
Russia	4,556	2,089
Finland	2,535	2,028
Denmark	1,156	1,036
Sweden	1,905	2,180
Norway	2,220	1,950
Iceland	388	233
Faroe Islands	454	475
Australia	1,315	400
Sumatra	726	823
Africa	335	452

* " People " includes the whole Lutheran population.

CHAPTER VIII.

LUTHERANISM AND LEARNING.

Up to the time of the Reformation, education was aristocratic, confined to the clergy and a few laymen of the higher classes. The common people could neither read nor write, and even noblemen signed their name with a cross.

It was a corollary of Luther's position that the people should be so trained as to be able to read Holy Scripture and think for themselves. He first discussed the subject in 1520, in his address to the German nobility. Four years later he wrote a book urging the civil magistrates to improve their schools and establish more of them. And his counsel was not unheeded, the Germans, through their incomparable educational systems, maintaining the highest rank among the nations of earth for their learning in all departments of knowledge.

That Luther is the father of the common-school idea and of the common school itself, is now generally acknowledged. "The German common schools, dating from Luther, may claim to be the oldest in Europe or America. They have for their chief end instruction in the art of reading, in order to enable the people to read the Bible and the Psalm Book."*

---

*Dr. John M. Gregory, of Urbana, Ill., one of the foremost educators of the times, spoken before the "National Educational Association of the United States," at an annual meeting held in Washington City, D. C., A. D. 1882. His paper is printed by the government, for general circulation among persons interested in education; and his assertion is thus endorsed by the educational department of our Government. Hence these words of one of the foremost educators of the time, spoken

"The Germans deserve in nothing greater thanks from mankind than for their efforts in behalf of education; for their deep and sagacious inquiries into its real nature and true objects; for their planning and organizing an effective system; for their admirable classification of the schools; for their internal arrangement—but far above all, for the extension of them to the whole population. They have been the first to exhibit the true thankfulness for the blessing of knowledge, by making, as far as their power extended, all mankind partakers with them. In this respect they have been the first to act on the great Christian maxim of doing as you would be done by; of loving your neighbor as yourself. As George III. wished that every man in his dominions might never want a Sunday's dinner and a Bible to read after it, so the Germans have wished that every man, woman and child should have an education; and they not only wished it, but decreed it. This glorious advance in the true science of government has raised no little sensation throughout Europe, and has created a large party in England, who, ashamed of our own neglect, ashamed of the stride which Germany has made ahead of us in this respect, are zealous to achieve the like grand object."

"Education in all German schools alike has this general character. It is methodically, actively, and perseveringly pursued. The children are kept hard at work. Their business is admirably arranged, and such a circle of languages and branches of instruction taught as would astonish the greater part of our parents and teachers. Having not only observed for myself, but watched the progress of my own boys, I can speak confidently on this head. Thus are habits of diligence and acquisition laid, which are so marked

---

before leading educators gathered from all parts of our nation, printed and circulated at its own expense by the Government for the information of its citizens, come to us with all the force that can be given to the words of men.

a feature in the German character. The young men of the higher classes are in consequence a thoroughly well educated class; and possess, besides, the accomplishments of music and singing almost universally, to a degree uncommon amongst our young men of a similar station."*

As Lutheran lands gave birth to the idea of schools for the people, so they have been first to carry the idea into practice, setting up a school house within reach of every home and compelling attendance.

The same lands have crowned their people's schools with systems of gymnasiums, or colleges, and universities, for which the world shows few equals and no superiors.

And as a result, in the most Lutheran lands of the earth, the education of the people is most general and thorough. "Germany is the most learned land on the globe,"† and the United States Government reports show that, in that "most learned land," the most learned States are those which are most overwhelmingly Lutheran. Paul Du Chaillu awards to Norway and Sweden the palm which Joseph Cook would bestow upon Germany, but Norway and Sweden are even more generally Lutheran than any of the States of Germany.

The recruits for the army are, generally, the test of a people's education. Tried by this standard, there were unable to read and write in the province of Pomerania, 0.32 per cent.; province of Saxony, 0.17; in Schleswig-Holstein,

---

* Rural and Domestic Life in Germany, 184. The name of the author, William Howitt, is familiar to all who have acquaintance with English literature. A native of England and a member of the Society of Friends, he wrote many very popular works, and his "Colonization and Christianity" is credited with having modified the management of England's colonies. He and his wife moved to Germany, and lived there for some years, in part to study the people, and in part to give their children the advantages of the German schools. Chambers' Encyclopedia of English Literature says that his "Rural Life in Germany" is admitted to be the best account of that country ever written by a foreigner. † Joseph Cook.

0.11; in Hanover, 0.53; in the two Mecklenburgs, 0.56; in Oldenburg, 0.27; in the Saxon duchies, 0.60; and in the kingdom of Saxony, 0.15.* In other words, these figures show that, in the whole population, the average number of persons unable to read and write is between one and six in a thousand.

In those States where the spirit of Lutheranism has shaped the affairs of the people, education is most universal, and there is less of illiteracy than is to be found elsewhere in Germany. Especially is this true of Würtemberg, where Lutheranism has been largely moulded by what is known as its Pietistic element. This kingdom has a public school for every thirty families; has four schools of Protestant theology; a university with over 90 professors and 1,400 students; with gymnasiums, grammar, trades and high schools, in all the principal towns.

There the ratio of illiterates is the lowest on the globe, excepting, perhaps, in the Scandinavian lands. The report of the United States Commissioner of Education for 1880 says that the ratio of illiterates to population, in the German Empire, is 2.37 per cent.; but in Würtemberg, it is only 0.02 per cent. This means that in 10,000 persons in the German Empire, there are 237 who cannot read and write, while but two in 10,000 are found in Würtemberg.

The Educational Department of our Government has published a special report on Illiteracy in the United States.† In it, p. 17, it is said that the ratio of illiterates to population 10 years old and upwards, for our country in 1880, was

---

* In Germany, every parent must send his child to school from the age of six to fourteen, or be held an enemy of the State. "So complete is the attendance at school, that in 1888 of about five millions of German children only 5,145 were absent from school without cause. In Berlin in the same year, only fourteen boys and one girl of school age evaded the law. In the United States, ten years ago, 11 per cent. of the entire adult population could not read or write."—*Harper's Weekly.*

† *Circulars of Information,* No. 3. 1884.

170 to every 1,000 ; for every 10,000, 1,700—eight hundred and fifty times as great as that of Würtemberg.

Or compare the illiteracy of Würtemberg with that of Massachusetts, or with that of New York, Pennsylvania and Ohio, which are fairly representative of our general educational status. The same " Circular of Information," p. 75, puts the illiteracy of white persons, 10 years old and upwards, in 1880, in Massachusetts at 6.4 per cent. of population, in New York, Pennsylvania and Ohio, respectively, at 5.3, 6.6, and 4.9 per cent. In other words, in Würtemberg, in every 10,000 of the population there are two persons who cannot read and write ; in Massachusetts, 640 ; in New York, 530 ; in Pennsylvania, 670 ; in Ohio, 490.

After all, Germany is the schoolmaster of the world, and the most Lutheran States of Germany are the schoolmaster of the schoolmaster.*

According to the recently published educational statistics of Prussia, constituting about two-thirds of the whole Empire, that kingdom had in its employ in 1886 a total of 66,500 masters in the public schools. The average salary was 1,274 marks. The teachers engaged in the city schools

---

* From the time of Frederick's father to the present day, the rulers of Prussia have sought to bring all the wisdom they could get to bear on this problem : they have sought for the men best skilled in the science and art of education to guide them in all educational legislation. German writers, statesmen, and teachers, have bestowed more thought on the problems of education, than have the same classes in any, or all, other countries together.

The results are now manifest to the world. It is not creditable to English and American teachers and educators, that a literature so rich in thorough historical research, profound speculation, and wise and varied experience, from infant training to the broadest university culture, should have been so long neglected.—*Barnard's Educational Journal.*

The *Independent* reports that the President of Cornell University, in a lecture before the American Geographical Society, declared, among other things, that "*Germany points out to us the path out of our own educational chaos.*"

I.

averaged 1,559 marks, while the 42,331 in the country villages averaged 1,134 marks annually. The salaries of teachers in the gymnasiums range from 6,000 to 9,000 marks.

The teachers of all grades of schools are entitled to a government pension in case of physical or mental disability, and pensions to the widows and orphans of all teachers are paid from the funds of various savings institutions established by them for that purpose. Sometimes the municipalities make additional provisions for small pensions. All teachers are bound to join the teachers' pension association. The amount of the annual pension depends on the number of years in service and the former salary. All pensions are paid quarterly in advance.

For 1890-1, Prussia appropriated 3,000,000 marks to teachers, because of long service, or in the way of aid. All salaries, after ten years' service, are increased 100 marks, and an additional 100 marks is added for every additional five years' service. In other words, if a teacher's salary is 1,250 marks yearly for the first ten years, it becomes 1,350 yearly for the next five, 1,450 yearly for the next five; and thus on until it has become 1,750. For women teachers, the increase is thirty marks less for the years from ten to fifteen, and seventy marks more are added at the close of each five years, until the total increase reaches 350 marks.

In Prussia, 12,000 women are teachers.* To prepare teachers for their work, 109 teachers' seminaries were in existence, attended by 9,892 persons. The tax for school purposes, in many districts amounts to 35 to 45 per cent. of the whole tax-levy.

The elementary schools in larger cities and towns, as a rule, consist of eight classes, and children have to attend them from their sixth to their fourteenth year. The regular course of study in these schools comprises the following

---

* *Amtskalender*, etc., 1891. A late United States Educational Report gave the number at 35,000.

subjects: religion, reading, writing, common rules of arithmetic, and the rudiments of algebra, the elements of geometry, history, drawing, geography, the elements of physics, and natural history, German composition and grammar, and compulsory gymnastics. In addition, the girls are taught sewing and knitting.

Demand is made for about a thousand new teachers each year. The whole kingdom is divided into school districts,* of which the latest report at hand mentions over eleven hun-

* The Prussian Minister of the Interior, in a circular dated April 10, 1883, called the attention of the provincial authorities to an association called the *Knabenhort*, which has existed in Munich since 1881. The object of this association is to place boys of school age who are sons of poor parents in charge of suitable persons during part of the time they are not in school, and give them some useful occupation, such as woodworking, etc., or amuse them in a way to stimulate and develop their understanding and sensibilities. The boys in this way become accustomed to habits of obedience, order, industry, and cleanliness, and are kept from the influences of bad company.

Moreover, the expenses of such a society as the one at Munich are small, the subscription in that city being only one mark, and yet the Knabenhort has been able to take care of over a hundred boys in less than two years. The minister recommended the formation of similar societies wherever local circumstances make it desirable. The boys are admitted at 2 o'clock Wednesday and Saturday afternoons, and at 4 on other work days. They get only bread to eat in the Munich Knabenhort, because the popular schools of that city have kitchens attached, where the poor children can get both bread and soup.

Similar institutions have since been started in Hanover, Fürth, and Bamberg, while Nuremberg also reports in favor of a Knabenhort. As far back as 1829 Darmstadt undertook to look after her boys out of school hours, and now between 400 and 500 boys are cared for. Erlangen, Baümenheim, Augsburg and Dresden have had like establishments under way in past years. In some of these "refuges for boys," soup and meat are given at noon. At Hanover each boy is given a plot of ground to cultivate. At present 25 boys are learning, under charge of two instructors, to hoe, chop, plant, water flowers, keep paths clean, etc. The fruits or vegetables raised may be carried off for home consumption. In wet weather indoor industries are taught, and already a straw matting has been made for the shop floor. Whether all these institutions are called "Knabenhort" is not stated, but the plan is said to be the same.

dred, each presided over by a director, or superintendent. Of the whole number, nearly one-fourth are professional superintendents, and are paid like our county superintendents; the others are clergymen, who devote a part of their time to the inspection of the schools with or without remuneration.

" For a really trifling sum a first-class education for boys and girls may be had in Germany. Many English parents are finding this out, and are migrating to Germany to avail themselves of this great privilege. This, of course, the wealthy can do; but not those who are tied down by their business. They must send their children to inferior English establishments, where for a third rate education they pay an exhorbitant price.

" A German school-master, who had English boys under him as well as those of his own nation, said to me: 'I cannot understand English boys. They play at their work, and they work at their play.' This is a true remark. As a general rule, they do not take interest in their lessons; and they do take a lively, vigorous, exhausting interest in cricket and foot-ball. German boys have no public games. All their energies are used up in their studies. School work is exhausting, and in it they do take an interest.

" But this is not all. The German masters have the knack —the art, rather, for it is the result of experience and study —of making their teaching interesting to their pupils. The system is simply this: the development of the reasoning powers in the boy. This is the great aim of German education, to make thinking men; there is no effort made to store the mind with a multitude of facts, but there is every effort made to train the mind to build something out of any number of facts tossed capriciously before it—to teach it, to analyze, compare and classify them."*

As Germany insists that her doctors, pastors and lawyers,

---
* Baring-Gould; Germany, etc.; 184.

shall be men of culture; she also demands that her instructors* of youth shall be men properly trained and qualified for that work. The masters are provided from colleges —government institutions, where the instruction is distributed over three years. Then the student is examined; if he passes, he goes for three years as an assistant in a large school, where he may learn the practical application of his knowledge. He is then prepared to take charge of a parish school, and his position is one of respectability. The pastor, the schoolmaster, and the apothecary are the magnates of the village.

Almost everywhere, the village schoolmaster is a person with whom it is a pleasure and a profit to associate. He is intelligent, well read, and full of interest in political and social questions, and always ready to impart local information on antiquarian and historical subjects, or matters of natural history.†

Before the Evangelical Alliance in New York, the younger Krummacher said: We must enlarge our boundary if we would watch Christian life in Germany. Let us look at the schools. In the elementary schools all Protestant children learn from infancy the stories and sentences of the Bible, and the hymns of the church; and whilst there are some teachers who perform their work mechanically, there are on the other side, a great many who endeavor diligently to watch for the souls of the children, and to lead them to the Lord.

Likewise among the principals and teachers of the higher schools many are to be found who, while they mount with

---

* "In 1886 only nine of our States reported upon the training of teachers, and in these States only one teacher in seventeen was a normal school graduate—that is, especially trained for teaching—and one-fourth of all our teachers leave the schools every year. In Germany, on the other hand, every teacher, even of the lowest grades, must have had three and sometimes four years' professional normal training, and at least one or two years of trial or practice."—*Harper's Weekly.*

† Baring-Gould; *Germany.*

enthusiasm the Olympus of Greece and the hills of Rome, nevertheless acknowledge willingly that the mountain of the house of the Lord is exalted above all the mountains of the world.

We point to ministers and generals like Roon and Moltke, and to the Emperor, who preaches during the war the gospel of the grace of God. Whatever may be said of the schools in any other particular period of German history, those of these latter decades, in most places, are a powerful force in acquainting the young with the truths of Revelation. Our Church's conception of education is that all the powers of the man should be developed, that he should be educated and trained in morals and religion, and that to miss this is to miss the great end for which schools have been established. The Word of God—in Bible, Catechism, Hymnbook, etc.,—is made the one great means for developing Christian manhood; and the Church insists that, especially in the formative period of a child's life, the mind be brought into contact daily with that Word which is spirit and life to men,—that it be stored deep in the mind through the daily memorizing of its precious facts and passages, and that this be made an important part of the child's work during all the years of youth. All this, with absolute faith in the declaration: "My Word shall not return unto Me void, but it shall accomplish that which I please."

"In the Intermediate Schools, usually entered at the age of nine, and with a course of nine years, three hours a week are devoted to religious instruction during the first year; and two for the other eight. The official programme states that the instruction of Protestant children shall include the biblical history of the Old and of the New Testament, particularly the latter; the Catechism, with the Scripture passages necessary for understanding it; explanation of the Church Year; committing important hymns: the contents of Scripture, with the emphasis on the New Testament, together with the established facts pertaining to the writing of the various books ; the principal points in dogmatics and ethics ; the leading epochs of ecclesiastical history, and the chief actors in the same.

"It is the avowed aim of the instruction to make the pupil familiar with the doctrines, precepts, and historical development of his Church, and to enable him to form a correct view of its relations to other churches, and to peculiar tendencies of the day."

George Moritz Wahl, himself a "University man," from Germany, and for many years one of the most successful educators in New England, tells of the German Gymnasium in its Working Order, as follows :

"The subject which is always placed first in the catalogue of any gymnasium, is religion. It absorbs three hours a week in the lower forms, and two in the upper. The course includes Bible History ; Catechism, with memorizing of Bible verses and references, and of old church hymns ; Bible readings, with exegesis ; moral philosophy as based upon the teachings of Christianity, and Church History.

The teachers of religion are, invariably, theologians, it being the law that no religious instruction shall be given— at least in the upper and in the middle forms—by any but a teacher who is a graduate in theology ; and a graduate in theology is one who has passed through the gymnasium, and pursued the study of theology for three or four years at one of the universities. It has always seemed strange to me that, while in all other branches we should demand skilled men as instructors, religion should be considered a subject which anybody might undertake to teach.

The predominant feature of the work which the theologians do in these schools is that they set forth the history of the Bible scientifically, teach its doctrines of belief and morals systematically, and adapt these doctrines to the present age judiciously."

Not only do the people of our churches practice on the theory that the state ought to furnish every child a religious education, but not a few go farther and, in their schools, teach their children the needs of the heathen world, with the avowed design of interesting them in heathen missions. At a Mission Conference in Saxony, a few years ago, attended by over a third of all the ministers of that Kingdom, in response to a request from these pastors of the churches, Dr. Warneck announced that he was preparing a hand-book of missions for teachers. Since then it has appeared, and passed into a fifth edition. It is being used in hundreds of German schools, and is helping shape the thought of the coming generation in behalf of mission work among the heathen.

What has been said of general culture in Germany, is true also of Scandinavia. Education has been compulsory for over forty years; the school term averages eight months, and over 97 per cent. of all the population of school age are in attendance at schools of some kind—" a percentage which is probably not exceeded by any other nation." *

President Cattell reports to the Educational Bureau of our Government that such a thing as a man signing X (" his mark ") because he never had learned to write, can scarcely occur there. †

Du Chaillu testifies that there is scarcely a Swede, having any claim to education, that does not speak at least one, and

---

* U. S. Bureau of Education.

† It will be remembered that, at the Centennial Exposition in Philadelphia, to the Swedish school house was awarded the first prize.

Kent, the celebrated American commentator on law, whose works are generally regarded as necessary text-books on the shelves of every lawyer's library, speaks as follows of the provisions made for the education of the people under the different governments of the world:

Distinguished exertions have been made in several parts of modern Europe, and with which none of the educational institutions of antiquity are to be compared, for the introduction of elementary instruction accessible to the young of all classes. This has been the case particularly in Denmark, Norway, Sweden, Prussia, some parts of Germany and Switzerland.

generally two, foreign languages. What most forcibly strikes a stranger traveling in Sweden is the fine school buildings scattered all over the kingdom, even to the farthest north. Entering a town or village, almost invariably the structure that is the most conspicuous is the school-house, in which the people take great pride. When he gains a better acquaintance with the country, he is astonished at the number of institutions of learning it contains. He wonders that in that far-away and barren corner of Europe the people, though poor, have such a love of knowledge; that the study of the sciences and of the foreign languages is very common, and that the inhabitants strive to root out ignorance from their land.

Visiting their schools, he is surprised to see how well managed they are, and that a gymnastic hall, fully equipped, is attached to each one, showing that the body is as well taken care of as the mind. He finds that among the regulations, the younger children have to go out of the building every hour for an airing, and play in the yard for about ten minutes. Every school has a library and additions of books are made at each term. I have seen in some more than 30,000 volumes. Many besides have museums, with zoölogical, geological, and botanical collections. The smaller scholars learn from a blackboard to read music. The children of the poor are neatly dressed, for the parents feel that it would be a shame to send them otherwise.

To supply the primary education, there are 9,925 national schools, with 5,216 male and 6,832 female teachers. For higher educational purposes there are 98 gymnasiums, &c., with 967 teachers and 14,617 students, and two universities. Upsala with 900, and Lund with 800 students. Another university is in course of formation, for which private individuals have given large sums. There are, also, a large number of government schools for the military and naval service, for the technical sciences, for metallurgy, for agriculture, for nautical science, and for the blind, and the deaf and dumb. All instruction at the national schools, the public schools and the universities is free.

The instruction in the people's schools, like that in the schools of Germany, is in reading, religion, Biblical history, Bible reading, and the memorizing of hymns and selected pieces out of a reader,—combining natural history, the elements of natural sciences, and the history of the country,— besides singing, writing, reading, written arithmetic, and, if circumstances allow, gymnastics and military exercises. The schools, generally, are open for eight months in the year in the southern parts of the country, and for nine or ten months elsewhere. The average salary of a Norwegian or Swedish country teacher is about 500 kronor, besides use of a house and a piece of land.

People's high schools have come into existence lately, designed for young men and young women of the working classes, who have already passed beyond the legal school age. The studies comprise a more extended course of the subjects taught in the common schools, besides the elements of the useful sciences and their application.

The Elementary Schools, the Swedish term for gymnasiums, are of two grades; the one having five classes, the other seven. In both, the studies are the same for the five classes; but graduates of the lower grade institutions must take up the studies of the two higher classes of the higher grade before they can enter the universities. The course of study requires five years for the first five classes; and four years for the last two; *i. e.*, the full course of the higher grade prepares for admission to a university and requires nine years of study. The year is divided into two terms of eighteen weeks each. The morning exercises begin with a prayer, the reading of the Bible, and the singing of a hymn, which exercises occupy half an hour. These schools are so distributed that all have first-class educational opportunities near home. To be accepted as a pupil in one of these schools, the applicant must pass an examination in the reading of the Swedish language, both in the Gothic and in the Roman characters, be able to repeat any passage read to him, write a plain hand, spell at least tolerably, know the simple rules of arithmetic, practice mental calculation, and possess a knowledge of the Geography of Denmark, Norway and Sweden. In the institutions, the tuition, fees, &c., are 25 kronor ($6.00) a year. To become an instructor in such a school, it is necessary to have taken the degree of Doctor of Philosophy, to have taught on trial for one year, and to have passed a competitive examination.

The higher schools in Germany are well adapted to the training of the pupils for their future professions and callings, and show a very high standard of mental discipline. They comprise the gymnasiums, the progymnasiums, the realgymnasiums, the realprogymnasiums, the oberrealschulen, and the höhere bürgerschulen. The gymnasium, realgymnasiums and oberrealschulen have a nine years' course, while the progymnasiums, realprogymnasiums and higher burgher schools have only a five or six years' course.

The gymnasiums are the preparatory schools for the admission into the universities, and are attended by pupils who, on entering the universities will devote themselves to the study of jurisprudence, medicine, theology, philology, and philosophy ; in short, who aspire to a professional or governmental career. Much attention is paid to the ancient languages.*

---

* The regular gymnasia in Germany have six classes; each of the upper three forms require two years each, and each of the lower three, one year. To enter, a boy must have passed the age of nine, and pass an examination in the ordinary school studies in his native tongue, and in the fundamental principles of the Latin tongue. It is generally said that our colleges and the gymnasia have about the same rank ; but the gymnasia do the more of preparatory training.

The realgymnasiums have a nine years' course, including Latin, but no Greek. Great stress is laid on mathematics, natural sciences, and modern languages. The graduates of the realgymnasiums are admitted to one university faculty only, that of philosophy with its numerous departments of natural sciences and modern languages. As a rule the graduates pass from the realgymnasiums to the higher technical schools.

The higher realschulen aim at a more practical education, and are generally patronized by pupils who intend to follow technical, industrial, or mercantile pursuits, or who are seeking a training for entrance into subordinate governmental offices. No ancient languages are taught, while French and English form prominent educational branches.

The instruction in the gymnasium and the realgymnasium in Prussia, according to the latest decree of the minister of public instruction, is uniform up to the grade of "tertia" (fourth year,) when in the gymnasium the study of Greek is commenced and in the realgymnasium English enters into the schedule of studies.

The gewerbeschulen, higher realschulen, and higher burgher schools have for their chief object the training of the pupils for practical business men, artisans, and mechanics. The classics are entirely excluded from the gewerbeschulen French and English are much cultivated, and much stress is laid on drawing and instruction in the various commercial branches. The graduates of these schools may be admitted into the higher technical and industrial schools.[*]

The latest reports give the number of gymnasiums in Germany at 422 ; while the higher schools of the other classes number 564. In these institutions for higher education, the number of students is given at over 177,000. Nineteen other gymnasiums and *real-schools* are now being established.

---
[*] Report of Commissioner of Education, (U. S.) 1881, p. ccxlviii.

Almost every large city has one or more such classical schools. Berlin had half a dozen of them thirty years ago, and the latest reports credit her with sixteen.

What is true of these higher institutions of learning in Germany, is also true of them in Scandinavia. The universities stand above them as they stand above the common schools.*

A university, some one has said, is a school in which one can lean something about everything, and everything about some one thing. Each university has four " faculties." A faulty includes both the professors who teach a science and the science itself.† The four faculties or schools, of the

---

* The " Elementary " school in Scandinavia corresponds to the German gymnasium and the American college. They prepare youths for the universities, and have courses of study which require from five to nine years' time.

In Sweden their number is, ... 98
In Norway their number is, ... 20
In these institutions (1875) there were—
    Professors, ... 1,202
    Students, ... 19,838
Three Universities, additional, had—
    Professors, ... 219
    Students, ... 2,834
Total Colleges and Universities, ... 121
Total Professors, ... 1,421
Total Students, ... 22,772

The population of these countries was then reported at 6,338,000, which gives an average of one student in these institutions for every 278 of the population.

In 1882, the United States reported within her bounds like institutions to the number of 365; the number of professors was 4,413; the number of students, 64,096. Her population then was over fifty millions, which gives an average of one student to every 780 of population. Or viewed in regard to the average number of these institutions as compared with the population the figures show that Scandinavia has one for about every fifty-three thousand, and the United States one for about every one hundred and forty thousand of the population.

† Germany has 21 universities, and in them are 2,200 teachers—an average of nearly 110 to each institution. Of the whole number there is not one who is not an author.

great universities are those of theology, philosophy, law and medicine. The theological faculty has the supremacy of honor, inasmuch as theology has always been deemed the queen of sciences, to which all others are tributary.

In each institution, each faculty has its dean, who is elected annually by the professors of that faculty. At the head of the whole university body is the chancellor, or rector, who is also chosen for one year from the regular professors of the various faculties in turn, and who is entrusted with the government of the institution.

Such institutions are very different from our American higher institutions of learning. We have scores of so-called universities; but so long as we desire to restrict particular words to signify particular things, we must insist that very few of these institutions have any right to the use of the word, university. A good authority has said that we have but one institution of learning in the United States that can use this word in the sense which has attached to it for generations, and in which it now is used in Europe. Our colleges are preparatory schools for the studies of the German universities.

The universities are the pride and glory of Germany. They exert more influence than any similar institutions in any other country. They reflect a picture of the whole world of nature and of mind under its ideal form. They exert a powerful influence upon other countries. Situated in the heart of Europe, and visited by strangers from all quarters of the globe, they are the firmest anchors of general learning and literature; and amongst the principal strongholds of modern European and American culture under its highest aspect. The late Sir William Hamilton truly remarks: "We saw these institutions accomplishing their end to an extent and in a degree elsewhere unexampled."*

* *Germany; Its Universities, &c.*

There are three classes of teachers in the German and Scandinavian universities, viz: the ordinary, the extraordinary and the private lecturers. The ordinary professors are regular members of the faculty, receive a full support from the state, independent of the proceeds of their lectures, and may be elected to the academical senate and the rectorship. The extraordinary professors have no seat in the faculty or in the senate, and a smaller income, but are generally promoted to a regular professorship when a vacancy occurs. The private lecturers have passed their *examen*, and deliver lectures as do the regular professors, but are without appointment, and receive, with a few exceptions, no salary from the state. They earn a small sum from the students they can draw around them in competition with the regular professors. They do not go into the work to make a living from it. They must have money to support them in part through this tutorship. All the private lecturers are aiming at regular professorships; and it is from their ranks that the professors are chosen. It must not be supposed that these are men of mediocre ability. Many of them are authors of books that become authorities. It is usually through publishing that they seek for promotion. This often comes within a few years; but many grow old and die without gaining the object of their hopes. So able a man as Kant was private lecturer at Koenigsberg for fifteen years, and even for a considerable time after he had become widely known through his writings. Beside the regular salary each professor receives the greater part of the fees paid by the students in his department. With the more popular professors, these fees make a handsome addition to the regular salary. The fees are low. One hears a course of four hours a week the entire semester, about five months, for about $4; a course of two hours for $2.50. There are also courses of public lectures, generally of an hour a week, for which nothing is paid.

Germany, in 1889, had 21 universities, with 2,199 professors and 29,481 students. The Lutheran church has either the exclusive or a partial authority in the direction of fourteen of them, in which there are 1,620 professors and teachers, and 20,637 students. In Germany, 72 per cent. of the cost of the universities is defrayed by the state, the appropriations for this purpose, for 1889, being 7,563,396 marks. In the way of fees, students pay but 9.3 per cent. of the total cost of maintenance. The proportion of professors and teachers to students is about 1 to 14 *

In 1869, there was one student for every 2,296 inhabitants; in 1889, one for every 1,409. The increase of population, meantime, was 20 per cent. The greatest proportionate increase has been in Prussia, where also there has been the greatest increase of the higher institutions for education. In 1881, these numbered 362; in 1889, 493. In 1867, in Prussia, there was one student at these schools for every 273 residents in the kingdom; in 1888, one for every 215; then, there was a student at a gymnasium for every 418 residents, now there is one for every 348.

Prussia's expenditures for the various church and educational purposes of the state, from April, 1889, to April, 1890, amount to 91,580,951 marks. Of this amount, nearly 55,500,000 marks were for the primary schools; over 7,500,000 for the universities, and nearly 5,500,000 for the other higher schools. In other words, for support of its universities and gymnasiums the state paid over thirteen millions of marks. As the universities received over 7,500,000 marks; the average for each must have been about 340,000 marks. For the three classes of institutions above named, the total expenditures were about 70,000,000 marks; and for

---

* In the English universities the proportion is much greater, and in the Scotch, 1 to over 50. The increase in the teaching force keeps pace with the increase of students. In 1880, there were 1,809 teachers, of all ranks, in the universities; in 1889, there were 2,199. For total of students and professors, see table at close of this chapter.

purposes allied to these, 13,000,000 more were given, making a total for educational purposes of about 83,000,000 marks.*

The universities are very sparing of honorary degrees, and as a rule grant them only after examination.† The D. D. degree is considered the highest academic honor, and may be acquired by the regular process of a written work, and a Latin debate in which all the members of the university may enter the lists against the published theses of the candidate. The degree is given, also, but rarely, in acknowledgement of distinguished literary merit or of eminent usefulness in the Church.

The German universities are State institutions, open to all citizens as a matter of right, and are just as much national property as the public schools, the courts, and the post office.

In Germany there has been an unprecedented increase in the number of university students during the last decade. From a population of 45,250,000 there are 29,491 students attending the universities, while in England, with a total population of 26,000,000, there are but 5,500 students at Oxford and Cambridge. The governments of Germany display great zeal in the cause of education, especially of University education. They watch over the universities with sleepless vigilance, and literally drive students within their walls by making them the only doors of admission to the learned professions and to the higher departments of the Civil Service. During the last few years there has been "a sudden crowding to theology," the number of divinity stu-

---
* *Amtskalender;* 1890.

† It has been said that there are in New York city more Doctors of Divinity than in all of Germany. Whether this condition be due to superabundance of Divinity or its need of Doctors, recent events indicate that, like the woman in the gospel who had suffered many things of many physicians and was nothing bettered, New York's theology seems to have grown steadily " worse."

dents, especially of Protestant students, having been increased in a remarkable degree.*

The students pay a matriculation fee ; and, in addition, a sum varying from two to ten dollars for each course of lectures, for the benefit of the teachers whose salaries vary from a few hundred to several thousand dollars, according to age, merit and reputation.

Nearly all of the students live in rented quarters of one or two furnished rooms, take the regulation German break fast of a cup of coffee and a roll served in one's room, and dine at restaurants. The prices, of course, vary. From four to six dollars a month are the prevailing prices for large, well furnished rooms. One's dinner costs from $12\frac{1}{2}$ to 25 cents; and the landlady will serve supper in one's room for eight cents. A student may live in Leipsic on from $15 to $18 a month for necessary expenses.

The University of Leipsic, founded in 1409, is the richest, excepting Heidelberg the oldest, and one of the most Lutheran of all the German universities. While many others depend largely upon the State for support, it is said this university could dismiss 500 students at once without reducing the professors' salaries. Of its principal buildings, three are occupied as lecture rooms; one contains the Library, Infirmary and the *Carcer;†* while a fifth is the *Senat*, in which are the corporation's business offices. These buildings, both without and within, are extremely plain. Adjoining them is the University Church, while in the newer part of the city are the other and more attractive buildings. The library contains 500,000 volumes and 4,000 manuscripts. In the University reading room, for the sum of 75 cents a semester, the students have access to more than 500 periodicals, theological, medical, philological, literary and miscellaneous.

---

* Hart: *German Universities.*

† The carcer is the prison in which for various offences students are held in durance.

Leipsic is highly distinguished for its vast philological and antiquarian learning and immense literary industry. In theology it is strictly Lutheran and "as to the number of students, far ahead of Heidelberg and Tübingen in the south, throws Erlangen into the provincial ranks, eclipses its nearest neighbor, dear, muddy, crooked, cobble-paved Halle, and is in advance of even the youngest and proudest of German schools, Berlin."* The Theological Faculty has a dozen or more professors, among them occurring such names as Fricke, Lechler, Luthardt, Gregory, Hoffman, and that of the senior Delitzsch until his death. The theological students in recent years average from 500 to 700. The whole number of instructors is 180; of students, 3,322.

The glory of Jena always has been its university. Founded by John Frederick, Elector of Saxony, in 1558, in certain periods of its history it has had great celebrity because of the philosophers resident there either as professors or as private gentlemen. About the end of the last, and the beginning of the present century, Fries, Fichte, Schelling, Hegel, and the poets and critics, Schiller, Schlegel, Tieck and Novalis, were found here. During the same period, Weimar, the capital of the grand-duchy, but fifteen miles distant, deserved and often received the name of the Athens of Germany, being the residence, until their death, of the immortals of German poetry, Goethe, Schiller, Wicland and Herder, who also was an enthusiastic admirer of the poetry and religion of the Bible.

About the middle of the eighteenth century, the number of students at the university reached 3,000. Since then, the opening of new universities, the organization of the "Burschenschaft," and the suspicions aroused among various German governments as to the spirit of the teachings of Jena, have greatly reduced that number. As auxiliaries, Jena has seminaries of philology, theology and education; insti-

---

* Dr. Schaff in the *Independent*.

tutes of chemistry, pharmacy, zoölogy, botany, (with a botanical garden,) and meteorology, (with an observatory); veterinary and surgical institutions, and the various physical and archæological collections which now are found in the castle. A clinical institute and the several hospitals assist the study of medicine. The university issues the *Jenaer Literaturzeitung für Deutschland.*

The University of Göttingen was founded by George II. of England, who also was Elector of Hanover; and, owing to the connection of the crown of Hanover with that of England, it was frequented by many English students up to the days of Queen Victoria. Two of America's most gifted writers, Bancroft and Everett, graduated at Göttingen. For many decades the university held its place among the very first institutions of learning in Europe. Since the middle of the last century it has been favored with professors of great learning and much fame. Prominent among them have been Mosheim, Walch, Planck and Gieseler, in church history; Spittler and Heeren, in secular history; Michaelis, Eichhorn and Ewald, in oriental literature; Heyne and Müller, in classical learning; the brothers Grimm, in German antiquities; Hugo, Blumenbach, Gauss and Herbert, in jurisprudence and science. Of a later date may be named Dorner, Weber, Latze, Lagard and Ritschl, while Neander, Ewald, and the distinguished chemist, Bunsen, were natives of this place.

The institution was named the "Georgia Augusta," and about 1825 had an attendance of from 1,500 to 1,600 students. Political disturbances, in which both professors and students were interested, and certain high-handed proceedings of the ruler, Ernest Augustus, which drove out not a few professors into exile, greatly reduced the attendance of students. It now has a teaching staff of 124, and the number of students is from 1,000 to 1,150 annually. It has a library of 500,000 printed volumes and 5,000 manuscripts.

It is one of the best selected and arranged libraries in the world, and is especially rich in foreign literature.* Connected with it are an art museum, with collections of old oil paintings, engravings, coins, models of all sorts, and some casts from the antique; a lying-in hospital and chemical laboratory; and the botanical gardens, laid out under Haller's superintendence in 1739, and one of the chief ornaments of the town.

The University of Tübingen, founded by Duke Eberhard in 1477, afterward became a " United " institution, even the Roman Catholics having a faculty in it since 1817. Its leading faculty has been that of theology, and the theology often has been of a questionable shade. Its staff of teachers and professors number 93; its students, 1,400; its library 235,000 volumes.

One who spent two years at Tübingen writes as follows: This university is distinguished for its thorough and systematic way of teaching and studying. This is especially the case with the theological students, who live together in one building, the Protestants in the so-called *Stift*, the Roman Catholics in the *Convict*, and are supported by the state to the conclusion of their course. It is impossible to find anywhere closer application and more fervent devotion to study. The *Würtemberger Gründlichkeit* has become proverbial. The late excellent Dr. Schmid never finished any course of lectures, although he kept the class from five to ten minutes beyond the time, and continued to lecture to the very last day of the session. He would, for instance, spend six hours a week for six months, in explaining grammatically, critically, historically, dogmatically, ethically, practically, etc., the first eight chapters of the Epistle to the Romans, promising to finish the rest the next session.

The prescribed theological course in Tübingen, to which no exception is made, extends over four years, or eight long

---

* *Germany; Its Universities, &c.*, p. 78.

sessions, there being but five or six weeks' vacation, in spring and autumn.

The well-known university of Halle was founded by Frederick I., in 1694; but was enlarged and enriched by its union with Wittenberg in 1816, when the latter ceased to exist. From its beginning it has been recognized as one of the leading schools of Protestant theology; and the theological department generally has numbered more professors and students than any other in Germany, often as many as from 800–900 students at a single term. Such men as Francke, Knapp and Tholuck have filled chairs in this faculty. In the earlier days of the present century it fell into the hands of the rationalists; but with the advent of Tholuck in 1827, a change gradually took place, and sound Christian teachers again make up the theological faculty. For a long time many of the lectures were delivered in Latin. The institution has an imposing new edifice, built in 1834; a library of 120,000 volumes. Connected with it, also, are a thelogical and normal seminary, a medical and surgical clinical institute, a maternity hospital, an observatory, and a botanical garden.

Königsberg is the seat of the university, founded by Albert I., Duke of Prussia, in 1544. Kant was born in this place and became a professor in the university, where, also, Herder, Bessel, and Neumann have been among the teaching force. The library numbers 200,000 volumes; teaching force, 94; and the students, 753.

The university of Berlin was founded in 1810, and though one of the youngest German universities, its reputation is widely extended. In 1889 the total of students was 4,939. In point of numbers, it stands at the head. It has, at different times, numbered on its teaching staff such men as Schleiermacher, Fichte, De Wette, Neander, Marheineke, Eichhorn, Hegel, Raumer, Niebuhr, Hengstenberg, Nitzsch,

Stahl, Schelling, the brothers Grimm, Carl Ritter, Dorner, Virchow, Von Ranke, Mommsen, Lepsius, Hoffman.

The total teaching force for the four faculties of theology, law, medicine and philosophy, numbers 241. Of this number sixty have no salary guaranteed them by the authorities, and depend on fees from students. Their aim is a professor's chair, and they are obliged to pass through this apprenticeship—it may last for years or for life—as a preparatory step.

The number of students varies. They gather there not only from the different German states, but from America, Russia, Austria, Switzerland, Greece, Great Britain, Japan, and elsewhere. Not infrequently American doctors of divinity attend the institution as students. The ordinary prerequisite for admission is graduation in a gymnasium, which is equal to that of a good classical college; and the studies are what in our land would be called post-graduate courses.

The University of Dorpat, with its observatory, anatomical theatre, and a remarkable botanical garden containing many plants not to be found elsewhere in Europe, was founded in 1632, by Gustavus Adolphus, but in its present form dates from 1802. Since that date it has had considerable of prosperity, and now is the intellectual centre of Livonia. It is true to the Teutonic traditions of its earlier days, and is much more German than Russian in its culture; and because of this it is not in favor with Russian authorities. It has 42 regular professors, a total teaching staff of 73, and about 900 students. Its library numbers 250,000 volumes; and its observatory is one of the most renowned in Europe, possessing a great refracting telescope presented by the Emperor, Alexander I.

This old Lutheran university now seems doomed. Established to meet the wants of German residents of the Baltic provinces, the ukase of the Czar orders that it shall be manned with Russian professors, governed by Russian laws, transformed into a Russian seat of learning. The Czar wants unity and is imbued with the tyrant's idea as to the means of attaining it—"Believe, teach, do, as I command, and there will be unity." What will be the ultimate result of this iniquitous proceeding, time alone can tell.

The University of Upsala, located in the ancient capital of Sweden, had its beginning in 1250, and was dedicated as a university in 1477. Its principal endowment was by Gustavus Adolphus, who presented it lands valued at $1,196,000, and now yielding a revenue of about $37,000, which is supplemented to the amount of about $100,000 annually by the State. Its total property valuation is over $1,500,000, and its annual expenses $171,000.

In 1887, the teachers numbered 119; the students, 1,928. About $36,000 are distributed annually in scholarships. The library has 250,000 volumes, 11,000 manuscripts, and its own building. In addition to a zoölogical institution, a botanical garden presented by Gustavus III., and a hospital, chemical, anatomical and other institutions belonging to the medical faculty, there are institutes of astronomy, meteorology, and chemistry, each with its own building of recent date. The Royal Society of Science has a house of its own and a valuable library.

The University of Lund was founded in 1663 by Charles XI., and the town of Lund is known chiefly because of it. Tegner, the poet, was a professor there, and Linnaeus was one of its alumni. The institution has the four faculties of philosophy, law, medicine and theology. Its professors and teachers number 70, and the students 800. The library has 120,000 volumes and 2,000 manuscripts. Connected with it, also, are valuable collections of archæology and natural history.

The University of Copenhagen was founded in 1479, and has five faculties,—the mathematical being in addition to the ones usually existing. Its professors number 50; students,

1,200 ; and the library, 240,000 volumes, besides a great collection of ancient Persian, and another collection of ancient Northern manuscripts,—upwards of 4,000 in all. Both collections were arranged by Rask. In addition to the regular professors, the university has, since 1831, an English, and, since 1852, an Anglo-Saxon lectureship. All the professors are bound to give a series of lectures open to the public free of charge. In connection with the university are an observatory, a chemical laboratory, a surgical academy, and a botanic garden. The Royal Library in Copenhagen has 500,000 volumes, with great treasures of Sanscrit and other manuscripts.

The University of Helsingfors stands at the head of the educational system of Finland. Founded at Albo in 1640, taken to Helsingfors in 1829, it has the usual four faculties, 100 professors and teachers, 1,300 students, and a library of 150,000 volumes. Connected with it are a hospital, a botanic garden, an observatory, and a museum with a very extensive collection of mineralogical and natural-history specimens. The Theological Faculty gives instruction in the Swedish and Finnish tongues.*

The Scandanavian universities afford, practically, a free education. At the University of Copenhagen there is a large old building where 100 students reside gratuitously, and receive, beside, a small monthly grant of money. There are also smaller houses erected by private beneficence to the same end. In addition, there are both private and public funds to aid the poorer students in the purchase of books and instruments needful in the prosecution of their studies. The course extends over a period of about four to six years.

At Upsala tuition is free and the student can find board and lodging suited to his means. If his resources are small, he can find a home, presided over by a pious woman, in

---

* For facts and statistics concerning other great Lutheran centres of learning, see the table of universities at close of chapter.

which the inmates live as members of a family and the expenses range from $30 to $50 a year.

Candidates for admission must pass examination on a course* substantially equivalent to that of an American college. Once admitted, all progress depends on the student. There is no class-drill, instruction is by lecture, and the student may graduate whenever he passes the examination, for which he may present himself at any time.

As a rule, lawyers, physicians, clergymen, and teachers and professors in the gymnasiums and other high schools in Germany, Scandinavia and throughout the Lutheran portions of Russia, must be graduates of a university. The May Laws, fixing the requirements for admission into the ranks of the clergy in Germany, declare that no priest shall enter on a cure of souls who has not passed examination in a German gymnasium,† spent three years in a German university, and passed examination in three faculties, of which theology shall not be one.

We may safely regard the books of a nation as a fair index to the degree of intelligence among its people. Tried by this test, Lutheran lands stand forth among the nations as Saul among his brethren, head and shoulders above them

---

* Here is the course of study upon which a candidate to enter the University must pass examination:

Latin : Cornelius Nepos; Virgil, three books; Horace, two books; Cicero, Tusc. Disp.; Livy, two books, and prose composition.

Greek : Xenophon, two books of Anab.; Homer, two books of Odyssey; New Testament, the Gospels or the Acts.

Religion : Biblical History, Church History, Dogmatics, outline, Luther's Catechism.

Modern Languages : German, French, English.

Science : Botany, Zoology, Physics, Euclid, Logic, etc., etc.

How many of the pastors in America now voting money to "convert" the Scandinavian Lutherans, could pass this examination, which is only the beginning of preparation for the Scandinavian Lutheran ministry? And the Church permits no short-cuts into that sacred office.

† Equivalent to an American college.

all! Take Germany as an illustration. The reports for 1890 emphasize the fact that the German Empire is the paradise of the book-maker, the book-buyer, and the book-reader. The Publisher's Circular states that the number of books issued in England in 1888, was 6,591; in America, 4,631; in France, about 4,000; in Germany, 18,800, or more than England, America, and France together. The German is a great book-buyer, not because he is rich, but because he is willing to forego luxuries which others think necessary to their existence, in order to be able to have the best works published in his department.*

The character of the books produced also hints at the intellectual tastes, not only of the authors, but of the people for whom they were prepared. In the publications of the United States more than one-fifth, and in England more than one-sixth of all the works produced, are classed as romances, or novels, while this class is not even named in the catalogue of German publications: but, instead, this home of learning present 372 works classed as Encyclopedias, Bibliography, and Scientific Literature, and which are not named in the publications of England or of the United States. While the country last named reports 123 almanacs, and England sent out 243 Year-Books and Annuals; the German reports say nothing about this class of publications, but have instead, classes of Antiquities, Oriental Languages, Statistics, Natural Science, Chemistry, Pharmacy, Military Works, Architecture, Mining, Engineering, Navigation.

While we of the United States produced 469 romances, the depth of our religious interest was manifested by the production of 271 religious works—a very few over half the number of our romances. Germany, however, has no class of romances, and gives out 1.253 works on theology, and 1,259 on history, oriental languages and antiquities. Of the latter, we suppose it safe to assume that not fewer than

---

* S. S. Times.

one-half have more or less reference also to affairs of religion, and might properly be referred to this class, as is also true of the encyclopedias and bibliography.

We may, then, safely write Germany's theological and religious productions at about 2,000, or over seven times the number of such works produced in the United States.

A query of no little interest in this connection is this: Certain sectarists proclaim from the house-tops in trumpet tones that religion is dead among the Germans. If this be true, why do German publishers persist, year after year, in publishing so many more religious books than are published in our "land of churches and of school-houses;" and what do they do with them? It is hardly reasonable to suppose that they print simply to enjoy the fun of throwing the volumes into the sea; these works are not printed for free distribution, as we have had occasion to know by experience; and if there is no religion in Germany, it is not likely that there is any home demand for religious publications, for only the hungry care for bread. As the facts are indisputable, the sectarists need to look around for some other plea to justify their sending missionaries to Germany.

The same love of learning that leads to the printing of many books, leads also to the founding of many libraries. In this again our Lutheran nations outstrip all others. Three other nations * have single libraries, each larger than any single one owned by any Lutheran people; but when it comes to the question of many great libraries scattered among towns and cities where people can get at them, no other lands can equal the Lutheran.

Of libraries having 100,000 volumes or more each, the great nations report as follows: Great Britain and Ireland, 10; France, 15; Russia, 8; United States, 12; Scandinavian States, 6; Germany, 45.

Two of the great libraries of Russia are the property of

---
* France, England and Russia.

the Lutheran universities of Dorpat and Helsingfors. Russia deserves no credit for them except that she has not burned them—at least the records show only this.

The Scandinavian population is about wholly Lutheran, and the German largely so. In these we find 51 great libraries, each containing over 100,000 volumes. In Great Britain and Ireland, France, Russia and the United States together, we find 51, if we include the two Lutheran ones in Russia which the Czar "annexed" when he "annexed" the people who own them. In other words, in the Protestant world, Lutheran countries, with a population of fifty-five millions, have more great libraries than the foremost non-Lutheran countries with a population of two hundred and twenty millions.

Of the fifty-three great Lutheran libraries, twenty-six have over 200,000 volumes each; of the forty-nine non-Lutheran ones, but seventeen have over 200,000 volumes each. Russia, with eighty-five millions of a population, has, properly, six great libraries; Germany, with half that population, has seven and a half times as many. The Scandinavian countries, with but eight or nine millions population, have five great libraries with over 200,000 volumes each; the United States, over sixty millions of people, have two college libraries, each numbering 200,000 or more volumes, and four others each, with a like number of volumes.

We may turn away from the great institutions of learning, and find evidences of the same love of books where, often, we least expect them. In cities and towns of Germany and Scandinavia it is a common thing to have public libraries containing an average of from two to ten volumes for every resident, man, woman and child. This average applies to as large a capital as Copenhagen, which, with a population of, say, 286,000, has three great libraries, apart from that of the university, containing, in all, 575,000 volumes. The average often is much higher in the smaller cities. In Gotha, population 28,000, there is a library with 245,000 volumes; in Oldenburg, population 24,700, two libraries with 200,000 volumes; and in Darmstadt, where the population numbers 50,000, the library numbers 500,000 volumes. In many yet smaller cities, an equally high average is maintained. In Detmold, where the population is 8,000, the library has 50,000 volumes; in Coburg, with 16,- 000 people, the library numbers 50,000; in Rudolstadt, with 8,800 people, the library has 65,000 volumes; in Wernigerode, with 9,100 people, the library has 87,000; in Weimar, with 21,600 people, the library has 200,000; and in Wölfenbüttel, with a population of 13,500, the library has 300,000 volumes. Reykjavik, Iceland, with 2,500 people, has two libraries, with 39,000 volumes.

It is seen, in these figures, that the high average of from two to ten volumes in the public library for every resident of the place not only is common, but that the much higher average of twenty volumes or more to each inhabitant is not uncommon. Not a few of the common and the elementary schools of these countries report libraries of which the most of our colleges and seminaries would feel proud. For example, the elementary school in Vesteras, Sweden, north of Stockholm, has a library of 12,000 volumes; that of a like school in Gothenburg numbers 15,000 volumes; and that of such a school in Linköping numbers 30,000. Travelers also find evidences of culture in private residences of the far north, in museums of natural history, rich cabinets of coins and collections of arms, engravings, sculpture, painting, and rare collections of books, etc. In Gripsholm Castle, on the Gripsholm fiord, Sweden, for example, there is a great collection of portraits in oil, numbering over 2,000, many of them rare, some of them dating from the fourteenth century, and together constituting one of the most valuable collections in all Europe.* Of private libraries may be mentioned two

---
*Du Chaillu.

belonging to two branches of the Bonde family, in Sodermanland, Sweden, each of which has about 10,000 volumes, rich in northern history, and not a few of them dating from A. D. 1300; or such as that belonging to the owner of Skokloster, on Lake Malar, and containing 30,000 volumes, with many additional valuable manuscripts.

The ungrateful world moves but slowly toward the realization of how much it owes to the great Lutheran communion, a church which, in the Fatherland, presents a literature unequaled in all the world; a science going hand in hand with deep, earnest, fervent piety; a theology and philosophy at whose overflowing wells the nations gather for refreshment; and a type of religion which preaches a pure Gospel, as no other church preaches it, in almost all the tongues of earth.

LUTHERAN UNIVERSITIES.

Location—Towns.	State.	When Founded.	Professors & Teachers.	Students.	Volumes in Library.
Copenhagen	Denmark	1479	50	1,200	240,000 and many MSS.
Christiania	Norway	1811	50	1,000	280,000
Dorpat	Livonia	1632	73	900	145,000
Goettingen	Hanover	1736	124	950	500,000 and many MSS.
Helsingfors	Finland	1640	100	1,300	150,000
Jena	Saxe-Weimar	1558	87	629	180,000
Kiel	Schleswig-Holstein	1665	78	576	200,000
Leipsic	Saxony	1409	180	3,322	500,000 and many MSS.
Lund	Sweden	1668	70	800	120,000
Rostock	Mecklenburg	1419	39	360	140,000
Upsala	Sweden	1477	119	1,900	250,000 and 11,000 MSS.

UNIVERSITIES LARGELY LUTHERAN ("UNITED.")

Name	State	Year			
Berlin.	Prussia.	1809	241	4,039	200,000
*Erlangen	Bavaria	1742	61	970	147,000
Giessen	Hesse	1607	59	616	160,000
Griefswald.	Pomerania	1456	82	887	120,000
Halle	Saxony	1694	110	1,701	220,000
Heidelberg	Baden	1386	106	1,060	300,000 and many MSS.
‡Koenigsberg	E. Prussia	1544	94	753	200,000
†Tuebingen	Würtemberg	1477	93	1,410	235,000
†Breslau	Silesia	1702	131	1,329	350,000
†Bonn	Rhenish Prussia	1818	122	1,404	250,000

SOME LUTHERAN LIBRARIES.

Name.	Town.	State.	No. of Volumes.
The Royal, of.	Copenhagen	Denmark	482,000
The University	Copenhagen	Denmark	240,000
The University	Christiania	Norway	280,000
The University	Lund	Sweden	120,000
The University	Upsala	Sweden	250,000
The Royal, of.	Stockholm	Sweden	250,000
The University	Dorpat	Livonia	145,000
The University	Helsingfors	Finland	150,000
The Royal, of.	Darmstadt	Germany	500,000
The Royal, of.	Dresden	Saxony	350,000
The Royal, of.	Gotha	Gotha	245,000
The University of	Goettingen	Hanover	500,000
The City, of	Hamburg	Germany	350,000
The Royal, of.	Hanover	Hanover	170,000
The University of	Jena	Saxe-Weimar	180,000
The University of	Kiel	Sch.-Holstein	200,000
The University of	Leipsic	Saxony	500,000
The City, of.	Leipsic	Saxony	100,000
The City, of.	Lübeck	Lübeck	100,000
The Royal, of.	Oldenburg	Oldenburg	150,000
The University of	Rostock	Mecklenburg	140,000
The Royal, of.	Stuttgart	Würtemburg	425,000
The Royal, of.	Weimar	Saxe-Weimar	180,000
The Royal, of.	Wolfenbüttel	Brunswick	300,000
The German Churches, of	St. Petersburg	Russia	100,000

* Erlangen is often classed as Lutheran, its professors being required to conform their teaching to that of the symbols of the Lutheran church.

† Tübingen, Breslau and Bonn have each a Roman Catholic Theological Faculty also.

‡ Koenigsburg originally was Lutheran and a graduate as Master, in the Faculty of Philosophy, ranked as a noble.

SOME LIBRARIES PREDOMINANTLY LUTHERAN.

Name.	Town.	Country.	No. of Volumes.
Royal	Berlin	Germany	750,000
University	Berlin	Germany	200,000*
Over a dozen others in	Berlin	Of which four have..	234,000
University of	Bonn	Rhenish Prussia	250,000
Public, of	Bremen	Bremen	100,000
City, of	Breslau	Silesia	200,000
University of	Breslau	Silesia	350,000
" "	Erlangen	Bavaria	147,000
" "	Giessen	Hesse	160,000
" "	Griefswald	Pomerania	120,000*
" "	Halle	Würtemberg	220,000*
" "	Heidelberg	Baden	300,000
" "	Tübingen	Würtemberg	235,000
Royal, of	Königsberg	Prussia	200,000

SOME LIBRARIES IN LUTHERAN TOWNS.

Town.	State.	Population of Town.	Volumes in Library.
Wolfenbüttel	Brunswick	13,500	300,000
Darmstadt	Hesse	50,000	500,000
Gotha	Saxe-Gotha	28,100	245,000
Weimar	Saxe-Weimar	21,600	200,000
Oldenburg	Oldenburg	24,700	150,000
Oldenburg	Oldenburg	24,700	50,000 Ducal Library.
Rudolstadt	Schwarz-Rudolstadt	8,800	65,000
Wernigerode	Pr. Saxony	9,000	87,000
Coburg	Saxe-Coburg	16,000	50,000
Detmold	Lippe-Detmold	8,000	50,000
Odense	Denmark	21,000	25,000
Reykjavik	Iceland	2,500	39,000
Helmstaedt	Brunswick	8,700	40,000
Drontheim	Norway	24,000	50,000
Vesteras	Sweden	....	12,000 School Library.
Gothenburg	Sweden	....	15,000 School Library.
Linköping	Sweden	....	30,000 School Library.
Dresden	Saxony	....	Has 49 public libraries.

* The Ducal Library of Gotha has some rare volumes, and about 7,000 manuscripts. The Royal, of Saxe-Weimar, has a large and valuable collection of portraits, busts, etc. The Royal, of Stuttgart, has the largest collection of Bibles in the world, and many manuscripts of great rarity. The public library of Göttingen is one of the largest, best selected and arranged in the world, and is especially rich in foreign litera--

CHAPTER IX.

INNER MISSIONS.

WICHERN, FLIEDNER, DAS RAUHE HAUS, AND THE DEACONESSES.

Under the spreading branches of a venerable and gigantic chestnut tree in the village of Horn, three miles from Hamburg, Germany, on the 1st of November, 1833, three boys, in rags, came timidly knocking at the door of an old, uninviting, thatched-roof little house, which, with its low eaves and small windows, looked as humble as themselves. They were the advance guard of applicants for admission to the Orphan's Home that day opened there. A young Lutheran pastor, just graduated from the universities of Goettingen and Berlin, then and there began a work for the neglected youth of the nation which has been felt not only throughout Germany, but all over Europe and other parts of Protestant Christendom.

That pastor's name was John Henry Wichern. He had been born and brought up in Hamburg, which, next to Lon-

---

ture. For the use of the books in the public libraries of Germany and Scandinavia, the most liberal provisions prevail. In Berlin, any adult person is allowed to have books in the reading-rooms. Books are lent to almost any one recommended by persons of standing. By leave of the librarian, books and manuscripts may be sent to a scholar at a distance; or, if specially valuable, may be deposited in a public library where he can use them. There appears to be no limit to the number of books which may be borrowed, although it is prescribed that not more than "three works" must be asked for in one day. Substantially the same regulations prevail generally, although it is generally presumed that the borrower's financial circumstances afford a sufficient guaranty against loss.

don, is the greatest commercial exchange in Europe. There he came into contact with great wealth and abject poverty; there met the blessings of a high civilization and the miseries of that barbarism which is to be found in every great city. His heart was touched by the sufferings of the poor, he yearned over the sinning, the sorrowing and the dying. Though poor in this world's goods he was rich in faith, and with such a capital he set out to devise ways and means for the relief of those in need.

His first step was to buy the old house under the chestnut tree. It had been owned by a person named *Ruge*. In the German patois this name unfortunately took the form of *Rauhe*, whence the place came to be called the *Rauhe Haus*. That means in English, "rough-house," though the term cannot be properly applied to any feature of life in the great Christian Home which has grown from that humble beginning.

Wichern believed that mere political reforms could effect no real cure of the many evils which continually threaten society. He saw that a moral regeneration was necessary; that works of Christian philanthropy alone could relieve the sufferings of the poor, destroy the envy and jealousy of the lower against the higher ranks, and recommend Christianity to the great body of people so perfectly alienated from it. And he proved his faith by his works. He said: "If the Church is to be the fountain of Christian life in the nation, it must, in its confederate capacity, make the work of *Inner Missions* its own."

He accordingly began the practical work of helping the orphan. His institution took up the homeless and outcasts from the filth and squalor of the dark cellars and vicious corners of the city, with the intention of rescuing them from temporal and eternal ruin, and transforming them into useful men and pious Christians. He met with desperate cases, but succeeded with boys of whom the very devil seemed to have taken full possession. The work grew. A girls' home was established. For many wicked boys and girls *Das Rauhe Haus* has become the birthplace of a new life, devoted to the service of God and the benefit of man.

In addition to the work already mentioned, a *Pensionat* has been established, where the sons of wealthy parents, troublesome or insubordinate at home, are received and educated.*

The old farm-house under the chestnut tree has developed into a noble establishment in a large park full of trees, with walks, flowers, gardens and fields. Several comfortable houses have been erected around the main building, and a pleasant chapel gives character to the surroundings.†

These houses number twenty-six in all, and the premises comprise a tract of one hundred and twenty acres.

In harmony with the idea of caring for neglected and vicious children, is that of caring for the inmates of prisons. Only during the present century has it been deemed possible to deal with convicts in the spirit of Christian love. Dr. Wichern said : " One of the first duties of the Inner Mission is to look after the imprisoned, not only through the printed Word, but in the living person, who, quickened and strengthened by that Word, and in the spirit of love and wisdom, through earnest work and loving deed can approach these erring brethren in the flesh." He accordingly set about training young men for this work. His effort was not limited to Hamburg. Those trained under his oversight have charge of other orphan-houses, workhouse schools, bridewells and prisons, teaching thousands of children. They are em-

---

* The $500 per year received from each of the eighty boys now in this department, forms no inconsiderable item in the income upon which the institution is supported.

† Shoe-making, tailoring, spinning, baking, etc., a commercial agency for the sale of articles made by the boys, a printing and publishing house, a lithographing and wood-engraving shop and a book-bindery, re energetically and successfully carried on.

ployed in reformatories, as turnkeys in jails, as catechists and chaplains in prisons, and attendants on the sick in city hospitals. They are visitors of the poor in many large cities, superintendents of city missions, agents of charitable societies, and officials in poor-houses. They are to be found today engaged in these and similar duties in London, Paris, Constantinople, Vienna, Berlin, and outlying cities in Germany, as schoolmasters and missionaries, colporteurs and Bible agents, under the shadow of Turkish mosques, at the base of Vesuvius, among the Lapps of Russia, and by the great lakes of North America—faithful, steady, manly men, an honor to the Rauhe Haus and a blessing to the world.*

In 1842 King Wilhelm, earnestly desiring to inaugurate a reform in German prisons, applied to Dr. Wichern for Brothers from the Rauhe Haus to undertake the work. Twenty-two were sent out. So successful were they, that in 1857 King Frederic William IV. called Dr. Wichern to the superintendency of his prisons.

In the times of George I. of England the German Lutherans of London had their own church and parochial school. The King, who had been born and brought up in the Lutheran faith, granted them rooms for their school in the old Savoy palace. After this school outgrew its quarters, it was removed from the palace and put in charge of Brothers from the Rauhe Haus, and other mission schools were organized under their control.

---

* They are distributed over half the earth. In a work published at the celebration of their jubilee, they were reported at work in Hamburg, Bremen, Lübeck, Mecklenburg, Schleswig-Holstein, East Prussia, West Prussia, Pomerania, Silesia, Berlin, Brandenburg, Province of Saxony, Hanover, Westphalia, Thuringia, Rhine Province, Kingdom of Saxony, Hungary, Roumania, England, Russia, Asia and America. They were engaged in houses of correction, Christian schools, as city missionaries, directors of Christian inns, directors of Christian society houses, port missionaries, colonial preachers, colporteurs, nurses of the sick, supervisors of houses for the poor, directors of orphans' homes, superintendents of prisons.

An orphanage was founded in London as a memorial of the golden wedding of Emperor Wilhelm, the Germans of that city contributing 80,000 marks for that purpose. His Majesty, the Emperor, assumed the protectorate of the institution, and in his honor it is named the Emperor Wilhelm Institute. It is under the control of Rauhe House Brothers.

In the realm of the Czar twelve of these Brothers are at work as managers of institutions for the care and training of children, and as city missionaries. At Mitau they have a home for neglected children with 34 inmates; near Riga another with 46; at Eich.uheim an Orphanage and Pensionat, caring for respectively, 90 and 20 pupils; an orphanage at Riga with 75 children; at Narwa a home for poor children of Esthonian, Finn, Russian and German parentage, of which the Empress is protectress; at Reval an asylum, and at St. Petersburg, where there are 80,000 Protestants, chiefly Finnish, German and Esthonian Lutherans, a house for sick men, an asylum for sick children, and a Convalescents' Home. At Kronstadt they have a Seamen's Home: and a Home for Aged and Invalid Missionaries, for which funds are being gathered, is to be built. Other houses of mercy are in charge of the Brothers of the Rauhe Haus, which it were tedious to mention. Four of the Brothers and two Deaconesses from the Rauhe Haus went to East Africa as nurses of the sick. Five others were to follow. They are in Zanzibar, at a station on the mainland, and in the lazaretto.

Many excellent books, tracts and papers are issued yearly from the institution, and a monthly periodical—*Fliegende Blätter*—which is the organ of the central committee for Inner Missions.

It is difficult, indeed, to specify the many forms of active Christian enterprise which Wichern's work has assumed. It aims at the relief of all kinds of spiritual and temporal misery by works of faith and charity, the quickening of nominal Christianity into active life and the general reform of society on the basis of the Gospel and the creed of the Reformation. *

One department of the Inner Mission work for which the Rauhe Haus has trained Brothers, is that of conducting Christian Inns or lodging-houses. These are established in nearly all the great cities of Europe. They are designed to shield young men from the evils of the public drinking house, and to provide them with the means of resisting temptation. They offer cheap and clean lodgings and meals, a friendly Christian word, and frequently provide the work necessary for the young men who go from the country to the cities and large towns.

It is well known that, in Germany especially, young men who have learned trades are expected to travel from place to place to work with the masters of their respective crafts in the different towns and cities, that they may become the more skilled in their handicraft and learn to know something of the world. No man is acknowledged a skilled workman until he has spent a few years in this way. The term of wandering varies from three to six years; and when a youth has done with this, he goes home, makes his "Masterpiece," and if it be successfully accomplished he obtains permission to enter business for himself.

---

* It comprises the care of the poor, the sick, the captive, the prisoner, the traveling journeymen, the emigrant and the laboring classes in general; it seeks to promote the better observance of the Lord's Day, helps in temperance and social reform; it trains laborers for their work in orphanages and asylums; organizes brotherhoods and sisterhoods; erects new buildings for destitute children; promotes family religion; provides every newly married couple making application with a copy of the Bible; sees to the spiritual welfare of orphans, widows, sailors, mechanics, emigrants, the poor, and the destitute; christianizes prison discipline; cares for discharged convicts; provides people's libraries; has benevolent institutions among collieries; distributes books and tracts; arranges courses of lectures on useful topics and aids in supplying destitute congregations with the Word and Sacraments. Its moving spirit is the love which comes of faith in Christ.

Of course, with such regulations, and in such a hive of mechanical industry as Germany, multitudes of young men —many but mere boys—are away from home and subjected to all manner of temptation. To meet this want of home influences, to help guard against the seductive influences of the tempter, these Christian Hotel-Homes, are established by the Society for Inner Missions. They furnish lodging at five, seven, or ten cents per night; food is supplied at correspondingly low rates, and daily religious services are provided. Connected with many of these homes are very comfortable quarters for other travelers, theological students, and ministers. In addititon to the staple commodities for the table, good books, papers and music are provided, and not infrequently, in one of their tasty chapels, can be heard from two to five hundred voices rendering Luther's chorals in a style that would bring no discredit to a first class conservatory of music.*

Remembering that the Inner Mission workers of Europe have established over three hundred and fifty of these Inns to keep young men out of the hands of those who would

---

* Some idea of the extent of this work of providing Christian lodgings for the young men and the Christian public of Germany, and the spirit with which it is undertaken and supported, may be inferred from such isolated facts as the following :

Some time previous to 1875, it was thought necessary to open a Christian Inn in the city of Chemnitz, in Saxony, Germany. It was opened September 1st, 1875, at a cost of 68,214 marks—perhaps fairly representative of as many dollars in America. In the beginning, it was provided with forty beds; but soon these were found insufficient, and thirty-six more were added. In 1882, 10,896 wanderers, traveling mechanics, etc., were entertained in it, for an average of about three nights each, or 32,088 nights for one. This gives an average of about 90 persons for each day of the year.

The Inn in Barmen was opened in 1857. In 1882, it had 4,500 guests, and gave them lodgings equivalent to 25,696 nights, an average of over seventy for each day of the year. This home had a net income, for that year, of 10,348 marks. In fifteen months, the second of these Inns in Berlin lodged 16,060 young men, 39,000 nights.

lead them into evil ways—drinking, carousing, gambling, etc.,—for the sake of gain; remembering that there is a network of them that spreads over Germany and into some of the surrounding countries, and that every one presents clean and inviting lodgings at the cheapest possible rates, and is provided with good books, periodicals, musical instruments and with pious House-Fathers who hold morning and evening devotional services, give all necessary advice and directions to guests, etc., we can conceive something of the blessed work that is thus done for the young men of Germany, in keeping them out of temptation's reach. *

These Inns aim not only to provide board and lodgings for travelers and traveling journeymen; but also for those who have regular employment, and have neither a home, nor an employer's house, in which they can find food and shelter. For these classes they aim to provide the necessary accommodations that they may be saved from the temptations which beset them at houses set up and carried on exclusively for financial gain, and in which, too often, any means are used that induce them to part with their money.

Christian Inns and Training Institutions for self-supporting girls and young women, under direct oversight of the Central Directory for Inner Missions, exist in 33 of the larger cities of Germany; Christian Inns alone, without the "Training" department, in 28 additional places; and Training Institutions, without the "Inns," at 9 other places. A

---

* The establishing of Christian Inns began about 1854. Up to 1863, the increase in their number was slow; but 19 existed at the end of their first decade. From that time, however, the increase has been more rapid. Twelve new ones were established in 1870. By 1873, 101 were in existence; and by 1884, the number was increased to 194. The next two years added 58; the next year, 30; the year following, 45; and the year following brought the number up to 332. In the province of Brandenburg alone, 25 such Inns were opened in 1885 and the four following years. In January, 1890, the whole number reported was 353, of which 21 were outside of Germany. This list embraced those in existence up to September, 1889.

full list of these 70 houses, their location—city, street and house-number—is printed and given out for the benefit of the classes interested. The aim is to give a home to girls and young women who go to the cities to find employment, where they are protected against all temptations, and through which they may be qualified for their work, and eventually helped to a position. As is true of the Inns for men also, these for young women aim to give good accommodations at the lowest possible rates.†

The Y. M. C. A. of the United States have a great deal to say about "saving young men." They professedly exist for no other purpose. They are very ready to complain when churches refuse to extend them that financial aid which they think they so richly merit. They declare that the saloon is the young man's deadliest enemy. They have repeated that declaration for years and years. They have talked about this thing, and written about it, and, doubtless, prayed about it.

Yet it seems not to have occurred to them that it would be a good and Christian thing to open Christian Inns or Coffee-Houses, in the great cities of the land, as a practical help in keeping young men out of the saloon. There may not be much sentimentality about such work. Providing houses, clean rooms and beds, healthful food, and the like, is a very real, humdrum affair. The washing of pots, dusting of rooms and looking after fires are things that drive romance and sentimentality out at the window. Yet they are the very things that must be done in the "saving" of men of all ages.

"Song-Service," "Gospel-Meetings for men only," &c., may be good and helpful when conducted by properly qualified persons; but to a young man who is a stranger in our large towns or cities, vastly more can be done to keep him out of the ways of evil when a Christian (Hotel) Home is

---
† *Fl. Blätter*, Sept. '90, pp. 269, 270.

opened as a place where he can lodge comfortably and decently, at reasonable rates, and at any time, than would likely be done by any "Gospel Meeting for men only." Why not try it?

Wichern's ideas took root, not only in other parts of Germany, but also in France, England, Holland, the United States, and other countries. When he died, in '81, he left an enduring monument in the cleansed hearts and the changed lives of thousands of earth's abandoned children, who at the last day will rise up and call him blessed. And the end is not yet. Each year extends the influences to which he gave shape. His works do follow him.

A number of other institutions, doing substantially the same work as the Rauhe Haus, have come into existence in other parts of Germany. The institution at Neinstedt, for example, has a four-fold purpose, viz.: the training of young men to work as Deacons, the bringing up of neglected and morally deformed children, the care of weak minded and imbecile persons, and, also, of epileptics.*

The "Pilgrim Mission" Institution at Crischona, near Basel, has done a great work in training Brothers to serve as evangelists, deacons, house fathers, &c., in addition to the work done by it in training men to work as missionaries among scattered Germans in foreign lands.†

---

* In the last year, 38 young men applied for admission into the institution, of whom but 14 could be received. Since its establishment in 1850, 123 candidates have been sent out into different fields of Inner Mission work, of whom 43 are in the institutions for the safety of the young, 22 are in Christian Inns and 14 are city missionaries. The departments for weak-minded and for epileptics have room for 492 patients, and always are full. Many applicants cannot be received for lack of room.

† Since 1840, it has trained 545 young men, of whom 407 are still actively engaged. Of this number, 196 are at work as ordained ministers of the Gospel in America; the rest are serving in the different spheres of Inner Mission work in various parts of Germany, Switzerland and Austria.

In all, we have reports from eighteen institutions which train Brothers for the service of Inner Missions, although some of them prepare their students to work as missionary pastors among their countrymen in foreign lands. Two thousand Brothers, or Deacons, are to-day at work in different parts of the world, as missionaries in one sphere or another, who have been prepared and sent out by these institutions, specially established for this work. They are working, principally, in Orphans' Homes, in Hospitals, in Christian Inns, as city missionaries, as teachers in schools, and as preachers among immigrants. Three hundred more are in the institutions, now being prepared for the work.

The Brotherhood which cares for the sick and wounded in time of war is a product of the spirit of the times in Germany; because its leaders are thoroughly trained for the work by competent teachers, and because it is no less Christian to care for the sick and dying in times of war than in times of peace.*

Theodore Fliedner, an active young Lutheran pastor, in 1833 began, in a very humble way, the training of teachers

---

* The Brotherhood of Free Will Nurses of sick in time of War, now has 14 district organizations, and over 1,050 members. Of this number 450 are honorary, and 1,200 active. Of the active members, 960 have had training under physicians, and 590 of them have enjoyed a full course of such drill. The 14 district organizations are directed by as many committees,—one for each,—which have 163 members, the majority of whom are teachers from the high schools of Prussia. The members of the Brotherhood are instructed and trained in 25 different clinics and lazarettos, and 125 different physicians conduct or direct the instruction and the training. Over eight hundred of the active members have had gymnasium or university culture.

Apart from the Brotherhood above-named, 801 women nurses are ready for orders in time of War. Of this number, 206 are Sisters of the Order of St. John; and 595 are Deaconesses. In 1889, the order of St. John expended 13,300 marks for the training of sisters; and in the two previous years, about thirty thousand. Two thousand four hundred persons, therefore, are ready to respond to a call for nurses for sick in time of war.

and nurses to take care of the sick and neglected. His "stock in trade" to begin with was reported thus: "One table, some broken chairs, a few worn knives and two pronged forks, seven sheets, and four cases of severe illness." He took into a summer house a discharged convict who wished to reform. After a short time he bought a house without any money to pay for it, but with a great supply of faith that the money would be provided. And this was the begining of the revival of the Order of Christian Deaconesses in the Protestant Church, the planting of the little seed which has grown into a great tree whose branches spread over the earth. The charter of one of these Deaconesses' Hospitals says it is established that the "suffering and the sick may be cared for and relieved in a becoming and Christian manner, without distinction of color, creed, or condition."

These hospitals are not, like private institutions, founded as financial investments. They do not close their doors against all who are not able and willing to pay well for all needed attention. Even when patients are able to pay for their care, these institutions do not make exorbitant demands, and charge from $10 to $50 a week. They open their doors to all who need their care. They furnish trained nurses, skilled physicians and surgeons, and the best possible accommodations in the way of house-accommodations, food, etc. Such as are able to pay for these accommodations are asked for a nominal sum—perhaps $5 a week—to cover the actual expenses of providing the nursing, the medicines, the food, light, heat, etc. The destitute receive them all free, as fruits of Christian love.

It is a work of Christian well-doing. The founders of the institutions and the nurses—Deaconesses, when possible—give their skill, their time, and their toils for mercy's sake. The labor is great; the most of it is not pleasant; the earthly rewards are few. But it is God's will that it be done. In doing it, we but follow the example of Him, a part of whose mission was to heal the sick, and who bade the disciples, "Go, preach; heal the sick," (Matt. x: 8.) And it has the promise, "Inasmuch as ye have ministered unto me; come, ye blessed of my Father."*

Another important sphere of the Deaconess work is in the congregation or parish, where, under the supervision of the pastor, they seek out the sick, nurse and care for them; clothe the naked; visit the abodes of disorder and filth, and have them put in healthful condition; teach order and cleanliness; strive to have neglected children sent to school and assembled in Sunday school; assist the unemployed to find work; teach the unskilled to darn, to patch, to sew, to

---

*In 1886 Deaconesses were at work in 645 of these institutions in Europe, Asia, Africa and America. The total of their work done in this sphere may, perhaps, be inferred from an account of what was done in one year in one institution. The German Hospital at Philadelphia has been under their care for years. A late report says that there, in one year, they nursed 1,250 patients, and that thirty-two thousand four hundred and eighty-five days nursing were given them. In addition, over 18,000 examinations of sick were made outside the hospital. All was done at an expense of less than thirty thousand dollars to the institution, and of less than half that sum to the patients. All physicians' work was a free gift, as well as the shelter, beds, medicines and medical appliances; giving all these free, less than a dollar a day was paid out by the Hospital for the care and nursing of a sick man, and for the bread and meat necessary to life, and an average of about forty cents the day paid by those who received all this care and attention.

Please remember, all the surroundings are first-class; all medicines and medical appliances, all physicians' services, nursing, etc., the best that can be had, and vastly better than ordinarily is had; and the world cannot show, outside of similar institutions, any responsible provision for the relief of the sick poor that is equally as effective and equally as economical.

When a poor man, even though "sick nigh unto death," can be cared for free of all charges to himself, or at an average cost to himself and his friends of but forty cents a day for physicians, medicines, nursing, shelter and food of the best that can be had, there certainly no longer is need that any should die of neglect. Blessings be on the devoted servants of our good Lord through whose efforts of Christian love alone these things are possible!

mend, to knit; aim to restore peace in households when it has been disturbed; look after factory girls and others employed in great cities away from home, and with motherly love and care provide for them suitable meeting places and services on Sunday afternoons and evenings; seek to acquaint the rich with the necessities of the poor and if possible secure from them relief for those in want. In a word, they diligently observe and strive to supply each individual need which in our busy times may be so easily overlooked. About 8,000 of these Deaconesses are now employed, one-third of them in the parish work, the others in hospitals, orphans' homes and asylums.

Another very important sphere of Deaconess work is in the education and training of the young. "They who have the children, have the future." That the church may have the future, this wing of her working forces aims to have the children. To reach this aim, the Deaconesses have found it expedient and necessary to look after all ages of childhood, particularly among the poorer and more careless classes.

Infancy is first of all ages. Thousands of mothers must go away from home to daily toil, while the child is yet at the breast. Need drives them to this. How shall such mothers be able to do daily toil among strangers? What is to become of the child while the mother is thus at work? The mother's earnings are so small that she can not afford to engage a nurse to care for the infant, which may be but one of several children depending on her toil for daily bread. Here the Deaconess comes to her aid with the Day Nursery, ("die Krippe"); and, for a very small charge, cares for the child day after day, or, if need be, by day and by night. Some charge is made so that parents may have no temptation to wholly give over the care of their young children to the nursery, and that something may be gathered thus for the support of the work; but the charge is made light, that worthy mothers may be assisted in earning the daily bread for their children.

Stuttgart, Würtemberg, has one of these Day Nurseries, largely as a gift from the late Emperor William and his queen, on the occasion of the 50th anniversary of their marriage. It has 60 beds, and is managed by four Deaconesses, with four assistants. The average daily number of children in it is 34. Lovely is the sight of the little ones, when each is set up in his baby carriage, neat and clean, apparently proud as a young lord, or sweetly sleeping as though the Angel of Peace watched over them. They are generally cared for, here, from 6 A. M. to 6 P. M. There is joy all around when the day's work is done and the mothers reach the Nursery to take their children into their own care for the night.

Part of the work of caring for children is done thus; but provision has to be made, also, for those of a larger growth. Next door to the Nursery, often, is found the home for children from two to six years of age, generally named the School for Little Children. After this, is the Elementary School for Children over six years of age, and in which they may be trained until they reach mature years. These schools are scattered all over Europe, principally in the great centers of population. Their one great aim is to keep the children away from temptation, and instruct them in the things they ought to believe and do. They were established, specially, to care for the children of parents who daily work away from home; but they reach out, also, to care for such as are liable to be neglected from any other cause.

Six years ago, over five hundred such institutions, including orphanages and high schools, were under the care of Deaconesses. Some of them have been established for a quarter of a century in Egypt and Palestine, as regular mission schools, into which the dark-eyed, sun-browned native girls of all classes have been gathered and instructed in Christian Truth, and trained in the ways of Christian civilization. Hundreds of the girls of the East, thus instructed and trained, have gone back among their people to give out again the leaven of the Gospel; and have become veritable missionaries of the cross through the power of the these Deaconess schools.

A Mother House is an institution that trains Deaconesses for their work, at the same time that it ministers to the particular needs of the sick and distressed who find care within its walls. Of these, in 1886, there were 57. In management and working, each Deaconess house is an independent establishment, relying on the training and experience of its sisters, and on the voluntary enlistment of recruits for the work, who come from the people among whom the Mother House is situated. Experienced and trained sisters are put at the head of such an institution to give their care and guidance for the training of all who may desire to fit themselves for any brance of the Deaconess work.

The prescribed course of study includes instruction in English and German, reading, writing, arithmetic, composition, geography, singing, religious exercises, medical and surgical studies under the direction of the medical and surgical staff, and the moral and religious, as well as the physical, care of the patients. The Evangelical Deaconess is not cut loose from her family relations. With perfect freedom each one can return to the care of her parents, if these think this necessary. She may always enter into the marriage relation. With her relatives she has free communication. Every two or three years she receives means from her Mother House to visit her friends. In nothing is there a yoke like that laid on the Romish nuns; although such regulations as preserve order must prevail, as this is the fundamental principle of the Gospel.

An appreciative Presbyterian writer says of the Deaconesses—and his words are reproduced, because substantially correct: "There are no social distinctions among them, and one sees the personal characteristics of all classes of society.

o

Side by side are the full rosy countenance and somewhat shame-faced manner of the peasant girl who has come up from her village community, and the intelligent, delicately-tinted face, the soft, slender hand, and the unobtrusive but graceful, self-reliant manner of the child of noble family. Each is useful in her own way, and each lives with the other as with a sister, forgetting differences in the overwhelming power of their agreement; serving the Lord with all their strength, and drawn to one another by the bonds of that common service. 'One Fold; one Shepherd.'"*

Are not these the very works to which the Divine Master referred, when John's disciples went to him asking, "Art thou He that should come, or look we for another?" Was not the reply given thus: "Shew John again the things ye do hear and see: the blind receive their sight, the lame walk, the lepers are cleansed, the deaf hear, the dead are raised up, and the poor have the Gospel preached to them."

If such works were evidences of Him that should come, then, are they not evidences of the same thing to-day? If they were necessary to prove His divinity then, are they not equally necessary to day? And if necessary to-day to prove a Christ-like spirit, what can we say of those spirits which claim to be Christian and yet know nothing of such works?

---

* The money value of the work thus done yearly is past computation. The minimum wages of a competent trained nurse may be written at $15 a week, or, say $700 a year. There are 8,000 Deaconesses in the Order, the great majority of whom act as nurses. Write this number at 4,000 and allow the others to be engaged in other branches of the Deaconess work. The yearly value of these services, then, on the basis furnished by the above-mentioned disinterested authority, is found to be $2,800,000. Add to this sum the value of the services of the 4,000 engaged in other works of mercy, estimated at half the yearly allowance of the nurses; add, also, over $1,500,000 collected and expended by the Order each year to alleviate the sufferings and miseries of the children of men in all quarters of the earth, and you find the magnificent contribution of over five and a half millions of dollars made by and through the noble Order of Deaconesses every year.

CHAPTER X.

CITY MISSIONS.

In all Europe, perhaps, there is no city whose moral and religious condition is so often under discussion as that of the capital of the German Empire. Owing to its wonderful growth,* the rapid appreciation of real estate values, and the consequent herding together of human beings wherever shelter can be found, the moral and religious conditions presented in Berlin have been singularly unfavorable. This has been the croaker's opportunity, and over and over again Berlin's Christianity has been pronounced dead, or dying beyond a doubt.

Owing to the Church's connection with the State, to wrestle with such problems as are presented in the German capital is vastly more difficult than in America. There people may not associate themselves at their pleasure for the erection of a church. The matter must first go before the authorities, and even when they are favorable, long time elapses before the desired end can be attained. Thrown thus upon their own resources, the Christian people of Berlin have been carrying on a work of Christian love the equal of which probably cannot be found in any city of the Western Continent. And as the city mission work of Berlin is conducted practically on the same lines as that of other Lutheran

---

* Probably no city on the Continent presents so startling statistics of growth. With a population in 1860 of 500,000, 1880 found it with 1,122,000, and 1890 with 1,550,000. Real estate values and rents so advanced that wage-workers were driven to cellars and attics. In 1872 there were over 50 inhabitants to a house, about 80,000 lived in cellars, and in 300 houses there were ten to twenty persons to each room.

cities,* we go somewhat into the details, that from one we may learn all.

When a man of sense starts out in quest of virtue, he will not seek its strongest evidences in the alleys and gutters of a great city. Admitting that there is fearful ungodliness in the German capital, the facts being fully known, we also must admit that the measures for the removal and correction of that ungodliness and the alleviation of its miseries are as complete, far-reaching, thorough and evangelical as any yet devised.

Church edifices are not so numerous in Berlin as they should be, there being but seventy-one† for the whole city. But here a careless observer may easily fall into error. Religion is not a Sunday affair. The churches of Berlin are open every day from 11 A. M. to 4 P. M., and the Sunday services in many of the churches are almost continuous, one audience dispersing while another takes its place. When it is considered that the churches are very large, that services are held every day in the week, and, beginning as early as 8 o'clock A. M., almost continuously on Sunday, that there are a number of pastors to each parish and that these are aided by lay-helpers, Deacons and Deaconesses, and that in the schools the young receive more hours‡ of religious

---

* There is need of mission work in the cities of Germany and Scandinavia. No one denies it. But the state of morals and religion in Lutheran lands is easily misrepresented by superficial observers, who judge by appearances and disregard the deep, quiet under-currents of religious life. Lutheranism has not much in the show-window, but it keeps the staple article in stock.

† Quite a number of new churches of very large dimensions are now in process of erection.

‡ The city has 184 parish schools, with 172,778 pupils. The schools throughout are compulsory, and impart religious instruction regularly and constantly as part of the curriculum, including Bible history, the catechism, memorizing of Scripture passages, and the essential doctrines of Christianity. "Sunday school" is thus kept every day in the week, and the acquaintance with Scripture teaching on the part of these Ger-

instruction in a month, and by thoroughly educated teachers, than the Sunday-school scholar of America receives in a year, the religious needs of Berlin may not seem so dreadful *as when it is said, without qualification, that the German capital has no Sunday schools and but one church for every 20,000 of population.

One of the results of the thorough religious instruction of the children, is that those ranked as non-church going classes in Berlin are more easily reached by the Gospel than are the same classes in America.†

Statistics reveal another good result of the thorough religious instruction of the children of the German capital in the relatively few crimes committed as compared with those of other large cities.‡

The Inner Mission authorities say that Berlin numbers

---

man children is far more thorough than where but a half-hour's instruction is given once a week and by teachers having no special training for the work.

* It is reported that over 90 per cent. of the total population is baptized. In 1889, 36,762 children were baptized, 20,443 confirmed, and there were 181,046 communicants. Would the statistics of any American city make so good a showing?

† Some years ago, the Court preacher arranged with Von Schluemberg to hold services in the capital, naming three conditions on which he might labor as an Evangelist with the approval of the authorities. The third condition was that he should not preach to the people as if they were heathens. Von Schluemberg said he must first see whether this third condition was true. After some experience he acknowledged that he had found nowhere in America such receptivity to Gospel truth.

‡ Ex-Court Chaplain Stoecker, in an address on Inner Mission work, has had occasion to draw some comparisons and is reported as saying that Berlin, with respect to morals, is far ahead of the English capital. While London had been the scene of over 16,000 burglaries the past year, only 34 were committed in Berlin. While nearly 17,000 women in London were arrested for drunkenness, there were only 580 in Berlin. While London had 60,000 paupers on its hands and expended on them 40 million dollars, Berlin had but 1,000 and maintained them at a cost of two million dollars.

300,000 young men among its population and that 54,000 girls flock thither annually. To aid the churches in caring for so vast a number cut loose from home-restraints and in counteracting the evils arising from this unnatural condition, the City Mission society was organized. The impulse to it dates from the dark days of 1848, to Wichern it owes its origin and to Stoecker its present form. At its head is a committee of fifteen with whom rests the control. The practical direction of the work is in the hands of four pastors of the State church, each having his specific department. Working under the society's direction are 35 city missionaries, laboring, in the interests of the regular congregations, in fields designated by the respective pastors. Their principal duties are to visit, from house to house,* sick and well, poor and rich, church-goers and non-church goers alike.

Five City Mission Sisters are engaged in visiting women who are in danger of going astray. The police furnish a weekly record of those in danger of arrest on suspicion of evil-doing, and they are visited, that if possible they may be turned from sin. Those who are living in violation of the marriage-laws and those who neglect the baptism and training of their children, receive the attention of the mission-visitors, that they may be brought into the right way.†

* These visits are classified as follows: Free visits—where they never before have gone; sick-visits: visits where the religious instruction of the children is being neglected; and visits of investigation. Of these latter, are several kinds. Among the poor, to learn the true condition of those asking aid either of the society or of individuals. In 1888, of this kind of visits, 1,220 were made at request of Her Majesty the Empress, 1,690 for the Society, and 2,434 for private persons. Another kind is at request of persons at a distance, asking information concerning, or that attention be given, to some particular person. Everything possible is done to answer and meet such requests.

† For one or other of these objects, during the past year their city missionaries visited no fewer than 9,000 families, many of them several times.

Oftentimes these visits result in the gathering of those visited into halls in their neighborhood for religious instruction, Sunday schools, bible hours, &c.* Each missionary is required to keep a daily record of visits, the substance of conversations held and whatever else he does in the line of his work. From this he makes out a report which goes before the authorities, affording a view of the whole field. The work begun in the Sunday schools by the missionaries, the Mission endeavors to keep up, for the youth, in Young People's Societies; and for adults, in societies for men, and for women.

Among the many societies helping the Mission, are seven Young Women's associations, in reality so many aid societies, caring for the poor and gathering means for the work. The City Mission as such does not give aid to those suffering only from bodily wants, but when advised through the missionaries' numerous societies of beneficence, care for the sick or those otherwise in bodily distress.

Four organizations, with 4,000 members, have as their purpose the quickening of Christian life and churchly interest, and are centers of Christian activity within the general organization. In addition to these sub-societies, there is an organization to gather money for heathen missions and a children's society, holding weekly meetings, to gather means for the City Mission.

The Societies of Young Men and of Young Women are agents of the Mission for particular parts of its work, the former having in charge a large portion of the Mission's work for young men. Six such organizations are directed by the City Missionaries, seven others connected with parish churches coöperating with them. Many other such societies, called into life by the City Mission, have been given into the hands of the pastors. Besides there are the Men's

---

* No such meetings may be held without the assent of the mission authorities.

Societies and the Women's Societies, in the different congregations—in all, 32 churchly organizations standing in close relation to the City Mission, in addition to several others, to care for girls in factories, for girls lately confirmed, and for such as have fallen.

Eight boy choirs sing the gospel into the hearts of the people and give such other assistance in song-service as may be desired of them. The city is districted, each choir has its part, and it is traveled over again and again so that no house be missed. The choirs visit from ten to a dozen courts daily, bringing the gospel to as many thousand, in the old and familiar hymns and chorals of the church. On Sundays, sermons and other devotional writings are distributed.

In the midst of the parish of the Holy Cross, the City Mission has its headquarters, a large five-story structure, having an assembly room* with a seating capacity of 1,200; rooms for the various societies forming part of the mission force; rooms for the schools of Industry where girls are taught sewing, knitting, and other handiwork; also a dozen large rooms for young women who seek the comfort and safety of a Christian home† while sojourning for a time in the city.

For twenty years now the City Mission has cared for those who have been in prison, giving them board and lodging, and finding work for them, while it aims to lift them to a better way of life. Finding it difficult to get work for them, the Society established several industries to give them employment. A fair price is paid for the work done and a diligent laborer is able to save about one-half of his earnings.‡

---

* In the assembly room, public services and other meetings are held during the week, and on Sundays three or four services by the pastors connected with the society.

† The charges are 1½ marks per day for room and single bed, and 2½ to 3 marks for room with double bed.

‡ The Society boards and lodges them at a cost to each of 18 to 24 cents a day.

In addition to the buildings thus utilized, the Society owns several others which it leases, and it rents fifteen halls for its various uses, in different parts of the city.

The Society's book store gives employment to 25 persons. One of its chief aims is to circulate good literature, sermons, papers for Sunday reading, for young people, for the advancement of public morality, &c., and its success has been remarkable.*

The "Sunday Friend," published in the interests of the Society, is an illustrated Christian weekly† intended to counteract the influence of a prostituted secular press, to rouse the sleeping, strengthen the weak, and lead the erring to a better life. The "Union Messenger" and the *Correspondenzblatt* are from the Society's Book Store, while the "Evangelical Church Paper" is edited by the late Court Preacher, Stoecker,‡ with several assistants.

In addition to periodicals, the society also publishes books. Among these are volumes of Stöcker's sermons since 1884, of which the earlier volumes have passed through several editions. Libraries for children; Christmas

---

* Up to 1883 the weekly issue of Sunday sermons was 13,000. Court-Preacher Stoecker was then asked to furnish the sermons and the weekly issue ran up to 40,000 within a year. Two years later the figures reached 115,500 weekly, with larger editions on festivals and special occasions. The issue for the Christmas Festival, 1888, was 171,000 copies. About 2,500 are in Polish, the rest in German. The cost is one pfennig each. More than half the entire weekly edition now goes beyond the confines of the capital city.

† Founded in 1885, its regular weekly issue is 44,000, with special editions for Posen, Frankfort and Falkenberg-Kirchberg. The price is 2 marks, 20 pfennig.

‡ It is in heartiest sympathy with all efforts to free the church from state control; and, in its first number, said: "This periodical is Evangelical in the sense that it accepts the Word of God, as the same is expounded in the Reformation confessions,—especially in the Augsburg Confession—as the God-given foundation principle of all work in the Kingdom of God and in the Evangelical Church." Its subscription price is ten marks, yearly.

Bells; Thorns and Gleanings from Mission fields; works on varies phases of mission life at home and abroad; devotional works; hymn books for Young People's Societies, etc., are among the Society's publications. It also keeps healthful publications of other houses in stock; and through its many friends and agents in Berlin, throughout the German states, and in foreign lands, it exercises great power in behalf of the circulation of Christian literature. *

The Society has its own editorial rooms where four persons are kept constantly employed. In addition to matter for the Society's own publications, they prepare articles for the local and provincial press. From the beginning, the publication house has paid its own way and usually has a surplus of some thousands of marks to pay into the City Mission treasury.

The Hospice is another institution of the City Mission. It has 70 guest-rooms, two dining rooms, a conference room, and rooms for employees. A room for devotional exercises mornings, evenings and Sundays, serves the guests also as a reading and correspondence room.†

The Society aims also to prevent evil by cultivating the idea of self-help among the poorly paid who are specially exposed to temptation.‡

The income of the Society proper is derived from various

---

* Attention is also given to the publication of lithographs, and an edition of 3,000 copies of " Jesus blessing little children," was exhausted in four weeks. Busts of Luther, Melancthon and others; wall-mottoes, festival cards are published and circulated in large numbers.

† A full dinner is served at the Hospice for 1½ marks. Each room contains a price-list of everything that the house furnishes. In three months of 1888, it gave 7,000 nights' lodging to guests.

‡ Of the Society's practical way of meeting a difficulty, the following is an illustration: Recently it bought a row of houses in the neighborhood of its hall, intending to convert them into lodgings for workingmen's families. The houses were formerly inhabited by lewd characters. It is the intention of the society to continue the purchase of such houses and to crowd out vice by opening a home to virtue.

sources, such as yearly and occasional gifts from friends; regular subscriptions; collections from the churches; donations from individual congregations; offerings made on occasions of special services for Bible study or in mission interests; contributions from regularly organized aid societies in the provinces, and from the Evangelical Church Aid Society of Berlin; as, also, the aid given by hundreds of women friends in the Capital. Twenty-five sewing societies work in its interests, preparing clothing for the very poor and otherwise giving assistance. In the Capital itself there are two collecting societies, and thirty women's societies, in addition to the sewing societies; while thirteen others exist in the suburbs. In the provinces of Brandenburg, Saxony, Silesia and in Thuringia, twenty-two other aid societies exist; while those in other parts number thirty-four,—a total of 126 branch or aid organizations. The woman's Society af the Good Shepherd, to aid in reclaiming fallen girls, is an independent organization, but works in the closest relations with the City Mission. "Chapel Societies," whose members are chiefly girls and young women, and whose object is to aid in building new churches, also work in sympathy with the City Mission Society. In Berlin itself, 19 district chapel societies are reported; in Charlottenburg, one; and in Potsdam, four, in addition to the three general organizations. Branch societies exist throughout most of the provinces: Brandenburg, Saxony and Pomerania, each have ten; Silesia has eight; the "Altmark" and Mecklenburg each have five; Westphalia, the Rhine Provinces, East Prussia, West Prussia, Hanover, Hesse Nassau and Thuringia, each two; and several other divisions have one each. In all, these societies number 101, and report 2,800 members, each of whom pays from three to ten marks yearly into the treasury. The visible results of their work are seen in the "Memorial" church, in Zion's parish, Berlin; erected to the memory of William I. and of Frederic III. *

---

* *Jahrbuch der Berliner Stadtmission, I.* 1889.

Working as a branch of the City Mission, is a society * for the circulation of good literature, with an income of 52,638 marks, and making a weekly distribution of 90,000 to 100,000 periodicals.

Berlin's Society of Christian Young Men may be termed the City Mission's right hand. Its building, at No. 34 Wilhelmstrasse, costing 950,000 marks, has rooms for evening worship, for Bible Hours, Mission Hours, library,† and a hall seating 1,000 persons for Sunday services and other assemblages. It now numbers about 2,000 members, of whom 185 of the most experienced aid the Mission Society in various ways, while 34 are engaged, under direction of the proper authorities, in conducting Mission Sunday schools. Other works of the young men are to help the needy to employment, visit the sick and the stranger, distribute sermons, arrange courses of instruction, lectures, &c. Sixty of the city pastors belong to it and the whole character of the organization is churchly. Warm welcome is given to the stranger. In the society's rooms he may spend the day and the Hospice or Christian Inn receives him for the night.‡

---

* It has over 900 members, and agents in all parts of the Fatherland. It furnishes papers to 546 reading circles; sends its agents into 2,190 factories; publishes the *Arbeiterfreund* in 125,000 copies; sends 5,000 free copies every week to vacant congregations; provides 151 prisons and 300 hospitals with weeklies; distributes 18,000 Sunday papers of the right kind in 205 garrisons, and has its agents among the sailors in the seaports and even among the fishers on the North Sea.

† The character of the society may be judged by the classification of its library, which is as follows: Theological, Devotional, Philosophical and Social, German Literature, Foreign Literature, History, History of Culture and Literature, Geography and Travel, Physical Science, Technical and *Varia*, each class again sub-divided.

In its Periodical Room are on file the best of each kind, among them periodicals from Germany, Switzerland, Denmark, Sweden, Italy, England, Palestine, Austria, France, Holland, Australia and more than a score from America.

‡ This we should call a Young Men's Christian Association on practical principles. Its many committees and their practical way of meeting the difficulties before them, are worthy of study by the well-

In addition to the work done by the City Mission Society, there are, in Berlin, four Deaconess Mother Houses, with about 500 Deaconesses ministering to the bodies and the souls of sufferers in 125 different fields. About 200 of them nurse 7,000 sick persons annually, another hundred labor among the needy poor in the parishes, about forty care for the sick at home, and the rest are engaged in training neglected children, raising up the fallen, and doing such other works of love and mercy as circumstances suggest.*

The Lazarus Deaconess Home in Berlin last year cared for 1,853 patients, with a total of 46,118 nursing days. The Policlinic, during the same period, was attended by 16,230 persons seeking medical and surgical aid. The number of Deaconesses belonging to the Home in 53, of whom some are laboring in outside stations.

The Bethania Deaconess Institute, having 252 Deaconesses and enjoying the protectorate of her Majesty, Augusta Victoria, last year nursed 3,076 sick persons, a total of 102,755 days—an equivalent of nearly 350 years' care of one patient. In addition, 187 of these Deaconesses cared for 13,700 sick at 33 stations outside of Berlin.† Great as is the number of Deaconesses, the supply is not equal to the need.‡

---

meaning but so often impractical directors of the costly institutions of similar name in America. For full particulars see *Jahrebuch, Christlicher Vereins Jungen Männer, Berlin.*

* All service on the part of Deaconesses is free of charge. Two of these four Deaconess Houses report yearly expenses of 392,000 marks.

† Figures cannot express the value of the loving service rendered by these Christ-like women. It is known to God alone and will be recognized when He comes to make up His Jewels.

‡ A year ago a meeting was called in Berlin to consider the Deaconess work. In response 2,000 women assembled. The Rector of the Paul Gerhardt-Stift addressed them in behalf of the dependent women of the city, of whom, he said, there are 226,000, and an average addition of 13,000 yearly. To give them such sympathy, counsel and aid as are needed to save them from want and ruin, at least two Deaconesses should be at work in every parish of 10,000 souls. These should be but the leaders in the work, authorized to urge others to come to their help. In addition,

Deacons as well as Deaconesses are at work in the German Capital. In 1856, Frederick William, of Prussia, called Deacons or Brothers from Wichern's Rauhe Haus, to the oversight of the prisons and they have remained to this day, thirty of them being so employed. Several more are in the prisons for boys.* Others conduct the Gossner Home for neglected girls of school age; still others, a like Home for Boys, an Orphanage, two Christian Inns, and a Hospice.†

The Institute of St. John, in Berlin, established by Wichern in 1858, consists of an Educational Institute and a Training House for Deacons. With the former is a boarding school for boys; with the latter a pro-seminary for the training of preachers for the German congregations in America. The Training House for Deacons has 66 Brothers busy in the Inner Mission work in Germany, and 37 elsewhere. It has established a health-resort by the sea and sends invalid children thither to recuperate.

The Society for Released Prisoners is under the protectorate of the Emperor and achieves a noble work. Of 3,000 applicants during the year, it secured employment for 2,420. Of the 12,687 persons released from prison during the past six years and finding employment through the Society, more then half were from country places. The Society has a fund of 42,000 marks, its yearly expenses are about 20,000 marks,

---
young women and mothers ought to be found for the care of the sick and for schools for little children. Every parish should have two Institutes for little children and a Nursing and Training Home.

To secure the needed helpers, he advocated a Society for the Promotion of Womanly Deeds of Christian Love. The call is to all Christian workers, to Deaconesses and to societies.

* These Brothers live with the boys in prison, working, praying, singing, playing with them, in order to fit them for a useful life when once released.

† The good accomplished by such institutions may be imagined when it is known that these three, in one year, sheltered 36,256 guests—that is, gave that many strangers the comforts of a Christian home. Friends of the Inner Mission say Berlin needs at least six more Christian Inns with 100 beds each.

and the deficit is made up by the Royal Family, churches, and the members of the organization.

The Bethabara Institute is an organization to help fallen girls.* It has in its service a pastor and four women helpers and within a year aided 301 rescued girls.

Their is also in Berlin a Women's Alliance, founded by the City Mission, for the rescue of fallen women. A periodical is published in its interests.

The Men's Alliance † for the suppression of open immorality, aided by a periodical in its interests, is another factor of Berlin's warfare against sin. It has its own bureau and employs its own agent. The Brandenburg Provincial Directory for Inner Mission grants it aid.

The Central Committee for Inner Missions also arranges to take poor children from unhealthful homes in the city to places where they can enjoy pure air. Some are sent to Christian families in the country, others to stations specially prepared for them there, others to the sea coast. A society exists, under the Central Committee, for the summer-care of these classes and reports, in 1888, having provided thus for 20,074 children. The bathing-resorts number 34. The total of contributions for this purpose the past year was nearly 1,000,000 marks. The same privileges are also being extended to wage-workers, both men and women, who through sickness or misfortune had been reduced to want.‡

---

* The method of this society is practical. After caring for the repentant, it places them in good Christian families. On its own grounds, it has two roomy houses for released women picked up in the streets. It has also a house, erected at a cost of 50,000 marks, for children born out of wedlock.

† There is a West German Society with like object having headquarters in Düsseldorf, and others in Kiel, Stuttgart and Dresden. These societies have a committee for the Empire and propose similar organizations in all the provinces and large cities of Germany where they do not now exist.

‡ One Women's Society in Berlin, the "Edelweiss," thus provided for 254 sewing-women and 240 children.

In addition to all the many agencies, societies, institutions, &c., already named and the many others unnamed, doing loving service for the Master in the person of His needy children, the German Capital has also an invested fund of $6,500,000, the income of which is devoted chiefly to the care of invalids and their needy families—a class among which especially Deacons and Deaconesses carry on their merciful work. And if all this many-sided ministry of love and mercy is evidence that "religion in Berlin* is dead or dying," where in all the regions of emptiness is religion alive?

* We have reports from over thirty other City Mission Societies in Germany, found scattered as follows: In Breslau and five other cities in Silesia; in Königsberg and Gumbinnen, in the Prussias; in Wittenberg and Wernigerode, Saxony; in Frankfort-on-the-Main; in Hesse; in Hanover and Schleswig, Leipsic, Dresden and Potschappel; in Lübeck, Hamburg, Bremen, Schwerin, Pottsdam, Strassburg, Mülhausen, Oldenburg, and elsewhere. Anything like a detailed report of their workings would fill a volume.

CHAPTER XI.

EXAMPLES OF PRACTICAL CHRISTIANITY.

"Preaching the Gospel," in the popular conception of that term, is but a part of the great work which the Church of Christ is called to do. To approach the ignorant and unbelieving with a tract or a sermon, may evince utmost sincerity and the innocence of the dove; but to prepare the way for that approach by a practical act of mercy, love, sympathy, is more in accord with the wisdom of the serpent not only, but also with the method of the Master.

The realization of this broader view of preaching in the Lutheran Church has resulted in a marvelous multiplicity of organization for the relief of the suffering and forsaken. It is known under the general name of the Inner Mission. Faith and works are related as cause and effect, as fire and heat, and there is no proper preaching of the gospel where either is lacking. The popular humanitarianism which tacitly denies the existence of the soul in its engrossment with the needs of the body, is equally at fault with the ranting "evangelism" which ignores the body in anxiety for the soul. Man is made up of body and soul, and a gospel which disregards either is not the Gospel of Christ.

Anything like a presentation* of the Inner Mission work of the Lutheran Church is, of course, not contemplated here.

---

* Such a history of the Inner Mission work of the Lutheran Church was begun in Germany about twelve years ago. At this writing, six volumes of good size have appeared, and they cover but six of the political divisions of the German Empire. The facts and figures of this chapter are gleaned from that work.

P

All that is attempted is to show some examples, and, by calling attention to the practical Christian common sense in them, to lead to the more general introduction of like methods in the work of our dear Lutheran Church in America.

As an example, the province of Schleswig-Holstein may be cited. In addition to a general organization for Inner Mission work, in the province, there exist also various district and city societies, such as societies for maintaining neglected children,* for nursing the poor and sick, for caring for little children while their mothers go out to work, for care and employment of released prisoners, for the prevention and suppression of drunkenness, for the circulation of good literature, for the founding of libraries, for the culture of young people, &c.

These purely voluntary local societies not being able fully to cope with the difficulties, the aid of Deaconesses has been sought. Women's societies to the same end have been organized, and generally when a family, on account of sickness, is in need of aid, a woman is put in charge or a committee sees that the need is supplied. Many women's societies exist also for the support of day nurseries for little children whose mothers are at work. Most of these are now under direction of Deaconesses.

Schleswig-Holstein has two Deaconess Homes—one in

---

* In Kiel, for 100 years, such a society has been in existence. Two hundred of its members, under direction of a central committee, meet monthly in the society's interests. These are sub-divided into a Helping-Hand Committee, with a sub-committee for each section of the city; a Women's Committee for nursing the sick, with same divisions; the Education Committee; the Committee for Released Prisoners; the Labor Committee; the Committee for People's Libraries, &c. The aim, of course, is to labor among the classes from which the neglected children come, and thus lighten the society's burdens.

In Altona, a Women's Society for Caring for the Sick has a hospital with four Deaconesses, nursing 30 to 40 children daily. During 1885, it cared for sick persons in 265 families. It has a balance of nearly 25,000 marks in its treasury.

Flensburg, one in Altona. The latter was established* in 1868, and the following year founded an institution to train women to take charge of Day Nurseries, with a course of instruction covering a half year, at a cost of 30 marks a month. Next was added an Asylum for Infants, where children born in wedlock are cared for by two Deaconesses and three assistants, at a cost of one mark a week each. Then followed at short intervals a rural asylum for sick children, a home for invalids, a hospital for sick men, and the establishment of so-called stations, *i. e.*, fields of labor filled by Deaconesses in the service of other institutes or societies. Among these latter, in 1886, were twelve parishes, two to four Deaconesses each, and three hospitals, with three or four each.

The Deaconess Home in Flensburg started from the gift of a magistrate and his wife. A Deacon from the Rauhe Haus assists the Deaconesses. Outside the home parish,† the Deaconesses serve at forty-two stations, twelve of which are parishes, five are little children's schools, and six are hospitals.

Near Flensburg is "Martin Foundation" for neglected children ; also a Training Society for other parts of the province. In 1886, the members of the Training Society numbered 1,026, and they had 68 children in charge.‡

Altona has a Mission Society employing three missionaries, one of whom reports his year's work as follows : 889

---

* The original building cost 152,500 marks, and was opened with two Sisters. In 1886 an addition was built at a cost of 50,000 marks. In 1884, the expenses of the institution were 99,300 marks. In 1885, about 3,000 sick persons were nursed and 1,300 children cared for. Pastor Schäfer publishes the *Correspondenzblatt* in the interest of the Deaconess work, and the *Monatschrift* in behalf of the Inner Mission proper.

† The property of the institution has cost over 350,000 marks; its income in 1885 was 111,140 marks, and the number of Sisters employed was 73.

‡ The aim is to place the children in good homes. The society pays 120 marks a year for their care. Friends and relatives sometimes assist.

families on visiting list; 2,400 visits made; 117 sick persons visited, and care given to their bodily and spiritual wants; 38 heads of families helped to employment; in 38 households where children were neglected, better order introduced; a library of 300 volumes established for the parents and children; children's services established and the chapel filled, and the claims of those asking assistance investigated, so as to protect the worthy against the unworthy claimants.

These missionaries conduct industrial schools, one for the boys,* two for girls. The latter are in charge of a committee of women who instruct the children in sewing, knitting, mending and other handiwork.

To keep the children faithful after Confirmation, there exist three societies, two for young men, one for young women, each under direction of a city missionary. During the week instruction is given in German, music and reckoning, the members' house is open every evening and a short devotional service is held Sunday evening.

In Flensburg there is a Christian Inn erected at a cost of 32,372 marks, with an average of about forty guests a day. The Society for Young Men has its home in the Inn and its Bible Hours, &c., are attended by about 150 persons. In Neumünster is another such Inn, also the home of the Society for Young Men and the headquarters of compositors and pressmen. Ploen and Kiel have like establishments,† the one in the latter city sheltering nearly 14,000 guests annually.

---

* Open during the hours when the boys are not in school. The boys saw and split wood and are taught to make brushes and mats. After a period of probation, they receive pay for their work. In 1882, the earnings were 7,760 marks, less cost of raw materials.

† In the whole province of Schleswig-Holstein in 1890, there were 24 Christian Inns, conducted at immense cost. Means for the maintenance are secured through collections, societies, and private gift and bequest. The worth of the work they do in shielding young men from temptation and surrounding them with Christian influence is beyond computation.

In Altona there is a Christian Inn for maid-servants. It gives them temporary board and lodging at nominal cost, aids them to secure employment, and affords them pleasant rooms where they may read, write, &c., free from temptation. In 1885, this Inn had 257 guests.

Not far from Neumünster, in 1883, a Labor Colony was founded. The grounds were purchased, from the proceeds of a general call issued for the purpose, at a cost of 140,000 marks. In 1885, the colonists numbered 190, in twenty months 1,375 were received, of whom 588 were helped to places of employment. The maintenance stations in the Province in 1886, numbered thirty six.

The Young People's Societies of the Province, both for young men and young women, as also the societies for men, usually have their place of meeting in the local Christian Inns. The purpose of the organizations is seen in the following: Certain evenings of the week are given to general culture; they cultivate music, assist in church concerts and anniversary celebrations; the majority of them aid in the circulation of good literature.*

The Schleswig-Holstein Publication Society is a branch of the Province's Inner Mission Society. It employes colporteurs, establishes parish libraries, and thus aims to circulate good books, papers, and pictures. It has a book-store in Neumünster which is also a depository for any literature which is not unchristian.†

The Society for Inner Mission employs ten messengers who go through the Province, visit families, hold Bible-Hours, sell or give away good books, and report their work quarterly to the officials.

---

* For example, in one year, the Men's and the Young Men's Societies of Kiel distributed 22,100 sermons for the people among the poor, the sick and the desecrators of the Lord's Day.

† The circulation of printed sermons, which has grown to great dimensions, is secured largely through the aid of the Young People's Societies, helpers in the Sunday schools, and the newly confirmed.

Since 1874, collections have been taken by the Churches of the Province for the Deaconess Home at Altona, for the Inner Mission work, and for the Asylum for released female prisoners. The total contributions for the Inner Mission work in Schleswig-Holstein are about 500,000 marks.

Since 1876 an institution has existed in Brecklum to train missionaries for the home and foreign field. Its foreign field is in India, where it has five stations and eleven missionaries. Kropp also has various institutions to a like end. A pro-seminary, a Preacher's Seminary, a Boy's School with the special design of aiding boys without means, in preparing for the gymnasium.

The Kingdom of Würtemberg * may be cited as another illustration of thoroughness of organization for works of mercy among the suffering and destitute. It has a general organization for Inner Mission work, with headquarters at Stuttgart, and local organizations covering almost every form of need.

For many years Würtemberg has ranked among the highest in activity and liberality in behalf of both home and foreign missions. Two hundred and forty of her sons are in the foreign mission fields. One of her mission institutes has sent over a hundred pastors to labor among Germans in America. Much of the support of the Basel Mission House is from her churches, which also make offerings for the Bible Society, for the Gustavus Adolphus Union, for numerous orphans' homes, refuges for neglected children, asylums for the deaf, the dumb, and the blind, an institution for epileptics and idiots and a Magdalen asylum.†

---

* In 1876 the little kingdom's provident institutions and charities numbered 105 and 4,311 respectively, had a capital of over $15,000,000 and an annual income of $1,570,000. These are independent of the Inner Mission proper, though working to the same end.

† Pfleidner quotes Wichern as saying: "There is no country in all Germany where inner missions are so fostered or so blessed as in Würtemberg and its capital." At the time of his writing, the *Ev. Sontaggs-*

The Würtemberg Society of Beneficence is now in existence over 72 years, has a capital of 408,000 marks, and an income of 337,500 marks. It aids 43 societies and institutions in caring for neglected children;* 150 poor young men and women in fitting themselves for gaining a livelihood; 228 institutions to care for little children; a school at Heilbronn to train nurses for the sick; 32 institutions devoted to the care of the sick and the suffering; the National Industrial Institute in Stuttgart; congregations in establishing local libraries and reading rooms, and especially 27 societies and institutions directly under its control. It aids in all possible ways the course of instruction for Inner Missions established in Stuttgart, works with the Women's Societies, with the Würtemberg Sanitary Society of the Red Cross, and circulates *Blättern für das Armenwesen*, which is now in its 43d year. †

In 1880 Würtemberg reported 288 schools for little children, with 23,927 children cared for by 312 trained attendants and 52 helpers. The Kaiserswerth Seminary for training teachers for such schools, at that time had sent out over 1,000 candidates.‡ Not only in Germany, but in England, France, Austro-Hungary, Switzerland, Italy, Russia, and among the Kaffirs and the Hottentots such schools were then in existence.

The Evangelical Association of Stuttgart employs six city missionaries and nine mission workers through the Kingdom. Among its other works are the publication and

blatt, published at Stuttgart, had a circulation of 115,000, and the *Christenbote*, at the same place, 30,000.

* Würtemberg has an area of about one-sixth that of Pennsylvania. It has one of these institutions for every 175 square miles, or for every district 12x14½ miles in size. A like proportion would give Pennsylvania 260 of them.

† *Fliegende Blätter*, April, 1890.

‡ Schaefer—*Weibliche Diakonie*, II: 15, 261.

circulation of good literature, * care of released prisoners, gathering of funds to build chapels, the establishing of courses of instruction to train men for the Inner Mission work.

The School Teachers' Aid Society in one year assisted 41 teachers, 25 teachers' orphans, and 221 teachers' widows.

The Stuttgart Young Men's Society, now in existence 25 years, has two society houses and a home for apprentices, † with 70 beds. One of the houses is now a Christian Home for Journeymen, by its side is a Christian Inn sheltering about 10,000 travelers annually, and another society is erecting another guest-house with which a hospice is to be connected.

The Society for the Care of Factory Girls in Stuttgart has an Inn with 148 beds, for the use of which a charge of one mark per week is made. Board is furnished at equally low cost, and not a few of the guests have been there for years.

The Zoar home for the day-care of little children, an asylum for little children, a society for the care of sick country people, which aided 309 families in a year, the Good Samaritan Society, caring for men and women released from prison, an institution for eye diseases, caring for over 2,000 patients within a year, and a society to aid students preparing for the ministry—are some of the other organizations of Stuttgart to carry on the Master's work among His needy people.

The Kingdom of Würtemberg, not unmindful of those to whom, under God, it owes the enviable place it holds, has an invested fund of $460,000 for the relief of needy pastors, their widows and orphans.

---

* The Literature Committee distributes about a million copies of papers and magazines annually.

† A Young People's Society has a home for apprentices and with it an eating house where breakfast is served for 12 pfennig, dinner for 30, and supper for 23, and applicants have to be turned away.

The Provincial Society for Inner Missions of the Lutheran Church of Saxony numbers 454 members, of whom more than half are pastors or laymen trained for the work. The Christian Inns of the province number 47, with 1,400 beds and 800 guests daily: there are 19 Central Stations for the care of the poor and the sick; a labor colony flourishes and societies of men and young men number 106, under direction of the Provincial Society. The Deaconess Home in Dresden has 302 sisters, of whom 193 labor at 102 outside stations, the rest in the home parish. The Brothers' House in Ober-Gorbits has 45 Brothers, of whom 32 have charge of institutions for neglected children, Christian Inns, &c. In Leipsic and Dresden there are 104 members of the order of the Red Cross, for works of mercy. A publication society circulates 31,000 copies of its *Volkskalender*, about 12,000 copies of sermons each week, and sells books annually to the amount of 40,000 marks. Six labor societies are managed.

The Provincial Society has 30 city and district societies as helpers. A committee issues, for the guidance of the people, catalogues of the best publications for people's libraries. Saxony has ten asylums for neglected children, four of which are managed by Rauhe House Brothers. Brothers from the same institution direct a Christian Inn in Chemnitz, costing 68,214 marks, having last year nearly 11,000 transient guests, besides regular lodgers, and a home for the poor with 200 inmates.

The Dresden Society for Inner Missions conducts a kindergarten for children of the poor. Its average attendance last year was 77, with an average attendance for each child of 260 days. A sewing society for instruction of girls of 12 to 14 years, during the last quarter of the past year had sixty pupils. The society also conducts a boys' labor and saving society, having a membership of 300, the object being to train boys to habits of industry and economy. During the past year the society provided for 34 neglected children of the dangerous classes, and held many childrens' services. One of the aims of the society is to keep young men and young women in close connection with the church.* To this end they are visited, the former are invited to join the Learners' or the Young Men's Society; the latter, the Sunday Society. As a result, there are in Dresden seven Young Men's Societies, two Learners' Societies, and two Sunday Societies for confirmed girls.

Another practical idea of the City Mission Society of Dresden is a committee to oversee the erection of healthful houses of low cost, to be rented or sold to the worthy on easy payments. During the past five years, the committee has provided such houses with a total of 240 rooms.

Dresden also has a Training Institute for Inner Missions.

Deacons and Deaconesses work side by side in works of mercy in the various districts of Saxony.† Among their works are the care of numerous hospitals ; 140 kindergartens for very small children of needy parents; 10 training schools for wayward children ; 3 asylums for sickly children ; 47 Christian Inns‡ which last year sheltered 220,000 guests ; 5 homes for servant girls ; 1 home for tramps ; 2 Magdalen homes for fallen girls.

The Brandenburg Society for Inner Missions has 38 Chris-

* The Church Extension Society of Leipsic has resolved to imitate the example of other German cities in the construction of a portable church, to be used by newly organized congregations until they can be provided with permanent houses of worship. Why might not this plan be practicable in the rapidly growing mission work in American cities?

† The annual offering of the people for Inner and Foreign Missions are about 375,000 marks, representing as many days' labor of a laboring man. The gratuitous work done by Deacons, Deaconesses and freewill helpers, who serve without money compensation, is beyond computation.

‡ More than half of these Inns provide free shelter and board for those destitute of means, and they all furnish board and lodging at figures ridiculously small.

tian Inns outside of Berlin. They are for traveling journeymen or mechanics, for mechanics located at work, and for places of assembly for all kinds of Christian Societies. They provide abundance of the best papers and usually a library of good books. The authorities say 20 more are needed. In 107 cities and towns of the Province there are 998 guilds, of which 468 have a care for Christian Inns.

The Society, assisted by other organizations, provides maintenance for poor wanderers, in exchange for work, cares for released prisoners, has aided in organizing a society against the misuse of strong drinks, in the erection of an institution for the reformation of drunkards, and aids the mission work among sailors and boatmen.

In this Province the Society has 85 little children's schools, 115 places for children's services, 40 houses for correction, 45 Young People's Societies, 48 Girls' Sunday Societies, 38 Christian Inns, 2 inns for servant girls, 73 societies for the care of the poor and the sick. Aiding all these, in 41 parishes Deaconesses are at work, and 11 Brothers * labor in nine different institutions of mercy or correction, while six city societies and as many district societies work toward the same end.†

The Churches in Hanover are active in relief of the needy and an account of their merciful ministration is but a repetition of that which characterizes the whole German Church. A few of its provisions deserve special attention. For example—fourteen Women's Homes for single or widowed women in need of help; an island in the sea at the disposal

---

* An idea of the work of the Deacons or Brothers may be gotten from the following: Four conduct Houses of Safety for children; three manage Christian Inns; two are in the Training Home for Children; while one is in charge of a Home and School for Incorrigibles, with 80 children in his care, and another in an Institute for weak-minded and epileptics, having charge of 60 patients.

† A benevolent building society of Frankfort is doing practical mission work. It has erected 55 houses for poor people, at a cost of 78,000 marks, and 1,008 persons have homes in them.

of pastors and teachers, where at nominal cost, they may enjoy the benefits of surf-bathing and sea-air; a labor institution conducted by a Brother, for the benefit of those who do not like to work; in the city of Hanover, a home for young women employed in fancy stores; a servants' home where they have a safe retreat when out of employment, or a place where, in leisure hours, they may read, write, or meet friends; and coffee-houses.*

One of the oldest and most widely known institutions of mercy in Europe is at Halle, Prussian-Saxony. It was begun in 1695 by Augustus Hermann Francke. At his death it consisted of a training college in which 80 pupils and 70 teachers were receiving instruction; the Latin School of the Orphan Asylum, with 3 inspectors, 32 teachers, 400 pupils, and 10 servants; schools for poor children in the town, with 4 inspectors, 106 teachers and 1,725 boys and girls; and the orphanage proper, with 100 boys, 34 girls, and 10 attendants. He also had established a cheap dining-table, which was attended by 250 students and 360 other poor scholars, an apothecary's shop and a book-store.

A leader among the Pietists, any instruction which neglected the religious nature of the pupil, to Francke was an abomination. All the instruction in his institutions was on a strictly Christian basis. Even in his Latin School, the heathen classics were treated with slight respect and homilies took the place of heathen history.

To the institutions left at his death, many others have been added. The whole number of pupils in the orphanage and schools is now 3,500. The instruction imparted still retains its deep religious character, though the severely ascetic character of the discipline has been somewhat relaxed.

---

* In the city of Hanover, the societies against the misuse of intoxicating drinks have taken the matter in hand in earnest. They have established coffee-houses to draw men away from the saloons, and so successful have they been that it is now proposed to establish a net-work of them to cover the kingdom.

Pomerania has one feature of christian endeavor which is worthy of consideration because of the possibilities it suggests. It is a labor colony * in farther Pomerania. During the year it had 305 colonists and the daily cost of providing for each was 26 pfennig, about 6¼ cents. The originator of labor-colonies is Pastor Bodelschwing, director of the celebrated colony near Bielefield in Westphalia. The labor colony touches closely upon the peace and good order of the State and is receiving more and more of the attention of public men.†

---

* Twenty-one of these colonies now exist in Germany. Because of them the number of homeless tramps in Central Germany has decreased 40 per cent. within ten years. In Saxony, from 1883 to 1887, the number of persons committed to houses of correction decreased from 1,805 to 1,260 a year; and in Prussia, from 1882 to 1887, the numbers decreased from 24,327 to 15,252. See *Amtskalender*, 1890, p. 194.

† An interesting experiment in the way of furnishing labor for people out of employment is reviewed by an article on the "German man Labor Colonies" in the *Quarterly Journal of Economics*. The German labor-colonies are established by a charitable organization, founded by a clergyman named Bodelschwing eight years ago. Twenty-one of them have been located in various parts of the empire, all but one of them being in the wilder agricultural sections. Men also, for lack of better work, obtain admission to them, work at tilling the ground, the reclamation of waste land, forest culture and the trades necessary to supply the wants of the colonies. For two weeks their work is only paid by their board and lodging, after which they are paid small wages, considerably below the current pay; but sufficient to permit most of the men to have a small sum to their credit when they leave the colonies.

This experiment, it is alleged, has materially diminished vagrancy and mendicancy in the localities where these colonies have been established. It takes away the pretext of the begging tramp that he cannot obtain employment, by offering him a means of earning his living; and if such a wanderer refuses the employment offered to him he can be turned over to the authorities.

The plan, though evidently incomplete, has a foundation of strength in its recognition of the duty of society to organize practical means of recognizing that it owes every man a living. If it is Socialism to assert that, it is a class of socialism that has been fully established in the poor laws of England and America for many years; but the trouble is that the discharge of the debt is generally incomplete and careless. Society

In Westphalia, near Bielefeld, is a colony* for epileptics, especially for those who are no longer able to follow their usual vocations. For the 800 and more patients, forty houses have been erected, and they have their own church edifice.

As experience has shown it hurtful for patients to be idle, the aim is to keep every one employed. Many work-stations are therefore maintained; agricultural stations for those who were farmers, stations for gardeners, painters, tailors, shoemakers, bakers, printers, bookbinders, &c. There are also schools for the young, and special houses for those who suffer from other diseases beside epilepsy. In addition to the earnings of the patients, the yearly expenses of the colony are about 150,000 marks.

The Evangelical Workingmen's Societies are another feature of German Inner Mission work. They are organized on the basis of the Church Confessions and of fidelity to Kaiser and Fatherland. Their aims are: to strengthen evangelical consciousness among the members of the Church; to cherish love for the Fatherland and the lawfully reigning House; to further the moral uplifting and the general culture of the members; to strengthen friendly relations between employers and employed; to assist members to work and keep free from debt in times of labor troubles. The papers for workingmen, published by the Inner Mission Society, are widely circulated among them. Each society has its own place of assembly, meets regularly, has its own library. To counteract socialism, the libraries are well upplied with works on the labor question. Physicians address the assemblies on health topics, lawyers on legal topics of gen-

---

owes every man the opportunity to earn a living, and every man owes to society the earning of that living when he has the opportunity.—*The Public Ledger, Philadelphia.*

* Similar colonies exist at Stettin, near Reinstedt, near Rastenburg, Potsdam, and at Rothenberg in Hanover. Westphalia has its own Brothers' House for training men to care for these unfortunates.

eral interest, and members of other professions add their services, each in his own line.*

Societies of Christian Young Men, also, in large number, exist in Germany, as also in Scandinavia. Their aim is to protect the confirmed youth against the dangers of the world, to cultivate personal piety and the habit of the study of God's Word, and by all right means to cultivate a spirit of fidelity to the Church and patriotism to the Fatherland. There is a central organization for East Germany, one for West Germany, one for North, one for Thuringia, and one for Southeast Germany. Each society has its library. The West German Alliance has 263 local societies and a membership† of 15,279, and has 433 workers in Inner or Foreign Missions.

At a recent Inner Mission Congress in Germany, one of the speakers, appointed to discuss "Inner Missions and the Press," prefaced his address with the remark that if the Apostle Paul were living to-day, he would be the editor of a religious paper. What papers are now, the pamphlets were in the Reformation, and to them we owe it, in large part, that nine-tenths of Germany became evangelical. The quantity of such literature circulated and its influence are enormous.‡ Societies for its dissemination exist throughout the empire, and special attention is given to having it read in factories, workshops, hotels, Christian Inns, restaurants, and on boats, ships, and among railroad men and such as are obliged to work on Sundays. These same societies also labor to establish people's libraries, and to see that they are

---

* Music constitutes a part of each meeting's program. "Family evenings" are usually held quarterly, and are of a social character. The latest statistics at hand give the total of members, 186 societies, at 92,000.

† This organization has its own organ, the *Youth's Messenger*. The "Alliance Harp," a book of hymns and songs for the society's use, is in its second edition.

‡ For the work that good literature is doing in Germany, consult the chapter on City Missions.

supplied with the very brightest and purest literature in existence. The best minds have given time and labor without stint to the examination of books, and published catalogues of the most helpful of them for the guidance of those to whom is committed the duty of replenishing the people's libraries. Colportage houses and societies work along with them, keeping men ever going from house to house to gain admission for good literature.

Mission literature is not popular in the United States. A periodical devoted to such literature may live and it may not. But in Lutheran lands across the sea, scores of papers devoted to such work attain a circulation of 10,000 to 115,000 each, while monographs on religious subjects have reached a circulation of 240,000 each, and at least one book on Missions * has attained the enormous sale of 755,000 copies. The principal Inner Mission Societies have each its own organ. The leading Deaconess Homes also. The Norwegian Foreign Mission periodical appears in an edition of 10,000, while the Friend of the Lord's Day, in Berlin, has a circulation of 44,000, and Kaiserswerth Volkskalender, 113,000.

Perhaps the first society ever formed with the sole purpose of providing the Holy Scriptures for those who were without them, was by Baron von Canstein. He obtained a large amount of money by subscription and was the first to issue the Bible from sterotype plates. An edition appeared in 1712,† the New Testament at a cost of about eight cents, and the whole Bible for about twenty-five cents. Up to 1854, 4,612,000 Bibles and 2,630,000 New Testaments had been sold.

---

* In the line of Mission-publications, Finland has regular issues of 12,000 copies; Sweden, of 14,000; Norway, of 18,000; Denmark, of 21,600, while nearly everything coming from Warneck's pen, in Germany, attains a circulation of 20,000 to 25,000 copies.

† This Lutheran Bible Society in Halle antedates all others. The British and Foreign Bible Society bears date, 1802; the American Bible Society, 1817.

Four of ten women's societies in the Fatherland, organized purely for works of mercy, report yearly receipts of 561,000 marks ; six of the ten report 54,430 members, and eight of the ten report 300 persons employed by them in charitable work.

Inner Mission authorities rejoice greatly over a late report of the German Privy Councillor in which are given statistics, covering the years from 1881 to 1889, of arrests ‡ made in Prussia. They are as follows: Number of persons arrested and detained in Prussian jails, for the year 1881-1882, 620,404. For 1888-1889, 384,927. The decrease in the period named is about 37 per cent. The decrease the last year was 66,222, or nearly 14 per cent. of the total of arrests for the previous year. And it can hardly be doubted that the wonderful development of the Inner mission work has had much to do with these gratifying results.

The number of arrests and convictions on serious charges are not numerous. A list of convictions for all Prussia, including the crimes of duelling, treason, false coining, robbery, incendiarism, child-murder, murder with robbery, manslaughter and murder, covering a period of 37 years, shows only 988 sentences, an average of about $26\frac{1}{2}$ for each year. Of these, 404 were for murder, an average of 11 per year; 391 were for manslaughter, murder with robbery, and child-murder, an average of $10\frac{2}{3}$ per year; giving an average of convictions in cases in which life was taken of about 22 per year,* or about one for each million of population.†

---

‡ Most of the arrests are for what we should call trivial offenses, from one-half to two-thirds of them being for violation of the forest laws.

* Kolb, Condition of Nations.

† In a single issue of the *Public Ledger*, Philadelphia, recently, under the head of criminal news, there were reports of nine murders, eight other murderous attacks, and one suicide.

Q

CHAPTER XII.

AMONG THE DIASPORA, THE ISRAELITES, THE SEAMEN AND
IN CITIES.

Nowhere, perhaps, are family relationships more closely knit, birthdays more joyously celebrated, parents more highly honored, than among the Germans. And as the love of kindred is thus marked, a like interest may be expected when the appeal is to the higher motives of Christian fellowship and sympathy. And this expectation is realized in the care with which German Lutherans have endeavored to provide for the spiritual wants of their countrymen in other lands.

To meet their needs, the Diaspora Conference was organized. Its object is to acquaint the church with their condition and provide them with the Means of Grace. It is now sending young men, trained in German gymnasiums, to America, to finish their theological education here and to labor among German immigrants. Four of the Foreign Mission Societies have sent out 350 Diaspora Missionaries, most of them to North America, others to South America and Australia. Five Inner Mission Institutes have sent nearly 800 to North America, and six other institutes have been established especially to train such missionaries. About 1,500 of these men, generally in deep privation, are now at work among their scattered brethren.*

---
* Of the Societies sending laborers to North America, the following have Mission Schools in which they are prepared.

It is now a little more than two hundred and fifty years since Gustavus Adolphus, in defence of Protestantism, laid down his life on the battlefield of Lützen. When the two hundredth anniversary of that event was celebrated (in 1832) it was proposed in Germany to erect a monument in his honor. A Lutheran pastor suggested that the best monument would be a society to propagate the faith for which he died. From this suggestion sprang the Gustavus Adolphus Union, which has for its object the aiding of feeble Protestant churches in predominantly Roman Catholic countries. It has auxiliary societies all over Germany, in Scandinavia and in the Netherlands.* It has done a glorious work for Protestantism.

In the 51 years of its existence it has expended 22,566,620 marks. Outside of Germany it aids congregations in Austria, Italy, Spain, France, South America and the Orient. In 1889 it erected four schools, ten churches and gave aid to 1,444 congregations.‡ The liberal basis of the Gustavus Adolphus Union, aiding Lutheran, Reformed and United Protestants, not being satisfactory to all, gave occa-

Basel,	No. of Students,	90	St. Crischona,	No. of Students	56
Herrmannsburg,	" "	48	Neuendettelsau,	" "	23
Gossner,	" "	?	Steeden,	" "	24
Berlin,	" "	30	Gross Ingersheim,	" "	?
Brecklum,	" "	?	Rauhe Haus,	" "	33
Kropp,	" "	64	Duisburg,	" "	32

Twenty societies and institutions have sent pastors, theolgical students or teachers hither, about two-thirds of whom have identified themselves with the Lutheran Church, the others having gone into the United or Reformed communions.

* There are 45 principal and 1,810 auxiliaries, with receipts aggregating $278,000 per annum. Of the auxiliaries 461 are managed by women and contributed $30,000.

‡ It has aided in all 3,015 missions; built wholly or in part 1,925 churches and schools; erected 864 parsonages; bought sites for 1,055 parsonages and churches; raised endowments for 624 churches and schools; aided 1,603 pastors and teachers; secured 1,270 places for divine services; furnished 820 schools or churches; operates 303 deaconess or orphan institutes and homes; established 49 gymnasiums and seminaries; supported traveling preachers; bought cemeteries and aided widows.

sion for the organization of another society known as the *Gotteskasten*, which confines its work to the Lutheran Diaspora.

The Evangelical League, formed to resist the aggresions of the Roman Catholics, in Germany, consists of 30 principal and more than 400 auxiliaries, with 76,000 members. Since Socialism has become prominent, it resists also its advances, and, indeed, opposes whatever hinders the progress or endangers the peace of the Evangelical Church. In its convention at Stuttgart, 1890, it adopted these four ringing resolutions: First, That the Socialistic agitations can be quelled only through the moral and spiritual power of the principles of the Reformation. Second, That it distrusts the Roman professions of peace and good-will so long as the Pope is proclaimed the head of the one only Christian Church. Third, That it protests against the recall of the Jesuits; and Fourth, That it protests against Roman interference in the school affairs of the Empire.

If anything could show the supremacy of the Pope in the dark conspiracy for the enslavement of man, it would be such opposition to his encroachments arising in opposite quarters of the earth, for the same battle must be fought here in America, against the same insidious power, as that which has been waged for centuries in Europe.

The Lutherstiftung is a society in Germany with 18 principal and 140 auxiliary organizations and a capital of 224,500 marks. Last year 24,123 marks were divided among the needy families of deceased pastors and teachers.

The Aid Society for Evangelical Churches, reported in 1890 an income of 175,400 marks. The Berlin City Mission was aided to the extent of 40,000 marks. The Emperor and Empress gave 6,000 marks. This is a recent organization formed to meet the need for city evangelization arising from the rapid growth of German cities. The State has been either unwilling or unable to provide adequate church accommodations for the rapidly increasing population of the great centres of commerce and manufacture. As a result the city parishes have become unmanageable, Zion's parish in Berlin, for example, having 140,000 souls. Naturally a new heathenism is growing up in the midst of Christianity in such cities as Berlin, Leipsic, Munich, Frankfort, Breslau and Hamburg, a heathenism which is not passive but active in its opposition to Christianity. When the Statistical Bereau announced, recently, that since the compulsory baptismal law had been abrogated, ten thousand children had been allowed to remain unbaptized in the capital city, the fiendish shout of triumph went up from one of the prominent journals: "Hurrah for the first ten thousand heathens in Berlin!" This was simply giving tongue to the infidel and pagan diabolism which the Aid Society is contending against.

Largely through the influence of Court Chaplain Stoecker, a work was begun in Berlin which is spreading through all the cities of Germany. Sermons are distributed in editions of more than 100,000 weekly; mission houses have been built, several dozen missionaries appointed for Berlin alone, a house to house visitation of the great metropolis organized, prayer-meetings instituted, Sunday schools opened, and all the machinery of evangelization brought into the service by members of the church, independently of the church, but with the welfare of the church in view.

Missions for seamen are carried on by members of the German churches, in Swedish and Norwegian ports, in Rotterdam, Stettin, Hamburg, in various ports in Great Britain, among the rivermen in Germany, and aboard German merchantmen. The work consists in preaching, distributing good books and papers, and, wherever it is possible, in building Seamen's Homes and chapels.

To lead the Jews to Christ was a desire that lay near to Luther's heart. The same desire moved the warm hearts of Spener, Edzardus and others to an effort to acquaint the children of Abraham with the truths of the Gospel. Here and there pastors labored to instruct such Jews as were resident in their neighborhoods, but the effort was not systematic and little was accomplished.

In the early years of the eighteenth century, John Henry Callenberg came forth as the earnest friend of the Jews, revealing his love in his works. By his side labored Fromman, a young physician, a Jew by birth, a Christian by conviction. Beginning with the printing of books in the Jewish-German dialect, they issued the Gospel according to St. Luke, the Acts of the Apostles and other books, secured the sympathy and help of Francke, and established the Institutum Judaicum to train men for work among the Jews. A printing press was bought and, in the Jewish-German type and later, in the type for the Turkish, Persian and Malayan tongues, the works that came from it went to Russia, to Holland, to Farther India. Books were also printed in Arabic, in the hope that the Mohammedans might be reached.

One of the aims of the Institute was to translate Christian literature into the Hebrew tongue, that being the preference of both the learned and half-learned of the class which the aim was to reach. It was found expedient, also, to make translations into Italian; and to reduce the ever-increasing cost, a house was purchased in which the work might be done with the least expense. Students of theology volunteered to act as colporteurs.*

In the first four years of their work, 21,500 copies of the Institute's publications were circulated among Jews; they were, often, read with interest; and one of the leading missionaries reported that, during the first 40 years of the work, not fewer than 1,000 Jews were converted to the Christian faith.

The work soon went beyond Germany,‡ into Bohemia,

---
* Their pay was two florins a week, about 96 cents—enough to meet only their most necessary expenses. They were to circulate the books and instruct all who would receive instruction.

‡ The proposal of a contribution of $50 yearly, by a pastor in

Poland, Denmark, and in England received the attention of the Society for the Propagation of the Gospel, to which Callenberg sent official reports of the work and the plans of the Institute.

Toward the close of the century, this mission among the Jews, which had been prosecuted with considerable of success, was taken up and carried forward by friends of Israel in Saxony, Bavaria, Norway and England, and thus was the eighteenth century endeavor in behalf of the Israelites, connected with that of the nineteenth.

The most prominent worker in behalf of the Jews in our century, has been Dr. Delitzsch. More than fifty years have elapsed since he began the translation of the New Testament into Hebrew. On the fiftieth anniversary of that event, an appeal was issued to his former students for a jubilee fund to distribute the work among Israelites. The translation met with a warm reception and perhaps no other agency in modern times has done more than it to bring the Jews to their true Messiah. It has now passed through nine editions and the tenth is in preparation.

The total of societies now laboring among Israelites is 47 —more than double the number of ten years ago: the missionaries number 377; the stations, 135. In Germany, including the Central organization, seven societies exist for Jewish work, having an income of 63,780 marks. Thirty-eight missionaries are employed among the Israelites, in addition to missionaries to the same classes in the larger cities, of whom there are 30, Berlin having three and Hamburg and Breslau, each six.

Sweden, for a third missionary, resulted in the appointment of Stephen Shultz, who labored in Germany, England, Holland, Denmark, Sweden, Russia, Poland, Hungary, Illyria, Italy, Egypt, Syria and Lesser Asia. He began preparation for his 6,000 mile journey, by a study of the Arabic, Turkish, Armenian and later-Greek tongues, understood twenty-five languages, and used fifteen of them as his mother tongue. On his return from the Orient, he was called to a pulpit in Halle, and with the death of the founder of the Institute, he became its head.

The Evangelical Lutheran Central Society for missions among the Jews, is composed of societies in Saxony, Würtemberg, Mecklenburg-Schwerin, Bavaria, Denmark and Norway. It has its seat in Leipsic.*

The Leipsic Seminary for the training of theological candidates for the mission among Israelites is under the direction of The Leipsic Central Society. Dr. Delitzsch, in his day, was the Director; under him, instruction was given by four other professors. Students' Jewish Mission Societies exist in many of the German universities,—Leipsic, Erlangen, Breslau, Berlin, Halle, Rostock, Bonn. They also exist in Upsala, Sweden; in the seminary at Gnadenfeld; and the academical mission societies of Christiania and Copenhagen work, also, in the interests of these missions.

Societies to better the outward condition of the Jews exist in St. Petersburg, Frankfurt, Neuchatel, Schaffhausen, &c. A society in Berlin to aid converts, exists since 1836; an asylum for the same class exists in Kishineff; another exists in Basel, (since 1844,) and there is one also in Stockholm, Sweden. In Prussia and in Mecklenburg-Schwerin, offerings are gathered for these societies on each tenth Sunday after Trinity. Mission festivals are held in their interest in Leipsic, Stuttgart, &c. Seven Jewish mission periodicals are published in Germany.

The Berlin Society, established 1822, had for many years a firm frend in Tholuck. The Basel Society, organized in 1830, aims to provide for the wants of converts, and has an asylum for this purpose. The Evangelical Mission of Moscow labors among the Jews, as a part of its foreign work. Work has been begun along the same lines by the Evangelical Churches of the Baltic Provinces. In Denmark,

* Its directory consists of Count Vitzthum, Prof. Kohler of Erlangen, Director Fetzer in Stuttgart, and of another elected to fill the place left vacant by the death of Delitzsch. Its income is about 18,000 marks; and it owns a bookstore and a bazar. Its missionaries travel through the lands of the Carpathians, and aid in the training of proselyte children.

Sweden, Norway and Finland also, societies to the same end are in operation. The work is carried on chiefly by means of literature, the most effective of which has been Delitzsch's Hebrew translation of the New Testament. Within eight years 50,000 copies of this book have been distributed among the Jews of the East. The missionaries visit them in their homes, distribute tracts, sermons and the New Testament, preach wherever opportunity can be found, and in all things labor to show that the historical Christ is the fulfilment of the Law and the Prophets.

The missionary, de la Roi, of Breslau, states that within the present century, more than 100,000 Jews have been baptized. The Statistical Bureau of Prussia has reported 1,888 Jews baptized in the nine old provinces of that kingdom within the last fifteen years.*

---

* SOCIETIES FOR MISSIONS AMONG ISRAELITES.
  1. *Institutum Judaicum;* 5 profs.; Leipsic; trains missionaries for the work.
  2. University-Students' Soc's.; at Leipsic, Erlangen, Berlin, &c.
  3. "Jubilee Fund," to circulate Delitzsch's Hebrew New Testament: over 50,000 copies circulated in the East.

Name of Society.	Head Quarters.	When Org'd.	Receipts.	Fields.
			Marks.	
Berlin, for Promotion of Christianity Among the Jews	Berlin	1822	18,000	Berlin.
For Care of Jewish Proselytes	Berlin	1836	?	Berlin.
Basel, Friends of Israel	Basel	1834	8,000	Asylum for Converts.
Rhenish and Westphalian	?	1843	20,000	Antwerp and the Rhineland.
Ev. Lutheran Central	Leipsic	1849	63,800	Saxony, Bavaria, Hesse and South Russia.
Saxon Soc. for Jewish Mis'ns. Mecklenburg " " " "				Work with the Ev. Luth Centl.
Würtemberg Soc. for Jewish Mis'ns	?	1874	5,000	Cities in Würtemberg.
Bavarian Ev. Luth. for Jewish Mis'ns	?	?	7,600	Kishineff. &c.
Swedish Soc. for Jewish Mis'ns	Stockholm	1874	31,950	Beyrout, Algiers Stockholm.
Nowegian Soc. for Jewish Mis'ns				Christiania, &c.
Danish Soc. for Jewish Mis'ns				
Finnish Soc. for Jewish Mis'ns				Helsingfors.
Moscow Ev. Soc. for Jewish Mis'ns				Russia.
Baltic Provinces Soc. for Jewish Mis'ns		1865		
Kishineff Soc. for Jewish Mis'ns		1864		Kishineff.
Norwegian Conference Soc. for Jewish Mis'ns	Minneapolis			Baltimore and St. Petersburg.
Missouri Synod Soc. for Jewish Mis'ns				

By force of their surroundings, Norwegians are familiar with the sea. Thousands of them there are at home. Their ships plough its waves wherever a vessel can float. Fifty thousand of these hardy sons of the North are sailors. For many long years they lived, while abroad, without the care and services of religion.

In 1864, under the lead of a candidate of theology,* Stor Johann, the Society for Preaching the Gospel to Scandinavian Seamen in Foreign Ports, was organized, with headquarters at Bergen. Since then they have sent pastors to Leith, Grangemouth, Alba, Dysart, Dundee, Glasgow, and Greenock. In 1883, there landed at these ports 1,589 Scandinavian vessels, having on board about 14,000 men. Missionaries have been sent to England for London, Shields, Newcastle, Hartlepool, Sunderland, Middlesborough, and Gateshead, where 10,000 seamen of Norway land during the year; for Belgium, to Antwerp, Ghent, and Lowen, which have from 10,000 to 12,000 Scandinavian sailors yearly; for Wales, Cardiff, Bristol, Swansea, and Newport; to Havre, France, and to Honfleur and Rauen; to Amsterdam and Rotterdam, Holland; to Quebec, Canada; and to New York, Philadelphia, and Pensacola. The income of the Society ‡ during the last two years has been 130,000 crowns.

A society for mission work among Norwegian Laplanders was formed in 1883. It has sent out two itinerant preachers to visit the people in their huts and tents, and has begun

---

* Pastor Stor Johann is now Principal of a Latin School at Christiania, in which he seeks to prepare young men for the University with the view of their entering the ministry.

‡ It owns the large Norwegian Seamen's Church in Brooklyn, N. Y., and supports one or more missionaries among the numerous Norwegian sailors who land there and at New York. It supports eleven regular Seamen's Mission Stations, with twelve churches, served by twelve pastors and seven assistants. Church buildings have been erected at Leith, Scotland; Shields, London and Bristol, England; Havre, France; Antwerp, Belgium; Amsterdam, Holland; Cardiff, Wales; Quebec, Pensacola, New York and Philadelphia.

the publication of parts of Holy Scripture and other books in their language.*

Norway is active also in all departments of mission work. The Norwegian Lutheran Society † is one of the leading organizations of the church.

About 25,000 fishermen are engaged in work in the North Sea. The Lutherans of Sweden minister to them through an organization known as the Mission among Deep-Sea Fishers. The Mission owns eight ships, each with a chapel in which regular services are conducted. The Societies of Sweden also sustain missionaries ‡ among their sea-faring countrymen in foreign ports, at Dunkirk, West Hartlepool, Kiel, Liverpool, Marseilles, Constantinople, Alexandria.

The Fatherland Society of Sweden is largely devoted to Inner Mission work, and to Work among Seamen in Foreign Ports. A hundred and twenty local organizations are connected with it. Over three hundred representatives work in its interests, the most of them pastors. It is an immense publishing concern, and furnishes the best devotional literature at a merely nominal cost. It publishes and circulates Bibles, commentaries, the works of Baxter, Bengel, Bogatzsky, Bunyan, Christlieb, Frances Havergal, Luther, Bickersteth, Neander, &c., in great abundance. Its agents have sold or distributed over 60,000 copies of Luther's works, and a half million Bibles and New Testaments. The sum

---

* Provost Bahl in *Allgemeine Missions-Zeitschrift*.

† It has for its aims the circulation of Holy Scripture, the printing and circulation of approved religious books, the education of young men as pastors and teachers. During the past year it distributed by sale or gift no fewer than 410,750 copies of its publications. The Missionary Society of the Church of Norway owns a ship which carries missionaries and supplies for its extensive mission fields among the Zulu and other tribes of Africa and the natives of Madagascar.

‡ Our latest reports give the number of their Seamen's Missions as 35. We have no figures of the total cost of the work, but note that 10,000 crowns were paid in support of it in one year at Kiel, West Hartlepool and Dunkirk.

total of writings sold or distributed amounts to 22,700,000. It employs 18 traveling missionaries and 137 colporteurs.

The Hessleholm Mission Society works mainly in the southern part of Sweden. It has 30 preachers and 7 mission houses, that at Hessleholm having a seating capacity of 2,000. The yearly receipts are about 5,000 crowns.

Western Skane is another mission society in southern Sweden. It has 23 preachers in its service, and has projected the erection of a mission house to seat 2,500 persons, the proposed cost to be 10,000 crowns. It has 6,000 members.

The Lutheran Mission Society of Stockholm has 2,300 members, and contributes 5,000 crowns annually to foreign missions. It employs six preachers in Stockholm and suburbs.

Students' missionary societies exist in the Swedish universities. They aggregate 195 members. Their object is to arouse missionary interest among the students.

A mission school is under the control of Pastor Ahlberg, who is specially interested in the work among Swedes in America.

The Fjellstedt school, for the education of missionaries, has eighty students and good buildings in Upsala.

The Swedes are firm friends of the cause of Jewish missions. They employ four pastors, all pupils of the Home for Proselytes at Stockholm, and a deaconess, who labors among Jewish women and children. The receipts of the society were 31,950 crowns.

The Missionary Society of Sweden has four orphan homes, with 56 orphans, among the Laplanders. Last year 26,328 crowns were expended in mission work among the Lapps.

The Swedish Mission Union maintains missionaries at St. Petersburg, in the Caucasus, and on the shores of the Polar Sea.

Danes planted a fort in Tranquebar, India, 1620 and

1621, sent a pastor and soon thereafter erected a church. This was made a Danish colony, and was maintained until 1837, when England bought the Danish possessions there. Franke's Foreign Mission Society was connected with this colony.

The Danes sent an expedition to Hudson's Bay, 1619-1620, with 66 men. The chaplain died soon after Christmas; the vessels were frozen in the ice, and but three men were spared to return to Denmark.

About 1658, the Danes also secured a footing on the Gold Coast of Africa. Regular settlements were made and towns located. Fredericksborg and Christiansborg date from 1659; Friedensborg, from 1735; and Kongsten, from 1783. Pastors were sent there in 1662, and though several of them died from the unhealthful climate, the supply was kept up until 1851, when Denmark sold her territory and the mission came to an end.

A. D. 1665, a Danish expedition was sent to the West Indies. From this resulted the possession of the islands of St. Thomas, St. Croix, and St. Jan. Pastors were sent, and have been continued to the present. While some have ministered to the Danish colonists and to the Scandinavian seamen who touch those ports, others have toiled among the negroes, and none of our American Lutherans are more devoted to their church than are these colored Lutherans of the West Indies. Denmark prohibited the slave trade in these islands as early as 1792, years before other nations took such a step.

The Danes gave attention also to the spiritual needs of their seamen. From 1619 to 1637, no fewer than 22 men were ordained for the spiritual care of the seamen in the East and West Indies alone. Many ships in the carrying trade went to China, and their chaplains were known as "China Pastors."

Whenever Denmark sent a Minister of Legation to a

Roman Catholic country a chaplain was commissioned to accompany him. The same thing was done at Protestant courts where the tongue of the people was strange to the official. Hence, as early as 1663, Lutheran chaplains preached the gospel in Vienna; in 1682, in Paris; and were sent, also, to Madrid, Naples and St. Petersburg.

In the same way, a Lutheran church was established in Dublin, 1698; and at Smyrna, on the Mediterranean, in 1767. About 1666, German and Norwegian Lutheran services were held in London, and a few years later a church-building was erected there.

To-day there are Danish pastors in London, Hull, New Castle, Paris, Havre; in Queensland, New Zealand, and at Capetown, Africa, to say nothing of the congregations scattered through the United States, or of the missions among the Tamils, the Red Karens, and the Santhals in India.

The work of the Danish Church in the Faroe Islands has resulted in connecting the church there with the church of Denmark.

The Lutheran Church Association for Home Missions in Denmark employs 79 missionaries, with a few exceptions paid by the association, owns 66 mission houses, and the periodical published in its interests has a circulation of nearly 20,000.

The Danish American Mission Society has sent about forty missionaries to America. Its receipts for this work are on the increase. Several years ago a Women's Society was organized in Copenhagen, the object of which is to aid Danish pastors in America who may be in needy circumstances.

The Church Society for Inner Missions, in Copenhagen, has for its object the building up of the kingdom of God among the people of the capital. It seeks to reach this end by the preaching of the Word and through works of Christian love. It stands on the basis of the churchly confessions. Its works are directed from its own mission house and from a Magdalen Home, also the property of the society. Twelve working branches of the society exist. It publishes its own periodical and has its own bookstore. The paper appears weekly, and aims to spread news of the works of the society and of inner missions generally. This society maintains 19 Sunday schools, whose aim is to gather old and young alike, who are aloof from the church, and lead them to the truth. The plan of instruction is so arranged that a five years' course covers the principal contents of the Bible. Along with the Sunday School instruction, children's services are held in the mission house for pupils of the higher educational institutions, and are largely attended.

The Christian Society for Young Men meets weekly for an exposition of Scripture or an address on heathen missions; each Sunday evening, for purposes of spiritual growth ; and once each week, to develop musical talent in singing. It also has a regular course of gymnastic training, and one of ordinary instruction. The "Union Cadettes" is a branch of this society, made up of youth between the ages of 14 and 17.

A Society of Christian Brothers is made up, chiefly, of married men. It meets once a week for prayer and exposition of Scripture ; and its members are at work, Sundays, among the poor and the weak in the "General Hospital." There is, also, an organization to forward Christian song, with the special aim of giving its aid in mission work.

Provision is made to gather the female workers in shops and factories, the servants in families, &c., each Wednesday evening for social enjoyment. The same idea has been extended, and weekly meetings of this kind are arranged for women in stores, and for poor mothers. "Sewing evenings" are held for the poor ; the sick in the hospitals are visited, and, under all circumstances and at all times, the effort is made to give aid to the spirit as well as to the body. A Flower-mission is kept up, the Queen, several women of the aristocracy, and other well-to-do residents of the capital providing the flowers.

The City Mission Society also provides for regular work among the cafés, saloons, inns, on board ships in the harbor, and among those who are following the ways of uncleanness. Its messengers are out as late as one and two o'clock A. M. remonstrating with evil-doers, helping the repentant, holding song and gospel-services, distributing tracts, periodicals, and copies of the Gospels. Over 100,000 tracts and papers, and 8,000 copies of the Gospels have been thus distributed in one year.

The Magdalen Home aims especially to look after the younger girls who, through their own fault or through the sins of others, are walking in the ways of shame.*

The society, during the year, had an income of 22,168 marks, apart from the income of the Magdalen Home; and its expenses, 21,303 marks. The yearly report showed a balance in the treasury of the Mission House of 865 marks; and in that of the Magdalen Home of 1,615. Denmark raises, yearly, about 22,700 crowns for seamen's missions.†

In the Baltic Provinces, there are various Church Societies ‡ and funds for advancing important interests. Such is

---

* It is open to those aged from 14½ to 25; no one is brought in in opposition to her own will. Girls are instructed for domestic service, and, if found trustworthy, places are secured for them. Some remain in the institution for a period of three years. The expenses for a year were 28,136 marks.

† Dr. Kalkar summed up the mission work of the Danish Church, for the Evangelical Alliance at New York, as follows: Missions to Heathen. Society of Deaconesses. Society of released convicts. Societies for prisons. Societies for infant Schools. Missions to Sailors. Society for sending Danish preachers to America. Societies for taking care of the sick, the blind, the idiotic, and others.

‡ Mission festivals are held in many of the cities. The Synods in the Baltic provinces and St. Petersburg are endeavoring to increase the in--

the Esthonian Fund for the increase of the Ministry, with a capital of 46,000 roubles; the Esthonian Publication Fund, with a capital of 50,000 roubles; the Esthonian Tract Union, founded in 1878, which has issued seven tracts in 28,000 copies; the Riga Tract Union, which has published 432 tracts and sections of the Bible, in 1,559,500 copies; the Evangelical Bible Society in Russia, which has distributed over 945,000 copies of the Bible; and the Fund for the Support of Evangelical Lutheran Congregations in Russia, which, in 1881, distributed nearly $35,000, and has recently taken under its care the Armenian Lutherans. Under the auspices of the last organization, circulating libraries of evangelical books have been established among the congregations of the diaspora, after the model of the Evangelical Library in St. Petersburg, with its 60,000 volumes.

The Finnish Mission Society cares, also, for the Lapps, who, because of the lack of ministers, are in danger of lapsing into heathenism. In a single year, it distributed 70,426 marks.

The Inner Mission Society of Finland, sends missionaries and colporteurs to all parts of the land, and their annual receipts are about 36,000 marks. In Helsingfors a mission school has been founded to train missionaries, especially foreign missionaries. A fund is being raised to erect in Helsingfors a mission house, and other funds are being collected for a missionary ship, and also for the erection of an institution to rescue fallen women. There is interest in the Jewish mission, for which a society has been organized, while much

---

terest. Their contributions go mostly to the Leipsic Society, which received in 1881, from the Lutheran Church in Russia, 29,599 marks. Missions to the Jews are also maintained. The Baltic Synod has a missionary and three schools for Jewish children, with 90 pupils. In 1881, from this mission, eleven proselytes were baptized. There is a mission house also in Kischineff, in which, in 1882, there were six baptisms. In St. Petersburg, there is a similar home for Jewish girls, with fifteen inmates.

R

practical Christian work is done for her excellent seamen and needy emigrants.

The Lutheran Evangelistic Society for Finland, located at Helsingfors, has done a grand work in translating, publishing and circulating Luther's writings and the leading theological and devotional works of our Church, not only in Finnish, but also in Swedish. It has its own publication house. Among other works, it employs ten colporteurs, and its capital is large. The *Missionary Tidings* is devoted to Foreign Missions, and circulates 7,600 copies. A Home Missionary paper also is published.*

The Finnish Bible Society was founded in 1812, and in 1880 distributed 6,824 copies of the Scriptures.

The Lutheran Church of Finland devotes attention to the sea-faring part of its people. The "Seamen's Mission" has a yearly income of $15,000 and three ministers in its employ, who visit the English ports. A fourth missionary will shortly go to Bordeaux and a fifth will be stationed at San Francisco. The Church does not lose sight of the Finnish exiles in Siberia and stretches forth a motherly hand to dismissed criminals and to the depraved youths. The students of Helsingfors university take great interest in city mission-work and in the ragged schools.

The Society to Aid Evangelical Lutheran Congregations in Russia, with headquarters at St. Petersburg, was organized April 19, 1859. Over $700,000 have been received from the beginning, and two hundred and nineteen pastorates are helped from its treasury. With its aid seventy-two churches, seventy-six prayer-houses, and fifty-four school and prayer-houses have been erected. It aids one hundred and eight parochial school teachers.†

This society is to be regarded as executing the work of the entire Evangelical Lutheran Church of Russia. Its chief

---

* Rev. J. N. Lenker.
† *Amtskalender für Geistliche;* Leipzig, 1886.

object is to provide spiritual care for the many widely scattered congregations in the interior of this vast Empire, building churches and school-houses, and supporting ministers and school-teachers. The congregations in this part of the land have been greatly suffering from the various calamities which of late have befallen Russia.

The Lutheran Church in Russia has a sustentation fund, which enables it to give a helping hand to weak congregations. The fund has an investment of $50,000, and the yearly contributions from the churches amount to $30,000, which are generally disbursed to the last cent.* The fund advances loans without interest, makes large free grants, helps to build and to furnish churches, schools and parsonages, and supports a number of students, who in turn pledge themselves to serve as home missionaries for 4 years. The fund distributes good books and periodicals and is indefatigable in its exertions to disseminate the truth.

Much is done in other lines of Inner Mission work. The extent of it may be inferred from what is done in three of the principal cities where our Church is represented. In St. Petersburg, the congregations in one year contributed 97,606 roubles to their own orphan and poor houses, and the support of pensioners, besides coöperating with the Reformed in support of a hospital, deaconesses' home, Magdalen Asylum, Sewing and Labor School, Home for the Feeble-minded and Epileptic, etc., to which during the same year 88,314 roubles were contributed.

In Moscow, there are two Lutheran congregations, in which, in 1881, there were 4,581 communicants, and four church schools, including a gymnasium and Female Seminary with 1,258 scholars. Over 10,000 roubles were contributed in these churches for the poor, besides coöperating

* Church periodicals, for last year, report receipts amounting to $50,000.

with the Reformed in the support of two orphan houses, a home for the poor, a city mission, a young peoples' association, etc., for which 55,729 roubles were in all contributed.

The churches of Riga contributed in 1881 to institutions for the poor, sick, dumb, blind, Magdalen asylums, deaconesses' houses, 87,268 roubles. Reval supported the same year a deaconess' house, three children's homes, and three emigrant houses, at an expense of 31,000 roubles.* A "Luther Fund" was begun some years ago, which now amounts to $130,000. The interest of that sum will be used for the education of ministers and parochial teachers.

In the nine Consistorial districts outside of Finland and Poland, the churches of our faith have seventy-five different funds to aid the widows and orphans of ministers, which amount in all to over $520,000.†

What makes all this especially noteworthy, is the fact that it is all purely voluntary Christian work. The State churches, as such, do little; not even supplying sufficient churches and pastors for the people at home. They are rather political than religious divisions. They do not imply any real entire agreement in faith among the individuals belonging to them. Hence such work as is undertaken by the Inner Mission Societies cannot be accomplished by the State Church, the unity of the Spirit being lacking. It is and can only be the work of individual Christians, prompted by the Spirit of God, to meet the needs of the hour and voluntarily uniting or working individually, in these numberless and diverse spheres of Christian activity. And thus those who love the Lord do show their faith by their works in carrying forward, often at much sacrifice, the principles of Christianity into the living reality of good fruits which spring up so abundantly.

---

* Herzog-Plitt Encyclopedia.
† Rev. J. N. Lenker.

AND MISSIONS.

INNER MISSION SOCIETIES, &c.

Name of Organization.	Branches, or Training Institutes.	Laborers Sent Out.	Yearly Receipts.
1. Societies for immigrants......	20	1,600	?
2. Gustavus Adolphus Union.....	45	1,444	1,112 000 marks.
a. Women's Auxiliaries.....	461	....	120,000
3. Evangelical League............	400	76,000 members.	....
4. Gotteskasten.	?	....	62,000
5. Lutherstiftung................	18	....	Has fund of 224,500
a. Auxiliaries	140	....	35,000
6. Aid Soc. for Ev. Churches.....	?	?	175,400
7. Societies for Jewish Missions..	18	In Germany 38	154,300
8. Deacons' Institute	20	2,000	?
9. Deaconess' Institutes..........	63	8,478	6,500,000 marks in 1886.
10. Bible Societies................	25	....	125,000 marks.
a. Prussian Auxiliaries......	178	....	....
11. Funds for Pastors,Widows, &c.	....	....	....
a. Prussia............	....	....	....
b. Hanover.....	....	Aids 270	1,000,000
c. Würtemberg............	4,311	....	charitable funds, $1,570,000
aa. I. M. Society......	....	....	337,500 marks.
d. Bavaria...............	....	Aids 52 Pastors.	....
e. Saxony.	....	118 Mis'n Per'dicals	....
12. Pub Societies, (Christian,)	24	....	....
13. Christian Bookstores..........	150	....	....
14. Colportage Houses	910	....	....
15. Inner Mission Societies	60	?	?
16. Women's Societies for Sick ...	10	54,400 members }	560,000
a. Auxiliaries...........	725	.. ....	
17. Other Women's Societies......	23	300	....
18. Students' Missionary Societies.	12	....	....
19. I. M. Institutions*. ...			
Inner Mission Labor Colonies	21	....	....
Ev. Workingmen's Societies.	186	92,000 members.	....
			kr.
Seamen's Mission Societies..		19 (Missions) 35	65,000 8 ships in Deep Sea Fisheries. 22,700
		In Fin land—	
		4	15,000 25 collecting Soc's.
Ev. Aid Societies............	....	327	200 000
Sustentation Funds........ ..	....	....	2,000,000
Finland Inner Mission Soc...	?	?	35,856
Hesselholm, Sweden.........	....	30	5,000
Western Skane, "	....	23	10,000
Stockholm Soc . "	....	6	10,500
Fjellstedt Mission School....	....	....	35,000
Jewish Mission, Sweden.....	....	5	32,000
Asso'n for In. Miss'n, Danish.	....	79	87,500
Danish-American Society....	....	over 40	....
Women's Danish-Amer. Soc.	....	....	....
City Soc., Copenhagen......	12	....	22,200
Society of Young Men	3	....	....
Storjohann's School,Norway	....	....	....
Inner Mission Soc., "			
Stud-nts' Mission Societies. Scandinavia	....	195 members. 137 colporteurs,	....
Fatherland Soc., I. M. Dept..	120	300 agents, 18 missionaries, }	41,500

* 357 Christian Inns; 640 Hospitals; Sick in 788 Parishes cared for; 425 Schools for little children; 360 Correctional Homes and Orphanages; 582 Soc's Christian Young Men; 218 Institutions for Deaf, Blind, &c.; 118 Mission Periodicals.

CHAPTER XIII.

DEACONESS MOTHER-HOUSES, FIELDS OF LABOR, &c.

In the earthly life of our dear Saviour, the gospel of grace and mercy to the sinning is ever accompanied by the evangel of hope and help to the suffering. It was with well-doing that the Church of the Apostles strove to put to silence the foolishness of ignorant men. The offering was a part of the worship and, wherever possible, the local congregation had its buildings for the care and support of its sick, widows and orphans.* That this merciful work was organized and aimed to be thorough, is beyond doubt. It was under the church's direction and had official sanction, as the New Testament designations of deacon and deaconess plainly imply. Begotten of God, the spirit impelling to such work cannot die; and in the brotherhoods and sisterhoods of a corrupted Christianity, down through all the dreary wastes of the Dark Ages, even to the present day in the various orders of Charity and Mercy of the Roman Church, may be traced the evidences of its sickly life.

The restoration of the true, evangelical conception of the deaconess work was left to the nineteenth century, as the task of Lutherans. And this was the order of its coming:

In the little village of Kaiserswerth, Germany, about fifty years ago, a young German pastor was settled, Fliedner by name. To him came a woman, a discharged prisoner, pleading for help. Having no room in his own modest little home, he assigned her a place in a little summer-house

---
*See Kurtz, Ch. Hist. (1865) I : 345.

adjoining his, where she might be under the eye of his wife. Soon another abandoned woman came and she, too, was sheltered there. They slept in the attic, which was reached by a ladder which was removed after they had ascended.

Such was the origin of a work which has attained marvelous proportions. What is known as the Kaiserswerth Deaconess House is really eleven different institutions under one name, each with its own specific purpose. There is the Magdalen Home for fallen women, which provides a room for each, furnishes agreeable work, strict oversight and educational and spiritual care for all. Of the 895 inmates received, the authorities state that one-third have been reclaimed, of another third they are in doubt, and the rest proved irreclaimable. There is a school for little children, with an attendance of over 100, in which the Picture-Bible, the Hymn-Book, the Play-Songs, &c., prepared by Fliedner, are in use. There is a High School for girls, and a Seminary to prepare teachers for little children's schools, with an attendance of 98. A fifth institution is an orphanage for girls which has cared for 249 and trained them also in all kinds of household work.*

There is also a school to train girls for the Deaconess School proper, in which 221 have received the elements of general culture, besides, in many cases, knowledge of English, French and music, as also of handiwork pertaining to the house, kitchen and garden. At the head of all, is the Deaconess School proper, with 25 sisters in training, under charge of three deaconesses. There is also a home for weak-minded women, in which 830 of these most pitiable of all the sick, have received loving ministration. There is also a home for unmarried invalid women, which has received 72 patients. In addition to all this, there is the hospital, with an average of 100 to 120 patients daily, requiring the

---
*In 44 years but six of the children have died, and not one during the years 1848 to 1876.

services of 35 to 40 deaconesses. Extra work leaves the sisters often in need of rest. To this end, the Mother-House has erected a large home in the midst of a great garden surrounded by forest, valley and mountain. It is named Salem and about 100 sisters are sent thither for a season each year, for recuperation. And finally the institution has its business establishment, agricultural house and publishing department. The agricultural department, managed by farmers resident in buildings erected on the grounds, provides grain, vegetables, poultry, sheep, cattle, &c., for home use, while the publishing department returns annual net proceeds of 30,000 to 50,000 marks.

The support of the institution comes from various sources. In addition to the returns from its own farms and gardens, from its publishing department, and from those of the patients or pupils who are able to pay, it receives many gifts, numbering kings, queens, princes and princesses among its benefactors. The church authorities permit it to make house-to-house collections, and in the Provinces of the Rhine and of Westphalia collections are made in the churches. Twice in its history, house-collections in its aid have been made in all the provinces of Prussia. Certain friends send in a yearly offering of about 10,000 marks, and the Pfennig Societies last year contributed over 26,000 marks. A society composed chiefly of the nobility of Mecklenburg-Schwerin, and led by the Duchess herself, has sent in gifts for a quarter of a century, those of last year amounting to 23,014 marks. The officers of various guilds send in gifts of wood, coal, &c.; 24 women's societies furnish clothing and other articles needed in caring for the inmates, while 23 Zion's societies cöoperate with them. The railway and navigation companies carry the deaconesses and officials free, or at most charge but half rates.

The yearly expenses of the Kaiserswerth Institution are about 333,500 marks. At the time of Fliedner's death, its property was valued at 1,472,574 marks, which has been increased largely since then. The Sisters at work in the home institutions number 98, while 638 others connected with the Mother-House labor elsewhere.

Filial Institutions, established by the Kaiserswerth Mother-House, and yet connected with it as a daughter is connected with her mother's house, although herself at the head of a household, exist in 21 other places in charge of 118 deaconesses.

Near Düsseldorf a seminary for girls of the higher and middle classes, with 75 to 90 pupils, is in charge of ten deaconesses. Of the 672 pupils received, coming from Germany, Holland, Belgium, Russia, England and Switzerland, sixty graduates are engaged as evangelical teachers, and five natives of England are at work in their native land as deaconesses.

In Altdorf, Upper Silesia, is another filial, an orphanage for girls, in which 80 to 100 children are cared for by six deaconesses at an annual cost of about 27,000 marks.

In Berlin are three filials, a Servants' Home and Training School, a school for little children and an elementary school for girls. Years ago without a dollar in hand, for 25,000 thalers, Fliedner bought a plot of ground with five little houses, as a Home for Servants. Since then others have been added and now there are 130 beds and 11 deaconesses are in charge. In the little children's school are more than 200 little ones, and the school for girls has 350 pupils. In the Servants' Home and Training School 800 inmates were cared for last year at a cost of 55,497 marks.

In Düsseldorf are two filials. One is a Home and Training School for Servants, which offers a home to those of them out of employment, at a cost of 20 pfennig, about 5 cents, a day, and receives untrained servants and trains them, at double these rates. The number received since

1866 is 4,521. The other is a school for little children with a daily attendance of about 90.

In Erefeld are two similar institutions, with like purpose, also in charge of deaconesses.

In Brandenburg is a Magdalen Home, also a filial of Kaiserswerth, and with it an asylum for those of this class who are sick. Since 1868 it has had 470 inmates and the average daily number is now about 80.

Near Hattingen, a home for convalescent children and a recovery institution for deaconesses, care for about sixty and thirty patients, respectively.

At Potsdam another filial was about to be established when the last complete report was published—a Hospital and an Orphanage—through the munificence of a donor who withholds her name. Her gift was 306,000 marks.

Kaiserswerth has filial institutions also in Palestine and in other parts of the Orient. Thus in word and in deed, deaconesses carry the gospel back to the people who aforetime said, " We will not have this Man to rule over us." They are found in Jerusalem, where they have a hospital with 44 beds, and where, also, at the clinics, from 6,000 to 8,000 patients, annually, are prescribed for and attended. There they have special ministrations for the troops of blind children and others suffering from distressing ailments of the eye. There, also, these Christ-like women minister to the leper, mercilessly cast out to die piece-meal, and gather the dark-eyed Arab maidens, cast off by their fathers as a burden, for instruction in the way of life.

Among the people of Palestine, it is a popular saying that " the threshold of a house weeps forty days when a girl is born." When our deaconesses began the work of training these despised Mohammedan girls for better things, the prejudices of the ages and all the power of a fanatical people were against them. But they persevered. Encouraged by a gift from William I, of Germany, in 1855 they bought a house and began work with one scholar, and she was a slave whose freedom they had purchased. It was a long struggle against Mohammedan prejudices. Pupils came in slowly. But to-day more than 700 are under instruction, to say nothing of the many who have gone forth to spread the leaven among their countrywomen, some of them in other parts of Palestine, others in Syria, others, still, in Arabia. They are now found in Bethlehem, Lydda, Nablus, Damascus, Alexandria, Beyrout, and elsewhere, and wherever they are they set up a light to light those who sit in darkness. In addition to those who have been trained as teachers, at least a dozen are engaged as deaconesses in hospitals, and in Constantinople, Beyrout, Alexandria and Jerusalem, many Europeans and Americans, sick and among strangers, have been nursed and tended, with loving attention, by these dusky maids of the East. Others still, are engaged in translating German devotional works into their own tongue, and thus the little seed, placed again in Jerusalem's soil but 35 years ago, has already become a tree whose leaves are for the healing of the nations.

In the Zoar Orphanage, in Beyrout, 8 deaconesses give daily instruction to 125 girls and more than 800 have thus been trained during the 25 years of its existence. Not a few of these now employed as teachers in other towns and cities, are carrying the gospel again to Antioch, Tarsus, Baalbeck, Nazareth, Gaza, Jaffa, &c. In their high schools for girls, 8 sisters are instructing more than 100 of the daughters of the wealthier and more influential classes, and thus setting in operation another instrumentality for the regeneration of the East.

In Smyrna, these same things are being repeated. For nearly 40 years the deaconesses have there been at work. More than 2,000 girls have received Christian instruction in their schools, and almost 200 are now under their tuition. Americans, Greeks and Turks are gathered here, and day by day receive something of the Truth which maketh wise unto salvation.

The same work,* practically, is being done by the deaconesses elsewhere in the East—at Port Said, Alexandria, Täbris, Sarepta, Madeira, Constantinople, in the Cameroon region, West Africa, in Zanzibar, in Bombay and Madras; also in England and Russia, as well as in nearly all the states of Europe, and in America.

In response to a most earnest petition from American, English, German and Swiss residents in Cairo, Egypt,†

---

*To furnish some conception of the extent of the deaconess hospital work in the East, the following regarding that work in Alexandria, Egypt, is appended:

In the winter of 1856-7, the Consuls of England and Prussia, resident in Alexandria, petitioned Fliedner to establish a Deaconess Hospital in Alexandria, Egypt, for the reception of sick seamen and other strangers in that port. They pledged assistance from their governments to establish the Institution, and also yearly contributions for its maintenance.

He could not refuse the request; especially as Alexandria is a central point for the commerce of the Mediterranean, and the gateway between Europe, Austria and India, through which there pour masses of men East and West.

Fliedner was wintering in Egypt to benefit his health, and in the following spring, before he left, he rented the house of a Turkish Pascha in Alexandria for 7,500 piasters.

In November, 1857, three Deaconesses landed in Alexandria to begin the work, and they soon had more sick than they could care for, "of all the nations under heaven." In 1869 ground was purchased outside the city, that the inmates of the Institution might have the benefit of purer air, and a two-story building was erected to be used as a hospital. In this the Deaconesses care daily, for from 60 to 70 sick. In the last year, there were 1,100 to 1,200 different inmates, of the following nationalities: German, English, Austrian, Italian, Swiss, Scandinavian, Russians, Greeks, Alexandrians and residents of other parts of Egypt, dwellers in Soudan, Turkey, India, Abyssinia, Malta, China, Bulgaria, Malacca, etc. In 1885, the clinical treatments numbered 29,659. The current expenses for both the last years were something over 100,000 marks.

†In Egypt and the Holy Land 57 deaconesses are engaged in their work of mercy. They toil without salary, have no families to support, and the necessary expenses incident to their work are about 175,000 marks a year.

deaconesses were sent from Kaiserswerth to open a filial hospital in that center of Mohammedanism. Contributions were sent by the royal couple of Germany, the Khedive of Egypt and his father, the Kings of Saxony and Würtemberg, the cities of Leipsic and Manchester, the Egyptian government, and by friends in Germany and in the East, until in 1884, when the building was completed, the sum amounted to 175,000 francs. The patients the first year numbered 185, while those attending the clinics were numbered, often, by the hundred, in one day.

In Florence, Italy, since 1860, has existed another Kaiserswerth filial, a training institute for girls. Here seven deaconesses instruct about 120 girls, most of them Italians. The cost of the building was 80,000 marks, and the cost of maintenance is about 18,000 marks yearly. Apart from her filial institutions, with their 217 sisters, 428 Kaiserswerth deaconesses are also employed by 172 other beneficent societies and institutions. In the provinces of the Rhine, 116 institutions or fields of labor are served by 257 sisters. Of these, four are Christian Inns, 18 are institutions for orphans, for the poor, &c., 22 are schools for little children, 29 are hospitals, and 34 are parishes where they care for the sick, annually, in almost 6,000 families.

Westphalia furnishes 42 fields in which 109 sisters are engaged in similar work. In other parts of Germany, 62 sisters serve in 16 fields of work, while beyond the confines of the Fatherland, other fields are in Rome, Budapest, Bucharest and America.*

A summary of the whole Kaiserswerth work, so far as obtainable figures can show it, is about as follows: Seven Mother-Houses to train deaconesses, 54 hospitals, 22 homes for the poor, for invalids, &c., 4 health-resorts for overworked deaconesses, 50 parishes in which they labor, 24 homes for

---

*For the institutions at Pittsburg and Rochester, Pennsylvania, no figures have been obtained.

orphans and training-schools for girls and young women, 30 schools for little children, 2 Homes for Magdalens, and homes and training institutions for servants.

And if the work done be summarized, for the year 1886— the last for which full reports of all are published—it is about as follows, exclusive of the Mother-Houses, which have their existence through Kaisersweth, and now report about 1,010 deaconesses:—800 invalids and poor persons cared for; 850 servants aided when out of employment, and kept out of the tempter's way; 7,750 little children, generally of day laborers, kept from evil companions, cared for, and trained in the way of salvation; 8,800 families of the poor and distressed cared for in sickness and need; about 2,600 sick persons nursed daily, and over 22,700 within the year.

Thirty-five fields, employing 217 deaconesses, along with the mother-house, employing 98 more, report a total yearly income of 692,315 marks.

Thus far in this chapter, attention has been directed to the Kaiserswerth Deaconess House, its various filial institutions and fields of labor. But Kaiserswerth, whilst the oldest and largest, is but one of 58 such institutions, each of which trains its own deaconesses and has its own fields of labor. Of the 58, full reports are at hand, with exception of one of recent origin.

In addition to 43 Kaiserswerth sisters employed in Berlin, the Capital has four* Deaconess Mother-Houses, which in 1889 had 502 sisters. The first of the four, established through the labors of Gossner, named after Queen Elizabeth who assumed the protectorate of it, cares for 1,600 patients annually, with the aid of 50 sisters.

In Breslau, in 1848, Fliedner began the work of establishing a Mother-House, which now numbers a dozen institutions. Among them are one for sick children, with 24 beds; an

---
*For particulars, see chapter on City Missions.

invalids' home, with 40 rooms; an isolated hospital, with 16 beds; a house for the sick with 101 beds; a house for clinics, and the training house for deaconesses. Outside fields of labor number 26, employing 140 deaconesses, of whom 62 serve in 21 hospitals, 43 in 16 parishes, whilst others labor in homes for invalids, in orphanages, homes for training servants and in other institutions. In the Mother-House itself 66 are engaged. The yearly expenses are 113,860 marks.

Another Mother-House in Silesia is that at Eraschniss. Along with it are homes for the weak-minded, the epileptic, and for sick and invalid persons. In 43 outside fields 58 sisters are engaged: 14 in 7 hospitals, 38 in 21 parishes, others in orphanages and little children's schools. The whole number of sisters is 89, and the year's expenses 111,535 marks. Frankenstein, Silesia, has also a Mother-House. In 1889 it reported 135 sisters at work at 56 places. They have charge of 45 parishes, and maintain 51 schools for little children, 8 hospitals and homes for invalids, and one orphanage.

The Mother-House in Königsberg, Prussia, established by Fliedner, has 258 sisters, and an income of 190,000 marks. In the home hospital over a thousand patients are nursed annually, while the outside stations number 65, of which 27 are hospitals, 5 are orphanages, 15 are schools for little children, one is a home and training school for servants, and the others, parishes.

Danzig, Prussia, has a Mother-House, which in 1889 had 135 sisters. In addition to a home hospital for sick children, and one for adults, the sisters toil in 35 outside stations, conducting 7 hospitals, 4 orphanages, 19 schools for little children, and caring for the poor and distressed in 35 parishes. The income is 53,000 marks.

In Stettin, Pomerania, Fliedner called into being a Mother-House which now has 36 sisters, and an institution for invalid children. The sisters conduct a children's hospital in Stralsund, and are engaged also in parish work in Colberg and Lauenberg. The income is 18,225 marks.

The Deaconess House, Bethania, at Stettin, "Neu Torney," has 189 sisters, and cares for about 1,600 sick annually. Of the sisters 128 work in 55 outside stations, hospitals, orphanages, homes for invalids, asylums for children, training schools and parishes. Income, 140,000 marks.

The Provincial Deaconess House at Halle, in addition to its sisters' training institute, has a general hospital, a hospital for children, an isolated hospital, and an institution for the aged, invalids, &c. Outside stations number 29, of which 12 are hospitals, 11 are parishes, 4 are schools, one asylum for children, and clinics for all classes. The years's income is 335,000 marks.

In Hanover, in 1860, Queen Maria founded the Henrietta Deaconess Institute, naming it in honor of the Duchess of that name, of Würtemberg, who left a legacy of 24,000 marks for it, which sum was increased to 150,000 marks by the King of Hanover. It consists of a training school, a hospital with 30 sisters, two children's hospitals with 6 sisters, an invalids' home, &c. The outside stations are 38, with 31 hospitals, 4 asylums for children, 16 schools for little children, 3 industrial schools, and 35 parishes. The sisters number 223, and the yearly income is 125,000 marks.

Frankfort-on-the-Main has a Mother-House, with 65 sisters in 9 hospitals, 12 parishes, and one training school. The outside stations number 16, and most attention is given to work in parishes. Income, 60,000 marks.

The Mother-House in Hesse has 45 sisters, and an income of 73,250 marks.

The Deaconess House in Posen has a hospital, a training school and a home for aged women. Its outside fields include 10 parishes, 4 hospitals, two houses for the sick, and one lazaretto. It has, also, an affiliated institution, with 18 out-stations. The sisters number 80, and the income is over 63,000 marks.

The Deaconess Institute of Flensburg,* in addition to its training-school, has an invalids' home and a hospital. Sisters are at work, also, in 6 hospitals, 9 parishes, 5 waiting-schools for little children, an industrial school, and in the Marthastiftung in Hamburg. The number of deaconesses is 73.

Ranking next, in number of sisters, to Kaiserswerth, is the Mother-House at Bielefeld, for whose establishment Fliedner opened the way. In the women's department of the Bielefield Institution for Epileptics, 40 of the deaconesses are employed; 60 of them serve in 42 parishes, 58 are engaged in 42 schools for little children, 149 are in 33 hospitals, 11 in 3 invalids' homes, and the rest in homes for the erring, for servants, for little children, orphanages, schools of industry, &c. The sisters number 463, and the income, in 1886, was 288,300 marks.

Strasburg's Mother-House has 174 sisters, of whom 69 work in hospitals, and the rest in homes for little children, for the poor, &c. The income is from 150,000 to 225,000 marks.

Two sisters from Kaiserswerth, under Fliedner's direction, in 1844, opened the Mother-House in Dresden. Of its 266 sisters, 36 are in a hospital, 19 in an invalids' home, 12 in a school for little children, in schools for servants, and a Magdalen's home. Outside the institution, 44 are engaged in 19 hospitals and homes for invalids, 36 are in parishes, 22 in schools for little children, 9 in four homes for Magdalens, and others in schools for servants, in orphanages, &c.

The Bethlehem Mother-House, connected with the Lutheran Church of Mecklenburg, and for whose hospital-

---

*For further particulars concerning this institution, as also the Deaconess House at Altona, see Schleswig-Holstein.

building Grand Duke Frederick Franz III. gave 180,000 marks, has 172 sisters engaged at 47 different places, 69 managing 22 hospitals, 33 in 17 parishes, and others in various institutions of mercy. The income is from 91,000 to 117,000 marks.

In Karlsruhe, Baden, is a like institution with 109 sisters and a yearly income of 90,000 marks.

The Neuendettelsau Mother-House, established by Löhe, consists of a hospital, a home for the aged and invalids, a Magdalen home, a training school for girls, a home for weak-minded women, an industrial school, an hospice, a deaconess home, a physicians' home, a church, houses for the various laborers employed, a house for the rector. Outside stations number 86, with 219 sisters. Among them are 17 hospitals, with 79 sisters, 13 parishes with 46 sisters, 18 little children's schools, 6 training schools, asylums for servants, orphanages, &c. The number of sisters is 282.

In the famous city of Augsburg is located a* Mother-House for deaconesses.

The Mother-House at Speyer, in the Palatinate, has 109 sisters, managing 8 hospitals, laboring in parishes, and doing other merciful work, at a cost of 160,000 marks yearly.

Stuttgart's Mother-House consists of a house for the sisters, a church and parsonage, an invalids' home for women, an institution for women suffering from cancer, a house for convalescents, and a home for aged and invalid deaconesses. Away from Stuttgart 66 stations are occupied, 5 being asylums for children; 5 training institutes for girls; 2 orphanages; 25 parishes with 68 deaconesses, and 29 hospitals with 120. The number of sisters is 383, and the income 175,000 marks.

The Mother-House in Darmstadt has 150 sisters, and an income of 125,000 marks. Its sisters occupy 37 stations; among them, 9 schools for little children, 9 parishes, and 16 hospitals

* For particulars see City of Augsburg.

The Bethlehem Mother-House in Hamburg was erected to shelter the deaconesses called by the Ansgar Chapel to labor among the poor, and is under the directory of the pastor of this congregation. The sisters now serve in a house for the sick belonging to other congregations of the city, in a children's home, a children's nursery, and an asylum for girls who are without proper care. In 1885 the foundations were laid for a second deaconess home, a branch, to consist of four departments, a training house for girls not yet confirmed, another for girls destitute of proper care, a home for incurables, and a resting place for deaconesses.

Hamburg's Bethesda Mother-House dates from 1860. It has a house for deaconesses, a home for invalids, a day-nursery for little children, and 29 sisters, of whom 10 serve in parishes, and others have charge of an asylum for children. Its receipts for current expenses last year were 28,000 marks; for special purposes, 30,000.

The Mother-House in Bremen has a hospital, an invalids' home, an income of 42,250 marks, and 23 sisters, of whom some are at work in parishes.

Members of the Fatherland Women's Society founded the Deaconess Home of Brunswick, whose sisters number 42. They care for about 450 sick in the institution, and have, also, an invalids' home. They serve in 19 out-stations, 4 of which are hospitals, 7 are parishes, two are industrial schools, and two are schools for little children.

Switzerland has four Deaconess Houses, with 626 sisters in 120 fields, and an annual income of 500,000 marks. In France and Holland are four Mother-Houses, with 203 sisters, conducting 9 hospitals, 8 training schools for girls, &c. In France the income is over 200,000 francs; in Holland, it is 77,625 florins. Three Mother-Houses exist, also, in the Austro-Hungarian Empire; one at Budapest, Hungary; one in Gallneukirche, in the Tyrol; and one in Vienna. In Budapest the home was opened by the aid of Kaiserswerth sisters.

In Stockholm, Sweden, deaconess work was begun in 1851, in a hotel rented for a training institution. A hospital was soon erected; a children's home followed; next an orphanage; then an asylum for Magdalens; then a house of correction for girls; then a servants' school; then a chapel with room for 1,000 persons; then a home for aged and invalid deaconesses; and lastly, in 1885, an invalids' home. In these home institutions 34 sisters find their field of labor, while in outside fields there are 17 hospitals with 33 sisters, 19 parishes with 21 sisters, 9 children's homes with 12 sisters in charge, besides 3 homes for correction, 6 homes for the poor, 6 asylums for children, a school, &c. The total of deaconesses in Sweden is 145; the income for the work, 120,000 marks.

Princess Louise, of Denmark, headed a movement to found a Deaconess Home at Copenhagen. The widowed Queen, Caroline Amalie, aided in the work. Three sisters and a half dozen sick, in a little house capable of receiving but 10, constituted the beginning. Soon a house was bought, and the care of the sick in parishes was begun. Presently a school for girls was opened, then released prisoners were cared for, next a home for Magdalens was opened, and later, a home for servants.

In 1873, His Majesty, the King of Denmark, laid the corner-stone of a new building to be used as a mother-house, hospital and church, Bishop Martensen delivering the address. A rector's house soon followed, then a house for aged and infirm women, then a training school for girls, and lastly, at the sea-side, a health-resort for aged or invalid deaconesses. The income is 87,525 crowns; the sisters number 135, who are in charge of hospitals, orphanages, &c., in 54 stations outside of the capital.

The deaconess work of Norway began also in a rented house, in 1868, in Christiania. In 1872 the Mother-House was built, and already the merciful influence is felt beyond the Polar Circle. The income for the work is 75,000 crowns, the number of sisters is 201, and they are engaged in the usual spheres of work. Recently a deaconess from Norway went to take charge of a hospital in Madagascar.

In Russia there are Deaconess Homes in six great cities: St. Petersburg; Mitau, in Courland; Sarata; Riga, Livonia; Reval, Esthonia; and in Helsingfors, Finland.

In St. Petersburg is a Deaconess Home, with 33 sisters. They have charge of a hospital for women, an asylum for children of sick mothers, and a school for small children of poor parents. They also have an Evangelical hospital in Moscow, an Asylum for Israelites in St. Petersburg, and are at work in two of the large Lutheran parishes of the capital. The income is 45,000 roubles.

The Deaconess Home in Mitau consists of a hospital, an eye clinic, an invalids' home, and a home and training school for servants. The sisters number 14, and serve also, in parishes.

Löhe sent six deaconesses for one year to begin the work at Sarata, and a house was opened for the care and relief of all classes of sufferers. In the war with Turkey, sisters served on the field with the Order of the Red Cross, in giving relief to the sick and wounded. They are engaged in the usual deaconess work, and the expenses are about 6,000 roubles.

In Riga, a baron, a minister of State, a physician and a pastor began the deaconess work. Sisters from Dresden were sent to take it in charge. A hospital, an asylum for children, and a little children's school, constitute the institution, which has 9 sisters and an income of 15,000 roubles.

The Deaconess Home in Reval was opened by three sisters from Neuendettelsau, aided by a society, in Reval, organized to that end. It is subordinate to the St. Olaf congregation. A gift of 100,000 roubles, with other means, made possible the erection of the buildings: a hospital for women afflicted with acute diseases, and one for men with affliction of like nature; an asylum for aged women with chronic diseases; another for weak-minded persons; a school for little children of very poor parents, where they are both maintained and instructed. The sisters number 21, and the expenses are 12,000 roubles.

A lady of the nobility provided the edifice in which the Deaconess Home of Helsingfors was opened. A deaconess and a pastor were then called to begin the work. The institution now has 15 sisters, and annual expenses of 27,000 crowns. The home has 30 beds for sick, four rooms for clinics, a home for girls, and a school. The sisters are engaged, also, in a hospital at Borga, an orphanage at Frederickshamm, a home for the poor at Esbo, and in two parishes.

In England the Deaconess work was begun in London, in 1866, as an orphanage.* Soon after came a gift of 220,000 marks, by two brothers, and 80,000 more by other friends, to found a deaconess institution. A four-acre lot was bought, a Mother-House and a hospital built. The patients generally are from the German population of London. Outside the institution, two sisters labor in a hospital in Cork, Ireland; 18 in a hospital in Sunderland; 3 in a parish hospital in Dublin, and one in parish work in the same city. The sisters connected with this institution number 58, and the current expenses are 65,000 marks.

The Upper Austrian Evangelical Society for Inner Missions is now erecting a Mother-House for Deaconesses, along with its Institute for Epileptics. It has 22 sisters engaged in various works of mercy.

On the basis of the facts concerning deaconess work, given

---

* In the spirit of the Kaiserswerth work, in 1840, Mrs. Fry founded the Institute of Nursing Sisters, Devonshire Square, Bishopsgate, London. Since then a number of English Deaconess institutions have been opened, and in many of the Anglican Bishoprics Diocesan Sisterhoods now exist. Some of these English institutions send representatives to the General Deaconess Conferences held in Germany.

in the foregoing pages, the labors of these Christ-like women may be summarized, in the three chief departments, hospital, parish, and school, about as follows: Patients nursed in hospitals annually, 353,000 ; poor, sick and distressed cared for in 600 parishes, 118,800 families; daily care and instruction given to 46,750 children, to keep them from evil influences, and teach them the way of truth, whilst their parents are absent toiling for daily bread.

The spheres of work noted above are but three of fifteen in which deaconesses are employed. The total results, the eye of Omniscience alone can see.

The partial reports of 1890 give the whole number of deaconesses as over 8,000, and the yearly income at over $1,600,000. And this is the right hand of the Lutheran Inner Mission work. Whether there be another organization on earth which accomplishes for Christ, in the person of His suffering people, what is accomplished by this Order of Deaconesses, not yet, perhaps, has been shown.

Full reports of all the organized Inner Mission forces of our Church in Europe, are not at hand ; but from what are at hand the following summary is drawn, in the hope that it may impress and stimulate and cheer other workers in the cause of Christ.

1. *Christian Inns*, established to shield travelers, traveling journeymen and strangers, from temptation, afford them lodging and board at nominal cost, and surround them with Christian influences. In 1890 the number was 357. Thirteen of these Inns reported 145,101 guests in one year. One of them, in 18 years, reported 126,000 guests. Forty of them, managed by Rauhe Haus Brothers, reported 250,000 guests.

2. *Houses of Correction*, established to care for neglected and wayward children. The number is reported as 330, and in them the constant aim is, not so much repression as

nurture, the inmates being under the power of Christian training and instruction.

3. *Orphans' Homes.* Within the kingdom of Prussia alone, the number is given as 396, and the inmates 18,800. One-half of these are directly under control of the Church, 127 under direction of individuals, and the rest are controlled by civil powers.

4. *Homes for the Idiotic.* These number 36, with 800 teachers and 4,300 inmates, supported at a cost of $400,000.

5. We also have reports of Magdalen Institutions, 18; Institutions for Released Prisoners, 31; Christian Homes for the Poor, 23; Institutions for Epileptics, 6; for the Blind, 14; to help needy girls to employment or to an education, 29; for the Deaf and Dumb, 97. And these 218 Institutions are but a fraction of the number actually in existence.

6. *Labor Colonies,* established to provide shelter and work for men who, through misfortune, have been thrown out of employment and of means of earning daily bread.

7. *Associations of Christian Young Men,* under direction of the church, to protect the confirmed youth from the dangers of the world, number 582.

8. Reports are at hand, also, of the Luther Association, to aid in educating the children of pastors and teachers; the Society for the endowment of homes for pastors' daughters fallen sick, left orphans, or in need; the German Protestant Missionary Society to establish churches and schools in Japan, and the Evangelical League, organized to resist the aggressions of Rome.

9. *Bible Societies,* numbering 25, with many auxiliaries the society in Prussia reporting 178 branches.

10. *Book and Tract Societies*, 24 in number. One reports a membership of 7,900, and circulates, annually, nearly a million good books and tracts. These societies publish 36 foreign missionary papers, 6 in aid of Jewish missions, 11 in behalf of Protestants in Roman Catholic countries, and 65 in the interests of Home Mission work.

11. *Women's Societies*, numbering 33 general, with many branches. Ten general societies aid the sick and needy, six of the ten reporting 723 auxiliaries, with 54,430 members, and four of the six reporting yearly receipts of 561,000 marks. Two Women's Societies do mission work in China and the Orient, while 461 are connected with the Gustavus Adolphus Union.

12. To the 15 Institutes to train men for the Inner Mission work in Germany, must be added 15 others, which train men for the spiritual care of those of their countrymen who are in foreign lands. To America and Australia these Institutes have sent 1,500 men, and many to England, Italy and Africa.*

13. In Germany there are no fewer than 8 societies to spread the gospel among the Jews, with branches in nine leading universities. Five of these societies support 17 missionaries, the University branches have 300 men in training for the work, and a special Institute in its behalf has been opened in Leipsic.

---

* Warneck says that in Germany about 3,000,000 marks are contributed annually for Foreign Missions, and for Inner Missions from 12,000,000 to 16,000,000, in addition to the State contributions for like purposes of beneficence, which of course come from the people also in the way of taxation. Prussia is reported as paying out in one year, 55,000,000 marks for works of mercy.

DEACONESS MOTHER-HOUSES, ETC., 1891.*

NAME.	When Founded.	No. of Deaconesses	Income, 1890.	Fields of Labor	Hospitals.	Homes for Invalids, &c.	Parishes.	Other.†
			Marks.					
Kaiserswerth	1836	807	742,010	217	61	19	62	75
Berlin, Elizabeth	1837	120	221,848	38	8	3	12	15
Paris	1841	66	170,422	26	11	4	1	10
Strasburg	1842	182	220,339	35	16	3	10	6
St. Loup	1842	82	55,834	21	18	1	1	1
Dresden	1844	332	482,081	125	28	8	53	36
Utrecht	1844	70	126,186	10	4	1	5	
Bern	1845	337	168,000	64	38	5	11	10
Berlin, Bethania	1847	265	306,245	86	26	9	23	28
Stockholm	1849	165	74,670	73	18	8	28	19
Rochester ‡	1849	9		6	4			2
Breslau	1850	250	117,650	62	24	4	25	9
Königsberg	1850	320	237,223	119	32	11	89	37
Ludwigslust	1851	198	170,720	64	23	3	24	14
Karlsruhe	1851	157	90,520	50	14	4	28	4
Riehen, B'f'l	1852	235	135,335	70	26	4	19	21
Neuendettelsau	1854	334	220,000	102	25	8	20	49
Stuttgart	1854	434	242,527	93	44	1	32	16
Augsburg	1855	110	44,553	33	9	1	15	8
Halle	1857	117	268,234	51	14	4	26	7
Darmstadt	1858	171	121,208	50	18	3	16	13
Zürich	1858	115	73,350	34	18	2	11	3
St. Petersburg	1859	34	93,183	5	3		2	
Speyer	1859	140	73,834	41	9	1	20	11
Kraschnitz	1860	155	157,884	75	14	3	31	24
Hanover	1860	246	136,024	104	36	6	41	21
Hamburg	1860	38	57,856	8	1	1	5	1
Danzig	1862	178	78,631	83	15	8	42	23
Copenhagen	1863	171	116,067	69	18	6	27	18
Cassel	1864	86	210,074	40	7	4	14	15
Hague	1865	46	79,428	3	2		1	
Mitau	1865	26	29,710	13	7	1	2	3
Posen	1865	130	168,609	43	11	2	21	9
Pesth	1866	9	32,616	1	1			
Frankenstein	1866	161	7,221	88	6	5	24	58
Riga	1866	18	46,285	4	1		1	2
Berlin, III	1867	66	133,782	17	2		10	5
London, Tottenham	1867	69	92,041	13	4	2	6	1
Reval	1867	25	37,631	5	1		3	1
Helsingfors	1867	17	25,408	6	2	1	3	
Altona	1867	77	78,539	35	8	1	15	11
Sarata	1867	24	15,162	5	1	2		2
Bremen	1868	22	51,495	8	3	1	4	
Christiania	1868	285	126,535	77	27	3	35	12
Wiborg	1869	6	20,026	4	2			2
Bielefeld	1869	565	435,190	203	60	6	56	81
"Neutorney"	1869	208	166,407	99	11	1	54	33
Brunswick	1870	59	77,161	23	4	1	13	5
Frankfurt, A. M	1870	81	74,024	32	6	5	17	4
Flensburg	1874	118	94,039	44	11		17	16
Paris, II	1874	14	18,555	6	1		4	1
"Berl. P. G. G."	1876	134	93,920	45	6		26	13
Gallneukirchen	1877	23	42,070	7	4	1	1	1
Ingweiler	1877	15	17,061	4	1		3	
Nowawes	1879	135	102,773	83	7	4	33	39
Haarlem	1882	33	22,786	7	1		4	2
Mannheim	1884	36	43,508	11	2		9	
Arnheim	1885	30	87,781	5	1		4	
Helsen	1887	16	10,007	10	1	1		9
Berl. Mgdl. S	1888	32	48,442	5				5
Philadelphia ‡	1888	36	?	7	3	1	2	1
Sobernheim	1889	35	?	7	2		3	2
Witten	1890	3	130,113					
Total	1891	8478	7,680,810	2774	780	168	1017	809
"	1888	7090	6,353,394	2248				
Increase in three years		1398	1,327,416	526				

The figures given as yearly receipts are exclusively for the receipts of the Mother-

GROWTH OF THE DEACONESS WORK.

YEAR.	Mother-Houses.		Deaconesses.		Fields of Labor.		Yearly Income.
	Total.	Average Yearly Additions.	Total.	Average Yearly Increase.	Total.	Average Yearly Increase.	
1861...............	27	....	1,197	....	....	?	....
1864...............	30	1	1,592	132	386	....	813,273
1868...............	40	2½	2,106	128	526	35	1,258,242
1872...............	48	2	2,657	138	648	30	2,103,729
1875...............	50	1	3,239	194	866	73	3,016,256
1878...............	51	?	3,901	221	1,093	76	4,110,147
1881...............	53	⅔	4,748	228	1,436	114	4,824,176
1884...............	54	?	5,653	302	1,742	102	5,607,886
1888...............	57	1	7,129	369	2,263	130	6,401,337
1891...............	63	2	8,478	450	2,774	170	7,680,810

Houses and their branch institutions. Could the receipts of all the fields of labor where Deaconesses are engaged, and which pass through their hands for the relief of the poor and the suffering, be added, the figures would reach a surprising height.

*Condensed from Schäfer's *Monatsschrift für Innere Mission*, Sept., 1891. The figures vary somewhat from those in the body of the chapter. They were prepared by Pastor Fliedner, of Kaiserswerth, for the General Conference of Mother-House officials, Sept. 16 and 17, 1891, and are accurate.

†Of the "Other" institutions, 125 are Orphanages, etc.; 451 are Schools for Little Children; 75 are Day Nurseries and Training Homes; 16 are Industrial Schools; 50 are Institutes for Servants; 26 are Institutions for Epileptics, Weak-Minded and Idiotic; 39 are Magdalen Asylums; 16 are Prisons and Hospices; and the rest (11) are unclassified.

‡For other Deaconess Mother-Houses in America, see table of Institutions of Beneficence, at close of chapter on the Lutheran Church in the United States.

∥ The increase in the number of deaconesses from 1888 to 1891, was 19.7 per cent.; in the number of fields of labor, 23.4 per cent.; and in contributions, nearly 20 per cent. Since 1864, the number of Mother-Houses has been doubled; the number of deaconesses has increased five-fold; the fields of labor seven-fold; and the contributions nine-fold.

CHAPTER XIV.

FOREIGN MISSIONS.

Lutheran Foreign Missions date from the days of Luther. Already, in 1560, Primus Truber translated the New Testament into the language of the Croats and of the Wends, that they might become acquainted with the Gospel, and that its pure teachings might reach the Turks.

From 1550 to 1611, during the reign of Charles IX., of Sweden, many efforts were made for the conversion of the Laplanders. Churches and parsonages were erected, and many pastors sent among them. Under Gustavus Adolphus (1611-1632) the work was continued with vigor; a hymnbook and agendæ were translated into their tongue, and a seminary founded at Upsala, chiefly to train men for work in Lapland. A former tutor of the King became superintendent of the schools established among these heathen people, and a second mission seminary was opened (at Lycksele) for the training of native helpers. The work in this mission was continued through the reign of Queen Christina. More churches were built, native pastors were ordained, and Probst Tornäus translated other helpful books into the Lapp tongue. In 1648 Tornäus began mission work among the Finnish Lapps, erected several churches and sent ministers to them. These tribes were then living in utter heathenism.

About the same time the Church in Sweden began mission work among the inhabitants of the Baltic provinces, who clung to their heathen religion and practices with the greatest tenacity.

In 1637 the Swedes planted a colony on the Delaware, the pastors of which were instructed to minister not only to the colonists, but also to the Indians "in the spirit of the Gospel." This Swedish colony was intended to be a mission station of the Lutheran Church. Campanius, who was sent to it with Governor Printz, in 1642, translated Luther's Catechism into the language of the Virginia Indians.

The Bishop of Drontheim, about 1658, began mission work among the Norwegian Lapps.

The Danes planted a colony on the Coromandel coast of India, 1620; and in the Royal Letters confirming the establishment of the East India Company, it was ordered that all the clergy sent to that colony should strive to turn the heathen aborigines from error. Over the grave of Jacob Worm, who died near the close of that century, stands the inscription: "India's Danish Apostle."*

Early in the 17th century seven Lutheran jurists of Luebeck formed an association for mission work. Among them was Peter Heyling, who reached Abyssinia as a missionary in 1634, labored successfully for twenty years, and translated the New Testament into the Amhar language.

The somewhat famous embassy from Germany to Persia, 1635, seems to have been comparatively fruitless. A subsequent missionary wrote that its chief visible result was that the people praised the leading missionary and wished only that he had been of their religion, which would have found in him a very skillful advocate.

About the middle of the 17th century Justinianus von

---

* About the year 1663 Duke Ernst, the Pious, of Germany, sent a messenger to Abyssinia in the hope that a way might be found for the introduction of Christianity among the people of that country. Other potentates of Germany joined him in the effort, but no record of success has been discovered.

Welz published books and tracts earnestly advocating more zealous foreign mission work ; and he proved the sincerity of his plea by giving 12,000 thalers for the work. He gave up his title (Baron) and himself became a humble missionary to the heathen. He went to Cayenne and Essequibo, and was thenceforth lost to history. But "the Lord knoweth them that are His." He was not lost to God. It is supposed that he was torn to pieces by wild beasts, a martyr for Christ.*

From the time of Baron von Welz to the end of the century, prominent men in the Lutheran Church stood forth to urge a more earnest effort to give the gospel to the heathen. Among them were Dunte, of Reval; Havemann, general superintendent of Bremen ; Donnhauer, of Strassburg; Spener, of Halle; the eminent Christian Scriver; the great historian of the Reformation, Veit Ludwig von Seckendorf; and the world-renowned scholar and philosopher, Leibnitz, of Leipsic and Hanover.

Denmark established a colony in the West Indies in 1672. About the same time she founded Christiansborg on the Gold Coast of Africa, and also acquired territory peopled with heathen in Lapland and Greenland ; and although not so active as the Church might have been, yet in these things lay her first steps toward setting her light to shine among these nations in darkness.

In the beginning of the 18th century the German settlers in Pennsylvania began sending petitions back to the Fatherland that pastors be furnished them. Although the Pennsylvania settlement was not a heathen mission, strictly speaking, yet it required men and means from the Church abroad, and became a mission-field which has borne a rich harvest. Through their efforts in behalf of this 18th century

---

* An edition of his principal work was republished recently in Leipsic—
Der Missionsweckruf des Baron Justinian von Welz, in treuer Wiedergabe des Originaldrucks von Jahre, 1664. *Leipsic,* 1890.

mission, Rev. Drs. Ziegenhagen, German Court-Preacher in London; Urlsperger, of Augsburg; and Francke, of Halle, became the spiritual fathers of Lutheranism in America. In response to the petitions of the emigrant settlers, they sent out Muhlenberg, "German Evangelical Lutheran preacher in Pennsylvania, Maryland, New Jersey and New York."* Kunze, the successor of Muhlenberg, about 1790, addressed President Washington in a proposition to begin work among the Indians. Inasmuch, however, as the proposed plan called for an expenditure of 1,000 Spanish dollars for beginning the work, it was "pigeon-holed" in Congress.

The Eben-Ezer colonies in Georgia, although they numbered but 279 souls, were supplied with two pastors, through the efforts of Francke. Among the regulations given these colonial missionaries was one requiring that Eben-Ezer should be a mission-station for work among the surrounding Indians. For a time this work seemed hopeful; the natives took kindly to instruction and sent their youth to the mission schools. But the "conflict of the races" brought the whole undertaking in their behalf to an untimely end.

The mission at Tranquebar, India, was founded by Denmark. To it, in 1705, went out from Halle those renowned Lutherans who have added so much to the success and dignity of missions, Plutschau and Ziegenbalg. The Netherland missionaries on the field were attempting to win the natives by teaching them the Hollandish or German languages. The Lutheran missionaries began by learning the language of the natives, rightly judging it sufficiently difficult to teach them another religion without attempting to teach them another language. No books were then in existence which could aid a European in acquiring the Indian tongue. The first move of the missionaries was to hire a native teacher to hold his school in their house. They

---

* Plitt: "Lutheran Missions."—*Erlangen.*

seated themselves among the native children and began to learn the letters with them. Ziegenbalg gave special attention to the acquisition of the language, and as soon as he was able to read began to translate. For three years, in so far as it was possible, he gave up the use of the German and Latin and used only the Tamil language. Two years after his arrival in India he wrote Francke that he had read more than 150 Tamil books. To gain the correct pronunciation he had native readers to drill him daily. To gain the speech of the common people he went among them constantly and noted their manner of conversation. He thus mastered the Tamil language, and presently became the teacher of the natives. He read or caused to be read to him, the best of their books, over and over, and thus became proficient in in their literature. Experience soon taught him, as he wrote Francke, " if we would have good Christians we must diligently teach God's word to the young ;" wherefore his next move was to open schools. Christian books were prepared and published in the Tamil tongue. The hymns of the Church were added to the school-books already in use. Without any help he began the transalation of the New Testament. March 31, 1711, three years after it was begun, this work was completed. In 1713 he translated Luther's Smaller Catechism, and shortly after published a Tamil hymn book. Other books followed from the pen of this busy worker. Before 1715 he could report that he had 38 tracts and pamphlets and five books, one of which was the New Testament, all in the Tamil language. Plutschau, meanwhile, had been working in the Portuguese tongue, and was able to report 17 books which he had prepared therein for the benefit of the missions.* About 1715 Ziegenbalg

---

*Ziegenbalg compiled two lexicons, also, one of the common speech and the other of the poetical words of the Tamil tongue. In doing this, in two years he read more than 200 Tamil books. He wrote a grammar of the tongue, which was published in Halle; and prepared a new dic-

began the translation of the Old Testament and continued this until his death, which occurred in 1718, before the work was completed. Romish missionaries had been in India for 200 years, but Ziegenbalg was first to translate God's Word into one of the most widely known languages of the country: and "the man who translates the Bible into a new language is a greater benefactor than he who founds an empire."

A shining light among Lutheran missionaries in India, and one who followed in the path marked out by Ziegenbalg, was the late Dr. Blomstrand. He was born in Sweden, left a promising university career at Lund to enter the field of the Leipsic Mission Society, and through his great linguistic powers, did grand work for the cause. He began his literary work as soon as he reached Tranquebar by revising Ziegenbalg's translation of the Smaller Catechism. He translated nearly all the Lutheran Symbolical books, Zahn's Biblical History, Kurtz's Sacred History, Kurtz's Church History, Löhe's *Samenkoerner*, Arndt's True Christianity, Graul's Distinctive Doctrines, and the first part of *Paradiesgaertlein*. Beside this, he edited for fifteen years, the Tamil paper, *Aronodaja*, "The Dawn." Thus the foundation of a Christian Tamil literature was securely laid, known and pressing wants were supplied, and the seed of future harvests made secure.

"The Danish and German Lutherans, with rare courage and zeal, labored for ninety years to evangelize India, before Carey or any other Englishman definitely entered on the immense and splendid sphere."* "The Danes were the first Protestant missionaries in India, and they sheltered and be-

---

tionary, containing 40,000 words, in alphabetical order, exhibiting at one view the primitive words and their derivatives. The type for printing these Tamil words were cast in Halle and sent to Tranquebar.—*Plitt.* "*Luth. Mission.*"

* Missionary Review, April, 1890. † Ibid, Sept., 1890.

T

friended the first English missionaries against the persecutions of their own countrymen. English and American workers owe a tribute of thanks to their Danish kindred. The first Protestant king who was, definitely, a nursing father of Christian missions, was the King of Denmark."†

India has become a favorite mission field for all denominations. Work therein has been made comparatively easy by the labors of those early Danish and German missionaries. The societies engaged there now are gathering the harvests from the seed sown by them. Ziegenbalg, in the eleven years of his work, brought 450 of the natives into the Church, and in forty years after his death the number of Tamil converts reached 9,000. After Ziegenbalg, other missionaries were sent out from Europe, among whom was Schultz, well versed in Hebrew, who completed the Tamil version of the Old Testament. This version is the one in use among the Tamils ever since; and it was by such literary labors that these pioneer Lutheran missionaries laid broadly and solidly the deep foundation for successful spiritual work, and made light the labors of all missionaries who came after them, even unto this day. Other mission stations were opened at Madras and Trichinopoli. A seminary for the education of native helpers was founded. In 1733 the ordination of the first native-born East Indian pastor took place.

About 1750 Christian Frederic Schwartz, "the greatest missionary since the time of the Apostles," began his half-century of work on this field. He moved among all classes to bless them. He taught and preached in the English, Portuguese, Tamil, Hindostani, and Persian languages. He labored for the conversion of all alike—natives, Europeans, heathen, Roman Catholics, Mohammedans, citizens and soldiers. By his untiring activity the boundaries of the mission field were widely extended. No man in the land was more extensively known or more influential. He was universally beloved. The number of converts brought to Christ by his direct instrumentality in the Hands of the Spirit, reached almost seven thousand. Even at the present day there is scarcely any European name so well known in India as the name of Schwartz. His European co-workers honored him as a master, from whom all could learn; his converts loved him as a father; his praise was in all the churches. The congregations founded by him up to 1778, by 1800 embraced more than 2,900 souls. Whole villages, containing hundreds of people, came to Christ together and were baptized at once.

No man had such influence among the natives as he. When the government of Madras sought to arrange terms of peace with Hyder Ali, one of the greatest Mohammedan princes of India, who dictated his terms under the walls of Madras, Schwartz was the only man with whom he would treat. "Send me Schwartz," said that mild-mannered but determined and successful man; "him and no other, will I receive and trust." And when, in 1781–83, during another terrible war for which the missionary thought the English were to blame, the inhabitants and garrison of Tanjore were dying of starvation, neither the British nor the native Rajah could induce the native cultivators of the soil to sell any provisions, and it seemed as though famine and pestilence would do what the war had aimed at—extirpate the whole foreign population. In despair the English and native authorities appealed to Schwartz to interfere: when he sent out his requests for food and gave simply his word that all supplies would be paid for, the people sent in all that was necessary and ended the threatened famine. Thus the moral power of one humble Lutheran missionary did for the English garrison and the people of Tanjore what they could not do for themselves, and what all the force of England's prestige, in the time of direst need, failed to accomplish. All of which shows that the natives almost worshipped him. And to this day his name stands unrivalled in honor among them. Schwartz, the grand old Lutheran missionary, "the German oak in the land of palms."

During a visit of one of the earlier Lutheran missionaries to England he secured some aid for the India mission from the Society for the Spread of Christian Knowledge. Later, an English mission was begun, with the assistance of missionaries from the Lutheran force.* Then the Catechism of the Church of England was introduced. By-and-by the missionaries were required to subscribe to the Confession of that Church. When they quit the service rather than renounce their faith, the missionaries of the Church of England took possession of the churches established by the Lutherans and they ceased to be Lutheran from that day. It was a repetition of the old tactics: Give them a finger and they will take the hand; give them the hand and they will take the arm. By the end of the first quarter of the nineteenth century the majority of the Lutheran mission congregations in India had been gathered into the Church of England fold. The spread of Rationalism and the resulting indifference in Europe made matters worse for the Church in India. Moreover, the fact that the English Society for the Spread of the Gospel in Foreign Parts had drawn many missionaries from the Berlin Society, and had been aiding the Halle Mission Institute with means, all tended to make the transfer easier. After the camel's head was allowed in the tent the whole body soon followed, and the owner was obliged to get out. The pioneer work of the zealous and faithful Lutherans for a century and a quarter, with its rich fruits, nearly all passed under control of the Church of England mission societies. It was, however, a time

---

* Plitt: *Lutheran Mission.*

when denominational lines were not strictly drawn in the mission fields, and when unbelief in France and England, and Rationalism in Germany caused much indifference to churchly confessions. The general apathy which followed in the wake of Rationalism in Denmark and Germany, probably made it difficult for our Churches in those lands to care properly for their missions in India. It is possible, also, that the English Society had some justification in these things for gathering in the many mission stations founded by so many years of toil and sacrifice by the Lutherans. But if such be the case, it was unfortunate for the fair fame of the Lutheran Church that such a possibility should have existed. The fact that the English Society extended financial aid to the missionaries without any pledge from them that they should change their confessional standing, and then, with the civil government behind it, required not only that they use the Church of England Catechism, but also that they subscribe to the Thirty-nine Articles of the Church of England, does not bear the stamp of a disinterested undenominational zeal for the spread of the gospel. The additional fact that, when the Lutheran missionaries refused to change their confessional basis, and were forced to retire from their posts, the English took possession of them, hints broadly at a disposition to reap the harvest of seed which other hands had sown. The Lutheran Church was left with but a handful of converts, who had protested against being conveyed to a people in whom they, with reason, had not unbounded confidence.

While the march of events was thus robbing the Lutheran Church of her missions in India, Lutheranism began to regain a better knowledge of itself. It awakened to a new devotion to its own Confessions. Three of the young men who had been trained in the Mission Institute of Berlin refused to accede to the demands of the English Society, and asked to be sent out as Lutheran missionaries. They appealed to the Lutherans of Prussia and Saxony. A society was organized in Dresden, August 17th, 1836, on a strictly Lutheran basis; the first one pledged to an adherence to the Augsburg Confession since doctrinal indifference had poisoned the spiritual life of so many of our people. A call was issued inviting Lutherans everywhere to join it. The Basel Society, organized twenty years previously, seemed to have been blessed in its work, and the friends of missions questioned whether it would be right to break from it. But the influence which went forth from Hanover and Saxony increased in strength as the years rolled on, in behalf of the strictly Lutheran Society. In 1838 the Dresden Society sent two missionaries to South Australia; in 1840 two others were sent. But here again the English interfered with the work, the Governor virtually closing the mission schools, and the newly established bishop of Adelaide "annexing" the converts to the English Episcopal Church.* For the time this ended our mission work in Australia. Some of the missionaries, however, labored among their countrymen who were settling in Australia, and gathered them into congregations.

In the meantime, the remnants of the missions left in the hands of the Danish missionaries in India began to gather strength, and the progress was so marked that request was made to the Dresden society for aid. About 1840 the first missionary from Dresden reached Tranquebar. Shortly afterward, with money sent out from Germany, a house was bought at Poreiar, India, to be used as a seminary for the training of native helpers. Some of the native Christians had petitioned the Danish government not to transfer them to the Church of England Society, when the sale of the Danish possessions was completed in 1845, lest their spiritual interests should suffer as their temporal interests had suffered, and their

* Plitt: *Luth. Mission*, 245.

petition was granted. The Danish authorities then arranged with the Dresden Society to receive and care for the Lutheran mission interests at Tranquebar. It was now deemed expedient to remove the Mission Institute of Dresden to Leipsic, inasmuch as the latter was a University town. A central directory, called "The College of Evangelical Lutheran Missions at Leipsic," was organized and opened the work in the interest of Confessional Lutheranism about 1848. When the Society, about the same time, received the India missions of the Danish Church into its care, the mission at Tranquebar had been built up, so that the organization in the city numbered 1,000 members, that in Poreiar 500, with 5 catechists, 14 schools, 18 teachers, and 572 pupils. Eight missionaries were put in charge of the work. And this was the substantial harvest gathered by the Lutheran Church from nearly a century and a half of successful mission work in India.

The idea of missions to the heathen has not always and everywhere been a popular one. In 1796 the General Assembly of the Church of Scotland passed a resolution declaring that the idea of converting the heathen was highly preposterous. In the United States, in 1810, the men who founded the American Board were regarded by many as visionary and fanatical. When the application for a charter for that Society was made before the Legislature of Massachusetts, opposition was made to granting it. One member declared, "We have no religion to spare." About the same time Sydney Smith, an eminent English churchman, and a representative man of letters, hinted at the feeling which, for a long time, was general in England, when he laughingly said to one about to go as a missionary to heathen lands: "I hope you will agree with the man who eats you."

Such were the circumstances under which our Church began her mission work. The world was indifferent. Now we turn to a short account of the societies through which the Lutheran Church is working to-day. Up to 1836 the friends of missions in Saxony sent their contributions to Basel, but since that time the Leipsic Society has worked independently. An annual meeting is held in the week following Whitsun-tide. All the auxiliary societies are represented by delegates. A semi-monthly magazine is published, and under the title, *Blaetter fuer Mission,* bulletins on missions have been issued since 1863, which are translated into seventeen languages. The special territory of the Society is in Southern India. Its chief stations are Tranquebar, Poreiar, Majaveram, Tanjore, Trichinopoli, Madras and Bengaloor. It is a strictly Lutheran Society, and draws its funds from the Lutheran Churches in Saxony, Bavaria, Hanover, Mecklenburg and Russia. The missionaries of the State Church in Sweden coöperate with it at several stations in India.*

In Farther India this society opened a station in 1878, to accommodate those of its members who were drawn to Rangoon. The station has 160 members, mostly immigrant Tamils; a school with 60 pupils, and is served by a Tamil pastor. The Society recently sent out its first woman teacher to foreign mission fields. The Hindus of Madras are opposing the work of the mission, and have established a society for that purpose; but the work goes on. The Tamil Christians contributed 4,000 rupees in 1889 for church work. A seminary in Tranquebar is training native

* During recent famine years in Southern India the Leipsic Society received large additions, but many who were then admitted have since turned away. At Majaveram, also, not a few were proselyted to Roman Catholic missions. Enough remain, however, to show an encouraging increase. Several of the auxiliary stations have become self-supporting, and are under the care of native pastors. The annexed figures show the growth of the mission in the last ten years:

	Stations.	Missionaries.	Members.	Communicants.	Schools.	Pupils.
1878.	16	17	9,908	4,000	102	2,154
1888.	22	22	13,341	6,808	155	3,933

The native ordained pastors now number thirteen.

helpers, of whom 14 are now ordained pastors, and 4 are candidates for the holy office.

The Herrmannsburg Missionary Society has been rightly designated "the wonder of the world." A glance at its workings will show it to be one of the most colossal individual missionary enterprises of the age. No bolder act or conception can be found in the history of missions than that of Louis Harms, when he proposed to his parishioners that they be their own missionaries, when he undertook to inspire poor farmers, peasants, day-laborers, and mechanics, to volunteer for missionary purposes, and to create and sustain, both with money and men, their own missions. It was entirely "out of the usual course," but so was the first Pentecost, and, like that, it proved to be a moving of God.

The founder of the Society, a faithful Lutheran pastor at Herrmannsburg, Germany, formed his first little organization in January, 1834. It is still in active existence. It has established two mission-houses in Germany, and sustained teachers to train men for mission work among the heathen; it has built, at a cost of 19,000 thalers and worn out its own ship in sailing between Germany and its foreign mission stations; it has founded churches and schools in Africa, Asia and Australia, and sent more than 60 pastors to Germans dispersed throughout America; it has secured property for mission purposes in various parts of the world, to the value of 1,352,945 marks; it has nearly 400 missionaries at work in heathen lands; it sustains 60 mission stations at a yearly cost of from $60,000 to $80,000, and has gathered into them a membership of 16,000 souls.

How was it accomplished? In faith, by zeal, with hard work, and through much self-denial. The people, generally, were poor, but were not, therefore, without resources. They had faith, and the Lord is rich. One family dedicated a part of its vegetable crop to the work; another the produce of the best of its fruit trees; some faithful mothers and maidens gave ear-rings, finger-rings and old silver; even the children grew produce on land allowed by their parents for the purpose, and sold it for the benefit of the mission, while others gathered bones, rags and old iron, sold them and laid the money in the mission treasury. And in working to bless others they themselves were blessed. During the seventeen years in which Louis Harms conducted the enterprise the Herrmannsburg parish enjoyed one long-continued season of refreshing from on high. Ten thousand church members were gathered into it. Instead of narrowing their sympathies by such specific effort in one particular field, the result has been to expand their horizon, enrich their spirit, and to render them catholic and cosmopolitan. We accordingly find them sending their missionaries to all parts of the world. And let it be observed that this small and obscure parish in Hanover had no proxies or substitutes. The people constituted their own Board, became their own secretaries, edited their own missionary magazine, and organized and administered their own mission work.

Among the Zulus, where missionary Schröder met a martyr's death, the Society lost six of its stations on account of the recent war, but all have been regained. In Natal, the stations number sixteen. In all there are in this field 23 stations, 1,648 baptized members, 500 communicants, and 580 pupils in the schools.

This Society has important interests in the Transvaal and Orange Free State, where its membership has more than doubled in the last ten years. One station, Bethania, has a membership of 1,590 souls. In Berseba is a seminary for training native teachers. In 1884 the Society passed through a crisis in its history. Complaint was publicly made that the missionaries were giving attention to trade and secular pursuits to the injury of the missions. A thorough investigation showed that, while there was some slight ground for complaint in the case of a few missionaries, the chief trouble arose from the misrepresentations of Roman Catholic polemics. The whole field was visited in 1888 by Inspector Harms and Pastor Haccius.*

In New Zealand the Society has maintained a mission, under great difficulties, for some years. Several German congregations exist on the island, where from 75 to 100 heathen are under the care of the missionaries.

In Australia the work has been prosecuted under almost insurmountable difficulties. Drouths prevail to such an extent that from 1879 to 1885 there was but one general rain. The want in the wilderness is extreme, the connection with the settlements difficult and costly. The hope of a railway between North and South Australia appears to have been but a dream. The native language presents a peculiar obstacle in that it is almost impossible to use it for the expression of Christian ideas. The establishment of a school was a mighty task, but it was accomplished, and now has 20 pupils. The first baptisms (seven) occurred on Pentecost 1887, and since then the work has been slowly progressing.†

The elder Harms, founder of the Herrmannsburg Missionary Society, has been dead for more than twenty years; but his work goes on. "He, being dead, yet speaketh." His works follow him and tell that faith is not dead. They

---

* The growth of these missions in ten years is shown by the following figures:

	Stations.	Missionaries.	Members.	Communicants.	Schools.	Pupils.
1878.	18	18	4.191	1,800	14	460
1888.	24	24	11,085	5,000	?	?

The natives contributed more than 18,000 marks per annum for the support of their congregations. In 1890, in the mission adjoining the Zulus, there were 28 missionaries, 27 native teachers, and 120 helpers; 1,401 heathen were baptized; 13,315 members were enrolled, and the schools had 1,987 pupils in attendance.

† The reports for 1899 show some increase. The mission in India has nine stations and 783 members; in the Zulu mission each station has acquired 4,000 acres of land. The income of the Society was 20,000 marks greater than in the previous year.

show what is possible to them that believe—that faith can remove mountains. That a poor Lutheran congregation, composed of humble people and led by a lowly pastor, should found a missionary society and sustain it for more than fifty years; that these obscure people should erect mission-houses and train missionaries; that they should send forth these educated teachers to the ends of the earth and gather in a baptized membership of more than 16,000 souls; that they should do this work at an annual outlay of more than $60,000; all this is a story of success in doing the work of the Lord almost passing belief! Yet it is being accomplished. No one can deny it. The living evidences of it stand before the eyes of men.

Over at Herrmannsburg stand the Mission Houses, surrounded by the 400 acres of land now owned by the Society, and in the Houses are the teachers and the students who are in training for the work. Away in Africa, India, Australia, New Zealand and far off Tartary are the Mission stations, with their teachers and disciples, the visible evidences of the power of God and the faith of him who planned it all, though for long years, already, he has been gathered to his fathers.

The Gossner Mission among the Kohls was begun in 1844. The district inhabited by these people comprises an area of 44,000 square miles. The inhabitants were among the wildest and fiercest of all the tribes of India. For five years after work was begun among them they shunned the missionaries, but later they were won, and now, in the number of conversions, the mission is one of the most successful of all the missions of Germany.* These Kohls are said to be well fitted for evangelizing the empire. Great things are expected of them. When once instructed in the truth they are indefatigable in teaching others. The Truth completely

---

* The home organization publishes, as its organ, "*Die Biene auf dem Missions Felde.*" The yearly income is about 100,000 marks.

masters them. They are capable of enduring all things for the sake of Christ. If the entire province become, as there is reason to hope, a Christian province, the influence of the Kohls may be felt through all the Indian possessions of Great Britain.

Two Missionaries of the Gossner Society are working in connection with several others sent out from Utrecht, on the Sangi Islands, near the Celebes, in the Eastern Archipelago. They have 22 native helpers, 13 stations, about 1,000 members, 339 communicants and 152 catechumens. A seminary for teachers is being established. About 60 schools are maintained.*

In 1889 four of the Gossner missionaries were sent to East India, and are now at work along the Ganges River. The Society has to meet great opposition from the Jesuits on its mission field.

The Rhenish Mission Society was formed in 1828 by the union of two smaller societies. A mission seminary has been opened in Barmen, and the publication of a mission paper has been begun. This Society has sent out more than 300 missionaries, has between 40 and 50 auxiliary associations, and an annual income of 385,000 marks. It has 63 stations in heathen lands, and 33,000 converts are under its care.

In Cape Colony the congregations of this Society, except two, were supporting themselves financially, and making contributions for the assistance of others, when poverty and want came upon many and hindered the work. The

---

* The principal field of the Gossner Society, as has been indicated, is among the Kohls of Northern India. With a comparatively small force of European missionaries a great work has been accomplished among them. In 1888 the Society reported 33,800 members, 14 principal stations, 14 European missionaries, 17 native helpers ordained to the ministry. A theological seminary exists at Ranchi for training native pastors. The schools number 85, with 2,100 pupils. The communicants number 11,532.

churches in this field are organized into a Synod.* Namaqua Land, in S. W. Africa, has been a mission field of the Rhenish Society for many years. Because of its sterile soil, the evils of the "drink-plague" among the natives, and the wars between the Namaquas and Hereros, the missions have been hindered in their progress, and, in some cases, the results of many years of toil have been entirely destroyed.†

The same Society has a mission among the Hereros, neighbors of the Namaquas. From 1870 to 1880 there was peace between these peoples, and the missions flourished. But after 1880 there was war for seven years, in consequence of which the stations all suffered, and one was wholly abandoned. Many members of the missions perished on the field of battle; many others were led back into the ways of heathenism. A little seminary, with fifteen students, is in existence in this field. An important aid for future work has been furnished in the completion, by Missionary Brinker, of a grammar of the Herero and Ovambo languages ‡

In Sumatra, up to 1878, the work of the Rhenish Society progressed but slowly. Since then it has been otherwise. For several years, dating from January, 1879, the baptisms each year have reached from 1,000 to 1,500. Many capable native assistants have greatly helped in the work. The

---

* The Cape Colony Synod has 11 stations, 14 missionaries, 87 native helpers, 11,159 baptized members, 4,037 communicants, 13 schools, and 2,350 pupils. The annual contributions are 38,750 marks.

† The number of stations in 1888 was but 8, (2 less than in 1880,) and the number of missionaries was 9, (1 less than in 1880;) the native helpers are 32, the baptized members increased from 3,302 in 1880 to 4,127 in 1888, and the communicants from 1,458 to 1,629. The schools are attended by 700 pupils. In 1889 the baptized members numbered 4,414, and the natives paid 2,000 marks into the church treasury. The congregation at Berseba numbers 924 members, and is the largest in Namaqua Land.

‡ At the close of 1887 the stations of the Society among the Hereros numbered 7; the missionaries 8; baptized members 2,073; communicants 713; children in the schools 560. It is proposed, for the future, to give most attention to the training of evangelists in this mission.

Helper's Seminary at Pautjurna-Pitu has 70 students, and eleven others had to be sent to another institution for want of room. Congregational and synodical organization has been effected, and a Superintendent of Missions has his residence among a part of the people who are still cannibals. A third station has been opened to the northward, on the Toba Sea. Some of the stations recently passed through great peril by reason of the action of Mangaradja, the Mohammedan Priest-King, an avowed enemy of the Christians, who waged war against the whole country, and compelled many of the missionaries to flee for their lives. But his plans were overthrown, his forces defeated, and the missions came out of the ordeal with renewed vigor.*

In the southern part of the island of Nias, this Society was compelled to abandon their stations in 1886, because of native race-wars. In the northern part, however, work has gone forward at the three stations there established. A new station has been opened to receive the Sumatra Christians coming to this island. A Helper's Seminary is in connection with the station, Dahana, and its superintendent, Sundermann, is translating the Bible into the language of the people. From 1880 to 1888 the number of members increased from 238 to 613. There are 161 communicants and the schools have 50 pupils.†

---

* Each year now sees new congregations organized and new church-buildings erected with their own means by the zealous Christians. Three native Battas were ordained pastors in 1885. The greatest enemy of the work is Mohammedanism, but it is gradually losing its power over the people. The following table shows the state of the mission:

	Stations.	Missionaries.	Members.	Communicants.	Schools.	Pupils.
1880.	11	16	5,009	1,228	?	995
1888.	13	16	13,135	3,192	55	1,422

The European missionaries are assisted by 3 ordained natives and 280 unordained helpers, 202 of the latter working without salary.

† Several stations in the island of Borneo, occupied for long years without visible results, have been abandoned for the time, on account of

The Rhenish Society has a mission field in China. Formerly it had several stations, but now confines its labors to one located at "Fuk-wing," with several outposts served by native helpers. A promising medical mission has been opened. A seminary exists for training native assistants. The baptized members, in six years, increased from 211 to 265.*

Missionaries of this Society opened stations in 1888 in King William's Land, New Guinea. Four missionaries are engaged here and on the neighboring island, Siar, (Prince Henry's Haven,) where they have established two stations.

During the year 1890 seven new stations have been established by the Rhenish Society: one on the Dampier Archipelago, one at Nias, and five in Sumatra. An extension of the work among the Hereros is also at hand. The receipts of the Society increased 58,000 marks during the year. It receives some support from Reformed churches.

The Society for the Promotion of Evangelical Missions among the Heathen, commonly known as the Berlin Missionary Society, is a Lutheran organization, representing the more conservative tendency of the Prussian State Church. It has a large Mission-house in Berlin, where some 30 young men receive full preparation for the mission service. Its field is South Africa, where it has 65 European missionaries in the work.

In Cape Colony it has stations among the mixed populations of the southern districts, where the few remnants of

the bitter enmity of Islam. Yet in the northern part of the island re main':

	Stations.	Missionaries.	Members.	Communicants.	Schools.	Pupils.
1880.	6	7	663	322	?	298
1888.	6	8	1,159	583	?	365

Twenty-six native helpers assist the missionaries.

* Missionary Faber, formerly connected with the Rhenish Society, published, in the Chinese language, Commentaries on books of the Bible and other writings intended to reach the cultured classes of China with Christian ideas.

the Hottentot tribes maintain their existence. The churches here are all organized and chiefly self-supporting. Few heathen remain in these regions, and these are being assimilated in the Christian congregations year by year. During the last ten years its operations have been greatly extended in Cape Colony. It has a synodical organization there, but enters complaint that the Anglican missionaries and the Salvation Army interfere to proselyte its people.*

This Society has a mission among the Kaffirs,† and Dr. Krapf, one of its missionaries, was a member of a commission which, after nineteen years, finished the translation of the Bible into the tongue of the natives. Superintendent Krapf, for eleven years President of the Commission, carried the translation to Europe and saw it through the press. The theological faculty of Berlin, *causa honoris*, conferred on him the title of *Doctor Divinitatis*.

In Natal and Zulu Land the Society has six stations and six missionaries; the number of baptized members has increased in ten years from 879 to 1,356.

In the Orange Free State the Berlin Society has a synodical organization embracing some stations in West Griqua Land; it has a synod also in North Transvaal and one in the South Transvaal.‡ In South Transvaal the synod, formed in 1878, embraces thirteen stations. This district did not suffer much during the late wars, and the number of baptized members more than doubled in six years. The congregration in Pretoria tripled its membership in seven

---

* In 1878 the Society had:

	Stations.	Missionaries.	Members.	Schools.	Pupils.
	5	7	2,206	5	277
In 1888	8	8	4,288	8	639

† The Society has on their territory 5 stations, 5 missionaries, 804 baptized members, 5 schools and 256 pupils.

‡ In 1885 the Society celebrated the fiftieth anniversary of the commencement of its work in the old mission, Bethania, among the Korannas and Betchanas. The Synod in this section is not only self-supporting, but contributes toward carrying on the work in other parts.

U

years. That in Botschabelo, although many of its younger members leave it for the adjacent diamond fields, numbers 2,500 souls. A seminary for training native helpers is located here.

In the North Transvaal is also a synod. The superintendent, Konthe, has translated the New Testament into the native tongue. Mphome, one of the newer stations, has a teachers' seminary and a congregation of 800 souls.* (1888.)

This Society has a mission-field also in China. The principal point is Canton, whence seventeen congregations in four districts are cared for. Three are served by European missionaries, of whom there are four, the others by native deacons and catechists. The membership numbers 735, of whom 442 are communicants. They have 126 children in their schools.

The Parent Society at home is assisted by 300 auxiliaries. Its churches in South Africa are growing into an important church system. Several schools and industrial institutions are in a flourishing condition there. A seminary qualifies colored native helpers, and the people have made most encouraging progress in external civilization as well as in Christian life. In 1889-90 a number of the missions among the Bassutos erected themselves into a self-governing and self-supporting Bassuto National Church.

The Berlin Society quite recently opened another mission field, and now begins work in East Africa. The Moravian Society occupies territory adjacent, both being in the German East African possessions, north of Lake Nyassa. The

---

*In the three synods are two ordained native pastors and 289 other native helpers, of whom 220 render service without salary. The free-will offerings amount to about 15,000 marks a year. The following figures show the increase and present numerical strength of the mission:

	Stations.	Missionaries.	Members.	Communicants.	Schools.	Pupils.
1878.	27	29	6,729	2,961	?	1,712
1888.	30	35	13,555	6,613	?	2,535

The out-stations number 77.

stations of the two societies being near each other, may be able to assist one another if need should arise. The Moravians will work from their location to the west and northwest, while the Berlin laborers will move toward the east and northeast. The Moravians send out four missionaries under the direction of the free missionary, Gross, who has had five years' experience in the Nyassa country. The Berlin Society sends out four missionaries and three mechanics, under the direction of the veteran superintendent, Merensky. The reports for 1890 say that two stations have been opened on the coast; one at Dar-es-Salaam and one at Tanga. At the former station a hospital is open and doing its work of mercy. It is controlled by brothers from the Rauhe Haus, assisted by deaconesses. A third station is to be opened farther inland.

The first indications of returning mission life among the German churches, after Rationalism had accomplished its work, were seen in the organization of the Basel Mission Society. It was begun substantially on the broad basis of the New Testament as its Confession of Faith. It had the sympathy of practically all the friends of missions in our Church. It was organized September 25th, 1815. In the following year it began the publication of its mission magazine. To it all the new auxiliary and aid societies sent their offerings for the work. To it the majority of the young men who felt called to preach the gospel to the heathen made application. Basel commanded the mission-life in the Evangelical churches of Germany,* and also largely of Scandinavia. Although styled a " union " organization, the most of its teachers and students have been from the Lutheran churches of Würtemberg. It derives half its income, its largest contributions, and most of its workers from them. One-half the living men educated at the Basel Mission College were natives of Würtemberg. Of

---

* Plitt: *Luth. Mission.*

the graduates of this institution 211 have found a home in the United States. The Society uses Luther's Catechism and the Würtemberg *Spruch-buch* as "memorizing books," in the schools in India. These books are translated into the language of the natives. This Society has been at work for many years on the Gold Coast of Africa. Great difficulties were encountered there. Twenty-five years ago the communicants numbered only 250, but since then the work is more hopeful. The native congregations contribute willingly, averaging two and a quarter marks for each communicant, in behalf of the work. The schools are doing good work. In 1885 a medical station and a health station were added to the other new stations recently established. A congregation of 136 souls exists in an independent province formerly belonging to Ashanti. The growth of the mission is indicated in the fact that the number of pupils in the schools has doubled in the last ten years.[*]

The Basel Society has three mission districts in India. In the South Mahratta district the number of members has been tripled in the last ten years.[†] Up to the beginning of 1890 twelve missionaries have been sent to the Cameroon district of Africa. Four have died. Three others

---

[*] The following figures show its strength:

Missionaries:		Members.	Schools.	Pupils.
European.	Native.			
1879. 33	8	3,960	37	1,121
1888. 31	18	7,495	83	2,253

The returns for 1890 gave 10 principal and 70 auxiliary stations, with 9,000 baptized members and 3,000 children in the schools. Two European medical missionaries belong to the mission force.

[†] The following figures give a summary of this Society's missions:

	Stations.	Missionaries.	Members.	Communicants.	Schools.	Pupils.
1878.	20	63	6,037	3,070	62	2,654
1888.	23	68	9,237	4,941	102	5,330

Seventeen native ordained pastors assist in the work. The reports for 1889 show an increase of about 33,000 marks in the contributions over 1888.

are preparing to take their places. On the Gold Coast the number of members has increased to 8,224; in India, to 9,400; in China to 3,286; while the Cameroon district reports only 250, with 350 children in the schools. When, in 1884, the German flag was hoisted over this territory, the English Baptists, who had been laboring there for many years with little success, gave their mission over to the Basel Society, Three missionaries were put on the field about Christmas, 1886; one of them died in a short time of African fever and in a few months a second was laid in his grave. Others went out to take the place of the fallen. Several of the smaller stations were united, and became independent congregations. The latest reports indicate a more hopeful state of affairs, although the Roman Catholics and the German Baptists have opened missions on the same field. The climate is deadly to Europeans. In 1890 four missionaries died. The director of the work was obliged, because of ill health, to return to Europe. Ten missionaries, assisted by twenty native helpers, are at work in this territory.

The missions of this Society in China have been steadily moving forward. Ten years ago the stations numbered four; now they number eleven; then the members numbered 1,627, now 3,127; the children in school were 372, now 692. This increase is the more notable because it is made in the face of constant migrations of the people to other districts. By this migration Christian colonies and congregations have been planted in Hawaii, Demarara and North Borneo. Hong Kong sends out the most of these emigrants. The missionaries visit these congregations as they have opportunity.

The North German or Bremen missionaries have been working on the deadly shores of the Slave Coast of Africa since 1847. Along with some Basel missionaries they have gone among the Ewei people, with the kingdom of Dahomey northeast and Ashanti northwest, and there, with much suffering and many tears, they have sown the precious seed. On this Slave Coast the North German Society has sealed its devotion to the evangelization of Africa with the lives of many of its messengers. In the 38 years preceding 1885, it sent out 110 missionaries—71 men and 39 women. Of this number 54 died under the deadly influence of the climate; 40 were obliged to leave the mission because of broken health, and but 16 were left to carry on the work. For many years the outlook seemed hopeless. After 30 years of toil and sacrifice the number of baptisms was but 200. Lately, however, the work is more encouraging. It is now concentrated at Keta, on the coast, Ho, and a health station in the interior, and twelve out-stations.*

The Society has recently taken steps to begin a work long planned in Togoland. An important movement was also made in providing a health-resort for the missionaries on its West Coast stations. With the aid of friends in Hamburg, four deaconesses have been sent to take charge of this health-station and a deaconess-house has been opened in Keta, but it is to be permanently established at a point inland. In Keta is also a seminary where 27 natives are in training for teachers and preachers. The New Testament and part of the Old, a Hymn-book, a Prayer-book, a Biblical History, and some school-books, have been translated into the difficult native language. One of the four deaconesses has already fallen a victim to the terrible, deadly climate, and with broken health has returned to Europe.

The Evangelical Lutheran Foreign Missionary Society of Bavaria has begun independent mission-work in East Africa. For a time the Church in Bavaria sent its offerings to the Leipsic Society. Loehe's organization at Neuendettelsau, existing since 1840, aided also in Foreign Mission work, although its principal object was to prepare men to accompany German

* The mission now employs 8 missionaries, 6 catechists, 14 teachers, has 664 baptized members, 409 communicants, 5 schools and 321 pupils.

emigrants to America and Australia, and there supply them with the means of grace. But it has engaged in work among the heathen also, and has coöperated with the Immanuel Synod of Australia in carrying on missions among the Papuans of New Guinea. The Bavarian Society more recently has begun work on or near the Coast in East Africa, occupying two stations, the oldest at Jimba and a later one opened 1887. At the former station the natives themselves built the church. Six ordained missionaries and one woman helper are on the field. One has died and one gave up the work because of broken health. A tour of exploration was made by two of the missionaries in 1889, "eighty hours" into the interior, and it is proposed there to open a third station. The headquarters of the Society are in Hersbruck; its Director is Pastor Ittameier. Its income is 23,400 marks a year. The Neuendettlesau Society has an income of 28,100 marks.*

The Evangelical Lutheran Protestant Mission Society, for work in India, China and Japan, has its seat in Saxe-Weimar. Grand Duke Karl Alexander assumed the Protectorate of this organization. It was formed to provide properly qualified men to look after the Germans scattered throughout the countries wherein it proposes to labor; to gather them into church organizations, and then to make these the centres for regular mission work among the surrounding non-Christian and heathen inhabitants. It established a mission in Tokio, Japan, 1885, where it has two stations, four missionaries, one congregation and about 300 communicants. The theory of the somewhat liberal organizers of the Society was that a philosophical presentation of theology is a necessity, in order to reach the educated classes of Japan, but their first missionary reports that the old-time methods of the mission societies seem to be the only practical ones. One of their four missionaries is laboring among the Germans in Shang-

---
* Warneck: *Miss. Zeitschrift*, April, 1891.

hai. A native preacher aids the two missionaries residing in Tokio. There a building-lot has been secured near the University and adjoining institutions for higher education, and there it is proposed to establish a "theological academy," with recitation rooms, quarters for students, a place for the 10,000 volume library already on hand, and, in time, a residence for the missionaries. A sign of the need of such an institution is seen in the fact that a congregation of native Christians only a few miles from Tokio has been without a pastor for seven years. This Society was formed, 1884. Its yearly income is about 35,000 marks.

Nearly fifty years ago a missionary society was founded in Germany, and entitled "Woman's Society for the Christian Education of Women in the East." For the past twenty-five years it has had its own monthly mission paper. In four years after its organization the Society had 35 auxiliaries, which sent their offerings to the head society in Berlin. Already in 1846 its income was 10,579 marks. The activity of the superintendent in Berlin did much to arouse interest in the extraordinary work, to overcome prejudice against women's missions, to collect funds, and to render assistance to auxiliary associations. The principal aim of the Society was to send women, qualified as teachers, to India. Under its auspices Christian schools have been founded at Ghazapone and Bhagulpore; some heathen children, also, have been provided for in orphanages. The greater part of the harvest from the work of this mission, however, has been gathered by our brethren of the Church of England missions in India.

The Berlin Woman's Society for China is doing effective work in Hong Kong in caring for neglected children. It has a foundling hospital in that city with four deaconesses in charge, and Pastor Hartmann as director. The institution is maintained for Chinese girls, of whom 24 have been confirmed, 33 have been married and are scattered from

Honolulu to San Francisco; 26 are yet school children, and 27 are ranked as "play-children," yet too young for school. One leading object of the mission is to provide women of Christian training, who may become wives of the native-born helpers in the missions. The whole number now in the institution is 80. The income is 15,700 marks.

The Brecklum Society, founded in 1877, works in Farther India. There it has four stations and eleven missionaries, with one school and 20 pupils. Its income is 65,000 marks.

The Mission Society for China, whose headquarters are in Berlin, works with the Berlin Society in the city of Canton. They employ five missionaries, and their converts number about 800.

The Paris Ev. Foreign Mission Society belongs to the "united" wing of mission work. It reports eleven stations in Basutoland, with 17 French missionaries and about 20,000 baptized members and catechumens.* It has a congregation at Morija with 1,148 communicants. The yearly receipts are 240,000 marks.

The Jerusalem Society for Gospel Work in Palestine, organized 1845, works in Palestine and Egypt. It reports three stations, two European missionaries and seven natives ordained as helpers, 300 members and 200 children in its schools. Its yearly income is 30,000 marks.

The Evangelical Mission Society for German East Africa, founded 1885, whose work in caring for the sick was here most opportune, founded its first station, 1887, in Dar-es-Salaam, where a number of slave children were taken under its care. Since then the mission family removed to Zanzibar. Two ordained missionaries, one deacon and two deaconesses are in the employ of the society. In 1889 its income had increased to 35,000 marks.

Pastor Flierl was sent out by the Neuendettlesau Society, years ago, to work among the natives of Australia. When

---

* Warneck: *Missions Zeitschrift.*

Kaiser Wilhelm's Land in New Guinea was chosen as a field for mission work, Pastor Flierl was sent as the pioneer of that undertaking. He started thither in 1885, but did not reach his destination until 1886. Another missionary was sent out and in the harvest time of 1886 they began work at a station called Simbang,"1½ hours" southwest of Finch Haven. This society has a mission among the natives of Australia, also, since 1878. A second station, north of Cooktown, was opened 1885 and a missionary sent to it by the Immanuel Synod of South Australia. A Christian negro is his assistant. The mission is under control of the Neuendettlesau Society. Another station has been opened near Cape Bedford.

The Immanuel Synod and the Lutheran Synod of Queensland, together, have taken charge of the Mission Reserve, Bloomfield, south of Cooktown. The German-Scandinavian Lutheran Synod of Queensland has taken charge of a mission on the river Andromache, 65 miles north of Mackay. The work here is carried on by two missionaries and three young Scandinavian colonists.

In ten years the receipts of the Immanuel Synod for missions increased from 15,000 to 85,000 marks per year. Of this amount 6,000 marks came from Germany, but after the Neuendettlesau Society opened its missions in North Australia and New Guinea the receipts from Germany fell to no more than 1,000 marks.

The Evangelical Lutheran Foreign Mission of Holland,* with headquarters at Amsterdam, endeavored to open a station in the extreme south of Sumatra, Dutch East Indies; but the missionary died while awaiting permission from the government to begin work. Two successors, trained in the Barmen Institute, were sent to succeed him, but went to the Batu Islands, south of Nias. The tongue of Nias is spoken

---
* *Evangelisch " Lutherisch Genootschap voor In-en Uitwendige Zending,"* Amsterdam.

there, and these missionaries work on friendliest terms with those of the Rhenish Society. Yearly income, 5,000 marks.

The officials and friends of our mission societies fully understand that this is the age of printers' ink, and deem the use of the press an absolute necessity in their work. One says: " All live missionary societies, either for the heathen or for Israel, in order that their field may widen and the circle of their friends increase, find a missionary journal needful. On the one side the progress of the work must be reported, and on the other the friends of missions must be aroused." The mission literature of Germany is one of the significant features of church life in the Fatherland. The periodicals are numerous and widely-circulated. The regular editions of those published in Berlin in the interest of Inner Missions are reported at from 220 to 260,000 copies. In Bavaria, where there are fewer than two million Protestants, (say half a million communicants,) three periodicals on Inner Missions, (one weekly,) are published. In addition to the publications in behalf of particular objects, pamphlets, magazines and books are issued to forward the general mission work. Many of these emanate from men who are recognized authorities on mission topics. Dr. Warneck issues a monthly which gives a review of all foreign mission work, together with discussions on mission subjects. This periodical holds a front rank in mission literature. A valuable work, covering the whole foreign mission field up to 1880, now offered by the publisher for 20 marks, is the Burkhardt-Grundemann Little Mission Library: 4 volumes. Dr. Grundemann has published a fifth volume in continuation of the series, which brings the work down to 1883. He has issued also a Mission Atlas with 74 large plates, and a smaller one with 12 plates, which are to students of missions what a good geographical atlas is to the student of geography. "Missions in the Light of the Bible" and "Missions in Pictures from their History," are works from the pen of

Dr. Warneck. "Missions in the School—a Hand-Book for Teachers," is from the same scholarly and prolific pen. In a very short time after the last-named work appeared three editions were exhausted, and a translation was made into the Hollandish tongue. Church papers report it now in its fifth edition. It was published in 1887.

Dr. Christlieb published "The Present Condition of Evangelical Heathen Missions" in 1880. It passed through four or more editions and was translated into English. Dr. Gundert is the author of "Evangelical Missions, their Lands, People and Works," Stuttgart, 1881: 2d Ed. 1886. Dr. Grundemann has issued "Statistics of Missions," 1886. The "Liberals" have issued "Missions Then and Now," Frankfort, 1883. Dr. Wangemann has published "The History of the Berlin Society's Missions;" and two pastors have each written a "History of the Gossner Society's Work among the Kohls." Herrmannsburg authorities have issued a history of their work in Africa. We may name also: "In the Danish West Indies," "In the Western Himalayas," and "Mission Work in Australia," which deal principally with the Moravian missions. Merensky's "Mission Life in the Transvaal" is a most interesting work: 1888. Petrich's Pomerania Mission-Book is an excellent presentation of the mission life of Pomerania and adjacent provinces.

The Calwer Mission Journal and the publications of the different mission societies, although given out specially in behalf of the respective societies, always give attention to general mission topics. The "Reports from the East India Institute at Halle," the oldest of the German mission journals, are now appearing as an annual under the editorial supervision of Drs. Warneck, Grundemann and Frick. The title is "Narratives and Pictures from the Mission Fields," and the work is illustrated with many wood cuts. In this new form it was circulated to the extent of 20,000 copies yearly; but of late the circulation has fallen off somewhat.

The Brandenburg Mission Conference published (1887,) "Thorns and Gleanings from the Mission Field," which went into the 3d edition already in 1888. Scores of mission papers, more than one hundred, at least one hundred and twenty-five, are published regularly, most of them monthly, in the interest of the various missions.

The Mission Conferences began, in 1836, to be a feature of the work. The officials of the different societies came together to confer concerning the interests of the cause. These conferences soon included representatives from Holland, the Scandinavian kingdoms, and the Evangelical organizations in France and French Switzerland. A friend of the cause has provided a house in Bremen where they always receive a hearty welcome. In addition to these official assemblies, pastors and friends of the cause in various parts of Germany have established other convocations of a more popular character. These are intended to awaken among the people more interest in the work. In Posen such organizations have existed for many years. In 1879, through the influence of Dr. Warneck, a Mission Conference was formed in Halle. In the second year of its existence it had 560 members; now it has 1,300. It circulates the mission pamphlets of Dr. Warneck to the extent of 20 to 25,000 copies each. The yearly meeting is held in the week following Sexagesima Sunday. The sermons, addresses and papers are heard by a large proportion of the pastors in the province as well as by large assemblies of the laity. Great good is thus accomplished in the way of extending news from the mission fields, making known their wants and arousing sympathy with the work. A similar organization exists in Brandenburg. It has held its annual meetings in Berlin in the week following Septuagesima Sunday, but now holds them alternately in the principal cities of the province. It applies all the means which come into its treasury to deepen the interest of the home churches in the mission work. It extends aid to theological students who show special inclination for mission work, and assists them in attending Mission Institutes in order that they may become acquainted with missionary operations in all their bearings. It publishes regularly and gives to its members a Year-Book filled with facts and all the matter necessary in holding "Mission-Hours." It circulates mission literature at the lowest possible rate and publishes popular writings on the subject. It establishes Mission-Preaching Circles, providing speakers and topics wherever needed. It has a Mission-Library which is free to all its members. It has arranged with the secular press for the insertion of articles every two months upon mission topics, and this arrangement has extended to the periodicals everywhere throughout the province. These articles are prepared by authorities on the subject and secure an astonishing circulation.

In Pomerania the Mission Conference pursues its work on about the same plan. It has, however, added a course of instruction on mission subjects which is given gratuitously to all students of theology. The course occupies fourteen days. These courses are arranged by men of ripe experience in mission affairs and are held in the mission house in Berlin. Other Conferences are taking up this plan as well as the regular publication of well prepared articles on mission topics in the secular press of the provinces. Mission Conferences are held in Silesia, Thuringia, Würtemburg, Kingdom of Saxony, etc. In some they pursue substantially the plan followed in Brandenburg and Pomerania, in others the work is restricted to the delivery of sermons and addresses on mission topics. The conference which assembles each May in Stuttgart, is one of those famous in Germany and is always well attended. The one great aim of these Conferences is not to gather funds, but to spread information which shall assist the regular mission organizations in doing so. The fourteen University Students' Mission Societies of Germany have substantially the same object in view. A significant token of the German interest in mission work is seen in the fact that the universities have conferred the degree of Doctor of Divinity on men who have given special study to mission work and become' authorities upon it. These institution are exceedingly careful and very sparing of their honorary titles and laugh at the freedom with which American institutions deal them out. Yet Halle gave Dr. Warneck his degree because of his service in the mission cause; the first instance of the kind in the history of the universities. Two years later Dr. Grundemann was honored in the same manner and for the same cause by the University of Berlin. Shortly after that, Heidelberg honored the founder of the General Protestant Mission Society in the same way; Jena, Missionary Faber; and Berlin, Mission Superintendent Krapf.

The first Protestant missionaries sent to convert the heathen anywhere, were those commissioned by the Lutheran King of Sweden, Gustavus Vasa, to preach the Gospel to the Laplanders. Traders had penetrated into Lapland before the missionaries and, when they found that many of their ungodly practices were denounced by these servants of Christ, raised great opposition to their work. The suspicions of the heathen natives, added to the opposition of the traders, made the work of the missionaries exceedingly difficult. In 1619 a hymn-book with liturgical forms was issued in the native tongue and a missionary institute established. A school for educating native pastors was founded at Lycksele, the new Testament was translated, and other schools established as centres of Christian effort.* Catechists were trained to follow the people in their hunting and fishing expeditions and as they wandered about herding their reindeer. Then arose Thomas Von Westen, the Apostle to the Laplanders, (born 1682,) and Denmark united with Norway

---
* Plitt: *Luth. Missions*, 27 *seq.*

and Sweden in carrying on the work. The heathen Finns were then included. Half a dozen other pastors aided von Westen in his efforts and requested the government to assist in carrying forward the proposed missionary work. A *Mission Collegium* was established at Copenhagen, 1717. It was found necessary, also, to establish a seminary at Trondhjens, Norway, to prepare men for work among the Lapps. In his efforts von Westen was nobly aided by Isaac Alsen, a schoolmaster, who fourteen years in succession, labored unweariedly and without any financial support, teaching the heathen the blessed truths of our most holy faith. He shared with them their smoky, filthy huts. He exposed certain sorcerers in their deceit and these aroused the natives against him so that they tried in every way possible without actually laying violent hands upon him, to cause his death. They denied him pure water, allowed him only spoiled victuals and decayed meat to eat, and gave him untamed reindeers to drive, in order that he might lose his life. The people among whom these men and their successors labored were without any fixed habitations and were scattered over a territory about twice as large as Pennsylvania. That territory was filled with treacherous swamps, wide morasses, bleak plateaus and towering mountains, which for the greater part were composed of naught but naked rock. Here the Storm King had his home and from those desolate peaks and dark rock-walls sent forth the biting winds and snow which often filled the valleys ten feet deep. The cold was intense, the thermometer registering not infrequently from 20 to 45 degrees below zero. In the bitter wind men's hands were frozen before they could pick up and replace the deer skin mittens accidentally dropped for a moment. The houses of the people were but tents of cloth or skins, without windows, chimneys or furniture. An opening in the top allowed the smoke to escape from the small fire which was to save them from the storm and cold. The skins of sheep and bear and reindeer formed their mattresses, blankets, seats and the material from which their clothing was made. What was their degradation and misery when our missionaries reached them three and a quarter centuries ago we can scarcely know or conceive. But among these poor ignorant and degraded heathen, into their rigorous climate, among the ice and snow and glaciers, wild valleys and bleak mountains, these devoted heralds of the Cross immured themselves to teach them the Way of Life. Their toils, privations, sufferings and self-denial never can be told on earth. Like the Great Apostle they too were "in journeyings often, in weariness and painfulness, in hunger and thirst, in fastings often, in cold and nakedness, in perils of waters, in perils of robbers, in perils by the heathen, in perils in the wilderness and in perils in the sea." But they persevered and the result is that Christ is known and His name confessed among all the 17,000 Lapps and their condition, temporally and spiritually, vastly improved.

In the beginning of this century the Swedish missionaries among the Lapps took the lead in an attempt to prepare them for a more settled life. They established schools, at Lycksele, Arjeplog, Jockmock and Sellivare, as centres from which they might work to Christianize the people. They also arranged to receive Lapp children and place them under the care of Christian farmers in Sweden and Finland, in order that they might receive Christian culture and at the same time be weaned from the nomadic life of their parents and gradually fitted for the duties of a more settled mode of living. But the opposition of the natives was so determined that the mission authorities were obliged to abandon the plan and return to the former method of preparing Catechists to go with them in their wanderings and teach them there the Word of God. The schools, however, were maintained and and finally won the confidence of the natives. Many Lapps trained in them now accompany their people

V

in their annual migrations and, being themselves firmly rooted in the true faith, carry on mission work privately, wherefore in many a Lapp home the Gospel is regularly read where, formerly, its sound was not heard. This is, in fact, almost the only way in which effective mission work can be accomplished among these people. To find pasturage for their flocks of sheep and immense herds of reindeer they are ever on the move. It is next to impossible that a missionary should follow them in their migrations and, if he could, but one or at most a very few families could have the benefit of his labors.*

The Lapps of Norway, Sweden, and Finland are estimated to number from fifteen to twenty thousand. Churches are to-day found all over their country and are well attended. The people often are so far away that they must start on snow shoes or with reindeer, the day before, in order to reach the church in time for the service. To them the church is sacred and beloved ; in it they are baptized and around it they are buried. Every church has a school beside it wherein the children are diligently instructed in the principles of religion. Teachers travel also from hamlet to hamlet and nearly all the children of proper age, as well as the younger generation of adults, can read and write. Before confirmation the youth must pass a rigid examination in the Catechism, one by one, that it may be known they have learned it well. Our Church in the northern countries deserves great honor for the long and earnest endeavors she has made to establish these people in the Gospel of Christ. " In the extensive territory occupied by the Lapps in Scandinavia, law and order prevail as in other parts of the land, lawlessness and brigandage are unknown, the wildest and least inhabited districts being as safe as any other in this most honest land." †

The judgment of the renowned traveler, Bayard Taylor,

---

* Fjellstedt, quoted by Plitt.   † Du Chaillu : Midnight Sun.

concerning them is given in these words: The Lapps are frightfully pious and commonplace. As human beings, the change, incomplete as it is, is nevertheless to their endless profit, but it has destroyed the materials for weird stories and romantic adventures. No wizards now ply their trade of selling favorable winds to Norwegian coasters, or mutter incantations to discover the concealed grottoes of silver in the Kiölen mountains. It would be far more picturesque to describe a Sabaoth of Lapland witches than a prayer meeting of shouting converts, yet no friend of his kind could help rejoicing to see the latter substituted for the former. We found them as universally honest and honorable in their dealings as the Northern Swedes, who are not surpassed in the world in this respect. Love for each other, trust in each other, faith in God, are all vital among them.

As early as 1626, Gustavus Adolphus planned to establish a colony in the New World. But the storms of the Thirty Years' War which were then gathering in fury around Sweden prevented the immediate accomplishment of his desire. Ten years later, however, in accordance with the plan of their illustrious King, a little Swedish colony landed on a natural warf, "The Rocks," curiously prepared for them on the Christiana River, where Wilmington, Delaware, now stands. Before they sailed it had been determined that their career should be kept free from the errors which disfigured the history of almost every other colony that had been planted on these shores. The rapacity of avarice, the ambition of conquest, the proscriptions of religious bigotry and the cruelties of slavery, were all carefully excluded from the course marked out for the Swedish colony. Said the King: "This colony to be planted in America may prove to the advantage of all Christendom." Religious toleration was part of the original plan and it was practiced when, in 1640, the Dutch (Reformed) sailed up the Bay to join the colony. The Swedes assured them of the free exercise of all their rights and full liberty in the use of the Calvinistic religion and its forms, provided only that they would "abstain from all scandal and from all abuse."

With the Indians they always lived in peace. It does not appear that a single life was taken on either side. The dark history of conflicts which saturated the soil of all the New England settlements with human blood had no counterpart in the history of New Sweden. While the witches were hung in New England, the Quakers persecuted and the Baptists driven into the forests: while in Virginia all who refused to conform to the established (Episcopal English) Church were summarily banished; and in New York the Dutch were flogging, imprisoning, mulcting in fines and driving away Lutherans; the Lutherans on the Delaware were, in accordance with the spirit of their Saviour, opening their homes as a refuge for the persecuted people of all nations. Instead of robbing and murdering the Red Man they were proving to him by their deeds of love and mercy that they had come to do him good, not work him wrong and injury. At every opportunity they exerted themselves that the wild men of the forest might be won and instructed in the truth, and in the worship of the God of the Christian. The Catechism of Luther was translated into the dialect of the Delaware Indians, that they might learn from it the fundamental doctrines of the Gospel.

These facts stand out conspicuous amid the cruelty and barbarism of the times. The fundamental plan of the colony was not only in advance of the new country in which it was being wrought out, but far above the ideas of colonization then prevailing in Europe. The seeds of the Declaration of American Independence were in that plan. Nothing detracts from the fame of these Swedish Pilgrims but the paucity of their numbers. They have suffered in history solely because they were too few to sustain themselves against their numerous opponents, or to stamp upon so wide a country the deep and enduring impression of their heroism and virtues. Had they been the offspring of a more prolific fatherland, whose steadily following reinforcements would have supported their feeble beginnings, the history of the Scandinavian colonization of the Valley of the Delaware would have taken a prominent if not conspicuous place in the early annals of the nation.

Speaking of the monument to the Puritan Fathers the *Inter-Ocean*, of Chicago, said: "The monument now completed ought to be supplemented by a chain of monuments extending from Plymouth to St. Augustine; one in Rhode Island, one in New York, two in Philadelphia, and so on along the coast, where the first seeds of this Nation were sown. To Philadelphia belong two such landmarks, because long before William Penn's day Scandinavian and German enterprise had laid there the foundation of an asylum for the oppressed of all nations; their purpose being the broadest and grandest of all our primitive fathers."

To all of which the assent due the truth must be accorded, for it is the truth. Let the Pilgrim Fathers of New England have their due. With all their faults they were men of courage and men with convictions; and as such all true men honor them. But while we honor them, let not the Swedes and Germans on the Delaware be forgotten. They were men who brought with them a breadth of view regarding individual freedom in matters of religion, utterly unknown to those of New England. They have a monument in the hearts of millions to whom this principle of religious toleration has become a blessing.

The Church Mission Society is the oldest of the Foreign Mission Societies existing in Sweden. In its early years it worked with the Wesleyan Society, of London, inasmuch as it was missionating in the island of St. Bartholomew, then the property of Sweden. It also assisted the Mission Institute in Basel. In 1845, ten years after its organization, the friends of missions in Lund organized another society in that city. Previous to this time mission contributions had been sent to Halle, but a union was now formed with the Leipsic Society, on a strictly Lutheran basis, and was maintained even after the two Swedish Societies were consolidated in 1855. Some years ago, however, this society opened its own mission field in South Africa and expends 26,500 marks yearly in its support. It expends an average of 13,-000 marks a year in India. The official mission collections of the State Church of Sweden go into the treasury of this Society, and it is always supplied with funds. The overplus has been invested as a fund in its interests. It supports a Missionary Seminary, founded 1863, at Johannelund. Its receipts average 94,000 marks per annum. It sent out three missionaries in 1889. It is trying to reach the Zulus, but has not been able as yet to get beyond the frontiers of Natal. At the stations Amoibie, Appleborch and Oskarsberg small congregations of Zulus have been gathered under the care of a zealous missionary, the Rev. Mr. Witt. An Orphan's Home exists in each of these places. Much is hoped from the influence of a young nephew of the late King Cetewayo, who, having been studying in Sweden for several years, has recently returned and been well received by his relatives. To this field one of the three missionaries sent out in 1889 has also returned with his newly married wife, and accompanied by a young lady of noble family who is to act as governess to the children of one of the missionaries and to become herself a missionary. This mission has recently been inspected by the Secretary of the Church Mission Board, the Rev. Mr. Tottie, Professor of Church History at the University of Upsala.

The Swedish Mission Society has been extending its work in the East and has now three stations in China and one in Algiers among the Arabs and the Jews. It has been at work among the Lapps, the Tamils of East India, and the

Zulus in South Africa. Eleven missionaries are maintained in Congo. It has its servants employed in St. Petersburg, in the Caucasus, in Persia, and on the shores of the Polar Sea. It has a membership of 100,000 and a yearly income of 126,176 crowns.

The Ev. Fatherland Society is, perhaps, the largest of the General Mission Societies of Sweden. It is independent of the State Church, though all its members are in that organization. It devotes its energies largely to Inner Missions, though for twenty five years it has maintained a mission in East Africa. Its principal station is "seven hours" west of Massowa on the Red Sea. There labor has been kept up n training orphans of several nationalities, in giving shelter to freed slaves and to persons persecuted because of their faith, in caring for worn-out pilgrims, in distributing Bibles to merchants and caravans and in maintaining a regular medical dispensary. The Bibles are printed partly on the mission press. With the help of native Christians the missionaries have translated portions of it and other books of devotion, which they print at the mission. They have 8 schools and 560 pupils. Among the Gallas four native Christians are preaching the Gospel. One studied in Sweden and was recently ordained.*

The same society has a mission in India. Seven missionaries, assisted by several native Christians, are at work in four of the Central Provinces. They have seven principal stations, three schools and 66 pupils. Nine missionaries are employed among the sailors in foreign ports and two among the islands of the Baltic. The mission paper of this society has 14,000 subscribers. The income is 150,000 marks yearly. In the two years ending Oct., 1890, three ordained missionaries and two women were sent out.

---

* A writer in the New York *Independent* says of this mission, with special reference to the medical dispensary: Their institution is the one among all the institutes of this country that deserves the most admiration and respect.

The Swedish Mission Union is yet farther separated from the work of the State Church than the Society above named. When in 1881 the Congo (Livingstone) Inland Mission was divided this Society received one station and began its own work there.* Six years later it opened a mission on Behring's Sound, known as the Ice Sea Mission. Its receipts increased (1889) to 151,906 marks. In 1890 it began a new mission in China. In 1889, it sent out two ordained missionaries and one woman helper, and in 1890 four ordained and four women missionaries.

Sweden has also a " Free Mission " among the Santals in India. This organization has Committees in Upsala, Stockholm and Gothenburg. Its income is about 8,000 marks a year. Several Swedish Free Missionaries are connected with the China Inland Mission. In addition to these must be mentioned the Ansgarius Society of East Gothland, organized 1886. It works among the Gallas at a yearly expense of 4,500 marks. About 10,000 marks a year are sent from Sweden to the Moravian Society. University Students' Mission Societies are active at Upsala and Lund. They publish a mission journal. In 1887, they issued a Mission Hymn Book containing 100 hymns with music, 54 of which had never before been in print.

Now we turn to Greenland. Its northernmost town, Upernavik, is one of the most northern of human habitations. There the thermometer registers 68 degrees in February and rarely more than 54 degrees above in July which is the only month when the average temperature is above the freezing point. No trees grow on the island because of the intense cold. Ice has been known to choke up the iron flue of a stove constantly heated. It is impossible to make clay

---

* It soon founded a second, and in 1890 reported four stations, eleven ordained missionaries and seven women helpers. Parts of the New Testament and Luther's Catechism have been translated and printed in the tongue of the natives.

into brick or put stones together with mortar in such a climate. The houses of the natives are built of snow or ice. Shelts of fresh water ice are used for windows. The one essential piece of furniture is the family lamp. It stands on a little elevation in the centre of the hut. It is made of stone, in the form of an oval dish, in the hollow of which is placed a heap of blubber, to supply the oil, which is drawn up to the flame by a wick of moss, arranged around the edge of the lamp. And this is made to light the house, heat it, melt the snow for all the water needed, and serve as the family cooking-stove. The country supplies scarcely any vegetation and the climate is such that it is extremely doubtful whether much vegetable food could be used in the way of diet. The intense and continual cold demands carbon in a highly concentrated form to supply the proper amount of heat in the human system. The food of the natives is almost exclusively the flesh of the seal and the reindeer, the blubber and the fat being most highly prized.

In their persons the people are most untidy, and seem to thrive on grease and dirt. They have little acquaintance with soap and water as prime agents of the virtue next to godliness; in fact some travelers aver that they never wash from birth to death. The thought of performing such a service even for his face and hands seems never to enter the mind of an Eskimo, unless he learn it from a foreigner or from a native who has thus learned it. The hair is generally left uncombed through life and is filled with moss, hairs of the seal and reindeer, and with many other things too numerous to mention by name. Among these people, more than one hundred and fifty years ago, the Danish and Norwegian traders assisted the Rev. Hans Egede to plant a Lutheran mission. In that land of desolation, amid its snow and ice and degradation, this devoted servant of God began his testimony for evangelical truth, and labored on through incredible hardships and privations, until he saw his work prosper under the Divine blessing. In 1736 the son of Egede succeeded him in the Greenland mission. The first native pastor was Tobias Moerch. In 1883, two natives, Bernelson and Checeritz, were ordained as ministers of the Lutheran Church, by Bishop Martensen, in Copenhagen. They passed a creditable examination, and shortly after their ordination sailed for Greenland, where they have charge of churches among their countrymen.

Dr. Robert Brown, who visited Greenland in pursuit of botanical and geological studies, says: " Mission stations now appear at frequent intervals. From being a simple missionary the Greenland priest has become a ' parish minister,' for there is not now one professed pagan in all Danish-Greenland. Settlements are conducted solely by the Danish Government for the benefit of the natives. Their trade is so extensive as to employ seven ships and yield a profit of $55,000 per annum. They are established from Cape Farewell up to seventy-three degrees north latitude, where, at Kingatok, on a little islet, lives a solitary Dane, who has the eminent distinction of being the most northerly civilized man in the civilized world.

In the early years of the present century many Norwegians were in the service of the Danish Missionary Society, the Basel Society, and the Moravian Missionary Society. The Norwegian Missionary Society was organized in 1842. Of course it is Lutheran. It united with the Danish Society to send out Missionary Schreuder, in 1843, and to establish a mission school. The Schreuder Committee was dissolved in 1846, and the missionary went into the service of the Norwegian Society. He made an unsuccessful attempt to start a mission at Natal, and another in China; then returned to Natal in 1848 and founded a mission school, which has grown into sixteen stations. In 1865 a new mission was founded by this society in Madagascar. This society has average receipts of 375,000 marks. All Norway is divided into mission districts, in which 900 local societies and 3,000 women's societies exist. Each district is under the supervision of a Council, a member of which, or an agent, visits the district councils. The Norwegian *Mission Gazette* is the organ of the society, and circulates 5,400 copies. The Women's Mission paper has a circulation of 5,000. The Norwegians in the United States send from 60,000 to 70,000 marks yearly to this society. The Committee, for work among the Santals, publishes its own periodical. Its income in 1889 was 43,670 marks. The Schreuder Committee, reörganized, works among the Zulus, with an income of 7,000 marks. The University Students' Mission Society, organized at Christiania, 1881, with 30 members, now has 125. There is an average of one member of the Norwegian Church at work on mission stations for every 125 members of the home church.

The success of the Norwegian Mission in Madagascar is one of the wonders of mission history. The government has the mission in full favor. The following figures show its growth and standing:

	Stations.	Missionaries.	Members.	Schools.	Pupils.
1878.	17	22	900	50	4,000
1888.	22	26	15,950	304	30,620

There are many out-stations with native helpers, and 16 ordained native pastors. At the capital, Antanawarivo, a city of 80,000 inhabitants, there is a theological seminary in addition to the two seminaries for training native teachers. There is also a school for catechists and a pro-gymnasium.*

In addition to the mission on the island the Society has recently opened stations on the west and southeast coasts of the mainland.†

---

* Warneck, for 1890, reports the number of members at 25,000, and the pupils in the schools at 38,000.

† The division that has been mentioned as having occurred in the missionary effort of the country, still exists, having been reöpened in 1873 by the withdrawal of Schreuder—who was made a bishop in 1866—

One of the founders of the Indian Home Mission to the Santals was the Norwegian, Skrefsund, who was sent to India in 1863 by the Gossner Society, but left its service in 1865. Other Norwegians have joined him, and through the efforts of returned missionaries a deep interest in their work has been aroused in Norway. Committees have been formed in the larger towns. These have no united organization, but recognize the one at Christiania as their chief. Their receipts for 1888 were 37,141 marks. They have 14 stations and 5,272 members.

In Natal and Zulu Land the Norwegians have 11 stations with 500 members, and 2,000 pupils in their schools. The " Free East African Mission," organized in Christiania, 1888, sent two missionaries to Natal. One soon died. Another was sent to take his place, and a mission station has been established on the middle Tugela.

Eleven Norwegians are at work in China, under the direction of Taylor's Society. A home society aids them to the extent of about 9,000 marks a year.*

from the service of the Society. He preferred to be the missionary of the Norwegian Church rather than of an unofficial organization, and was not satisfied with the democratic administration of the Society. He claimed the station Entumi, which had been assigned to him, and his widow maintained the claim after his death in 1882. The Government of Natal decided that Entumi was the property of the Norwegian Missionary Society, but that the Schreuder Committee had a right to labor in it so long as they were able to supply the station with a Norwegian missionary. A new station was formed in 1875 at Untumjambili. Four missionaries have been sent out, with two helpers in the temporalities. The directory of this mission is a close committee, of which the Bishop and Provost of Christiana are *ex-officio* members. If the Norwegian Church should formally assume the care of heathen missions, the committee would have to dissolve and surrender its functions.

* This mission is on no Confessional basis. It is in connection with a similar one in East Africa. The founder of the latter went over to the Baptists, but he died in 1889 and his son in 1890. One of the Swedish missionaries also joined the " Free Mission " force. It receives aid from Norway to the extent of 16,500 marks a year. It appears, also, that the China mission receives considerable aid from Norwegians in America. —*Warneck, Missions-Zeitschrift*, Jan., 1891.]

The Norwegian missionaries in Madagascar have formed a leper colony, erecting twenty-two small houses, which are inhabited by 45 lepers, seven of whom are Christians. In the midst of these houses stands the church, where services are administered by one of the missionaries.

Recently a Norwegian Lutheran Society was formed to coöperate with a like organization in Sweden, to do mission work in China. It has 17 workers in the field, and double that number waiting to be sent. Not long since the Missionary Society of Norway sent 12 laborers to reinforce those in Madagascar, and two to the missions among the Zulus. Two native young women of Madagascar, who spent two years in Christiania, returned with the missionaries to help instruct their countrywomen in the ways of civilization.

Norway is not a very large country, being but little more than two and a half times the size of Pennsylvania. The population numbers less than half that of the Old Keystone State. In wealth and material resource the difference is still more marked in favor of "Penn's Woods." The country is scantily endowed by nature. The general barrenness of the soil is proverbial. Bleak moors and inhospitable mountains make up the greater part of its area. But in this far North Land these sons of the Lutheran Church are laboring in various ways with heroic devotion to extend the Gospel of Christ. They are engaged in inner missions, heathen missions, seamen's missions, and missions among the Jews. They are a missionary people. In almost every parish, from Lindesnoes to the North Cape, that is, from the most southern to the most northern part of the country, may be found a missionary association. And poor as the land is in natural resources, her people raised, without a cent of outlay for paid collectors or agents, in 1888, the gross sum of 374,800 marks. This great amount came by the regular societies, and does not include what went to the mission work through smaller organizations.

It has been shown how through the sale of the East Indian territories of Denmark in 1847, and the Gold Coast of Africa in 1851, many of the fruits of her early mission work passed into other hands. The Lutheran Church of Denmark, however, will always retain the honor of having been the first to send the gospel to East India, and also to the West Indies. Denmark took the lead in the new era in the history of Lutheran missions which opened with the eighteenth century. The work of her early missionaries was singularly successful. In 1730 the converts in the Madras mission numbered 415 souls; in Tanjore there were 1,140; and in Tranquebar 1,189. Ten years later the number rose to 4,000, and in 1845 to 9,000. Kiernander, a Danish missionary, arrived in Calcutta in 1758, and erected the church which still is known as " the Mission Church." Two years before his arrival eight European missionaries were in the field, and the converts numbered 11,000. Although Germany furnished some of the Danish Society's missionaries, and some of its money came from England, yet it was distinctively the Danish Society; its headquarters were in Denmark, and it was liberally assisted by the State Church. And yet the interest in its work was not so great as had been anticipated, partly because it was regarded as an outburst of Pietism, and partly because its reports were usually published only in German. The East India Mission, as well as those begun in Finmark, 1716, and in Greenland, 1721, are still continued, but, being incorporated in the regular administrative organization of the State Church, call for no further mention here.

Zinzendorf caught his inspiration for Foreign Missions at the Mission Seminary in Copenhagen ; and the early efforts of the Danes were followed by the establishment of missions by the Moravians in the Danish East Indies, the Danish West Indies, Greenland, Danish Guinea and other points. Many Danes were thus introduced to the service of the

Moravian missions. Such a step was easy, since the Confession of the Moravian Church was identical with that of the Lutheran Church, and the missions were being planted in Danish territory. The North-Schleswig Missionary Society was organized in 1843 to aid Moravian missions in the West Indies, and still receives aid for them from Denmark. It has several branches in Jutland.

The Danish Missionary Society, founded 1812, after much success in India, lost most of the results of its labor by the sale of Tranquebar in 1847, though it had the satisfaction of seeing some of them go to the Leipsic Society. The work in Southern India was begun anew in 1863, and at the end of 1888 had three stations, four missionaries and one native pastor, two native catechists and one deaconess. The number of Christians at the close of 1887 was 546, and the 10 schools had 110 pupils. Two smaller Danish organizations existed for a time, and then were incorporated with the Missionary Society. A small mission, established at Bellore, India, has 20 converts and 3 native helpers. It is under the care of a committee, whose receipts in 1888 were 8,981 marks.

The Dane, Borresen, and the Norwegian, Skrefsrud, who had been a year with Gossner's society in India, in 1865 applied to the Danish Missionary Society to be taken into its service. Borresen returned to Denmark in 1876, and aroused great interest among his countrymen in the work among the Santals. A special committee was appointed in the Danish Missionary Society to collect money for its support.*

A mission was founded at Pobia, among the Red Karens, in 1886, by H. Poulsen and H. Jenssen. It is supported by a "Committee for Karen Missions." Including three

---

* The Mission had, in 1888, 4 missionaries, 4 native pastors, 3 European teachers, 17 native deaconesses, 67 traveling elders, 10 catechists 15 itinerant teachers, 1 native physician, 220 pupils, and 4,840 converts.

persons engaged with societies, not of Denmark, there are now 19 Danes in active service in the mission field.†

In 1889 and 1890 the societies of the home Church were reörganized in order that the members of the congregations might be better informed concerning the missions. The intention is to organize a society in every parish, each to be composed of at least thirty members, and to contribute at least fifty crowns a year. The parish Societies will be united in District Mission Unions, and will send delegates annually to the General Mission Convention for the Kingdom. Up to 1890, 460 District Societies had been organized. The President of the General Convention is Provost Bahl. The duties of the Secretary require that he travel among the District Unions. Several men and women are ready to go out as missionaries, and it is probable that a new mission will be opened in China or Japan. In 1889 Missionary Borresen re-visited Denmark, Sweden and Norway in the interests of the Santal Mission. The receipts, in consequence of the increased interest awakened, arose from 24,500 marks in 1888 to 41,105 in 1889.* Lowenthal. a "free missionary" in India, is supported from Denmark. His work calls for an expenditure of 6,700 marks yearly. Two mission periodicals are published; their combined circulation is 22,850. The increase of contributions in the last ten years has been from 40,400 to 88,000 marks. The income from the State Church Missions in Greenland is about 60,000 marks. It is derived from the interest of funds invested for its support, or paid from the treasury of the State. A summary of the Danish Missions shows them to have increased from 9 missionaries and 10,664 members in 1878, to 14 missionaries and 12,386 members in 1888.

---

† Warneck: *Missions-Zeitschrift.*
* To this is to be added 17,000 marks contributed for the Karen missions, 60,000 appropriated for the support of the missions in Greenland, and the sums given small societies: making a total of 218,000 marks.—Warneck: *Missions-Zeitschrift*, 1891.

The Finnish Mission Society, organized in 1858, at first coöperated with the Berlin and Herrmannsburg Societies, but later began independent work. First a seminary for training missionaries was opened, and when, in 1867, Missionary Hugo Hahn invited them to begin work among the Ovambos of South Africa, who are neighbors of the Hereros, among whom he was laboring, the invitation was accepted, and five young Finns, in 1868, were ordained to the work. A sixth, from the Herrmannsburg Society, and four mechanics, were sent out. This Finnish Society is the organization through which the greater part of the mission spirit in Finland does its work; and, while the sum total does not appear large, yet the fact that the contributions have increased in eleven years from 38,000 to 88,000 marks, shows a healthful condition. In 1882, 5,000 Finnish and 1,600 Swedish periodicals were circulated; in 1887, 9,760 Finnish and 1,800 Swedish.* The Society publishes smaller mission papers, also, which are widely circulated. The Women's Sewing Societies, of which, in 1887, there were sixty, realized from the sale of their work the sum of 6,700 marks.* The Finnish Foreign Mission Society labored in South West Africa for thirteen years before the first convert was baptized. Now they have three stations in the Ondonga district of Ovamboland, where the six missionaries have 500 attendants upon their Sunday services, and in the three schools have 230 pupils. Luther's Catechism, the Psalms, a Hymn Book, and the Gospel of St. Luke, have been translated into the tongue of the Ondongas.†

In Russia, also, our Church has its own Foreign Mission Society. At Reval there is a school to train men as missionaries. The Lutheran Church of Poland supports a mission among the Kaffirs of South Africa. It has been

---

* In 1877, when the population of Finland was 1,980,000, the Swedes numbered 270,000. The population now is at least 2,150,000.—*Grundemann.* † Grundemann: *Ev. Mission.*

recently begun, and has as yet but one missionary and about 100 converts.

The Board of Foreign Missions of the General Synod of our Church in the United States, manages missions in India and Africa. In India there are three stations, of which Guntur is the oldest. The Mission College is located here, where it is proposed, also, to establish a hospital. The substations are six, and there are two medical dispensaries. The seven American missionaries are aided by 194 native helpers. There are two churches and 135 prayer houses, 371 congregations, and 13,556 baptized members, and 3,100 candidates for baptism. There are 220 schools, and 4,960 pupils; 655 students are in the College and its branches. The contributions of the natives for the two years ending April, 1891, were $2,600. The expenditures of the Board for the same period were $100,089. The treasury has a balance of $12,000. The Zenana department of the mission has two women missionaries and 18 assistants. They also conduct schools for high caste Hindu and Mohammedan girls. There are 14 of these schools with 47 teachers and helpers, and 800 pupils. The medical mission treated 300 sick persons in their homes, and had 3,100 patients at their dispensaries during the two years covered by the report for 1889.

In Africa there are two American missionaries, assisted by two ordained native pastors and nine other helpers. There are three congregations, with 159 members, and three schools, with 222 pupils. An industrial department is a special feature of the work in this field. Of it the authorities say: "It is utterly useless to attempt to educate and Christianize the people without at the same time teaching them agriculture and the mechanical arts, so that they may of themselves be able to meet and supply the wants created by a Christian civilization." The mission owns nearly 500 acres of land, of which about 100 acres are planted with coffee trees. Fifty thousand of these are growing, nearly a third of them bearing. Almost a thousand acres adjoining the mission lands are owned and cultivated by men who formerly were pupils of the mission, and are now members of the church. More than $20,000 have been contributed to establish the College in India, and additional sums have been expended for hospital and other purposes on the mission field. Nearly 14,000 women are organized in Women's Mission Societies, and many Children's Mission Societies have aided the work of the Board. The contributions of the Women's Societies, in the last two years, exclusive of the thank-offering, were $36,240. The thank-offering was $5,500.

The Committee for Foreign Missions of the General Council of the Lutheran Church in the United States has a mission in India, with headquarters at Rajahmundry. There were four missionaries and three on the field at the beginning of 1889. There were also two native ordained pastors, seven evangelists and catechists, and eighty-one teachers. The native Christians numbered 2,319, and the pupils in the schools 1,073. Two papers are published in the home field in the interest of the work—the *Missionsbote*, circulating 18,000 copies, and the *Foreign Missionary*, circulating 6,200 copies. From $12,000 to $13,000 a year are spent in this mission. Mission Leagues and Women's Mission Societies are working in its interest. In October, 1890, two young women missionaries, Miss Schade and Miss Sadtler, sailed to India to begin Zenana work there.

The Norwegian Synod of the United States has been working in connection with the Mission Society of the Church in Norway. The Norwegian Lutheran China Mission Society of America is of recent organization. The Missouri Synod has been preparing for work in Brazil. Other facts concerning the Foreign Mission work of the Lutheran bodies in America are given in the sketches of these bodies in Chapter fifteen.

LUTHERAN FOREIGN MISSIONS.

Society	Mission Field.	Prin. Stations	Missionaries	Laymen.	Native Helpers.	Baptized Members.	Schools.	Pupils.	Society's Income.
LEIPSIC:	Southern India	24	25	nat. ord.	500	14,000	177	4,500	
	Farther India	1	1			160	1	60	313,000
HERRMANNSBURG:	Zulus, Natal	23	25		50	1,548	?	580	
	Transvaal and Orange Free State	24	28		147	13,815			By natives, 12,350
	New Zealand	3	3			100			
	Australia	1	3						
	India	9	11	?	27	917	1	20	275,000
GOSSNER:	Kohls, India	12	17 & 17 nat.	?	300	37,400	85	2,100	
	On the Ganges	?	5			600			
	Santi Islands	13	2		22	1,000	60	2,350	160,000
RHENISH:	Cape Colony	11	14		87	11,159	13	700	38,750
	Namaqualand	8	9		32	4,417	?	560	2,000
	Hereros	6	8		35	2,073	?	1,422	1.730
	Sumatra	18	16		280	13,135	55	305	
	Borneo	6	8 & 3 natives		26	1,195	?	50	
	Nias	5	6			613	?	37	
	China	3	1 native.		?	265	?		
	New Guinea and Prince Henry's Haven	2	4						
	Solomon Islands	?	?						
	On "Toba-See"	2	?			3,000	?	?	385,400
	Dampier Archipelago	1	?						
BERLIN:	Cape Colony	8	8		74	4,335	8	639	19,537
	Kaffirs of Cape Colony	5	5			804	5	256	
	Zulu Land and Natal	6	6		51	1,356			
	Transvaal, S. Africa	23	29		312	13,554			
	Orange Free State	6	6		19				
NYASSA:	East Africa	2	4	3	24	735	?	2,535	110,000
BASEL:	Gold Coast, Africa	16	3 & 4 natives	2		9,000	9	126	320,000
	Cameroon District	80	35 & 18 nat.			930	63	3,000	
	China	4	12 since 1856	88		3,286		920	114.500
	Hawaii and Demarara, colonists of the China	11	14					622	
	India	23	68					5,340	
					489	9,400	102	5,340	1,21,073

AND FOREIGN MISSIONS. 365

Society							
N. German: Slave Coast, Africa	12	8 & 17 natives.		20			105,500
" Togoland		1					
Bavarian: Australia			1 since 1886				
East Africa	2	5	2				23,400
Evangelical Society: E. Africa	1	3					35,000
Ev. Protestant: Japan	2	4		300	1	80	35,000
Berlin Woman's: China	1	1 & 1 native.		110			15,700
Berlin Society, for China	1	5		800	1		With Berlin Soc.
Brecklum: Farther India	5	11		?		20	65,000
Woman's Society for East: India	2	?					?
Holland Ev. Lutr.: Batu Island		2					5,000
Immanuel Synod: Australia	1	9 since 1886.					35,000
Neuendettelsau: New Guinea	3	1 native.					26,100
" Australia	2	2	3				?
Queensland Society: Australia							
Jerusalem Society: Palestine	3	2 & 7 natives.		300	4	430	30,000
Egypt.							
Paris Ev. Soc.: Bassutoland	11	17					240,000
Senegambia and Tahiti		12	2				
Berlin Evangelical: East Africa	1	1		2,000	1 Hosp.		41,200
Swedes: Alaska	2						
Scandinavian Societies: Lapland		Norway 2 Sweden 4	6 women.	17,500	8	560	Crowns, 231,400
Swedish Fosterland: Abyssinia	2		several.		8		
" India	6	7 & 4 natives			3	450	94,000
Church Society: Zulus	4	3			3		
" India	7	7		50		66	
Lapland	4		?				4 orphanages. 4 schools.
Mission Union:* Congoland	1	11					151,900
Behring's Sound	1						
Swedish Committee for Santals							8,000
" China		In 1887 Swedish Societies had 34 missionaries in the foreign field.					
" with China Inland Mission							
Ansgarius, East Africa							4,500
Women's Society for China							12,000
Falun Soc. for Syrian Orphanage							18,000

* In the last two years this Society sent out six ordained and five women missionaries, whose destination is not given.

Society.	Mission Field.	Prin. Stations.	Missionaries.	Laymen.	Native Helpers.	Baptized Members.	Schools.	Pupils.	Society's Income.
Jönköping Union with Paris Evangelical Society. Sent to Madagascar									10,000
Moravian Society									Works with Norwegian Society
LUTHERAN SOC. for China since 1887.									
NORWAY, NORWEGIAN SOCIETY: Madagascar		300 Cong	38 & 16 nativs.		900	25,000	304	33,000	374,300
	West Coast, Madagascar	3	?		?	100	?	50	
	Zulu Land	10	16		16	500	?	450	7,000
SCHREUDER COM.: Natal		2	2		1 woman.	352		124	43,675
Committee for Santals			Natives, 4 } 6 }		105	5,272 ?		284	16,500
EAST AFRICA FREE MISSION		14	2						
LUTHERAN SOC. FOR CHINA		1	17 including Swedish Missionaries.						9,000
China Free Mission		?	11, with women.		3	546	10	110	86,800
DANISH MISSION SOC.: S. India		3	8		3	20	?	?	8,900
Com. for Bellore, India		1	1 & 1 native.		68	4,840	?	226	41,100 ?
Com. for Santals			4						17,000
Com. for Karens, India			2,& 19 natives.						6,700
Free Missionary, India			1			8,000			60,000
Church Society, Greenland			3			500 Ch.attend }			
FINNISH SOC.: Ovambos, Africa		3	6 & 3 natives.		4	100	3	230	86,000
Luth. Church of Poland ; Kaffirs, S. Africa		1							
U. S. G. C. COM.: India		1	4		86	2,319	81 teach.	1,073	$12,500
G S. COM.: India		3	7 & 2 natives.		194	13 556	220	4,960	$50,000
	Liberia, Africa		2 & 2 natives		9	159	3	222	
Ohio Synod, works with Herrmannsburg, Germany.									
Norwegian ; China, recently begun.									
Missouri : beginning work in Brazil and the East.									
United Syn. S.: Japan, beginning.									

* Slight discrepancies exist between these figures and those given in the text. These are the latest statistics available, compiled from the Guetersloh *Amtskalender fur Geistliche*; Grundemann's *Entwickelung der Ev. Missions*, and Warneck's *Allgemeine Missions-Zeitschrift*.

CONTRIBUTIONS FOR FOREIGN MISSIONS * IN GERMANY, SHOWING INCREASE IN TEN YEARS. ‡

Name of Society.	Average for Years 1875-7.	1885-7.	+ or −	Average for Years 1875-7.	1885-7.	+ or −
	Yearly Income.			Yearly Outlay.		
1. Basel................	700,600	794,200	} +137,800	659,000	796,200	+184,500
" in Cameroon...		44,200			47,300	
2. Berlin I..............	279,000	297,000	+18,000	281,000	310,500	+29,500
3. Rhenish........	312,700	351,500	+38,800	340,300	350,800	+10,500
4. North German	81,000	90 000	+9,000	83,000	81,200	−1,800
5. Berlin II.............	110,000	148,000	+38 000	133,800	172,900	+39,100
6. Leipsic	242,700	305,700	+63,000	220,600	276,300	+55,700
7. Hermansburg	211,600	224,700	+13,100	254,800	224,700	−30,100
8. Berlin Women's Soc.	27,400	19,500	−7,900	21,500	17,900	−3,600
9. Jerusalem Soc.......	18,100	36,000	+17,900	17,800	35,000	+17,200
10. Schleswig-Holstein..	25,600	56,600	+31,000	25,600	54,000	+28,400
11. Neukircher.........		16,500	} +110,400		18,500	} +101,600
12. Protestant Mission ..		23,100			23,100	
13. Berlin East Africa...		20,600			30,100	
14. Bavarian East Africa		23,400			12,600	
15. Neuendettelsau......		17,801			17,800	
Appendix.	2,008,700	2,477,800	+469,100	2,037,400	2,468,400	+431,600
16. Women's Soc. for the East......	8,300	10,900	+2,600	6,600	10,400	+3,800
17. Syrian Orphanage...	16,700	43,500	+26,800	16,000	47,000	+31,000
18. Among Mohammedans Deaconess Work	131,400	213,100	+82,000	95,800	189,800	+94,000
	156,400	267,800	+111,400	118,400	247,200	+128,800
Sum Total.........	2,165,100	2,745,600	+580,500	2,155,800	2,715,600	+560,400

* Grundemann, Entwickelung Ev. Mission; Leipsic, 1890.
† *Protokol Diaspora Konferenz.*
‡ The Moravians who acknowledge the Augsburg Confession as their confessional basis, report the following, under the same heads, respectively, as in the table above:

	326,700	365,700	+39,000	414,800	396,200	−18,600
Total for Germany....	2,491,800	3,111,300	†619,000	2,570,600	3,111,800	†541,800

The increase in contributions, during these ten years, was 619,500 marks, or about 25 per cent.; and the increase in the number of societies was six, or about 50 per cent. The increase in the population, in the same time, was from 27,000,000 to 30,025,000; or about twelve per cent.

University Students' Foreign Mission Societies have increased in number from nine in 1877, to fourteen in 1887; and the increase in the number of members, in the same time, has been from less than 200 to over 400.

GERMAN SOCIETIES AND INSTITUTIONS * SENDING OUT MISSIONARIES AMONG EMIGRANTS.†

	When Founded.	Total Number Sent.	To N. A.	To S. A.	Australia, &c.	To What Churches.
I. Foreign Mission Societies.						
1. Basel............................	1815	239	211	15	13	Lutheran; Ref'd; United.
2. Berlin Mission Society........	1824	15	12	..	3	Lutheran—Mo. and G. C.
3. Gossner Mission Society......	1836	13	9	..	4	Lutheran and United.
4. Brecklum Society.............	1876	8	8	..	..	Lutheran—G. C. and G. S.
5. Hermansburg Society.........	1849	55	37	..	18	Lutheran—Mo., Ohio, Iowa, &c.
6. Kropp Society	1882	10	10	..	..	Lutheran—G. C. and G. S.
II. Societies for Inner Mission.						
1. Rauhe Haus....................	1833	19	17	..	2	United.
2. Johannes Stift, Berlin........	1858	12	11	..	1	United.
3. Pilgrim Mission...............	1840	203	196	7	..	Lutheran; Ref'd; United.
4. Duisburg Deacon Institute....	1845	20	20	..	..	United.
5. Puckenhof Deacon Institute..	1850	7	7	..	..	Not Stated.
III. Soc's for Miss. among Ger. Protest's.						
1. Barmen, for America..........	1837	123	95	28	..	Lutheran; Ref'd; United.
			over			
2. Neuendettelsau, Bavaria.....	1841	350	300	..	7	Lutheran—Iowa, &c.
3. Berlin Soc. for America......	1852	62	62	..	..	Lutheran and United.
4. Gotteskasten, Mecklenburg ..	1853	28	28	..	..	Lutheran—Iowa.
5. Pro-Seminary, Steeden.......	1861	215	215	..	..	Lutheran—Mo. (closed.)
6. Ev. Seminary, Mülheim......	1872	10	10	..	..	Reformed. (closed.)
7. Reinertzau, Würtemberg.....	1885	9	9	..	..	United.
8. Gross-Ingersheim, Würtemberg....	1881	100	100	..	..	Lutheran—All branches.
9. Diaspora Conference.........	1882	6	6	..	..	Lutheran; Ref'd; United.
Total.........................		1,501	1,363	50	..	

With two exceptions, the figures all are for 1885.

* *Protokol Diaspora Konferenz.*

† The most recent figures slightly alter the totals of men sent out, but means are not at hand to ascertain the church relations of the additional laborers. The whole number now reported as sent out by the six societies named below, is as follows: Brecklum, 60; Berlin Mission House, 37; Pilgrim Mission, 196; Duisburg Deacon Institute, 80; Barmen Soc for N. America, 190; Neuendettelsau, 350. These figures increase the numbers sent, to which also are to be added about 125 men sent by the Supreme Church Council, of Prussia, making a total of 1,677 Diaspora Missionaries, sent out by the Protestant Churches of Germany, among German immigrants in America, Australia, South Europe, Turkey and Egypt.

An institution at Strackholt, East Frisia, prepares men for theological seminaries in America, and several well-known pastors labor, privately, to the same end.

LUTHERAN MISSION-INSTITUTES.

Location.	Managed by	Students	For What Work.
Barmen, Rh., Prussia	Rhenish Mission Society	40	Foreign Missions, and Emigrants.
Basel, Switzerland	Evangelical Mission Society	90	" " "
Brecklum, Holstein	Schles. Holstein Mission Society	....	" " "
Berlin, Germany	Evangelical Mis Society, (Gossner.)	....	" " "
Hermansburg, Hanover	Hermansburg Mission Society	25	" " "
Leipsic, Saxony	Evangelical Lutheran Mis. Society	12–15	" " "
Upsala, Sweden	Fjellstedt Institute	80	
Duisburg, Germany	Deacons' Institute	32	Inner Mission and Emigrants.
Packenhof, Bavaria(?)	Mission Institute	....	" " "
St. Crischona, Switzerland	Pilgrim Mission	56	" " "
Rauhe Haus, Hamburg	Mission House	33	
Helsingfors, Finland	Evangelical Lutheran Mis. Society	6	Foreign and Inner Missions.
Johannelund, Sweden	Fatherland Mission Society	9	" " "
Berlin, Germany	Society for Foreign Missions	30	Foreign Missions.
Copenhagen, Denmark	Danish Mission Society	....	" "
Bielefeld	For. Mission Society	....	" "
Sweden	Society for Lapland	?	" "
Lyksele, (?)	Society for Lapland	?	" "
Ludwigsburg, Germany	Brothers' Institute	79	Inner Missions.
Neuendettelsau, Bavaria	Löhe's Mission Institute	30	American and Foreign Missions.
Berlin, Germany	Johannesstift	....	Among Emigrants in America.
Kropp, Holstein	Johannesstift	64	Inner Mission and Emigrants.
Steeden, Nassau	Pro-Seminary	24	Emigrants.
Gross-Ingersheim, Würtenberg	Mission School	....	"
Strackolt, Frisia	Institute for America	?	"
Christiania, Norway	Storjohan's Practical Seminary	?	
Copenhagen, Denmark	Mission Seminary	....	

*Several of these institutions are upon the "United" confessional basis.

HIGHER EDUCATIONAL INSTITUTIONS IN HEATHEN LANDS.

Location.	Rank of Institution.	Maintained by
Tranquebar, India	College	Leipsic Society.
Pareiar, "	Preachers' Seminary	" "
Tranquebar, "	Theological "	" "
Ranchi, "	" "	Gossner "
Guntur, "	Mission College	General Synod, U. S.
Keta, Africa	Theological Seminary	Bremen Society.
In the Transvaal, Africa	Sem. for Native Helpers	Berlin Society.
Botschabelo, "	" " "	" "
Oljimbingue, Herero-Land	" " "	Rhenish "
Dabana, Nias	" " "	" "
Antananarivo, Madagascar	Teacher's Seminary	Berlin "
" "	" "	Norwegian Society.
" "	II. "	" "
" "	Pro-Gymnasium	" "
" "	Theological Seminary	" "
" "	School for Catechists	" "
Hahndorf, Australia	Teachers' Seminary	German Societies.
" "	Gymnasium	" "
Jacobshaven, Greenland	Seminary for Helpers	Danish Church.
Godthaab, "	" " "	" "
Berseba, Africa	Teachers' Seminary	Hermansburg Soc.
Pantjurna Pitu, Sumatra	Seminary for Helpers	Rhenish Society.
Fuk-Wing, China	" " "	" "
Sangi Islands, China	" "	Gossner "
Tokio, Japan	" "	Ev. Protestant Soc.

Following are the names of Lutheran Foreign Mission Societies, with their addresses and the years of their founding:

1. *Society for the Furthering of Evangelical Missions among the Heathen:* Berlin, 1823. Mission House, No. 43, *Georgenkirchstrasse* 70. Director, Dr. Wangemann.
2. *Rhenish Mission Society.* Mission House, Barmen; 1828. Inspector, Dr. Schreiber.
3. *North German Mission Society:* 1836. Bremen, 26 *Ellhornstr.* Inspector, Zahn.
4. *Evangelical* (Gossner) *Mission Society:* 1836. Berlin, *W. Potsdamerstrasse*, 31. Inspector, Prof. Plath.
5. *Evangelical Lutheran Mission:* Leipsic, 1836. Mission House near Bavarian Railway Station. Director, Missionary Handmann.
6. *Hermansburg Mission Society:* Hermansburg, Hanover, 1849. Mission House, Hermansburg. Directors, Pastors Harms and Haccius.

INCREASE OF MISSIONARIES* AND OF CONVERTS IN GERMAN FOREIGN MISSION FIELDS. †

Name of Society.	Missionaries.		Members.	
	1877.	1887.	1877.	1887.
1. Basel	102	123	10,756	20,031
2. Berlin I	48	60	6,272	18,948
3. Rhenish Mission	68	68	ca. 20,000	31,043
4. North German	6	8	100	664
5. Gossner. (Berlin II.)	15	19	ca. 30,000	33,823
6. Leipsic Mission	17	22	9,908	13,505
7. Hermansburg	70	69	6,000	13,452
8. Woman's Society, Berlin	1	1	70	110
9. Society for Jerusalem	1	1	ca. 150	ca. 200
10. Schleswig-Holstein		8		11
11. Protestant Mission		3		33
12. Soc. for E. Africa, Berlin		4		
13. Neuendettelsau		5		
14. Luth. Soc. for E. Africa, Bavaria		2		
Total	328	393	83,256	131,820
Moravian	152	148	68,476	83,052
Total German	480	547	151,732	215,006

* Grundemann, *Ent. Ev. Mission*, Leipsic, 1890.

† The total increase of missionaries is 67, or about 14 per cent.; the increase in the number of Heathen-Christians is 63,273, or over 40 per cent.

---

7. *Jerusalem Society:* Berlin, 1845. Berlin, C. 2, Bischofstrasse, 4, 5.
8. *Schleswig-Holstein Society :* Brecklum, 1877. Inspector, Pastor Fiensch. Mission House, Brecklum.
9. *Berlin Women's Society for China:* Berlin, 1850. Pastor Knack, Berlin, S. W., 29 Wilhelmstrasse.
10. *Evangelical Protestant Mission Society:* 1884. President, Pastor Buss, Glarus.
11. *Bavarian Evangelical Lutheran Society for East Africa:* Hersbruck, 1886. Director, Pastor Ittameier, Reichenschwand.
12. *Neuendettelsau Mission Society:* 1843 and 1886. Inspector, J. Deinzer.
13. *Evangelical Mission Society for East Africa:* Berlin, 1886. Inspector, L. Beyer, Berlin, N., 24 *Kesselstrasse*.

SOME LUTHERAN CHURCH AND MISSION PERIODICALS, &C., IN OTHER LANDS.

Name of Publication.	Place of Publication.	Circulation.
Evangelical *Sonntagsblatt,*	Stuttgart,	115,000
The *Christenbote,*	"	30,000
Volkskalender,	Saxony,	31,000
Sonntagsblatt,	Thuringia,	30,000
"	Hanover,	33,500
Hanover *Kalender,*	"	46,250
The Neighbor,	Hamburg,	100,000
Arbeiterfreundes,	Berlin,	95,900
Warneck's Mission Papers, each,		ca. 25,000
Palm Branches, for children, 80 ed's,		240,000
Sunday Friend,	Berlin,	44,000
Sunday Sermons,	"	115,000
Book of Devotions,	"	40,000
Christliche Volkskalender,	Kaiserswerth,	113,500
Inner Mission Periodicals, reg. eds.,		334,000
Luther Jubilee Booklet,	Kaiserswerth,	755,000
Yearly Cirulation of Periodicals in	Stuttgart,	1,000,000
Missionsblatt,	Herrmannsburg,	9,500
Norwegian F. *Missionstidende,*	Norway,	10,000
" Women's Miss. Paper, &c.	"	8,000
" Sunday Paper for Inner Missions,	"	6,000
Swedish Foreign Mission Paper,	Sweden,	14,000
Finnish " " "	Finland,	11,600
Danish " " "	Denmark,	20,600

14. *Women's Society for Christian Training of Women in the East:* Berlin, 1842. President, Mrs. Gen'l von Daring, Berlin, W., 13 Schellingstr.
15. **Evangelical Mission Society of Basel:* Basel, 1815. Inspector, Th. Oehler. Address for Germany, Leopoldshöhe, Baden; the Mission Directory.
16. *Evangelical Lutheran Society:* Holland, 1882. Director, Dr. L. C. Lentz, Amsterdam.
17. *Danish Mission Society:* 1821. Director, Dr. Wilhelm Holm, Gladsaxe, at Herlöv Station, Denmark.
18. *Norwegian Mission Society:* 1842. Secretary, Pastor Lars Dahle, Stavanger, Norway.
19. *Evangelical Fatherland Institution,* of Sweden: 1860. Secretary, Montelius, Mäster Samuelsgatan 32, Stockholm.
20. *Finnish Mission Society,* of Finland: 1858. Director, Pastor K. G. Fätterman, Helsingfors.
21. *Board of Foreign Missions of the Lutheran Church in the United States,* (General Synod): 1842. General Secretary, Rev. Geo. Scholl, D. D., Baltimore, Md.

22. *Evangelical Lutheran Mission*, (General Council): 1869. President, Rev. A. Spaeth, D. D., 1615 Girard avenue, Philadelphia, Penn.
23. *Board of Home and Foreign Missions and Church Extension*, (United Synod): 1882. General Secretary, Rev. Luther K. Probst, Knoxville, Tennessee.
24. *Foreign Mission Committee*, (Missouri Synod): Rev. F. Sievers, Sr., Secretary, Salzburg, Michigan. Director, Rev. Willcome, Leipsic, Germany.
25. Swedish Church Mission Society.
26. " Mission Union, 1881.
27. " Committees for Free Missions among the Santals.
28. " Friends of China Inland Mission.
29. " Ansgarius Society of East Gothland.
30. " Societies for Aid of Syrian Orphanage, at Jerusalem.
31. " Women's Society for Missions in China.
32. " Friends of Moravian Missions.
33. Jönköping Union, works through Paris Evangelical Mission Society.
34. Norwegian, Schreuder Committee for Missions in Natal.
35. " Committee for Missions Among Santals.
• 36. " Friends of Missions in China.
37. Danish Committee for Missions in Bellore, India.
38. " Committee for Work among Santals, India.
39. " Free Mission, India.
40. " Church Mission, Greenland.
41. Lutheran Immanuel Synod, Australia.
42. *Paris Evangelical Society.
43. Norwegian Lutheran China Missionary Society, of America: Manager, Rev. O. A. Ostby, Franklin, Minn.
44. Mission Committee of the United Norwegian Church in America; works chiefly in China.

---

* The Societies thus marked are positively "Union;" a few others have more or less of the same spirit in their workings.

NOTE—The value of foreign coins mentioned is as follows: A *mark*, $23\frac{4}{5}$ cents; a *franc*, $19\frac{3}{10}$ cents; a *rouble* of 100 copeks, $73\frac{3}{4}$ cents; a *rupee* of 16 annas, $42\frac{2}{3}$ cents; a *crown*, $26\frac{4}{5}$ cents.

CHAPTER XV.

LUTHERANS IN THE UNITED STATES—THE GENERAL
BODIES—PAROCHIAL SCHOOLS, AND INSTITUTIONS OF
BENEFICENCE.

A great difference of opinion prevails as to the Lutheran population of the United States; some writers claiming that it numbers ten million souls, and others thinking these figures absurdly exaggerated. In 1860, Kurtz, the church historian, estimated it at 1,500,000 souls. He excluded from his reckoning a part of the emigrants from Germany as "for the most part rationalistic masses and wild demagogues, who have almost robbed the German name of all honor and reputation in North America." The actual communicant membership of the Church at that time was reported at 235,000. As we now have five times that number of communicants it is safe to estimate five times that population, *i. e.*, seven and a half millions.* Authorities on statistics estimate the American born children of these immigrants as being equal to the number of immigrants, which places the present German population of our country at about nine

---

* The immigration from 1820 to 1886, was as follows:

	Germans.	Scandinavians.
	4,140,941	831,512
In 1888	109,717	81,924
In 1889	99,584	56,968
Allow for 1887	100,000	56,000
	4,450,242	1,026,404

million and Scandinavian population at about 2,050,000.† The Encyclopedia Brittanica says, ¶ "Almost two-thirds of the population (of the German Empire) belong to the Evangelical Church, and rather more than one-third to the Church of Rome." The Cyclopedia of Education says, ‡ "It has been estimated that of the twenty five millions of Protestants in the German Empire, twenty millions, at least, are of Lutheran extraction." The testimony of these authorities is that two thirds of the people of Germany are Protestant and that four-fifths of the Protestants are Lutherans; that is, four-fifths of the two-thirds of the people, or over one-half of the whole population, are Lutherans.

Some years ago Zeller's Comparative Church Statistics of Germany gave the Lutherans three-sevenths of the Protestant population of Germany, and ranked all the people of the Prussian States as United. Collating all other accessible authorities leads to the conclusion that six-sevenths of all Protestant Germans are Lutherans and that four-sevenths of all Germans are born and bred in the Lutheran faith. And from this conclusion it is but a logical sequence to conclude that more than one-half of the Germans coming to the United States are Lutherans. Adding the Scandinavian and four-sevenths of the German populations together gives more than seven million souls of our faith now in the United States; the deaths among these classes being more than equaled by the births of those who are more than the second generation distant from the Fatherland. And when we remember that the bulk of the immigration has come in during the last twenty-five years and that in 1882 more immigrants came than from 1820 to 1840, inclusive, this esti-

---

† The United States Government officials find the German population of our country by multiplying the number of German immigrants by $2\frac{4}{10}$, and the Scandinavian by $1\frac{7}{10}$.

¶ Vol. X : 468.

‡ Kiddle and Schem, pub. by Steiger, New York.

mate is seen to be more than ample to cover all possible losses by death.

The Rev. J. N. Lenker, of Grand Island, Neb., has been giving special attention to Lutheran statistics during the last ten years. He has studied this subject in Germany, Finland, Sweden and Norway, as well as in America. In response to our inquiries he says, "Lutheranism is not acquainted with itself. I have published the Lutheran population of the United States at 6,500,000, which is too low a figure. I think it nearer correct to say 7,500,000. There are as many people in the United States of Lutheran blood as of Roman Catholic." The Rev. S. B. Barnitz, D. D., has been for years so active in the mission work of the Church as to have gained for himself the title of "Ubiquitous Secretary." His work has led him to study the Lutheran population of the United States. He says, "In connection with others, I have been trying to make an estimate of the number of Lutherans in the United States, and believe that we really have over six millions." On an average enough Lutheran immigrants come to America every day to make a congregation of 500 souls.

The modern migration of nations which is so wondrously affecting our Church in America shows itself in astonishing facts.

According to Professor Boyesen and Pastor Wenner, one quarter to one-third of the population of New York city is German-speaking. The school census of 1885 shows Chicago to have been then the same. The years 1882–1890, brought us 1,400,000 Germans. Wisconsin has 150,000 German voters. More than one-ninth of the population of New York State was German-speaking in 1880. About one seventh of the people in the states north of the Potomac and Ohio River parallel, at that time, spoke German. Texas has no great cities and is a remote state, but at the last census one twenty-fourth of the people on her immense territory spoke German. There are more than one-third as many Norwegians in America as in Norway itself. One-half the population of Minnesota is Scandinavian. Chicago is the fifth Scandinavian city in the world and Minneapolis is the sixth. There are more Lutherans in Minnesota than members of any other denomination. In North Dakota they number more than half the entire population. Some counties are almost solidly Scandinavian. In one county there are only six families not Scandinavian. And still they come. Train load after train load of new-comers is being deposited in the cities and on the prairies of the Northwest.

About one-half of these seven millions are more or less directly connected with Lutheran Church organizations. There are sixty-one synods in existence and about fifty congregations not in connection with any synod. Thirteen of these synods are not connected with any larger organization and are styled independent. The other forty-eight belong to one or the other of the four General Synodical bodies: The General Synod, The General Council, The Synodical Conference, and the United Synod of the Church in the South.

The oldest of the general synodical organizations of our Church in the United States is the General Synod. Its confessional basis is set forth in the following official declaration : " We receive and hold with the Evangelical Lutheran Church of our fathers, the Word of God, as contained in the Canonical Scriptures of the Old and New Testaments, as the only infallible rule of faith and practice, and the Augsburg Confession as a correct exhibition of the fundamental doctrines of the Divine Word, and of the faith of our Church founded upon that Word." The institutions for higher education under control of the General Synod, including the mission college in India, number fifteen. Five institutions of beneficence are maintained by its members and two others are being established. The educational instutions have prop-

x

erty and invested funds worth $1,400,000; 125 professors and 1,500 students. The Theological Seminaries are at Gettysburg and Selinsgrove, Penna.; Chicago, Ills.; Hartwick Seminary, N.Y.; and Springfield, Ohio. Its colleges are at Gettysburg, Pa.; Wittenberg, O.; Carthage, Ills.; Atchison, Kas.; and Guntur, India. The schools for young women are at Mechanicsburg, Pa.; Hagerstown and Lutherville, Md.; and the principal academies are at Selinsgrove and Hartwick Seminary. Orphans' Homes are established at Middletown and Loysville, Pa.; Frederick, Md.; and Syracuse, N. Y.* A Free Infirmary is in operation in Washington, D. C., and a Home for the Aged has been established there. Twenty-seven acres of land, with buildings, valued at $30,000, have been donated for the purpose. Ten acres of land have been donated near the Garden of the Gods, Manitou, Colorado, on which to open a home for invalid ministers.

To carry on the different branches of mission work this body has five different organizations. The Board of Home Missions has its headquarters in Baltimore and employs three secretaries; one has oversight of the whole field, a second is the Western Secretary and the third is known as the "Church-lot Secretary." According to the report of the Mission Secretary, rendered at Lebanon, Pa., the missions aided during the two years ending April 1st, 1891, numbered 135 and the missionaries 151. The mission congregations numbered 200; the new missions established, 50; new churches built or bought, 36; and the communicants enrolled, 11,587. For salaries of pastors, church property and local expenses the sum of $222,500 was paid; and for other purposes, $43,000. Twenty-one of these missions have become self-sustaining. They are distributed through six-

* The four Orphanages have property worth $115,000, 25 teachers and 299 orphans. The expense of maintaining 242 of these is reported at $26,500 per annum.

teen states and one territory. The money which passed through the hands of the Board of Home Missions during the two years amounted to $77,055. Two hundred and three other missions were maintained by members of the district synods.

The Board of Foreign Missions has its headquarters also in Baltimore.*

The work of the Board of Church extension is allied with that of Home Missions, but is managed on a different plan by its own officials, keeping its funds separate from those of the Home Mission treasury. Its special work is to help erect mission church buildings, which help is generally extended by loans of money, although when necessity demands it, donations outright are made.† The Women's Home and Foreign Missionary Society has been in existence for twelve years, and in this time has raised more than $140,000 for missions. April 1st, 1889, it reported 507 district societies and 13,800 members. The receipts for the two years covered by the report were $37,830. It also sent to home missionaries sixty-seven boxes of articles and goods for family use, worth $6,630.

A Children's Foreign Missionary Society, with 133 branch organizations and 9,240 members, was combined by the synod at Lebanon with the regular Board of Foreign Missions.

The Board of Education was organized recently to render financial aid to the Educational Institutions of the General Synod; to coöperate with the local agencies in determining sites for new institutions; to decide what institutions shall be aided; to assign to institutions seeking endowment the special fields open to their appeals; to receive and disburse

---

* For further information see chapter on Foreign Missions.

† The Treasurer reported the total amount in the treasury during the two years at $79,855 and the net assets of the Board at $201,120. Nearly $63,300 were contibuted in the same time.

contributions, donations and bequests for educational purposes, and do such other things under the direction of the General Synod, pertaining to and best calculated to promote the general educational interests of the Church. Its receipts for the two years preceding 1889 were $8,709, and its assets $96,500.

The Lutheran Publication Society was organized May 1, 1855, and has its offices and store in Philadelphia. It is established on the doctrinal basis of the General Synod, and has for its object the diffusion of religious knowledge, and the furnishing of a literature suited to the wants of the Church. Lutheran ministers and laymen may become members by the payment of $1 annually, or $10 at one time. For the year ending March 1st, 1891, its sales were $78,200. All its profits are appropriated to the work of the Church. Its assets were $73,100. It publishes the helps for Sunday schools generally in use among the schools of the General Synod.*

The German Publication Board, representing the German Publication Society of the General Synod, was organized Nov. 24, 1885, and has its headquarters in Chicago. Its publications are: Lutherische Hausfreund, Jugend Leuchte, Zum Feierabend, Sonntagsschul-Leitfaden, Kinder-Garten, and Kirchen-Kalender, besides Catechisms and Reading Books for Sunday-schools.

The Parent Education Society aids deserving young men

---

* The circulation of these periodicals as given for May, 1891, was as follows:

Lutheran Sunday-school *Herald*	38,000
Augsburg Sunday-school *Teacher*	10,100
Augsburg Lesson Book	55,000
Augsburg Junior Lesson Book	54,000
Augsburg Lesson Leaf	19,500
Augsburg Junior Lesson Leaf	11,500
The Little Ones	41,500
Total	229,600

in preparation for the ministry. Receipts were reported at $1,537. Similar societies exist in each of the district synods.

The Lutheran Historical Society was organized in Baltimore, in 1848, and has for its object the collection and preservation of works by Lutheran authors, and all such works as have a bearing on the history of the Lutheran Church.*

The Lutheran Ministers' Insurance League has for its object "the exercise of mutual benevolence, and the mutual insurance of relief to the families of its deceased members." At the death of a member each survivor pays $2.00, which goes to the family of the deceased. The amount thus paid out aggregates $70,000.

The American Lutheran Immigrant Missionary Society has its headquarters at Grand Island, Nebraska. Its object is to coöperate with all existing organizations in efforts which apply to Evangelical Lutheran Immigrants, without regard to synod or language.

The Pastors' Fund, to aid needy and disabled ministers, reports invested funds amounting to $6,600; and biennial receipts of $3,765.†

The General Council has set forth its confessional basis in the following declaration: "We accept and acknowledge the doctrines of the Unaltered Augsburg Confession in its original sense, as throughout in conformity with the pure truth, of which God's Word is the only rule. We accept its statements of truth as in perfect accordance with the Canonical Scriptures. We reject the errors it condemns, and believe that all which it commits to the liberty of the Church, of right belongs to that liberty.

---

* The second catalogue of books, pamphlets, manuscripts, photographs, etc., deposited in the Theological Seminary at Gettysburg, fills 66 pages, 9x5¾ inches in size ; the first thirty eight containing titles of books written by Lutherans in the United States.

† The statistics of synods and of institutions maintained by synods, societies and individuals, connected with the General Synod, are found on the two pages following:

"In thus formally accepting and acknowledging the Unaltered Augsburg Confession, we declare our conviction that the other Confessions of the Evangelical Lutheran Church, inasmuch as they set forth none other than its system of doctrine, and articles of faith, are of necessity pure and scriptural. Preëminent among such accordant, pure and scriptural statements of doctrine, by their intrinsic historical position, and by the general judgment of the Church, are these: The Apology of the Augsburg Confession, the

STATISTICS OF SYNODS.

Name.	Organized.	Pastors.	Congregations.	Communicant Members.	Sunday Schools.	Scholars.
Maryland Synod................	1820	84	105	17,925	115	17,585
West Pennsylvania Synod........	1825	90	130	21,774	143	20,356
Hartwick, (N. Y.) Synod.........	1830	32	33	4,650	39	3,962
East Ohio Synod.................	1836	37	74	5,760	68	7,135
Franckean, (N. Y.) Synod........	1837	26	34	2,379	26	1,886
Allegheny, (Pa.) Synod...........	1842	62	132	12,162	133	11,825
East Pennsylvania Synod.........	1842	78	111	17,702	118	19,836
Pittsburg Synod.................		42	77	7,378	69	6,312
Miami, (O.) Synod...............	1844	32	45	4,157	41	4,695
Wittenberg, (O.) Synod..........	1847	42	74	7,274	61	7,924
Olive Branch, (Ind.) Synod.......	1848	20	30	3,263	32	4,398
Northern Illinois Synod..........	1851	29	45	2,779	41	3,688
Central Pennsylvania Synod......	1855	38	84	7,996	93	9,297
Northern Indiana Synod.........	1855	35	73	4,406	60	4,970
Iowa Synod.....................	1855	27	24	1,612	22	1,532
Southern Illinois Synod..........	1857	8	10	1,124	13	820
Central Illinois Synod...........	1867	27	26	2,080	25	2,506
Susquehanna, (Pa.) Synod.......	1867	43	68	9,257	71	10,097
Kansas Synod...................	1868	49	49	3,039	43	3,847
New York and New Jersey Synod..	1872	54	48	10,623	51	7,882
Nebraska Synod.................	1871	79	87	4,022	68	4,161
Wartburg Synod.................	1876	39	47	3,230	39	1,864
Middle Tennessee Synod.........	1878	10	11	950	8	540
Nebraska, Ger., Synod...........	1890	17	21	1,750	...	......
California Synod................	1891	...	...	......	...	......
Colorado Synod.................	1891	...	...	......	...	......
Rocky Mountain Synod..........	1891	...	...	......	...	......
Total....................		1,000	1,447	157,292	1,379	157,118
Additional preaching places....		162				

Smalcald Articles, the Catechisms of Luther and the Formula of Concord, all of which are, with the Unaltered Augsburg Confession, in perfect harmony of one and the same scriptural faith."

This body dates its beginning from 1866. Its higher educational institutions number fourteen, of which two are theological seminaries, six are colleges and six academies. They report property and endowment worth $990,000, (with three unreported;) the number of professors is 108, and of students 1,974. The institutions of benevolence maintained or controlled by the General Council number thirty-four, with three others being founded. Twelve of these, and

INSTITUTIONS.

I. Educational.

Name.	Location.	Value of Property.	Endowment.	Volumes in Library.	Professors.	Students.
Theological Seminary*...	Hartwick Sem'y, N. Y.	$100,300	$ 50,000	4,000	...	...
Theological Seminary.....	Gettysburg, Pa......	75,000	92,000	11,000	5	59
Theological Seminary*...	Springfield. O........	......	......	......	3	23
Theological Seminary*...	Selin's Grove, Pa.....	25,000	26,000	2,000	2	14
Theological Seminary, Ger	Chicago. Ill..........	10,000	......	2,300	3	20
Pennsylvania College.....	Gettysburg, Pa.......	225,000	185,000	22,000	14	226
Wittenberg College.......	Springfield. O.......	150,000	175,000	10,000	13	287
Carthage College.........	Carthage, Ill	36,000	18,000	3,000	10	150
Midland College..........	Atchison. Kan........	51,000	25,000	1,000	8	85
Mission College..........	Guntur, India	25,000	......	......	19	253
Hartwick Clas. Institute..	Hartwick Sem'y, N. Y.	......	......	......	5	92
Classical Institute.	Selin's Grove, Pa.....	......	......	......	8	91
Young Women's Sem'ry..	Hagerstown. Md......	80,000	......	3,000	16	101
Young Women's Sem'y...	Lutherville, Md	50,000	......	1,000	11	92
Young Women's Sem'y...	Mechanicsburg, Pa....	15,000	......	200	8	39
Fifteen Institutions.		$841,300	$571,000	59,500	125	1.533

* Has its own faculty, but occupies building with College.

II. Beneficent.

Name.	Location.	Endowment and Property Value.	Teachers and Helpers.	Inmates.
Orphans' Home. for Girls.................	Frederick, Md....	$55,000	2	12
Emaus Orphans' Home...................	Middletown, Pa..	18,000	4	45
Tressler Orphans' Home..	Loysville, Pa.....	30,000	16	212
Evangelical Lutheran Orphans' Home.	Syracuse, N. Y...	12,000	3	30
Free Infirmary...........................	Washington, D.C.	......	......	*524
Home for Aged	Washington, D.C.	30,000	......	......
Home for Aged Ministers..............	Manitou, Colo..	......	......	......
Totals................		$145,000	25	823

*In year.

three more being established, are Orphans' Homes. Their property is valued at $380,000. They have forty teachers and helpers and 520 orphans. The other institutions are hospitals, homes for the aged and infirm, and missions among the immigrants at New York. These number twenty-one, and have property worth $1,100,000, (two institutions not included.) Four of the hospitals care for 1,150 patients in a year, and the Immigrant Missions receive about 12,000 persons annually. Pastors in Bremen, Hamburg, Stettin, Antwerp, Amsterdam and Rotterdam coöperate with the Immigrant Missions.

The Foreign Mission work of the General Council is managed by a committee. One field is occupied by its missionaries at Rajahmundry, India. Its yearly expenses are about $12,000.*

The Home Mission work of this body is managed chiefly by its district synods. The English, German and Swedish Home Mission Committees manage the missions outside the district synods, or aid the missions within their territory when the synods have more missions than they can support. The whole number of missions aided by the synods and the committees is 280; the number of mission congregations is 369; missionary pastors, 280; and the yearly expenditures $59,286. The amount raised and expended by the missions themselves is not reported.

A General Church Extension Society was organized some years ago, and local societies of a similar kind exist in New York city and Rock Island, Ill. Women's Mission Societies and Mission Leagues are being organized throughout the churches. Other organizations for various works of beneficence exist in most of the synods—the Ministerium of New York alone reporting 228 societies, of which 108 are for works of benevolence. No general organization of these societies exists, and full reports are not available.

The General Council's Committee on Publications issues

---
* For statistics see chapter on Foreign Missions.

Church Books, Catechisms and Sunday-school books. With other aid it also publishes three mission periodicals. Two of these are in the interests of foreign missions, one in the German, the other in the English language, and circulate about 20,000 copies each issue; the other is in the German tongue, is devoted to the home mission cause, and has a circulation of 1,000 copies.

The Lutheran bookstore in Philadelphia is a private enterprise supported by the churches of the General Council. It has published many Lutheran books and tracts and issues *The Lutheran*—to which Rowell's American Newspaper Directory credits a circulation of 2,500—the Busy Bee, the Helper, the Church Lesson Leaf, and a Church Almanac.

The Augustana Synod, connected with the General Council, is composed almost entirely of Swedes and their American-born children. The first Swedish church on this Synod's territory, was organized with ten members, in 1850. Then there was but one Swedish pastor here. Ten years later the Synod was formed. The people in the congregations were poor. They settled chiefly in the West and Northwest. They suffered from the vicissitudes of the climate, from drouths and storms, from Indian outbreaks particularly in Minnesota, and from unforeseen contingencies and calamities attending the settlement of a new country. They passed with the nation through the hardships of the civil war. They were enticed by Methodists, Baptists, Mormons and Congregationalists in detail, and by the Protestant Episcopalians by wholesale, as well as by others who sought to turn them away from the faith of their fathers.

Despite all these trials this Synod has flourished like a "green bay tree." To-day it numbers 308 ministers, 611 congregations, and more than 78,000 communicants. It has its own Theological Seminary; three colleges, with 47 professors and 835 students; five academies, with 24 professors and 488 students; and has $625,000 invested for these institutions of learning. The principal schools and colleges are managed especially to qualify teachers for the institutions of learning and preachers for the pulpits of the churches. The congregations bear nearly all the burden of providing for them. The entire cost of their maintenance last year was $75,400. They have 279 teachers and 12,900 children in their parochial schools. The cost of maintaining them was $30,000. They have five Orphans' Homes and three Hospitals, with property worth about $175,000. The church property of the synod is worth $2,650,000. Its contribution last year for benevolence was $76,000, not taking into account the immense amount of gratuitous work done for missions. Its local expenses for church purposes for the same time were $580,000.

The Lutheran Augustana Book Concern was organized for the publication and distribution of Lutheran literature as the Augustana Synod might direct. It has capital and assets of $38,000. It has a bookstore and issues five periodicals, of which four report a regular circulation of 54,000 copies each issue. "The Augustana" is a weekly, the official organ of the synod, and has a circulation of 13,400. *Bärne Vennen* is an illustrated Sunday-school monthly with a circulation of 25,500 copies. *Sondagsskolars Textblad* is also a monthly and circulates 5,000 copies. "The Olive Leaf" is an illustrated monthly for the Sunday-school, in the English tongue, circulating 10,000 copies. *Korsbaneret* is an illustrated annual.

Congregations in several synods of the General Council maintain parochial schools. Two, maintaining twenty schools, publish no report of the number of pupils in them. Four others report 399 teachers and 17,166 pupils. The Augustana reports 279 teachers and a total of "school-weeks" aggregating 2,981. The New York Ministerium reports 54 teachers and 14 pastors in its schools; the Ministerium of Pennsylvania, 29 teachers. All maintain these parochial schools in order that the children may receive religious instruction, wherefore the parochial school question is neither a question of politics nor language, but solely of religious instruction.

The statistics of synods and institutions maintained by synods, societies or individuals connected with the General Council, are as follows:

STATISTICS OF SYNODS AND INSTITUTIONS.

I. SYNODS.

Name.	Organized.	Pastors.	Congregations.	Communicant Members.	Sunday Sch'ls.	Teachers and Scholars.	Parochial Schools.	Pupils.
Ministerium of Pennsylvania	1748	269	448	110,917	520	86,105	17	1,255
Ministerium of New York,	1786	114	116	41,999	118	27,926	38	2,854
Pittsburg Synod	1845	120	196	21,229	168	14,983	...	......
Texas Synod	1851	27	66	7,711	25	1,442	6	188
Ohio (Dist.) Synod	1857	31	66	7,863	56	6,613	...	......
Augustana Synod	1860	307	611	78,295	332	29,772	259	12,909
Canada Synod	1861	38	81	8,800	63	3,425	18	1,000
Indiana Synod	1871	17	31	2,939	19	1,942	...	......
		923	1,615	279,753	1,301	172,188	338	18,206
Iowa (Ger.) Synod	...	283	493	45,700	......	......	230	?
Recently Ordained	...	40	......	......	......	......	......	......
		1,256	2,108	325,452				

II. INSTITUTIONS.

A. Educational.

Name.	Location.	Value of Property.	Endowment.	Volumes in Library.	Professors.	Students.
Theological Seminary	Mt. Airy, Pa	$130,000	$120,000	21,000	6	89
Augustana Seminary	Rock Island, Ill		None.	7,000	4	40
Augustana College	Rock Island, Ill	165,000	None.	......	15	250
Gustavus Adolphus College	St. Peter, Minn	60,000	None.	5,300	13	289
Muhlenberg College	Allentown, Pa	80,000	133,100	8,000	11	143
Thiel College	Greenville, Pa	50,000	50,000	6,000	10	127
Bethany College	Lindsborg, Kan	118,000	None.	4,000	15	306
Wagner Memorial College	Rochester, N. Y	25,000	......	500	4	42
Total, Seminaries and Colleges		$628,000	$303,000	51,800	78	1,286
Wartburg Seminary	Dubuque, Ia	50,000	......	......	3	39
Wartburg College	Waverly, Ia	18,000	......	1,400	6	65
Augustana Academy	Salt Lake City	......	......	......	3	31
Emanuel Academy	Minneapolis, Minn	......	......	......	4	112
Hope Academy	Moorehead, Minn	15,000	......	......	6	130
Luther Academy	Wahoo, Neb	18,000	......	700	5	100
Mamrelund Academy	Staunton, Ia	......	......	500	5	115
Greensburg Seminary	Greensburg, Pa	25,000	......	......	7	200
Total, Academies		$58,000	ca.	1,200	30	688

B. Beneficent.

Name.	Location.	Value of Property.	Endowment.	Vol's in Library.	Teachers and Helpers.	Inmates.
Orphans' Home............	Germantown, Pa...	$42,500	$25,000	1,100	4	70
Boys' Orphans' Home.........	Zelienople, Pa......	?	? Farm	?	4	36
Orphans' Home, Girls.........	Rochester, Pa......	80,000	?	?	4	30
Orphans' Home, Girls.........	Near Buffalo, N.Y	75,000	....	100	6	79
Orphans' Home, Boys.........	Buffalo, N. Y.....					
Orphans' Home..............	Jamestown, N. Y...	36.000	....	......	5	45
Orphans' Home..............	Jacksonville, Ill....	5,000	....	......	1	15
Orphans' Home..............	Vasa, Minn........	7,000	Farm of 123 Acres.	......	4	40
Orphans' Home..	Andover, Ill........	25,000	....	......	?	71
Orphans' Home..............	Mariedahl, Kan. ..	10,000	....	......	2	20
Orphans' Home..............	Stanton, Ia.........	12,500	....	100	4	19
Orphans' Home..............	Omaha, Neb........	with Deaconess Home			..	...
Orphans' Home..............	Joliet, Ill..........	? Being opened.....			..	...
Orphans' Home..............	Templeton, Cal., being established...			1,300	34	425
Wartburg O. H.	Mt. Vernon, N. Y...	100,000	....	1,500	5	95
Asylum for Orphans..........	Andrew, Ia........	8,000	....	100	6	28
Evangelical Lutheran O. H....	E. Toledo, O.......	20,000	....	50	2	43
Total...................		$371,000	....	2,950	47	591
Asylum for Aged............	Germantown, Pa..	$32,500	Yearly Exp'ses	....	3	31
1. Mary J. Drexel—Deaconess Home........................	Philadelphia, Pa...	500,000	$50,000	....	35	....
2. Children's Hospital........	Philadelphia, Pa...					In year 200
3. Girls' School..............	Philadelpeia, Pa ...					36
4. Hospital Nursing....... .	Philadelphia, Pa,,				20	150
5. Parish Work.............	Philadelphia, Pa...				2	....
6. Day Nursery..............	Philadelphia, Pa...				2	....
7. Hospital Work in Easton, Pa					1	....
Deaconess Home	Omaha, Neb	40,000	....	......	5	....
Hospital.....................	Omaha, Neb	In Deaconess Home...				Yearly
Hospital, (Swedish)...........	Chicago, Ill	35,000	....	......	..	103
Hospital.....................	St. Paul, Minn.....	35,000	....	......	..	Yearly
Deaconess Hospital...........	Milwaukee, Wis...	175,000	18,000	......	..	554
Deaconess Hospital...........	Jacksonville, Ill...	30,000	....	......	.	Room for 40
Deaconess Hospital...........	Chicago, Ill.......	40,000	6,500	....	..	Yearly 265
Deaconess Infirmary	Pittsburg. Pa......	50,000	....	......	..	....
Drexel Home for Aged........	Philadelphia	....	....	......	..	36
Ger. Luth. Immigrant Mission	New York, N. Y...	150,000	1,050	....	..	Yearly 12,000
Swedish " " "	New York, N. Y...	....	200	....	..	....
Ward's Island Mission........	New York. N. Y...	....	500	....	..	1,200
Swedish Seamen's Mission....	Boston, Mass......	....	....	......	..	....
Hospital.............	St. Peter, Minn....	....	....	......	..	....
Total		$1,087,500	In all	ca.	66	14,795

The Synodical Conference embraces four District Synods, namely: Joint Synod of Missouri, Ohio and other States, Wisconsin Synod and Minnesota Synod; to which must be added the English Conference of Missouri. It "acknowledges the canonical Scriptures of the Old and New Testaments as God's Word, and the Confession of the Evangelical Lutheran Church of 1580, called 'Concordia,' as its own."

The immigration of the first representatives of this body was begun to escape the Unionism which the King of Prussia was forcing on them in Saxony and other German provinces. Many in those days endured persecution there for conscience' sake. To escape at once the Unionism and the persecution, they came to America. They began to arrive in 1839. Soon, in the wilds of Missouri, many of them were reduced to want. Not a few perished from the hardships attendant upon their new settlement. But they were people of strong faith and stern moral fibre. They erected their humble log churches and schoolhouses in the midst of their settlements, and the blessing of heaven has been upon their labors. Home, school and church alike have prospered wondrously.

The Missouri Synod is, in an important sense, the *Mother Synod*, or General Synod of the Synodical Conference, having the following district synods connected with it, viz: The Eastern District; the Western; Michigan; Middle; Illinois; Iowa; Canada; Minnesota and Dakota; Wisconsin; Nebraska, Southern; Kansas; California and Oregon. The mother synod is now a delegate body, from two to seven congregations being entitled to send one clerical and one lay delegate. The district synods meet annually, but the general body only once in three years.

To day the Conference has $720,000 invested in institutions of higher learning and $300,000 in institutions of beneficence. It has in 15 educational institutions, 78 professors and 1,800 students. As all are managed in the interests of the church—to prepare young men as teachers in the church schools or as pastors of the congregations—the church willingly bears the burden of their support. The institutions of beneficence number 16, with branches in Bremen and Hamburg. Of these ten are homes for orphans. They have property worth $190,000. In them 36 teachers and helpers care for 510 children, who are maintained, instructed and trained as they would be in a well-ordered Christian family.* The other institutions of beneficence are two Hospitals, two Immigrant Missions and two Homes for the Aged and Infirm. The hospitals have property worth $55,000, and each year care for between 200 and 300 sick and wounded, chiefly poor persons unable to pay for needful attention. The hospital in East New York has connected with it a Home for Aged and Infirm, 72 of whom it sheltered during the past year. Its expenses, in the two departments, were $10,341. The Immigrant Mission at New York has a property for which $65,000 were paid. Its object is to protect those German Lutherans from imposition, who emigrate to North America, and furnish them with counsel and assistance. It received nearly 6,000 immigrants during the year and assisted them to the extent of $5,500. Missionaries connected with this institution are located at No. 8 State St., New York; at 1515 East Pratt St., Baltimore, and also at Hamburg and Bremen. The agency in Baltimore cared for more than 1,200 immigrants during the year, and advanced to them the sum of $1,470. The synod contributed $1,731 toward the support of the mission.

The Publishing House at St. Louis, Mo., issues most of the periodicals, schoolbooks and devotional works used in their schools and churches. It was established in 1860. It has no liabilities. Its assets aggregate $160,000. Its profits are paid into the synodical treasury.† The Missouri Synod

---

* Five of these Homes, which care for 274 children, report yearly expenses amounting to $24,700.

† The main building is 40x94 feet, and, including the ground floor, is four stories in height. The lower floor contains four steam presses, one other press, steam engine and other machinery. The boiler, 22 feet

has for years been sending money to certain of the Foreign Mission Societies of Germany to aid them in their work. At the meeting of the Synod held May, 1887, at Fort Wayne, Ind., it was resolved to begin their own foreign mission work, the Synod having on hand for this purpose the sum of $13,000; and at the convention of 1890 it was resolved that a Mission Director be called, into whose care the oversight of the work should be given. The contributions for 1890, including Negro and Jewish Missions, were $16,648. Negro missions are in successful operation at New Orleans, La., Little Rock, Ark., Meherrin, Va., and Springfield, Ills. Five ordained missionaries and four teachers are engaged in these fields; 600 adults are in connection with the churches and nearly as many children in the schools. More than $7,500 were expended on this work during the year.

---

long by 3 feet 10 inches in diameter, is placed in a brick annex 26x44 feet, one story in height. In the second story of the main building is the bookstore, office and packing room. In the third story is the bookbindery. The fourth story is used for type setting, and contains an assortment of type, which, at least as far as German types are concerned, is scarcely surpassed by any other office in the United States. In one corner of the edifice is a steam elevator, and a steam heating apparatus supplies all needed warmth. North of the main edifice stands the warehouse. Here printed sheets of unbound books are stored, and here also are fire-proof vaults which contain the valuable stereotype plates, the archives and safe. Sixty-six men are employed in the establishment. During the year past its productions were 45,000 hymn books; 13,000 Bible histories; 25,500 catechisms; 19,000 books of fables; 44,000 readers, of which 25,000 copies were in the English language: a total of 180,000 volumes. Last year it reported profits of $61,000. In addition to its book business this publishing house issues 7 periodicals which have an aggregate circulation of 81,000 copies each issue. *Der Lutheraner* circulates 22,000; *Die Missions-Taube*, 14,000; and the *Luth. Kinderblatt*, 29,000. Five of these seven papers are issued by the Missouri Synod, the other two by the Synodical Conference. Both the Wisconsin and the Minnesota Synods have their own periodicals; the former publishing two church papers in Milwaukee, and the latter one in New Ulm, Minnesota. Apart from these are 8 periodicals published by individuals in other parts of the church, yet devoted to the interests of the Synods to which their editors belong.

A missionary is maintained among the Israelites in New York City ; and it is now proposed to establish a colony of Hebrew Christians, to provide the converts with the means of honest self-support after they have been cast off by their co-religionists.

The Missouri Synod has always devoted its principal energy to gathering into the Church the immigrant Germans, organizing many new congregations every year. The work of Home Missions is under control of the district Synods, and only such funds as are not needed by each district are paid into the general fund. Great success has attended these efforts, as is shown by the fact that the little company of poor and unknown men who began the work only fifty years ago, has grown into an organization of fourteen hundred pastors who minister to 1,991 congregations of nearly 400,000 souls. The Statistical Year Book shows 548 stations supplied and more than a hundred additional preaching places visited by traveling preachers. The amount of money passing through the hands of the Central Committee in 1889 was $6,300. The thirteen district Synods expended $32,000. The total amount reported for missions, education and similar work during the last year reached $154,722 : the aggregate sum for the past five years being more than half a million.

The English language is receiving more attention now than formerly among the members of the Missouri Synod. Many of the younger pastors use it with fluency. The higher educational institutions are drilling candidates for the ministry forthcoming and the teachers in its use. English books are being issued from the publishing house. English missions are being organized and now exist in five States. Candidates for admission to their teachers' seminaries must be able to use the vernacular to the extent of reading simple stories and writing legible English, and in the Seminary they have English studies through the whole of the five years' course. Most of the instruction on non-religious topics is given in the same language.

The principal colleges, gymnasiums and the theological seminaries, as a matter of course, have been established to prepare pastors, who may go among the incoming Germans and break to them the Bread of Life. Every young man who has the requisite mental, moral and physical equipment, anywhere in the church or her twelve hundred congregational schools, who expresses a willingness to do the Lord's work in the holy office of the ministry, is taken in hand and trained for it. If he, or his friends, can pay the light expenses of his educational course it is expected that they do so; if not, the Church pays them. Thus it comes to pass that nearly $15,000 a year have been paid by the Church for the support of the college at Fort Wayne, and that the reported expenses of indigent students and current expenses in the colleges last year were almost $24,000.* It is the cause of Home Missions that is being advanced in the establishment and maintenance of the educational institutions of the Synodical Conference; the means being provided in part by collections in the churches and in part by the profits from the Publication House in St. Louis.

The course in the college at Fort Wayne covers six years. The curriculum embraces all the requisites of a good English education, from simple reading, writing and spelling up through composition, grammar, history, extemporaneous speech and the study of the standard authors. The Pro-Gymnasium in Milwaukee has substantially the same course, except that it covers only four years. In the Teachers' Seminary at Addison, Ill., English studies have a prominent place in the curriculum. Tuition and boarding in these institutions are furnished at a low rate. At Fort Wayne the whole cost is but $110 per year of 10 months, of which charge $40 are remitted to such stu-

---

* *Statistisches Jahrbuch:* St. Louis, 1890.

Y

dents as are studying for the church. At the Pro Gymnasium, Milwaukee, board, room rent, heat and light cost $61, but those who do not intend studying theology pay $20 per year for tuition. In the Teachers' Seminary at Addison, the total charges are $57 per year. In all cases "plain living and high thinking" are necessarily the rule.

Two of the eleven institutions named are theological seminaries, one at St. Louis, Mo., the other at Springfield, Ill. The former is intended for young men who are graduates from the college at Fort Wayne. It provides a three years' course in theology. The latter is for men more advanced in years, who commonly take a two years' preparatory course in the Pro-Seminary and then enter the three years' course in what is known as the Practical Seminary. In the former a nine years' course of study is required to prepare the candidate for final examination for admission to the ministry; in the latter this course is shortened to five years. The curriculum of the Springfield Institution embraces the following subjects of study, viz: Dietrich's Dogmatics; the Symbolical Books; Comparative Symbolics; Practical Exegesis of the Old and New Testaments; Church History; Homiletics, with Luther's Church-" Postille;" Themes of Casual and Festival Sermons; Homiletical and Catechetical exercises; Pastoral Theology; Reading of the Apology and the Book of Concord in Latin; English exercises; instructions for the organization of a "mixed" school; Violin lessons; and evening hours for English Debate.* In the "theoretical" Seminary at St. Louis the course includes Logic, Metaphysics, and History of Philosophy; Encyclopædia and Methodology; Isagogics; Hermeneutics; Exegesis of Old and New Testament according to the original texts; review of Hebrew Grammar; Reading of Original Text in course; Dogmatics, including Ethics and Polemics; Symbolics; Church History, including History of Doctrine,

---

* *Katalog Lehranstalten*, 1890.

Patristics, and Church Archæology; Catechetics and Homiletics; Liturgics; Exercises in Catechetics and Homiletics; Pastoral Theology; Evening Lectures on Questions of the Times; Lectures on Epoch-making Theological Works; Reading of Significant Writings of the Church Fathers; and Theological Discussions.

The whole educational system of the Missouri Synod began in a humble cabin in Perry county, Mo., not half a century ago. Even that humble beginning was possible only when the three pastors and three candidates of theology then in that new German settlement, went into the woods and with their own hands felled the trees and helped to lay the logs cut from them into the building wherein was to be organized the proposed school. Out of the gymnasiums and universities of Germany they came to be for the time "hewers of wood and drawers of water." The small building with but one rough door and one window in its front, located in the wilds of primitive Missouri, gave promise to the outward vision of no great things. But who shall despise the day of small things! In that humble edifice the Missouri authorities, looking with the eye of faith to the unseen things, began their work. Inside those lowly walls instruction was given first in religion, which has always been maintained as the first of all studies in their schools, in Latin, Greek, Hebrew, German, French and English, in History, Geography, Mathematics, Natural Philosophy, Natural History, Mental Philosophy and Music. And God wrought with these fathers in the faith. Out of their humble beginning has grown the whole system of educational institutions concerning which these pages speak.

Dr. Ruperti, an official of the Church in Germany, says of the seminary building in St. Louis: "In St. Louis there stands . . . Concordia Seminary, a magnificent building in Gothic style, which need not dread comparison with finest university buildings in Germany; and that, too, built not by the State, but by the spontaneous gifts of Lutheran Christians." With respect to the drill and instruction given there, Charles Dudley Warner has written: " The ministers of the denomination are distinguished for learning and earnest simplicity. The president, a very able man, only thirty-five years of age, is at least two centuries old in his opinions, and wholly undisturbed by any of the doubts which have agitated the world since the Reformation. He holds the faith 'Once for all,' delivered to the Saints. The *Seminar* has a hundred students. It is requisite to admission, said the president, that they be perfect Latin, Greek and Hebrew scholars. A large proportion of lectures are given in Latin, the remainder in German and English; the Latin is current in the institution, although German is the familiar speech. The course of study is exacting, the rules are rigid and the discipline severe. Social intercourse with the other sex is discouraged. The pursuit of love and learning are considered incompatible at the same time, and if a student were inconsiderate enough to become engaged, he would be expelled. Each student from abroad may select or be selected by a family in the Communion, at whose house he may visit once a week, which attends to his washing, and supplies to a certain extent the place of a home. The young men are trained in the highest scholarship and the strictest code of morals. I know of no other denomination which holds its members to such primitive theology and such strictness of life. Individual liberty and responsibility are stoutly asserted, without any latitude in belief. When I asked the president what he did with geology, he smiled and simply waved his hand. This Communion has thirteen flourishing churches in the city. In a town so largely German, and with so many free thinkers as well as free-livers, I cannot but consider this strict sect, of a simple, unquestioning faith and high moral demands, of the highest importance in the future of the city.

. . . It repudiates prohibition as an infringement of personal liberty, would make the use of wine or beer depend upon the individual conscience, but no member of the Communion would be permitted to sell intoxicating liquors or to go to a beer garden or theatre."*

"What this Synod has done for the upbuilding of the kingdom of God—for the education of ministers and teachers—for the circulation of truly Lutheran books and papers, is widely known; and by these operations she has gained the attention, if not the love, of her worst enemies. Her congregations though mostly small and poor, have been very liberal and brought large offerings, even beyond their means: and they were not brought to this under the lash of drivers, but did it of their own free will, with joy and gladness; not to obtain favor with men, but in thankfulness to God for mercies received. Nor did the ministers hold back; but with the utmost self-denial, often at the expense of health and strength, they went forth into 'the highways and hedges'—into the most distant regions and through the thickest forests—to seek the lost and scattered sheep. With the poor, they gladly became poor, that they might gain the poor:—with the hungry, they patiently suffered hunger to gain them, in many cases denying themselves the most necessary comforts of life, that God's work might go on. They lived in the poorest huts and on the poorest fare without murmuring or complaint, because they were in the service of the Master. They ceased not to teach and preach 'with all long-suffering and doctrine,' exhorting, rebuking, and comforting, regardless of the incivility and unthankfulness with which they often met. Nothing deterred them from their duty.

"With great industry they also established congregational schools everywhere—Christian schools—themselves becoming the teachers, in which the dear children and youth could

* In *Harper's Monthly.*

be brought to Christ and trained for the Kingdom of God; and the Lord has crowned their labors with abundant success."*

The venerable Dr. John G. Morris, writing of these brethren, has said: "Their activity in founding and supporting literary and theological schools of the highest order; their religious publications, the sales of which amounted to over $140,000 last year, and extensive book establishment at St. Louis; their numerous churches in the large cities of the West, especially their liberal contributions to every good cause within their own domain; the provision they make for their poor and disabled ministers, widows, orphans, and Home Missions, constitute a spectacle pleasant to look upon, and calculated to excite our admiration and sympathy." Truly a spectacle for men and angels. Would to God that all men looking upon it be moved not merely to gaze and wonder, but being "provoked unto good works," might go and do likewise according to the measure of their ability.

The statistics of the Synods and their institutions in connection with the Synodical Conference are given below:

STATISTICS OF SYNODS AND INSTITUTIONS.
I. SYNODS.

Name of Synod.	When Organized.	Pastors.	Cong's.	Communicant Members.	Parochial Schools.	Pupils.
Synod of Missouri, Ohio, etc.	1847	1,140	1,631	305,350	1,226	78,061
" Wisconsin	1850	152	248	73,784	176	?
" Minnesota	1860	62	99	16,100	46	2,023
Eng. (conference) Synod of Mo.	1888 / 1891	13	13	900	7	312
Total		1,367	1,991	396,134	1,455	80,396
Sunday Schools					178	12,000
Preaching Stations and Missions, additional, over				600		

* The late Rev. S. W. Harkey, D. D., in the *Lutheran Observer*.

The confessional basis of the United Synod of the Church South, is as follows: "The Holy Scriptures, the Inspired Writings of the Old and New Testaments, are the only standard of doctrine and church discipline. As a true and faithful exhibition of the doctrines of the Holy Scriptures in regard to matters of faith and practice, the three Ancient Symbols, the Apostolic, the Nicene, and the Athanasian Creeds, and the Unaltered Augsburg Confession of Faith, also the other Symbolical Books of the Evangelical Lutheran

II. INSTITUTIONS.

A. Beneficence.

Name.	Location.	Value of Property, &c.	Teachers & Helpers	Inmates.
Martin Luther Orphans' Home	West Roxbury, Mass.	$ 32,000	3	63
Institute for Deaf and Dumb..	Norris, Mich...	25,000	3	45
Ger. Ev. Luth. Orphans' Home	Adison, Ill...	50,000	6	106
Concordia " "	Delano, Penna	20,000	3	47
Ev. Lutheran " "	Des Peres, Mo.......	15,000	9	70
Bethlehem " "	New Orleans, La ...	6,000	2	20
Ger. Bethlehem " "	Indianapolis, Ind....	8,000	1	16
Bethlehem " "	College Point, L. I...	25,000	6	80
Martin Luther " "	Wittenberg, Wis.....	6,000	3	63
			36	510
				In Year.
Martin Luther	San Francisco, Cala.(	Being es	tabli	shed.)
Lutheran Hospital..........	East New York, N.Y.	40,000	?	124
Ev. Lutheran Hospital	St. Louis, Mo........	15,000	6	90
Wartburg Home for Aged....	East New York......	....	?	72
	(With hospital.)			
			6	286
Home for Aged.............	Delano, Penna. (Bei	ng estab	lish	ed.)
Immigrant Mission, German..	New York, N. Y.....	65,000	1	5,020
" " Scandinavian	" "	......	....	......
" "	Baltimore, Md......	....	1	1,515
An Emigrant Missionary is stationed at..........	Bremen, Germany...	....	1	......
Two Emigrant Missionaries are at	Hamburg, Germany..	....	2	... ..
Total.................		$307,000	55	6,535

Church, viz.: The Apology, the Smalcald Articles, the Smaller and Larger Catechisms of Luther, and the Formula of Concord, consisting of the Epitome and Full Declaration, as they are set forth, defined and published in the Christian Book of Concord, or the Symbolical Books of the Lutheran Church, published in the year 1580, are true and scriptural developments of the doctrines taught in the Augsburg Confession, and in perfect harmony of one and the same pure, scriptural faith." This is the smallest in numbers of the general bodies of our Church in the United States, reporting (Nov., 1889,) 189 ministers, 386 Churches and 29 mission stations, with a communicant membership of not quite 34,000. It stands in proportion to its numbers, best equipped of all in the number of educational institutions, having eighteen, ranging from academies, and schools for young

INSTITUTIONS.
Educational

Name and Class.	Location.	Value of Property, &c.	Volumes in library.	Professors.	Students.
Ev. Luth. Concordia Seminary.	St. Louis, Mo...	$200,000	10,000	5	141
Practical (Theol.) Seminary....	Springfield, Ill..	65,000	800	4	106
Theol. Seminary, (Wis. Synod.)	Milwaukee, Wis.	20,000	800	3	84
" " (Minn. Synod.)	New Ulm, Minn.			7	95
Concordia College	Ft. Wayne, Ind.	100,000	.....	7	225
North Western University....	Watertown, Wis.	60,000	2,500	8	175
Pro-Gymnasium..............	Milwaukee, Wis.	90,000	1,300	6	179
" "	Concordia, Mo..	15,000	500	6	83
" "	New York, N. Y.	?		5	34
Martin Luther College........	New Ulm, Minn.	30,000	?	7	95
Walther College..............	St. Louis, Mo...	32,500	.....	2	86
St. Matthew's Academy.......	New York, N.Y.	30,000	.....	7	280
Teachers' Seminary...........	Addison, Ill....	70,000	1,400	7	183
St. Luke's Academy	Brooklyn, N. Y.	7,000	....		
Pro-Seminary, ...	Springfield, Ill..			4	102
Total...................		$719,500	17,300	78	1,817

women, up to theological seminaries. They report property and endowment aggregating $395,000, have 109 professors and 1,650 students. One Orphans' Home exists at Salem, Va., with property worth $10,000, 3 teachers and 14 orphans—the number soon to be increased. A hospital is now being founded in Charleston, S. C.

The mission work shows 29 stations connected with regularly organized pastorates. The Board of Missions employs a General Secretary, whose headquarters are at Knoxville, Tenn. The report shows the receipts for the year past to have been $4,700, and asks for $6,000 for the current year. The Southwest Va. Synod is mentioned as being especially active in Home Mission work. The same Board has oversight of the Foreign Mission work of the Synod. Up to the present time they have been coöperating with the General Synod in its foreign work, but now have a missionary of their own and expect soon to have another and to open a mission in Japan. In all the Synods, both women and children are organized and active in the cause of missions. The receipts for Foreign Missions have been about $3,000 per year. "The Mission News" is published at Augusta, Ga., in the interest of Missions. About 8,000 copies of each issue are circulated. A church in Salem, Va., pledged itself to support one missionary in the foreign field. The United Synod has a Committee on Seamen's Aid Society which aims to coöperate with German and Scandinavian authorities in looking after the spiritual welfare of the 45,000 seamen who annually visit southern ports, and particularly in caring for the 15,000 among them who are brethren in the faith.

The Alpha Synod of Freedmen originated under the superintendency of the North Carolina Synod.

A Board of Education has been appointed whose duty it is to gather, tabulate and publish reports of all our church schools of whatever grade, to compare their courses of study, to advise with their trustees and faculties, and on the basis of the information thus gathered, to suggest to future conventions of the United Synod, appropriate action.

Publishing houses and book stores exist in Columbia, S. C., and in New Market, Va. The latter is under the control of Henkel & Co., has existed since 1806, and has issued many standard religious works, among them the first edition of the Book of Concord ever issued in the United States, or probably anywhere, in the English language. "Our Church Paper" and the "Lutheran Visitor" are the two principal periodicals issued in the interests of the Synods. The former has a circulation of 1,550 and the latter of 1,900. The total receipts for the different objects of benevolence during the past year among the churches of the United Synod aggregated $24,500, the local expenses for all objects were $92,700. Following are the statistics of the United Synod:

STATISTICS OF SYNODS AND INSTITUTIONS.

I. SYNODS.

Name.	Organized.	Pastors.	Cong's.	Communicant Members.	S. S's.	Scholars.	Preaching Places.
Synod of North Carolina.	1803	34	58	6,162	50	2,100	6
Tennessee Synod	1820	34	107	10,000	60	3,000	...
Synod of South Carolina.	1824	36	59	6,650	54	4,200	...
Synod of Virginia	1830	29	76	5,126	66	4,834	12
" South West Va.	1842	34	56	3,907	57	3,484	45
" Mississippi	1855	9	10	544	5	166	...
" Georgia	1860	9	19	1,456	13	1,059	...
Holston Synod	1861	11	28	2,226	15	700	2
Synod of Freedmen	1889	3	5	200	?	?	...
Total		199	414	36,271	320	19,543	65

The parochial reports of several Synods do not seem to be at all full.

II. INSTITUTIONS.
A. Educational.

Name.	Location.	Value of Property, &c.	Vols. in Library.	Professors.	Students.
Theological Seminary ...	Newberry, S. C....	$ 52,000	6,000	3	4
" " ...	Columbia	(Now closed.)			
Roanoke College.........	Salem, Va	135,000	17,000	11	123
Newberry "	Newberry, S. C....	40,000	6,000	7	123
North Carolina College...	Mt. Pleasant, N. C.	12,000	2,000	7	96
Concordia College........	Conover, N. C.....	5,000	500	6	139
Gaston "	Dallas, N. C......	10,000	600	8	60
Mosheim "	Mosheim, Tenn....	1,500		2	100
High School.............	Enochville, N. C...	500		3	108
Collegiate Institute.......	Beth Eden, Miss...	2,500		4	68
Eng. and Class. Institute.	Leesville. S. C.....	5,000	800	7	91
Holly Grove Academy....	Ilex, N. C.........	1,200	100	2	75
China Grove "	China Grove, N. C.	?		3	80
Wartbury Seminary.......	Graham, Va	100,000	400	4	75
Mill Point Institute......	Mill Point, Tenn...	2,000		2	100
Cleburne Institute........	Edwardsville,Tenn.	?		4	?
Young Women's Seminary	Mt. Pleasant, N. C.	4,000	200	5	87
" " "	Marion, Va.	25,000	250	9	113
" " "	Staunton, Va.	20,000	600	11	75
Trinity Seminary	Wytheville, Va....	10,000	1,000	5	43
Von Bora College........	Luray, Va	10,000		10	90
		$447,700	36,950	113	1,053

B. Beneficent.

SouthView Orphans' Home	Salem, Va........	10,000		3	20
Hospital and Home for Aged	Charleston, S. C... (Being established.)				

The Evangelical Lutheran Joint Synod of Ohio and other states now consists of ten District Synods, four having been erected at the last meeting of the general body in Columbus, Ohio, September, 1890. The older districts are the Eastern, Western, Northern, Northwestern, First English and Concordia; the new ones, the Minnesota and Dakota, Pacific, Kansas and Nebraska, and the Texas. The whole number of her pastors and professors is 326, of parochial school teachers 87, of congregations 486, and of members 66,480. Her pastors and people are found in twenty-three states and territories, although Ohio contains nearly the one half of all. Indiana ranks next and Wisconsin, Pennsylvania, Michigan and Minnesota follow in the order named.

The Home Mission work of this Synod stretches over a wide territory. The Mission Committee has 27 missionaries in its employ and some of them have from twelve to twenty preaching places. The continual lamentation is that as many more men cannot be had for this work. It is carried on chiefly among German immigrants in the West, although the English interests are not overlooked. The yearly expenses are about twelve thousand dollars. The work is carried on in seventeen states. One chief aim of the Synod's educational institutions is to prepare men to care for the thousands who are set down among us without proper church privileges. Most of its contributions to Foreign Missions go to the Herrmannsburg Society in Germany.

The "Book Concern" of this Synod is located at Columbus, Ohio, and has a capital stock of $40,000. Its profits in the last two years were $17,350, of which nearly $7,000 were turned into the general treasury and the remainder taken to increase the capital stock. In this time it published about twenty different books, besides tracts, brochures, &c. Including Sunday school lesson leaves, it publishes nine periodicals, five in English, four in German. During the year 1889-90, four of these returned a profit of $2,840 and five a loss of $875. The "Book Concern" is preparing to build and furnish for itself a home at a cost of about $30,000.

This Synod has four principal educational institutions. Three of them have both a classical and theological department. The Teachers' Seminary at Woodville, Ohio, is especially for training teachers for the parochial schools. The property of these schools is valued at $130,000, the professors number 24 and the students 364. The majority of these are preparing for the teachers' office or for the ministry. The Orphans' Home and Asylum for the Aged at Richmond, Indiana, has 115 inmates. The Treasurer's report shows that nearly $11,000 passed through his hands in the last year for the benefit of the institution.

As the educational institutions have been established to supply teachers and pastors, the churches make yearly contributions to them, both for helping to support indigent students and to pay the salaries of professors. Including $23,800 debt canceled, the Synod paid out in the past two years more than $68,152 for the support of these institutions. It supported sixty young men at Capital University, who are preparing for the pastoral office. The expenses of their board and professors' salaries in two years aggregated $36,000. The estimate for this year calls for $25,000. An additional building is being erected to accommodate the increased number of students at Columbus, and an additional professor has been given to each of the other theological and classical schools. Capital University, located at Columbus, Ohio, was founded in 1850, and is the principal institution of the Synod. According to its new prospectus, " the object it has in view is a truly liberal education of young men, which can take place only where the fear of God and the instruction in His Word are made the groundwork of all learning and wisdom." It has four departments, viz.: a grammar school, which gives a solid English education and prepares young men for college; a teachers' course, to prepare young men to teach in the public schools; the regular college department, with a classical and art course covering four years; and a theological department, which has existed since 1830, and has a course of study covering three years. Students are required not only to attend prayers every morning and evening in the college chapel, but also to study Bible History, Sacred History and the Catechism as part of the regular course. The study of the

Catechism and of Bible History is begun in the first year of the preparatory course, continued through the different sessions until, in the Senior year, Sacred History and the Catechism furnish the religious studies of the student.

In the Teachers' Seminary at Woodville, Ohio, the course of studies is designed to extend over a period of five years, three of which are employed in the preparatory department and two in the seminary proper. The expenses are $2 per week for board, and $40 per year for room-rent and tuition.

The German Practical Seminary at Afton, Minn., is really a Home Mission Institute, with a course of study extending through four years. Two of these years are in the preparatory department, which course fits the student for admission to the Freshman class at Capital University; the other two years are devoted to theology. Board is $60 and tuition $40 per year, for those who do not study theology. Young men of piety and talent, whose aim is to prepare for the ministry, but who have not the necessary funds, may receive beneficiary aid from Synod.

St. Paul's English Practical Seminary, at Hickory, N. C., is substantially the same in design and working as that at Afton, except that it has no official preparatory department. This department exists, but is in the hands of private individuals. German is taught to an extent that enables students to make use of German Lutheran literature. These institutions do not supply the demands for pastors, and candidates are being brought from Herrmannsburg to assist in meeting the needs of the Church in the Northwest and Southwest.

The Iowa German Synod is classed among the independent organizations, although it has a nominal connection with the General Council, which entitles it to representation in the Conventions of that body, without the right to vote. It has six district Synods, and numbers 75,400 souls. It has a Theological Seminary at Dubuque, Iowa, and a College at

Waverly, Iowa. The latter has a department for teachers. The buildings are valued at $70,000; there are nine professors and 104 students. Two Orphans' Homes are maintained by members of the Synod; one at Andrew, Iowa, and the other at East Toledo, Ohio. Eight teachers and helpers labor in them; the orphans number 71. In 1889 $2,900 were expended on these institutions. Parochial schools to the number of 230 are supported, the pupils in them numbering 8,900. As in nearly all the schools which exist among the German and Scandinavian members of our Church, which prepare young men to be teachers or ministers, the burden of their support, also, in this Synod is borne by the congregations. The Treasurer's report from June, 1888, to June, 1890, shows contributions to the educational institutions aggregating $17,330, in addition to donations amounting to $16,142, made toward the erection of a new Seminary.

The Iowa Synod has no independent foreign mission work, but assists that of the General Council in India, and the mission enterprises of Herrmannsburg and Neuendettelsau. Through the latter Society it sends funds to New Guinea and Australia. It also assists in supporting missions in East Africa, the Evangelical Orphanage in Jerusalem, missions among the Israelites, immigrant missions and the Mission Institutes of Brecklum and of Strackholt in Germany. The total of contributions for beneficence in the two years ending June 1st, 1890, was $43,525. This includes no funds which did not come directly into the synodical treasury. Last year the receipts were $27,360.

The Inner Mission work of the Synod is carried on under the direction of the Mission Committee, and by the district Synods. The Central Committee has under its supervision 82 missions, with 21 missionaries, in seven States, maintained at an expense of $3,000 per year. In addition to this, different pastors in five Synods maintain 113 missions as a labor of love, in connection with the congregations in which they labor.

The Synod has its own Publication House at Waverly, Ia., which last year did a business of $14,150, and returned a profit of $2,500. It has a book department, which supplies the congregations with devotional works of an orthodox Lutheran spirit, and a periodical department which issues the *Kirchen-Blatt* and the *Zeitschrift*. The former is published once in two weeks, the latter in magazine form, six times a year. *Blätter aus den Waisenhäusern* is issued in the interests of the orphanage at Andrew and is edited by the House-Father of that institution. The Wartburg *Kalender* also is issued by the Publication House, and circulates 6,000 copies. The *Kirchen-Blatt* has a circulation of 4,000.

The Synod is collecting a fund to aid aged and invalid pastors and teachers. Each pastor is expected, on the 1st of January, to remit to its treasurer one-half of one per cent. of his salary for the year; the churches are asked to make contributions to the fund.

A Church-Building Loan Treasury is also being established to aid feeble congregations to build churches. Its purpose is to gather funds, to be loaned not longer than five years at five per cent., and to receive church furniture and the like from the older congregations, and forward it to those newly organized and weak.

During the year 1889, the members of this Synod paid for the support of pastors $87,443; for teachers, additional, $8,920; for the alms-treasury, $10,766, and for other local purposes sufficient to make a total of $213,304. In the same time the contributions for beneficence were $27,360: a grand total of $240,665.

Since 1879 a mutual Aid Society has been in operation. Upon the death of a member in the first division the sum of $1,000 is paid to the family of the deceased, and for those being members also of the second division, an additional sum proportionate to the number of members, the maximum not to exceed $1,000. The society numbers 2,000 members in the first division and 70 in the second. From June, 1879, to 1891, the sum of $54,016 has been paid to beneficiaries of 58 deceased members. There have been 84 assessments. The Society has a reserve fund of $7,200, which is increasing at the rate of $1,500 a year.

Seven of the eight Scandinavian Synodical organizations in in the United States are among the independent Synods. "The Danish Evangelical Lutheran Church in America, with 49 pastors, 112 congregations and 11,000 members, maintains some connection with the State Church of Denmark. Its pastors and people are distributed through sixteen States, from Maine to California, although more than half of them are in Michigan, Iowa, Nebraska and Wisconsin. Maine, Massachusetts, Connecticut, New Jersey, Oregon and Utah have each one pastor. The territory of this body is virtually a mission field.

The Norwegian Evangelical Lutheran Church in America is an organization dating from 1853. Its pastors and congregations are found in twenty-three States, stretching from Massachusetts to Texas, and from California to Washington. The pastors and professors number 180; the congregations above 550, and the confirmed members 60,000. More than half the pastors and people are located in Minnesota, Wisconsin and Iowa. The Synod is divided into the Eastern, the Iowa, and the Minnesota districts: the first extending from Massachusetts to Nebraska, the second reaching on to California, and the third extending over the Northwest to the Dominion of Canada.

The Synod of the United Norwegian Lutheran Church in America was organized June, 1890, by the consolidation of three smaller bodies. Its pastors are in fifteen States, and two are missionaries in Madagascar. It numbers 260 ministers, 830 congregations,* and 83,500 communicants. Over one-third of the pastors and people are in Minnesota and the Dakotas. While many of the congregations number from one hundred to seven hundred members each; perhaps one-fourth of the whole number are really mission organizations, each numbering from six to fifty members, and are supplied by pastors whose main support comes from the older and abler congregations.

The Danish Church Association, (or Danish Synod,) has its pastors and members mainly in Nebraska, Minnesota, California, Iowa and Wisconsin. It numbers 22 pastors and 45 congregations.

The Hauge Norwegian Synod, with 65 pastors, about 160 congregations and 10,500 members, has its strength also in the Dakotas and Minnesota.

The Icelandic Church Union, with six pastors, has its chief strength in Dakota and Manitoba, where there are 17 congregations and 4,000 members. The Norwegian pastors of the Synods, which united in 1890, and who have not entered the United Synod, number about a dozen and a half, with some 30 congregations and 4,000 members.

The (Finnish) "Suomi" Synod dates its existence from December, 1889; numbers six pastors, as many more congregations, and about 2,000 members. Its strength is chiefly in Michigan.

In addition to the members of the independent organizations a number of pastors and congregations claiming to be Lutherans are outside of all synodical connection. Their numbers are variously reported at from fifty to one hundred and fifty pastors, and from 10,000 to 30,000 members. A goodly number of the pastors and people in the United Evangelical Church of America—a body resting on the confessional basis of the Church of Prussia—say they are Lu-

---

* This includes 187 congregations not regularly connected with it, but served by its pastors.

therans; but none of the Lutheran Synods have recognized them as such.

The Independent Scandinavian Synods support 24 institutions for higher education and have seven Orphans' Homes, Hospitals and Deaconesses' Institutes. Of the educational institutions eighteen report property worth $514,000. Four of them are theological seminaries with 16 professors and 124 students; four are colleges, (of which the one at Minneapolis is to be wholly given over to theology, after this year,) with 33 professors and 564 students; the others are academies with 56 professors and 991 students. In all the 24 institutions there are 105 professors and 1,697 students.

Both the Danish and Norwegian Synods maintain parochial schools. Reports at hand say 431 teachers are supported and 45 additional schools are kept open, from which it is safe to infer that 450 teachers of congregational schools are supported. Computing the expenditures for these schools at the low average given for the support of a teacher per year in the Missouri Synod, ($350) we find the

STATISTICS OF SYNODS AND INSTITUTIONS.
I. SYNODS.

Name.	Organized.	Pastors.	Congregations.	Communicant Members.	S. Ss.	Members.	Parochial Schools.	Pupils.
Synod of Ohio, etc..............	1818	326	486	66,480	214	8,000	288	8,500
Buffalo Synod.................	1845	23	32	5,000	8	?	18	1,010
Hauge Synod. Norwegian.	1846	68	164	10,900	106	?	86	?
*Norwegian Ev. Luth. Ch. in America............................	1853	171	483	50,661	....	......	217	t'chrs
Michigan Synod................	1860	37	76	8,700	32	1,500	27	1,037
*Danish Ev. Luth. Ch. in America, in connection with Ch. in Denmark	1872	49	192	6,678	....	......	30	?
*Augsburg Synod...............	1875	19	23	5,234	14	1,200	10	397
*Danish Ev. Luth. Ch. Association.	1884	22	45 ca.	3 000	....	......	10	t'chrs
Icelandic Church Association.......	1885	6	26	6,228	20	650	.....	......
Immanuel Synod	1886	19	19	5,420	20	1,000	?	265
Suomi Synod (Finnish)............	1889	6	12	2,400	...	......	.....	......
United Norwegian Ch. in America..	1890	285	830	83,500	...	......	468	?
Norwegians..Independent...........	....	20	30 ca.	4,000	...	......	......	......
Independent Pastors............	....	50	50	10,000	...	......	......	......
		1,074	2,470	268,201			1.094	11,209

* Reports not full.

II. INSTITUTIONS.

A.—Educational.

Name and Class.	Location.	Value of Property etc.	Vols. in Library.	Profess- ors.	Students.
Theological Seminary, (Ger.)	Columbus, Ohio...	$100,000	7,500	3	39
Augsburg Seminary......	Minneapolis, Minn	200,000	1,000	4	73
Theological Seminary......	Red Wing, Minn..	30,000	400	2	17
Practical Seminary........	Afton, Minn......	10,000	......	3	32
Ev. Lutheran Seminary...	Saginaw, Mich...	12,000	300	4	14
" " "	W. Denmark, Wis.	2,000	300	3	13
Martin Luther Seminary...	Buffalo, N. Y....	10,000	2,500	1	7
Practical Seminary........	Hickory, N. C...	10,000	500	2	17
Trinity Seminary..........	Blair, Neb.......	8,000	......	3	14
Luther Seminary..........	Minneapolis, Minn	......	......	4	44
Capital University........	Columbus, Ohio..	......	......	8	112
Martin Luther College.....	Buffalo, N. Y....	......	......	1	?
Luther College............	Decorah, Iowa..	82,000	5,000	8	158
Concordia College.........	Gravelton, Mo...	2,000	......	2	121
Norweg. Augustana College	Canton, S. Dak...	15,000	500	7	100
St. Olaf College...........	Northfield, Minn..	32,000	600	13	146
Augsburg College..........	Minneapolis, Minn	......	......	6	116
Pacific University.........	Tacoma, Wash...	(Being	establi	she'd)	
Co-Educational Institute...	Lima, Ohio.....	(Being	establi	she'd)	
Danish College............	Racine, Wis.....	(Proposed.)			
Danish High School.......	Elk Horn, Iowa..	8,000	1,000	3	48
Red Wing Seminary.......	Red Wing, Minn..	30.000	400	6	180
St. Ansgar Seminary......	St. Ansgar, Iowa..	4,000	200	5	40
Stoughton Academy.......	Stoughton, Wis...	......	......	5	103
Teachers' Seminary.......	Wittenberg, Wis..	......	......	3	36
Ev.Luth.Teachers'Seminary	Woodville, Ohio..	10,000	1,200	3	53
Willmar Seminary........	Willmar, Minn...	18,000	500	6	281
Danish High School.......	Ashland, Mich...	3,000	......	3	34
Pro-Seminary.............	Afton, Minn.....	......	......	3	28
Indian Mission School....	Wittenberg, Wis..	10,000	......	6	96
(Danish) Trinity Seminary..	Blair, Neb.......	......	......	......	......
Ev. Lutheran Seminary....	Saginaw City,Mich	......	......	......	......
St. Paul Academy.........	Hickory, N. C....	......	......	2	66
Albert Lea High School...	Albert Lea, Mich.	25,000	......	5	145
Danish High School......	Nysted, Neb.....	......	......	4	23
"Danebod" High School..	Tyler, Minn.....	5,000	1,500	4	32
Teachers' Seminary.......	Sioux Falls, S Dak	30,000	150	5	72
Bruflat Academy.........	Portland, N. Dak.	10,000	......	3	110
Luther Academy..........	Bode, Iowa......	3,000	......	3	50
Teachers' Seminary.......	GraniteFalls,Minn	15,000	(Being	est'ab.)	
Seminary.................	Ishpeming, Mich..	......	......	......	......
	(Being estab. by	"Suomi"	Synod		
Luther Academy..........	Winnipeg, Man...	Propos'd	by Ice	lan'ders.	
Total.............		$700,000	23,550	131	2,231

average cost of their maintenance each year to be about $157,500.

These synods have seven orphanages, a hospital and Deaconess Home in Brooklyn, N. Y., and a Deaconess Home in Minneapolis. Two of the orphanages are but recently established. The other institutions report property worth $88,000; 14 teachers and helpers, and 244 inmates cared for during the year. A hospital has been opened at Sioux Falls, Iowa, and another is being opened in connection with the Deaconess' work in Minneapolis.

B.—*Beneficence.*

Name and Class.	Location.	Value of Property.	Teachers and Helpers.	Inmates.	Yearly Expenses.
Orphans' Home	Wittenberg, Wis.	$10,000	5	70	$6000
Orphans' Home	Maplew'od, Chic'g.	3,000	2	30	
Orphans' Home	Madison, Wis.	20,000	3	34	
Martha and Mary Orp'ns' H.	Tacoma, Wash.	3,500	1	12	ca.
Wernle Orphans' Home	Richmond, Ind.	20,000		98	4500
Orphans' Home	Beloit, Iowa	12,000			
Orphans' Home	Elk Horn, Iowa	40 acres of land.	Rece'tly Ope n'd		
Norwegian Deac'esses Hptl.	New York	20,000		40	6000
Norwegian Deac'esses Hptl.	Minneapolis, Minn.		7	63	
St. Lukes' Deac'esses Hptl.	Sioux Falls, Ia.				
Norwegian Deac'esses Hme.	Minneapolis, Minn.	In Hospital Building.			
Norwegian Deac'esses Hme.	New York	In Hospital Building.			
Home for Aged	Richmond, Ind.	With O. H.			
Home for Aged	Wittenberg, Wis.	With O. H.			
(Norwegian) Immgt. Mission.	Brooklyn, N. Y.				
(Danish) Immigrant Mis'ion.	Brooklyn, N. Y.				
Scandinavian Seamen's Hm.	Brooklyn, N. Y.				
(Norwegian) Immgt. Mission.	Pensacola, Fla.	In winter.			
(Norwegian) Immgt Mission.	Quebec, Can.	In summer.			
(Finnish) Immigrant Mis'n.	New York.				
(Finnish) Immigrant Mis'n.	San Francisco, Cal				
(Danish) Seamen's Mission.	Boston, Mass.				
(Swedish) Seamen's Mission.	Boston, Mass.				

In order to a better understanding of the aims and methods of the parochial schools in the Lutheran congregations of the United States, it is proposed to give a somewhat detailed account of them here. And as a disinterested observer, the Rev. Dr. Robert Ellis Thompson, one of the most scholarly of the Faculty of the University of Pennsylvania, shall give the historical reason for their existence. He says :

"As most people know, the Protestants of Germany are divided into two parties, the Lutherans (or Evangelical) and the Reformed (or Calvinistic) Churches. The former were very much in the majority, but the Hohenzollerns of Prussia and several other dynasties belonged to the latter. Through the growth of religious indifference, and of Rationalism, the interest in the doctrines on which they had divided became very weak; and in 1817 the King of Prussia, Frederick William III., issued his royal order for the union of the two churches throughout his dominions. This was imitated by Saxony, Baden, Hesse, and several other German Governments of that time. But there were still left Lutherans who cared for the doctrines of their fathers, and these refused to go into the United Church. The Government tried to coerce them into obeying. It banished some, imprisoned others, silenced many. It locked the doors of the churches against Lutheran congregations which refused to lay aside their old prayer-books and pray in the words of that prepared by the King of Prussia, who thought himself a great authority in matters of liturgy and ritual. But these Prussians, and many Saxons also, refused to yield. They had been drilled to obey the Government in everything else, but in this they would not and could not. After nearly twenty years of official persecution, including almost every measure short of death, their clergy in 1835 formed a Lutheran Synod at Breslau, in Silesia, and declared themselves a separate communion. Then for five years there was a raging storm of police repression, until in 1840 the old king died and his son, Frederick William IV., put an end to the scandal.

"In the meantime large bodies of these faithful Lutherans had decided to leave their country and seek a new home in America. Some came to Buffalo and its neighborhood ; the more part sought the upper valley of the Mississippi. St. Louis became their headquarters and the seat of the Concordia College, in which they train their pastors. They had in 1888 no less than 1,743 congregations and 342,000 communicants, besides baptized children and others, making a population of close upon a million.

"These German Lutherans came to America on the supposition that here they would find liberty for both church and school. They fought for both at home. Believing that the instruction in schools controlled by the German Governments was such as to weaken their children's attachment to the truth of their Lutheran creed, they withdrew their children from them and founded schools of their own. Even when the emigration to America weakened their forces and in some cases made the maintenance of their schools impossible, they refused to obey its Compulsory Education laws and send their children to the schools maintained by the State. Doctor Buchrel, a pastor in the United Church and latterly court preacher in Berlin, writes : ' In Wallmow, against the urgent advice of the pastor, the police undertook to force a poor widow to send her son. Actually a *gens d' arm* in full equipment appeared every morning and amid the general attention of the village, carried the lad off to school, where the good teacher received him kindly ; but he never came back after recess. This scene was repeated for eight days running, to the amusement of the village. Then the *gens d' arm* stayed away, and the boy did the same.'

"That these Lutherans will not give up their own schools is as good as certain. They do not believe in merely secular education. They do not think that secular studies have a right to a child's whole mental and nervous energy for six days of every week, and that higher topics can be left safely to a day when the school-child is fagged and needs rest just as much as does the workingman. They do not believe that a balanced character can be produced by turning the mind downward and outward for six days in the week, and upward and inward for only one. They do not think that religion can be postponed in a child's case until some special season of excitement, when it can be jerked into him as if out of the skies, and that just as well as if he never had a lesson in his life that led up to its reception. They are not revivalists; they believe in Christian training, and therefore in Christian schools. And I agree with them."

To this, because it affords some additional light on the subject, and comes from a prominent man wholly outside of the Lutheran Church, and who, therefore, cannot be accused of speaking because of denominational prejudice, may be added the following, from the pen of the Rev. Dr. Kimball, of Boston:

" The idea of Luther was, that each church should have by its side and under its influence and control, a parish school. This true conception of the educational problem has been actualized wherever the Lutheran Church has been the controlling power, and religious as well as secular education to day is universal. In all the countries of the old world where this Church is the established religion, ignorance is not only a shame and a disgrace, but the parents of such children are punished as criminals, by fines and imprisonment.

" The early Lutheran immigrants who came to the new world, in the depths of their deep poverty, at once erected the school-house by the side of their humble sanctuaries, and these schools for more than a century, were the training places for the church, until they were swept away by the introduction of the public school system. So, over the whole land, where the emigration from Europe is sufficiently strong, parish schools are now established by our churches, and while our people uncomplainingly pay their taxes to keep up the public schools, they make the greatest sacrifices to maintain their own parochial schools, knowing well that no increase of mere secular learning can make up for the absence of that religious education which their children obtain in their own schools. This interest, instead of dying out, is coming to the front more and more prominently and one School Teacher's Seminary after another is being established by Western synods of our people. They find by experience that their parish schools are the strong arm of their strength, and that by means of them they not only ward off godless influences and associations, but train up and develop a generation to serve God and work righteousness. Many of these schools in Western towns and cities have large and elegant buildings, with four and even six teachers, and the pupils are numbered by the hundreds. Whole series of school books are published, in all of which the Christian idea is the ever present one, and the catechism, the holy Scriptures and the hymn book, are memorized, repeated, illustrated and 'said and sung' from the day of admission to the graduation of the pupils. That we, too, must come back to this old and true conception of Christian education is absolutely certain. In no other way can we hope for the highest good of those who are dearer to us than our own life."

Admirable as are these deliverances on the congregational school questions, it is yet to be supposed that the men who are supporting these schools at great expense at the same time that they willingly pay their school taxes for the support of the public schools, best know why they think this necessary. We, therefore, allow a Committee of the Missouri Synod to speak on this point. Their spokesman says :

You will readily admit that it is a right and duty of parents to instruct and educate their children. It is their right and duty to provide for them in every respect; it is their right and duty to give them raiment, bread and shelter; and it is their right and duty to teach them the elementary branches of knowledge. This right and duty parents have according to the laws of nature, and the word of God enjoins it upon them: I. Timothy 5, where Paul says, "But if any provide not for his own, and especially for those of his own house, he hath denied the faith and is worse than an infidel."

However, if that were the only obligation which parents have towards their children in regard to their education, to instruct them in secular matters, we Lutherans would never go to the expense of erecting denominational schools; because the public school system of this country affords ample opportunity for such an education, and it would be the greatest folly imaginable on our part to erect church-schools along side of our public institutions of learning, if they had one and the same purpose and end in view.

But we are conscious of a higher and more important duty towards our children. We know it to be imposed on us by God Almighty himself to afford them a thorough Christian education. That is the reason why we feel ourselves bound to establish schools where religious instruction is a chief part of the daily studies. True, we desire our children to be fit for the duties and pursuits of this life; but it is of greater importance to us that they be fit to walk in the narrow path which leads them to the life to come. We indeed want our children to study the histories and events of this world; but we would see them acquainted with the great histories and truths of the Bible, informing them of their creation, their lamentable fall, and their glorious redemption through Christ Jesus. We indeed do not intend our children should neglect the study of arithmetic, geography and grammar, but we consider it a paramount obligation towards them, to have them calculate the length and breadth, the depth and height of God's love; to have them look for the mountain, whence cometh their help; to have them know in what direction Jerusalem, the golden city with its dazzling gates of pearl, is situated, and to have them speak in the language and grammar of sincere children of God. In short we realize the imperative duty of giving our children a thorough instruction in the great truths and undefiled doctrines of Christianity pertaining to the salvation of their immortal souls, and that is the reason why we Lutherans make it a practice to educate our children in congregational schools.

But why do we believe and how do we know the Christian education of our children to be a sacred duty? We know it from the Bible, the unfailing and everlasting Word of God. I need hardly tell you, that true Christians should abide with the Bible always and everywhere, and refer to its precepts in all their doings. And when we take note of what the Bible says in regard to the education of children, we find their religious instruction enjoined upon the parents in the strongest terms. Psalm 78 : 5--7 . . Knowing and considering what the Bible teaches, we cannot and dare not deny our children a thorough Christian education. Besides, reflect but a moment on the tender relation that exists between us and our children. They are the most precious jewels and gems that we possess. All our money and property are of little or no value to us in comparison with our children. They are our very flesh and blood and hence ought to be and certainly are as dear to us as we are to ourselves. We are ever diligent in providing for them the necessaries of life. We are always mindful of their bodily ailments. Should we then neglect paying attention to their soul's salvation, knowing them to be depraved by Satan and sin? Should we neglect rearing them in the nurture and admonition of the Lord, since they even as children in simplicity of faith are capable of comprehending the teachings of the Holy Spirit? If we were negligent in these matters we should be making one of the greatest mistakes in our life. When on the great Day of Judgment we are called upon to render an account for the instruction and education of our children, our very sons and daughters would rise as witnesses against us and charge us with the neglect of one of the most sacred duties that we had during our sojourn in the land of the living here below. That is just how we feel about it! And this keen sense of duty in regard to the Christian education of our children prompts and induces us to estabish schools where religious instruction is the most important part in the daily exercises and studies.

But one says, you are overlooking our Sunday-schools; do not they afford our children a Christian education? You will allow me to say a few words in regard to the prevailing Sunday-school system. We have no inclination to detract from the merits of Sunday schools if they be properly conducted. But common sense and experience tell, that the Christian education which children derive by means of our Sunday-schools must needs be very superficial. Think of the little time that Sunday-schools allow for religious instruction, an hour a week, one out of 168! If I had a boy whom I intended to be a physician and become skilled in the art of surgery so that he would be capable of performing the most difficult surgical operations, and I made it a practice to send him an hour a week to some medical college, you would be right in considering that the greatest folly. We cannot be satisfied with having our children instructed an hour a week in matters that pertain to the eternal salvation of their immortal souls. We are convinced, and this conviction of ours is based upon experience, that if our children are to receive a thorough knowledge and lasting impression of the Bible, its divine truths and commandments, they are in need of daily religious instruction. The law of God will have to be called to their minds, explained to them, and brought home to their hearts by competent teachers day after day. And that is what we are aiming at in our parochial schools. In all discipline exercised in our schools we strive to make the word of God the governing element. And even the secular sciences taught in our schools are pervaded by a Christian spirit. That is what we, under present circumstances, deem the best, if not the only correct method of bringing up our children in the nurture and admonition of the Lord ; and that is the reason why we Lutherans make it a practice to establish, build and maintain parochial schools.*

That thoroughness is aimed at in these schools, and that competent instructors are demanded as teachers, is to be inferred from the course of study and drill through which they must pass before they can undergo the necessary examination for the teachers' office. The Missouri Synod is foremost in the number of these schools established, and we therefore take up the catalogue of its Teachers' Seminary at Addison, Illinois, and from it learn of the demands made in the way of study of him who is a candidate for the teacher's office.

That he may be admitted as a student, it is necessary that he be in good health, fourteen years or more old, a confirmed member of the Church, and present satisfactory testimonials as to his Christian conduct, diligence, &c. ; he must pledge himself to obedience, diligence in study, and declare it his intention to make teaching in Lutheran schools his life-vocation. The minimum demands as to mental attainments are that he shall be acquainted, at least, in Bible History, with the history of the Creation, the Fall, the Flood, the Patriarchs, with the principal events in the life of Christ, with the text-history of the festivals of the Church-Year, and with the Pericopes concerning the coming judgment. In German, the demands are such as might reasonably be made of one who has had the advantages of a school equivalent to

* From Report of Com. of Mo. Synod.

a fairly good common English school. In English, he must be able to read, easily and understandingly, anything in a first reader; and to write, plainly, anything contained therein. In music, he must be able to sing alone, at least, such melodies as are heard in his home church on Sundays, clearly and correctly.

Possessed of, at least, such qualifications, he may be admitted to the Teachers' Seminary. The course of study in it extends through five years.

First on the list of studies is Bible History In the first class (or year) he studies the New Testament, with recitations for two hours each week; the Catechism, with recitations for two hours; memorizing of a dozen hymns and six psalms, with recitation of the same for one hour each week; and Church song—108 melodies of the "Gesangbuch" of the Synod—recitations two hours per week. In the German language he has recitations for five hours, weekly; in the English language, recitations for same time; and recitations in arithmetic, geography, writing and drawing fill up the remainder of the time.

In the second year he memorizes extracts from the Old and New Testaments, and studies "Bible History for Upper Classes;" continues recitations in the Catechism for two hours a week and memorizes another dozen of hymns; in addition to the elementary studies in English and in German, he begins the History of the World, up to the times of Constantine the Great; Natural History, types of the animal kingdom; and continues his music, &c.

In the third year he continues the Biblical History; memorizes portions of the Psalms; continues the studies in the Catechism; memorizes 15 additional hymns, and the Nicene and Athanasian creeds; continues the elementary branches in German and in English; takes up the History of the World from Karl the Great to 1776; continues Natural History, with Magnetism and Electricity; continues, also, writing in German and in English, drawing and music. The studies and the drill of these three years are supposed to have fitted him for the Teachers' Seminary proper, which has a two years' course, and to which he is now admitted.

In the Seminary, the first year, the study of Bible History in both the Old and the New Testaments is continued, with recitations for two hours each week; Catechism is continued, recitations for two hours a week in the winter, and for four hours in the summer term; the Symbolical Books are taken up, and articles 1–10 of the Augsburg Confession are studied, with one hour's recitation weekly; the higher studies of both the German and the English tongues, such as the study of the national literature of Germany, and of such authors as Irving, Addison and Goldsmith, are given eight hours' weekly recitations; arithmetic, geography and history are continued, as also is Natural History, and the students have practical exercises in Bible History and the Catechism, with the lower classes of the preparatory department.

During the last year, the students study the Messianic Psalms, selections from the Book of Proverbs, from the prophecies of Isaiah, Jeremiah, Ezekiel, Micah, Zechariah and Malachi; and from Timothy, Philemon, Peter, and the Hebrews; the study of the Catechism is finished, the recitations being for three hours a week in the winter and six hours in the summer term; Church History is begun, and attention is given to the History of the Reformation, with an introduction to the writings of Luther, and the study of the Augsburg Confession is completed. Methods of teaching and school discipline have three recitations a week; the study of German national literature is continued, with special reference to grammar and style, and with oral exercises in narration. In English, the celebrated authors of the 17th to the 19th centuries are studied, and lectures given on them; there are " free " orations with subsequent discussion of the same; translations for four hours of recitations each week. In Mathematics, the students have practical teaching exercises in the classes of the preparatory department and in the parochial schools of the city. About the same is true of Geography. In Music, the students repeat the melodies from the Church's Hymn Book, and practice motet and choral singing. They also have practical teaching exercises, with the Catechism and Bible History, in the parochial schools of the city.

In most of the non-religious subjects of instruction, the English tongue is used in the class-room.* Eggleston's History of the United States is the text-book on the history of our country; but in most other branches, English works for use in the schools are published by the Synod, because the religious spirit in the popular text-books is kept so far in the back ground, or is altogether lacking. The student who studies faithfully through this course, and who has fair mental talent, will be qualified to pass the examination for the teacher's office. He is expected to be able to read, write and speak both the German and English tongues, and to be qualified to teach both.

We have been at considerable trouble to get full and reliable statistics of the Parochial schools of our Church. The greatest difficulty was met in the attempt to get the yearly cost of their maintenance. No official returns on this point can be had. The difficulty is increased by the fact that in nearly all the Synods in which these schools are maintained, many pastors act as teachers; in some of the smaller Synods, indeed, nearly all the teaching is done by pastors.

The Missouri Synod supports over twelve hundred schools. Pastor Walker, of York, Pa., who is good authority, says in reply to our inquiries: "There is no official estimate whatever to be had, . . and I cannot, on that account, claim any exact accuracy for the figures given here. Yet I do not think they are very far from the mark. The average cost of maintaining each school a year, I would put

---

* *Katalog der Lehranstalten . . der . . Synode von Missouri, &c.* 1889–90; p. 21.

down at $350; the figures being so low because of the fact that so many schools are taught by the pastors of the congregations, and therefore cause but little extra cost to the churches. The average salary paid the teachers per month is about $45. Our schools are, on the average, kept open nine months during the year." In the Augustana (Swedish) Synod, the average wages of teachers is about $30 per month, and we suppose it fair to infer that in the other Scandinavian bodies it is about the same. In the Ministerium of New York, where 68 teachers are maintained, Secretary Peterson estimates the yearly expenditure at $24,-350, about the same average cost reported by the other synods.

The facts given above show that the average cost of maintaining a school is about $350 a year. Our table shows 2,350 schools reported; and 506 teachers additional in three synods for which the number of schools is not given. Allowing each teacher to represent a school, and the total number to be 2,856, which, at an average cost each of $350, amounts to a yearly expenditure of $999,600. To all intents and purposes this is an expenditure for inner Mission work. These schools are maintained because the public schools make no attempt to teach religious truth. That the children may be educated and trained in a Christian spirit, and be taught day by day, by precept and by example, to know and to love the Father, the Son and the Holy Ghost, these schools are maintained. They are provided and supported for the same purpose served by churches and preachers, which is that men may learn to fear, love and trust in God above all things.

The "fruits of the Spirit" though diverse are always beautiful. The religion which has brought forth such abundant fruits in Europe as those manifested in the great circle of Inner Missions, is not unfruitful in America. The difficult circumstances under which the Church has been working in this new land, though delaying the harvest, has not destroyed it. By the grace of God it is coming. Fifty years ago there was scarcely a Hospital, an Orphanage, an Immigrants' Home, or any other institution of mercy within the bounds of the Luthern Church in America. Then, the blessed work of the Deaconesses had been revived for about twelve years in Germany, but even there it was but like a germinating mustard seed. A young pastor, (now the venerable Dr. Passavant, whose praise is in all the churches,) on a journey through Europe, became interested in that work, and made arrangements to have two good women, able to speak the English tongue, trained for like work in the United States. He practiced economy in personal expenses —walked where formerly he had hired a hack or cab, took plainer dinners, etc.—to save money to defray the cost of their training.

On the return of that young pastor to America he rented a small house in Pittsburg, Pa., for the purposes of a Hospital.

In June, 1849, Pastor Fliedner arrived at Pittsburg, with four Deaconesses from Kaiserswerth. In July following the Hospital was formally opened and the Sisters publicly given charge of the work. This was, so far as known, the beginning of our organized efforts to care for the distressed within our gates, in the United States.

The young institution had its sorrows as well as its joys— its dark hours as well as its bright ones. The Pittsburg Synod, of which the founder was a member, gladly commended its work to the confidence of the churches; but, while some were willing to give money to sustain it, it seemed that no Christian women could be found willing to undertake the work of Deaconesses. The money, too, not seldom seemed about to be wanting. The treasury once ran so low that the Director was obliged to go to market with but 25 cents to buy food for the sick and for the nurses.

When the cholera was cutting down its victims on the right and left, the last shirt was on the back of a patient.

"We *must* have more linen," said the matron to the Director. It was late on Saturday night; stores all were closed. There was no money in the treasury to buy, even if the stores had been open.

In such extremities, however, help came from unexpected sources. Provisions came in by the dray load, perhaps sent by men hundreds of miles away. Money came in, perhaps from strangers but passing through the city. Clothes, linens, etc., were sent in by societies of ladies who knew nothing of the pressing needs of the institution.

Thus God saved his own. The officials and nurses often were anxious, but never discouraged. They knew in Whom they trusted. He who watches over the sparrows, also watches over His servants when they are doing His will.

From these apparently unpromising financial beginnings has grown an institution of Christian mercy that is known far and near. In something less than forty years it cared for over 6,000 of the suffering children of men. The money cost of their care was over $200,000, to say nothing of the free attentions of nurses, physicians, officials, etc. Thus has the Lord shown that He "is able to do exceeding abundantly above all that we ask or think."

A few years after the opening of this institution, ("The Infirmary,") a call was heard for the establishment of a similar one in Milwaukee, Wis. It also was small, financially considered, in its beginning. A German Lutheran pastor of that city, an eye witness of the miseries of sick strangers and also of many sick residents, besought the Director of the institution at Pittsburg to establish a hospital in Milwaukee. When no answer was returned to his first letter, the pastor wrote a second, a third, and a fourth time. Then he received a dollar, and with it a note on which was written: "Begin your hospital; this is more than we had to start with at Pittsburg." In the course of another year a poor woman contributed a dollar. The pastor then wrote to the Director at Pittsburg that the time had come to build in Milwaukee.

The two pastors arranged to look over the ground. They rented a small house in the city, but the residents in the locality around were so strongly opposed to the establishing of a hospital in the midst of a dense population that it was abandoned. Then they found a suitable fifteen-acre-tract with buildings, all offered for $17,000. This, at length, was bought, and the money borrowed to pay for it. The cash was secured on personal notes of the Director, and the work of collecting and paying this amount was the work of many weary years. Nearly nineteen years later, the Director himself wrote of the work done by the institution, and of its expenses, in the following words:

"In the eighteen and a half years since the purchase, there have been upwards of 3,000 sick and wounded persons cared for within its limited walls. Many more than one-half of these were received 'without money and without price.' Of the remainder not over one-fourth could pay the sum of five dollars per week for board, nursing, medicine and medical attendance. For fifteen years all the small-pox cases of the city were cared for by its nurses, and upwards of 500 of these pest-stricken ones were ministered unto in their time of need. It will be seen from this, that the work of the hospital has been largely among the poor, the immigrant and the stranger within our gates. The outlays during this time have been almost $60,000 for the care of the sick, $22,000 for the cost of the buildings and grounds, and upwards of $19,000 for the making of streets on the three sides of the hospital property, with the endless assessments for paving, sewers, water mains, etc., etc."

Since these words were written, a new building has been erected, with all the modern appliances for the comfort and relief of patients, at a total cost of $96,000. The institution now has a location consisting of two entire squares, elevated, central and attractive in its surroundings, and a hospital building, with a frontage of 162 feet, beautiful, convenient and substantial, erected upon it. The value of the whole is certainly not less than $175,000, but the intrinsic value of the buildings and grounds for hospital purposes is much greater. It is constructed wth reference to the future, and when the north wing is finally erected, it will have a capacity for two hundred beds. There is also abundant room for pavilion buildings for special diseases. The ground work is secured for all future time.

In the first twenty-five years of its operation, 5,903 sick and injured persons were ministered to by our sisters and other nurses—many more than one-half gratuitously—while the remainder have paid for boarding, nursing and care, scarcely half the sum which would have been necessary had they been treated at a boarding-house or hotel. During the four years since the erection of the new hospital, the number of patients has been 1,803. Of these, 444 were received during the past year.* The total amount paid out for the support of the sick in the hospital in the twenty-five years of its existence, has not been far from $150,000, while the cost for buildings and grounds has been about $140,000.

An idea of the cost of conducting such an institution may be found from the following table of expenses during the year 1888: Subsistence, (bread, meat, groceries, milk, vegetables, etc.,) $5,042.98; medicines and medical instruments, $941.38; fuel, $1,653.06; gas, $291.40; water, $119.15; furniture and fixtures, $641.37; improvements and repairs, $469.19; removing old hospital and cleaning brick, $216.15; engineer and man of all work, $421.20; male nurses, $250.90; services of assistant superintendent, $300; street sprinkling, $30.67; female nurses and helpers, $1,159.58; domestics and washer-women, $842.82; traveling expenses of officers and employés, $140.87; insurance. $300; tele-

* *Workman*, March 21, 1889.

phone and telegrams, $38.87; stable expenses, $65.05; interest on debt, $1,935.64; miscellaneous expenses, $149.72: making a total of $15,017.00. The income during the same time (1888) from contributions for support of "charity beds," was $2,068.37; from articles sold and advances returned, $167.22; and from the board and nursing of pay patients, $13,248.36—making a total of $15,484.95 received during the year. This reveals the unusual result of a surplus in the current expenses of $467.95, which has been utilized towards paying the debt of the institution. It is the first and only instance of the kind in the history of the hospital during a period of more than a quarter of a century.

Elsewhere have been noted the humble beginnings of the work at Kaiserswerth. The beginnings in Pittsburg and Milwaukee, also, were sufficiently humble. While the work here has not grown as it has in Germany, yet the caring for 6,000 sorely distressed children of men—many of them homeless, friendless, penniless, with no place where to lay their heads, and not a few of them veritable outcasts—is, in itself, no small thing in a world where the curse of sin eats so deeply into the peace and happiness of men.

But if the little seed planted in America nearly forty years ago was dropped into a soil less fertile, and in a climate less congenial, than that of the Fatherland, it, nevertheless, has germinated and is now in process of development.

To day these deaconesses have institutions in Pittsburg, Pa., Jacksonville and Chicago, Ill., and Milwaukee, Wis., in addition to several orphanages under their care.

The first hospital building in Chicago was destroyed by the great fire. A new building was erected and furnished at a cost of $40,000. A tract of eight acres was bought on the outskirts of the city, on which a hospital may be erected in the future. The buildings and grounds at Jacksonville, formerly the home of Col. Hardin, are estimated to be worth $30,000. One deaconess and three assistants have charge of this institution. The Boys' Farm School at Zelienople, Pa.

has a farm of several hundred acres, and half a dozen valuable buildings, the value of which cannot be short of $50,000. The Girl's Home at Rochester, Pa., has extensive grounds and buildings, worth perhaps half that sum. Probably the most magnificent buildings in the world, used as a Deaconesses' Home, are those which stand opposite Girard College, Philadelphia. They were erected at a cost of $500,000, on one of the finest locations in the city, through the large-hearted Christian charity of Mr. John D. Lankenau, who has given another half million to the German hospital in the same city, and which has been for years under the care of the deaconesses for whom the magnificent Mother-House has been erected. No description of the home of the Deaconesses can do it justice. The buildings are constructed of stone and brick, are three stories high, and have a frontage of 250 feet, a wing at each end 300 feet long, a uniform width of 60 feet, with an open court between the wings; have sixty rooms on each floor, with all the appurtenances and furnishings, of the best which money can buy. The Order of Lutheran Deaconesses being thus provided with a permanent home, is assured of both position and influence in our land. A training-school or seminary for deaconesses, is in connection with the Home, which will supply successive classes of consecrated women, fitted by their training for the positions which will be open for them all over this country. The institution furnishes a home for them, to which, when worn out in the service, they may return to enjoy the comforts of a Christian family, without care or thought, and without any painful, tedious and too often unavailing efforts to wring a few drops of charity from unwilling hearts.

The work of the deaconesses covers the following departments: 1. The care of the German hospital, with 150 patients daily, and 4,100 in the dispensary during the year. Twenty sisters are engaged here, and the annual expenses are $50,000. 2. The Children's Hospital, with an average of 30 patients daily, and an equal number in the dispensary. Four sisters and several associates have charge. 3. The Old People's Home, with rooms for 36 inmates, and now containing 29. One sister has oversight here. 4. A School for Girls, conducted on a thoroughly Christian basis. It is held in the east wing of the building, and has 40 pupils in attendance. 5. The Sisters are engaged in parish work and in day nurseries in Germantown and Philadelphia, outside the institution, and two of them have gone to take charge of a hospital in Easton, Pa.

The Philadelphia Mother-House aims to adapt, as nearly as possible, the principal features of the Deaconess work in Germany to this country. The foundation of the whole work is to be the unity in the faith and love to the Lord Jesus Christ. The sisters seek no earthly gain, and do their work without wages; but in giving themselves fully up to this work, they are assured that they will be well provided with all the necessaries of life, have a comfortable home, enjoy, every summer, a vacation of three or four weeks, which they spend either in the homes of their relatives or in the beautiful sea-side home which Mr. Lankenau has just built for himself, and to which he invites those who are in need of the refreshing and invigorating sea breezes.

They are divided into full consecrated Deaconesses, Assistant Sisters and Probationers. The time of service as a Probationer and Assistant Sister generally covers a period of four years. During this time there is a regular course of instruction for the Sisters, both theoretical and practical, which is intended to prepare them, as well as possible, for the varies duties of the office. The Rector of the Mother-House, who must be a clergyman of the Lutheran Church, is the pastor of the Sisters. He conducts the services in the beautiful chapel of the Home on each Lord's Day, in the morning and afternoon, and also a daily Vesper service through the week in which the inmates of the Home participate.

There are at present in connection with the Philadelphia Mother-House 12 full consecrated Sisters, 8 Assistant Sisters, 12 Probationers and 4 Associates.

Mr. Lankenau has named this monumental charity "The Mary J. Drexel Home and Philadelphia Mother-House of Deaconesses."

"I have seen," says Dr. Morris, of Baltimore, "magnificent charity foundations abroad and at home; but nothing I have seen equals this in splendor of construction, convenience of arrangement and breadth of capacity. One man out of his private purse pays over $50,000 a year to support all the Deaconesses and their novitiates; the rector and his family; the thirty-six aged pensioners; the poor, sick children in the Hospital; and a large number of cooks, servants, male and female, porters, messengers, gardeners, and other helps. *Fifty-five thousand dollars* a year is a large sum to come out of one man's pocket; but that pocket is very deep and never gets empty. . . I advise all who ever go to Philadelphia, to visit the institution and see for themselves."

Deaconess Homes under the management of Lutherans, and connected with the Church, exist in Rochester and Pittsburg, Pa., Brooklyn, Minneapolis and Omaha, Neb. No answer to repeated requests for information has been received from the Rochester-Pittsburg Institution. The Home in Brooklyn is under the control of the Norwegian brethren, has several Sisters in charge and a property worth $20,000. A hospital and a training school are in connection with it. The Norwegians also have ownership of the Lutheran Deaconess Institute in Minneapolis, which has a hospital and a training school. Seven sisters are in charge. The Home at Omaha has an orphanage, a hospital, and is opening a training school.

About the time the Infirmary was being opened in Pittsburg, circumstances seemed to indicate that the Rev. Mr. Passavant should lead in the work of opening an Orphan's

Home. The dark days of the cholera scourge were then lowering over the land. It was master of the hour in most of the great cities. Fear took hold of multitudes, and led them to neglect their sick. The dead were buried without ceremony. So great was the death rate, that in most places rough boxes took the place of coffins, and funeral processions were neither desired or allowed. Often it was with much difficulty that persons could be found to prepare the dead for burial.

Out of that time of terror came one of the first orphanages of our Church in America. A Swedish Lutheran pastor in Chicago wrote to the Director of the (Deaconess) Infirmary in Pittsburg that with his own hands he was making coffins in which to bury the dead of his parish, but he said: "What shall I do with their orphan children?" That was the question which gave the deepest concern. The natural protectors of the helpless little ones were dead. In so far as he knew nobody but himself had any interest in the orphans, and he was too poor to supply even the necessaries of life to them. In despair, yet hoping against hope, he put the question to the Director of the Pittsburg Infirmary: "What shall I do with their orphan children?" Back flashed the reply: "I will take twelve of them." To him twelve were sent. He went to meet them as they came on the cars to the hospital at Pittsburg. He expected to meet neat, clean, fair-haired Scandinavian children, but he found them dirty, tear-stained, soiled, begrimed, and the romance of the work flew out of the window. The stern reality of an uninviting duty faced him. But he was not the man to flinch from duty. He, with another young Lutheran pastor, a short time previously, with their own hands, had washed, combed and dressed a wounded, filthy and exhausted Mexican soldier, the first patient in the Infirmary, and in that act had received a new revelation of the spirit which moves true preachers, and although disappointed in the appearance of the new addition to his family, was in no wise turned aside from his purpose. The children were received, cared for and brought up in the nurture and admonition of the Lord. Some of them have made men and women of mark and all of them good, honest citizens. On another occasion it was reported that thirty or forty people were starving at the Outer Depot. A friend of the Director went out to see them. He found them Swedes, unable to speak one word in English. Their wants were supplied and the children were taken to the hospital. Five of them were gaunt, horrible skeletons, but they all were saved. One is now the wife of an eminent physician, herself one of the directors of a similar institution in a great city.

From this came the Orphans' Farm School at Zelienople, and the Home for Girls at Rochester, Pa.

The local director at Zelienople went out every morning at 6 o'clock and read and prayed with the workmen for daily aid; and, although they knew no money was on hand, they completed and paid for a building costing $25,000.

It was a matter of daily deliverance.

After the house at Zelienople had been occupied some time, it was burned in a season of extreme cold in mid-winter. Thus seventy-five houseless, homeless children were on their hands. They were placed in families for the time, and in six months temporary barracks were erected until the home was again completed.

From the Rochester Home in Pennsylvania grew a similar one in New York. Mr. Moeller, a wealthy man, instead of erecting a costly monument in Greenwood to his son, gave $30,000, and his brother $10,000, for an orphan asylum, in which a model home and school have been conducted for the past 25 years. Wichern's Rauhe Haus sent over helpers trained in the work. Among them was the late Rev. G. C. Holls, once an instructor in that institution, and one of the world's most efficient instructors of the young. One of the chief cities of America held out to him flattering offers to take charge of her home for wayward and neglected youth.

He, however, remained faithful to the work he had undertaken in the name of the Church; served for a time as head master of the Home at Zelienople, and then took charge as director of the institution founded at Mt. Vernon, N. Y.

The history of the various orphanages established and maintained by our Church, or by individual members of it, would fill a volume. One hundred and fifty years ago, away in the South, our Church in America erected her first home for the fatherless. Many years passed before the second was established—1837—at Middletown, Pa. Then followed the one at Zelienople in 1855. And since then one after another has sprung into existence at the rate of one each year, until almost every section of the country has its own. A reference to the table devoted to Institutions and Beneficence will give most of the material facts for which the reader will care to seek.

Fourteen missions among immigrants and seamen are reported, eight of which are in New York and Brooklyn, two are in Boston, and one each in Quebec, Baltimore, Pensacola and San Francisco. The General Council's Mission has a property worth $150,000 on State street, New York, and near by it is the Missouri Synod's Mission, with property worth $65,000. The Scandinavians have a Sailors' Temperance Home in the same city, but no reports have been obtained from it. Three of these immigrant missions received and cared for 8,535 persons during the year.

The work of the immigrant missionary is very plain, prosaic and necessary. As a rule, the immigrant is a stranger in our nation, unacquainted with our tongue and unfamiliar with our ways. Formerly, too often, he was beset by land-sharks the moment he set foot on our shores, robbed, beaten, and left bleeding by the way. Now he is met on landing by the missionary, and is conducted to the Immigrant House—a Christian inn on a large scale—where he has a kind reception and comfortable accommodations, until the missionary can make the necessary arrangements to continue him on the journey to his destination. The religious life of the stranger is also most carefully provided for; and thousands of copies of tracts, periodicals, books, etc., are distributed each year at the Immigrant House.

And thus the Lutheran Church, true to the spirit of the Divine Head, works the works of love and mercy not only among and for the benefit of her own children, but among all classes and conditions of men, as God gives her opportunity. She meets the wanderer on the dock when first he makes his landing. She finds a shelter and safe resting place for him and his family in the Immigrant Mission. If he fall sick, she receives him in her hospital, nurses him with loving solicitude by the skilled hands of her Deaconesses, and when recovered sends him rejoicing on his way. She follows him through the agency of pastors and missionaries, and seeks him out on his prairie farm or in city shops, helps him into an organized congregation as soon as possible, and offers freely to him the bread and the water of eternal life. For his children she makes provision in her schools and pastoral ministrations, in order that they may be trained not only into good citizens, but also as good Christians, members not only of the commonwealth on earth, but also as members of the household of faith and fellow-citizens of the saints. And should he die and leave a family of helpless orphans, again the Church extends her helping hand, and in the name of the Lord Jesus gives them her care and shelter in her Orphans' Homes. And not to be unmindful of the injunction of her Lord, she sends her missionaries far over seas to carry the sweet invitations of the Gospel of Salvation to those who sit in darkness and the shadow of death in heathen lands. God bless the Lutheran Church. God help her to multiply her Christian activities. God speed her divine work with money and men, until like Moses at the offerings for the tabernacle, she shall cry, "It is enough and more than enough for all the work." And let all the people say, Amen.

EDUCATIONAL INSTITUTIONS.

I. THEOLOGICAL SEMINARIES.

Town.	State.	Name.	Synodical Connection.	Property.	Endowment.	Library.	Profs.	Students.
Gettysburg,	Pennsylvania,	Theo. Seminary,	G. S., Eng.	$ 75,000	$92,000	11,000	5	56
Hartwick Seminary,*	New York,	Seminary,	G. S., Eng.	100,285	50,000	4,000		
Columbus,	Ohio,	Evan. Lutheran,	Joint Ohio, Ger.,	100,000		7,500	3	39
Newberry,*	S. Carolina,	Seminary,	United, Eng.	30,000		6,000	3	4
St. Louis,	Missouri,	Concordia,	Missouri, Ger.	200,000	22,000	10,000	5	141
Springfield,*	Ohio,	Wittenburg,	G. S., Eng.	150,000	175,000	10,000	4	23
Springfield,	Illinois,	Concordia,	Missouri, Ger.	65,000		800	4	106
Dubuque,	Iowa,	Wartburg,	Iowa, Ger.	50,000			3	39
Seliusgrove,	Pennsylvania,	Mission Institute,	G. S., Eng.,	25,000	26,000	2,000	2	12
Rock Island,*	Illinois,	Augustana,	G. C., Swedish,	150,000		7,000	4	40
Philadelphia,*	Pennsylvania,	Evan. Lutheran,	G.C., Ger. and Eng	130,000	120,000	21,000	4	82
Minneapolis,*	Minnesota,	Luther,	Norwegian Conf.				4	44
Minneapolis, (P. O., Rob- insdale, Hennepin Co.	Minnesota,	Augsburg,	Ind. Norwegian,	85,000	115,000	ca.1,000	4	73
Milwaukee,‡	Wisconsin,	Evan. Lutheran,	Wisconsin Synod,	20,000		800	3	34
Red Wing,†	Minnesota,	Lutheran,	Ind. Norwegian,	35,000		650	2	17
Afton,	Minnesota,	Practical,	Ohio, Ger.				2	32
Chicago,	Illinois,	Evan. Lutheran,	G. S., Ger.	10,000		2,300	3	20
Saginaw,	Michigan,	Evan. Lutheran,	Ind., Ger.	12,000		300	4	14
Columbia,	S. Carolina,	Southern,	United, Eng. Tem porarily closed.					
Hickory,	N. Carolina,	Practical,	Ohio, Eng.	10,000		500	2	17
New Ulm,*	Minnesota,	Martin Luther,	German.	30,000		sev. hun.	7	95 ‖
Blair* and ‡,	Nebraska,	Trinity,	Ind., Danish	8,000			3	14
Buffalo,†	New York,	Martin Luther,	Ind., Ger.	10,000		2,500	1	7
West Denmark,‡	Wisconsin,	Evan. Lutheran,	Ind., Danish.				3	11
Atlantica,	Iowa,							
Totals,				$1,295,000	$600,000	87,350	73	920

* Occupy buildings with Colleges, &c., but have separate Faculties, Classes, &c. † U. S. Educational Report.
‡ From Reports in Church periodicals. ‖ Including students of Classical Department.

2. COLLEGES.

Gettysburg,	Pennsylvania,	Pennsylvania,	G. S., Eng.	$225,000	$185,000	22,000	14	226
Fort Wayne,	Indiana,	Concordia,	Mo., Ger.	100,000			7	225
Springfield,	Ohio,	Wittenberg,	G. S., Eng.	150,000	175,000	10,000	13	333
Columbus,	Ohio,	Cap'l University,	Ohio,	100,000		7,500	8	148
Salem,	Virginia,	Roanoke,	United, Eng.	75,000	60,000	17,000	11	123
Buffalo,*	New York,	Martin Luther,	Ind., Ger.	10,000		2,500	4	‡
Newberry,	S. Carolina,	Newberry,	United, Eng.	30,000	10,000	6,000	7	123
Mount Pleasant,	N. Carolina,	N. Carolina,	N. C., Eng.	10,000	2,000	2,000	7	96
Rock Island,	Illinois,	Augustana,	G. C., Swedish,	165,000		7,000	15	250
Decorah,	Iowa,	Luther,	Ind., Norwegian,	75,000	7,000	5,000	8	203
St. Peter,	Minnesota,	Gust. Adolphus,	G. C. Swedish,	60,000		5,300	13	274
Watertown,	Wisconsin,	N. W. University,	Syn. Conference.	60,000		2,500	8	175
Allentown,	Pennsylvania,	Muhlenberg,	G. C., Eng.	80,000	133,000	8,000	11	143
Greenville,	Pennsylvania,	Thiel,	G. C., Eng.	50,000	50,000	6,000	10	127
Carthage,	Illinois,	Carthage,	G. S., Eng.	36,000	18,000	3,000	10	150
Conover,	N. Carolina,	Concordia,	United, Eng.	5,000		500	6	139
Lindsborg,	Kansas,	Bethany,	G. C., Swedish	118,000		4,000	15	306
Milwaukee,	Wisconsin,	Concordia,	Syn. Conference.	90,000		1,300	6	179
Rochester,	New York,	Wagner,	G. C., Ger.	25,000		500	4	42
Concordia,	Missouri,	St. Paul,	Mo., Ger.	15,000		500	6	82
Gravelton,	Missouri,	Concordia,	Ind., Eng.	2,000		Sev. hun.	2	121
New Ulm,	Minnesota,	Martin Luther,	Syn. Conference.	30,000		500	7	95
Canton,	S. Dakota,	Augustana,	Univ., Norweg.	15,000			7	100
Waverly,	Iowa,	Wartburg,	Iowa, Ger.	18,000		1,400	6	65
Atchison,	Kansas,	Midland,	G. S., Eng.	50,000	25,000	1,000	8	86
St. Louis,	Missouri,	Walther,	Mo., Ger.	32,500			2	86
Northfield,	Minnesota,	St. Olaf,	Unit., Norweg.	38,000		600	13	140
Minneapolis,†	Minnesota,	Augsburg,	Unit., Norweg.	85,000	115,000	ca.1,000	4	160
Dallas,	N. Carolina,	Gaston,	Ind., Eng.	10,000		600	8	60
Moshein,	Tennessee,	Mo-heim,	United, Eng.	1,500			2	100
Guntur,	India,	Mission,	G. S.	25,000			19	253
Totals,				$1,786,000	$780,000	115,700	261	4,519

*Temporarily closed. † To be consolidated with St. Olaf, Northfield. ‡ From Church paper Report.
Lima, Ohio, Co-Educational—Proposed. Red River Valley—Proposed.
Tacoma, Wash., Pacific University; being established by Norwegians.

3. ACADEMIES.

Town.	State.	Name.	Synodical Connection.	Property.	Library.	Profs.	Students.
Hartwick Seminary,	New York,	H. Seminary,	G. S., Eng.	$100,285	4,000	5	92
New York City,*	New York,	St. Mathew's,				6	250
Selinsgrove,	Pennsylvania,	Miss. Institute,	G. S., Eng.	25,000	2,500	8	75
Addison,	Illinois,	Teachers' Sem'y,	Missouri,	70,000	1,400	7	183
Enochville,	N. Carolina,	Enochville,	United,	500		3	108
Beth Eden,*	Mississippi,	Collegiate Inst.	United,	2,500	2,000	4	68
Elk Horn,*	Iowa,	High School,	Ind., Danish.	8,000	1,000	3	27
Leesville,	S. Carolina,	Classical Inst.	Independent.	5,000	300	3	91
Red Wing,	Minnesota,	Red Wing,	Ind., Norweg.	35,000	400	7	130
St. Ansgar,	Iowa,	St. Ansgar Inst.	Unit., Norweg.	4,000	200	6	40
New York City,	New York,	Pro-Gymnasium.	Mo., Ger.	No report.		5	34
Woodville,	Ohio,	Teachers' Sem'y.	Ohio, Eng.	10,000		5	53
Willmar,	Minnesota,	Willmar,	Independent.	18,000	1,200	3	281
Ashland,	Michigan,	High School,	Ud., Danish.	3,000	500	6	34
Wahoo,	Nebraska,	Luther Acad.	G. C., Swedish.	18,000	700	3	77
Afton,	Minnesota,	Pro-Seminary,	Ohio, Ger.			5	27
Wittenburg,	Wisconsin,	Indian Mission,	Norwegian.			2	96
Blair,*	Nebraska,	Trinity Sem.	Ind., Danish.	10,000		6	14
Ilex,	N. Carolina,	Holly Grove,	United, Eng.	8,000	100	3	75
Saginaw City,	Michigan,	Evan. Lutheran,	Ind., Ger.	1,200	300	2	14
Brooklyn,	New York,	St. Luke's,	G. C., Ger.	12,000		4	
Adrian,	Michigan,	Ev. Luth. Sem.		7,000	‡		
Rock Island,	Illinois,	Cons'y of Music,	G. C., Swedish.	In College	property.	2	31
Hickory,	N. Carolina,	St. Paul's,	Ohio, Eng.			2	23
Moorhead,	Minnesota,	Hope,	G. C., Swedish.	15,000		6	114
Granite Falls,	Minnesota,	Luth. Seminary,	Unit., Norweg.	15,000		?	?
Albert Lea,	Michigan,	High School,	G. C., Swedish.	25,000		5	145

* Church paper Report.   † From Church paper Reports.   ‡ Temporarily dropped into a Congregational School.

IN THE UNITED STATES. 441

Town	State	Name	Synod				Profs	Students
Nysted,	Nebraska,	High School,	Ind., Danish	?			4	23
Tyler,	Minnesota,	Danebod,	Ind., Danish	5,000	1,500		4	32
Ishpeming,	Michigan,	Being established by Finns of Suomi Synod.						
China Grove,	N. Carolina,	China Grove,					3	80
Columbus,	Ohio,	Gran. School,	Ohio, Ind.	15,000	Being built.			
Greensburg,	Pennsylvania,	Greensburg Sem.	G. C., Eng.	25,000			7	150
Graham,	Virginia,	Wartburg,	United, Eng.	100,000†	400		4	75
Stanton,	Iowa,	Mamrelund,	G. C., Swedish		500		5	115
Minneapolis,	Minnesota,	Emanuel,	G. C., Swedish				4	112
Salt Lake,	Utah,	Augustana,	G. C., Swedish				3	31
Sioux Falls,	Dakotah,	Teachers' Sem	Ind., Norweg	30,000	150		5	72
Springfield,*	Illinois,	Pro-Seminary,	Mo., Ger.	65,000	800		4	102
Portland,	N. Dakotah,	Bruflat,	Ind., Norweg	10,000			3	110
Mill Point,	Tennessee,	M. P. Institute,	Eng.	2,000			2	ca. 100
Bode,	Iowa,	Luther,	Norweg	3,000			3	50
Winnipeg,	Manitoba,		Icelanders, proposed.					
Stoughton,	Wisconsin,	Academy,	Norweg., Ind.	8,000				
Murray Co.,	Minnesota,	Bethany Acad.	Swedish, lately opened					
St. Paul Park,	Minnesota,	Academy,	Norwegian. Being established.		300		5	120
Totals,				$660,500	18,250		164	3,254

* With Practical Seminary.   † And endowment of $12,000.

4. SEMINARIES FOR YOUNG WOMEN.

Town	State	Name	Synod	Ch. Property	Library	Mother House	Profs	Students
Hagerstown	Md.	Kee Mar College	G. S.	$80,000	3,000		16	101
Lutherville	Md.	Lutherville	G. S.	50,000	1,000		11	92
Mt. Pleasant	N. C.	Mt. Pleasant	United	4,000	200		5	87
Philadelphia	Pa.	West Greene Street Institute	G. C.				7	48
St. Joseph	Mo.	Y. L. Institute		30,000	250		10	107
Staunton*	Va.	Female Seminary	United	20,000	600		11	75
Marion	Va.	Female College	United	25,000	250		9	113
Dallas*	N. C.	Gaston Female		10,000			8	128
Wytheville	Va.	Trinity	United	10,000	1,000		5	43
Luray	Va.	Von Bora College	United	10,000			10	70
Mechanicsburg	Pa.	Irving College	G. S.	15,000	200		8	39
Philadelphia	Pa.	Deaconess School for Girls	G. C.	In Mother House.			8	40
				$254,000	6,500		108	943

* From Church paper reports.

TOTAL HIGHER EDUCATIONAL INSTITUTIONS.

	Endowment and Property.	Library.	Profs.	Students.
25 Theological Seminaries........	$1,895,000	87,350	73	912
32 Colleges...	2,566,000	115,700	261	4,519
48 Academies...................	660,000	18,250	164	3,254
12 Seminaries for Young Women..	254,000	6,500	108	943
117 Institutions...	$5,375,000	227,800	606	9,628

PAROCHIAL SCHOOLS, 1890.

Name of Synod.	Teachers.	Schools.	Pupils.
Swedish Augustana......................	279	....	12,909
Norwegian Church in America............	217	....	....
Missouri and Adjacent States...........	637 and over 400 pastors.	1,226	74,006
Missouri, English Conference.............	....	7	312
Norwegian Danish Conference........	204	322	....
"Joint" Synod of Ohio............ ...	81 and 134 pas-tors.	153	....
Buffalo..	....	18	1,010
Danish Church Association............ ....'	10	....	....
Danish Church in America..................	....	30	....
Wisconsin Synod........	....	176	....
Minnesota Synod........................	....	46	2,023
Ministerium of New York........ ....'	68	38	2,854
Ministerium of Pennsylvania.............	29	16	1,155
Michigan Synod..........................	......	27	1,037
Wartburg Synod.........................	....	7	....
Eng. District of Ohio.....................	....	2	....
Iowa, German...	....	230	8,903
Synod of Canada..	....	18	... .
Norwegian Augustana..	....	15	300
Augsburg Synod......	....	10	397
Texas Synod.............................	....	6	248
New York and New Jersey...............	2	1	120
		2,343	
In Synods mentioned above, but not reporting number of Schools, say 506, gives total	... .	2,854	

INSTITUTIONS OF BENEFICENCE.
1. ORPHANS' HOMES.

Where Located.	State.	Name.	Connection.	Property and Endowment.	Teachers and Helpers	Inmates.	Yearly Expenses.
Middletown	Pa.	Emaus	G. S.	$ 18,000	4	45	
Zelienaple	Pa.	Boys Farm School	G. C.		4	36	
Rochester*	Pa.	Girls	G. C.	30,000	4	30	
Germantown	Pa.	Ev. Lutheran	G. C.	75,000, and end.$19,000	4	74	ca. $11,000
Buffalo	N. Y.	F. L. St. Johns	G. C.	75,000	6	79	8,000
Sulphur Springs	N. Y.	" "	G. C.	7,000	4	40	3,500
Vasa	Minn.	House of Mercy	G. C.	100,000	5	95	10,500
Mt. Vernon	N. Y.	Wartburg	G. S.	30,000	16	212	ca. 23,600
Loysville	Pa.	Tressler	G. S.			71	
Andover*	Ill.		G. S.	12,000	3	30	3,500
Syracuse	N. Y.	Ev. Lutheran	Iowa, Ger.	8,000	6	28	
Andrew	Ia.	Asylum for Orphan and Destitute.	G. C.	5,000	1	15	
Jacksonville*	Ill.		Mo.	30,000, end. $2,000 25,000 and 20 acres	2	27	ca. 3,200
Wt.Roxbury(Brook Farm)	Mass.	Martin Luther	Mo.		3	45	3,500
Norris	Mich.	Ev. L. Deaf and Dumb	Mo.	50,000	6	106	ca. 12,000
Addison	Ill.	Ev. Lutheran	Ohio.	20,000		98	4,500
Richmond	Ind.	Wernle	G. C.	10,000	2	20	
Mariedahl	Kan.	O. Asylum	G. C.	12,500	4	19	
Stanton	Ia.	"	G. C.	20,000	3	47	
Delano	Pa.	Concordia	Mo.	20,000	2	43	
Toledo	Ohio.	Ger. Ev. Lutheran	Iowa	15,000	9	70	
Des Peres	Mo.	Ev. Lutheran	Mo.	36,000	5	45	ca. 2,200
Jamestown	N. Y.	Gus. Adolphus	G. C.	55,000	2	12	
Frederick	Md.	Loats Female	G. S.	3,000	2	30	
Maplewood, Chicago	Ill.	Ev. Lutheran	Danes	10,000	5	70	6,000
Wittenborg	Wis.	Ev. Lutheran	Private	6,000	2	20	
New Orleans	La.	Bethlehem	Mo.	8,000	1	16	ca. 2,000
Indianapolis	Ind.	Ger. Lutheran	Mo.				

444   LUTHERANISM

Where Located.	Name.	State.	Connection.	Property and Endowment.	Teachers and Helpers	Inmates.	Yearly Expenses.*
Salem	South View	Va.	United	10,000	3	20	
College Point, L. I.	Bethlehem	N. Y.	Mo.	20,000	6	80	ca. 4,000
San Francisco	Martin Luther	Cala.	Mo.				
Wittenberg	"	Wis.	Mo.	6,000	3	68	
Madison	"	Wis.	Norwegian	20,000	3	34	
Tacoma		Wash.	"	3,500	1	12	
Beloit		Iowa	"	12,000 in former college buildings.			
Templeton	Being established, 40 acres of land.	Cala.	Danes	40 acres of land.			
Elk Horn		Ia.					
Omaha	With Deaconess Hospital.	Neb.					
Joliet	Being established.	Ill.		Being established.			
Total				$764,000	16	1,608	

2. IMMIGRANT MISSIONS.

Where Located.	State.	Connection.	Property and Endowment.	Teachers and Helpers	Inmates.	Yearly Expenses.†
New York German Immigrant House	N. Y.	G. C.	$150,000	1	12,000	$1,229
New York Lutheran Pilger House	N. Y.	Mo.	65,000	1	5,020	1,731
New York Swedish Immigrant Mission	N. Y.	G. C.		1		
Brooklyn Norwegian Immigrant Mission				1		
Brooklyn Danish Immigrant Mission				?		
Brooklyn Seamen's Home				1		
Brooklyn Finnish Immigrant Mission				1	1,200	
Ward's Island Mission	Md.	Mo.		1	1,515	500
Baltimore Immigrant Mission				1		
Pensacola and Quebec Immigrant Mission				1		
San Francisco Immigrant Mission	Cala.	Finns		1		
Boston Immigrant Mission	Mass.	Danes		1		
Boston Immigrant Mission	Mass.	Swedes		1		
Total			$215,000	12	19,735	3,460

* Church paper report.
† All figures in this column are taken from reports in Church periodicals.

3. HOSPITALS.

Town.	State.	Name.	Connection.	Property.	Expenses.	Patients.
East New York	N. Y.	Luther	Mo.	$25,000	$10,341	124 in year.
Milwaukee*	Wis	Deaconess	G. C.	175,000	15,000	In year, 554; ca. 50 daily.
Jacksonville*	Ill.	Deaconess	G. C.	30,000		Room for 40.
Chicago*	Ill.	Deaconess Emergency	G. C.	40,000?	ca. 6,500	Time, 1890, 265.
St. Paul*	Minn.	Bethesda	G. C.	35,000		Room for 35.
Brooklyn	N. Y.	Norwegian Deaconess	Norwegian	20,000	ca. 6,000	ca. 40, and much out-door relief.
Chicago	Ill.	Swedish Augustana	G. C.	35,000	ca. 4,000	103 in year.
Pittsburg*	Pa.	Deaconess Infirmary	G. C.	50,000		220 in year.
St. Louis	Mo.	Ev. Lutheran	Mo.	15,000		90 in year.
Minneapolis	Minn.	Bethesda	G. C.			
Sioux Falls	Iowa.	St. Luke's	Norwegian			
Washington	D. C.	Free Infirmary	G. S.			150-200 calls a month.
St. Peter	Minn.	Bethesda				
Philadelphia	Pa.	Drexel Childrens	G. C.	In Deaconess Motherhouse		30 daily.
Philadelphia	Pa.	German Hospital	In charge of Deaconess.			In year, 1,900; 150 daily.
Omaha	Neb.	Deaconess	G. C.	50,000	With Deaconess Home.	
Charleston	S. C.	Proposed				
Totals				$475,000		

*From published reports. No reply to letters of inquiry.
†Deaconesses also have charge of the Hospital of the King's Daughters, Easton, Pa.

4. DEACONESS HOMES.

Town	State	Name	Connection	Property	Expenses	Patients
Rochester	Pa.	Deaconess Home	In G. C	$		9 Deaconesses.
Minneapolis	Minn.	Norwegian Luth.	Ind.			
Brooklyn	N. Y.	Norwegian Luth.	Ind.	20,000		In hospital building.
Omaha	Neb.	Deaconess Inst.	G. C.	50,000	Being established.	8 Deaconesses.
Philadelphia	Pa.	Mary J. Drexel Motherhouse.	G. C.	*500,000		35 Deaconesses.
Total				$570,000		

5. HOMES FOR AGED.

Town	State	Name	Connection	Property	Expenses	Patients
Germantown	Pa.	Asylum for...	G. C	(In O. H.)		See Orphans' Home. 31
Richmond	Ind.	Wernle	Ohio	$75,000		With Orphans' Home. 72
East New York	N. Y.	Wartburg	Mo.	25,000		With Hospital.
Delano	Pa.	Concordia	Mo.	25,000		With Orphans' Home.
Washington	D. C.	Lutheran Home	G. S.	20,000		Being opened.
Philadelphia	Pa.	Mary J. Drexel Home For Aged	G. C.	30,000		36
Manitou	Colo.	Invalid Ministers	G. S.	In Deaconess Moth'r House		
Charleston	S. C.		United	10 acres near "Garden of the Gods."		Being established.
Wittenberg	Wis †			Gathering Funds for		
Totals				$170,000		152

SUMMARY.

	Cash Value	Helpers	Inmates in Year
39 Orphans' Homes, (8 reports lacking)	$764,000	116	1,608
14 Immigrant Missions	215,000	12	19,735
17 Hospitals, (5 reports lacking)	475,000	?	ca. 3,700
5 Deaconess Homes, (2 reports lacking)	570,000	ca. 56	
9 Homes for Aged, (4 reports lacking)	170,000	?	152
Total	$2,194,000	184	25,195

*From published reports. †Reported by Church papers. No particulars.

PERIODICALS.

I. ENGLISH.

Name.	Editor.	Where Published.	Began.	Appears.	Circulation.	Price.
The Lutheran Observer*	Dr. F. W. Conrad, L.L. D., et al.	Lancaster and Philadelphia, Pa.	1831	Weekly.	over 10,000	$2.00
The Lutheran*	No names given.	Philadelphia, Pa.	1861	"	over 2,500	2.25
The Lutheran Evangelist.	S. A. Ort, D.D., and Rev. L. S. Keyser.	Springfield, O.	1876	"	6,000	1.50
The Lutheran Visitor.	J. Hawkins, D.D.	Newberry, N. C.	1868	"	1,900	1.50
Our Church Paper.	Rev. S. Henkel, D.D.	New Market, Va.	1873	"	1,550	1.00
The Lutheran Standard.	Rev. D. Simon.	Columbus, O.	1842	"	4,200	1.25
The Workman.	W. A. Passavant, D.D.	Pittsburg, Pa.	1880	Every 2 w'ks	3,500	1.25
Lutheran Witness*.	Rev. C. A. Frank.	Zanesville, O.	1881	Semi-mo'thly	over 1,500	1.00
Church Messenger.	S. A. Repass, D.D., et al.	Allentown, Pa.	1875	Monthly.	4,300	.50
Lutheran S. S. Herald.	M. Sheeleigh, D.D.	Philadelphia, Pa.	1860	"	38,000	.20
The Little Ones.	Robt. R. Kinsell.	Philadelphia, Pa.	1880	Weekly.	41,500	.20
Sunshine and Shadow.	Rev. W. H. Singley, D.D.	Springfield, O.	1878	Monthly.	6,000	?
The Busy Bee.	Rev. G. W. Frederick.	Philadelphia, Pa.	1866	"		
Lutheran Child's Paper.	Rev. Geo. W. Lose.	Columbus, O.	1875	"	6,000	.35
The Seed Sower	Miss M. Welden, Rev. W. A. Schaeffer, Publisher.					
The Olive Leaf.		Philadelphia, Pa.	1878	"	?	.25
The Christians' Guide.	P. Anstadt, D.D.	Rock Island, Ill.	1882	"	10,000	.30
Augsburg S. S. Teacher.	H. L. Baugher, D.D.	York, Pa.	1883	"	?	.25
Teachers' Journal*.	P. Anstadt, D.D.	Philadelphia, Pa.	1875	"	10,100	.55
The Helpert.	Rev. J F. Ohl.	York, Pa.	1874	"	over 3,000	.56
Augsburg Lesson Leaf.	H. L. Baugher, D.D.	Philadelphia, Pa.	1877	"		.50
Augsburg Junior Lesson Leaf	H. L. Baugher, D.D.	Philadelphia, Pa.	1874	Weekly.	19,500	.07¼
		Philadelphia, Pa.	1875	"	11,500	.07¼

Name.	Editor.	Where Published.	Began.	Appears.	Circulation.	Price.
Augsburg Lesson Book	H. L. Baugher, D.D.	Philadelphia, Pa.	1879	Quarterly.	55,000	.15
Augsburg Junior Lesson Book	H. L. Baugher, D.D.	Philadelphia, Pa.	1881	"	54,000	.15
Lesson Quarterly†	P. Anstadt, D.D.	York, Pa.	1874	"	?	.12
Intermediate Leaf†	P. Anstadt, D. D.	York, Pa.	1874	"	?	8
Primary Lesson Leaf †	"	"	"	"	?	6
Church Lesson Leaf †.	M. H. Richards, D. D.	Philadelphia, Pa.	1876	Monthly.		
Church Lesson Leaflet †	"	Philadelphia, Pa.	1884	"		
Luth. Missionary Journal *	Rev. H. H. Weber, et al.	York, Pa.	1880	"	over 15,000	30
The Home Missionary†	Rev. C. A. Evald	Chicago, Ill.	1888	"		
Mission Studies†	Mrs. A. V. Hamma, et al.	Baltimore, Md.	1888	Quarterly.		20
The Foreign Missionary†	Prof. C. W. Schaeffer, D. D.	Philadelphia, Pa.	1880	Monthly.		
Little Missionary†	Rev. Edward Pfeiffer	Columbus, O	1887	"		
The Lutheran Pioneer	Prof. R. A. Bischoff	St. Louis, Mo	1879	"	4,500	25
The Young Lutheran	Rev. T. B. Roth, et al.	Utica, N. Y.	1889	"	30,125	50
The Lutheran Protest†	Rev. N. Klock	Kent, Ill	1889	"		
Mission News†	Rev. S. T. Hallman	Augusta, Ga.	1889	"		
Theological Magazine†	M. Loy, D. D.	Columbus, O	1881	Bi-Monthly.		2 00
Theological Monthly†	Rev. Prof. C. H. R. Lange.	St. Louis, Mo	1881	Monthly.		
New and Old†	C. L. Ehrenfeld, Ph. D.	Springfield, O.	1890	"		
The Lutheran Quarterly†	P. M. Bikle, Ph. D.	Gettysburg, Pa.	1871	Quarterly.	520	3 00
Lutheran Church Review†	H. E. Jacobs, D. D., et al.	Philadelphia, Pa.	1882	"		2 00
Luth. Almanac and Year Book	M. Shlecleigh, D. D.	Philadelphia, Pa.	1831	Yearly.		10
Church Almanac†	Rev. G. W. Frederick	Philadelphia, Pa.	1866	"	13,500	
Ev. Lutheran Almanac†	Rev. D. Simon	Columbus, O.	1878	"		
Deaconess-House Messenger.	Rector A. Cordes	Philadelphia, Pa.	1890	Quarterly.	250	25

II. GERMAN.

Name	Editor	Place	Year	Frequency	Circulation	Price
Lutherische Hausfreund*	J. D. Severinghaus, D. D.	Chicago, Ill.	1885	Semi-mo'thly	over 1,000	1 00
Herold und Zeitschrift	T. H. Diehl	Allentown, Pa.	1856	Weekly	3,100	1 10
Lutherische Botschafter	Rev. J. H. Theiss	Oakland, Cal.	1884	Monthly		
Der Lutheraner	Fac. Concordia Sem.	St. Louis, Mo.	1844	Twice-mot'ly	22,000	1 00
Luth. Kirchen-Zeitung	Rev. C. H. Rohe	Columbus, O.	1859	"	6,000	1 25
Zeuge der Wahrheit	Rev. J. H. Sieker	New York	1877	Monthly	1,200	1 00
Das Kirchenblatt	Rev. E. M. Genzmer	Toronto, Can.	1860	Semi-mo'tbly		
Der Sonntagsgast	G. U. Wenner, D. D.	New York city	1871	Monthly	3,250	72
Kirchenblatt	Prof. G. Grossman, et al.	Waverly, Iowa	1857	Twice-mo'tly	4,000	1 00
Luth. Anzeiger	Rev. A. Biewend, et al.	Boston, Mass	1883	"	900	50
Wachende Kirche	Rev. M. Burk	Buffalo, N. Y.	1855	Monthly		
Lehre und Wehre	Seminary Faculty	St. Louis, Mo.	1855	"	2,000	2 00
Mag. für Ev-Luth. Homiletik	Seminary Faculty	St. Louis, Mo.	1877	"	1,800	2 00
Ev.-Luth. Schulblatt	Dir. E. A. W. Krauss	St. Louis, Mo.	1865	"	700	2 00
Ev.-Luth. Schulzeitung †	Rev. W. Notz	Milwaukee, Wis.	1877	"		
Kinder-Garten	J. D. Severinghaus, D. D.	Chicago, Ill.	1877	"	12	
Jugend Leuchte	J. D. Severinghaus, D. D.	Chicago, Ill.	1882	"	20	
Kinderblatt	Rev. J. P. Beyer	St. Louis, Mo.	1872	"	29,000	25
Der Jugend Freund	W. Wackernagel, D. D.	Allentown, Pa.	1847	"	18,000	30
Synodal Bote	Rev. C. J. Albrecht	New Ulm, Minn.	1886	Semi-mo'thly	2,000	1 00
Luth. Volksblatt	Rev. William Weinbach, et al.	Elmira, Can.	1870	Monthly	1,050	1 00
Luth. Friedensbote	Rev. R. Von Pirch	Berlin, Can.	1883	"	1,100	50
Monatsbote	Gen. Conference Pittsburg Synod	Reading, Pa.	1855	Weekly	1,500	25
Luth. Kirchenblatt	G. C. Pastors	Philadelphia, Pa.	1884	"	3,460	2 00
Sendbote von Augsburg	Rev. E. Scherbel	Madison, Wis.	1886	Semi-mo'thly		
Missionsbote	Rev. H. Grahn	Philadelphia, Pa.	1878	"		
Ev-Luth. Gemeindeblatt	Prof. E. K. Notz, et al.	Milwaukee, Wis.	1865	"	5,200	1 00
Der Diakonissenfreund	Rector A. Cordes	Philadelphia, Pa.	1890	Monthly	2,000	25
Der Kirchenbote	Rev. E. Meister	Lancaster, Pa.	1890	"	400	25
Synodal Freund	Rev. P. F. Huber	West Bay City, M.	1889	"		
Siloah	Rev. A. Richter	Rochester, N. Y.	1882	Semi-mo'thly		

Name.	Editor.	Where Published.	Began.	Appears.	Circulation.	Price.
Missions Taube	Rev. P. Hauser	St. Louis, Mo.	1879	Monthly.	14,000	25
Ev.-Luth. Blätter	Rev. G. J. Wegener, et al.	New Orleans, La.	1883	Semi-mo'thly	800	50
Luth. Botschafter	Rev. J. M. Buehler, et al.	San f'cisco, Cal.	1884	?	1,000	1 00
Illustrirte Jugendblätter	A. Bendel	Reading, Pa.	1885	Semi-mo'thly	31,000	25
Blätter aus der Waisenhaus'n	Rev. F. Lutz	Waverly, Iowa.	1869	"	5,800	25
Sonntags-Schul Leitfaden	J. D. Severinghaus, D. D.	Chicago, Ill.	1879	"		15
Hülfsbuch für S. S. Lehrer	Rev. J. C. J. Peterson, et al.	New York City.	1888	Monthly.		
Kinder-Blättchen	Rev. F. W. Weiskotten	Philadelphia, Pa.	1878	"		
Kinderfreude	Rev. E. A. Baehme	Columbus, O.	1878	"		
Kirchliche Zeitschrift	Faculty Wartburg Seminary.	Waverly, Iowa.	1875	Bi-monthly.	500	1 25
Theol. Zeitblätter	Prof. F. W. Stellhorn	Columbus, O.	1881	"	400	2 00
Familien Freund	Rev. E. Meister	Lancaster, Pa.	1880	Monthly.	1,400	50
Kirchen und Waisenbote	Past. Conference	Pittsburg, Pa.	1884	?	1,800	25
Kirchenglocke	Conference of Ohio Synod	Pittsburg, Pa.	1887	?		
Zions-Biene	Rev. J. Heininger	Nanticoke, Pa.	1889	Monthly.	500	50
Christl. Erziehungs Blätter	John L. Fehr	Woodville, O.	1890	"	2,200	75
Die Heimath (Illustruted.)	G. Lober	Hoboken, N. J.	1890	"		
Luth. Hausfreundes Kalender	J. D. Severinghaus, D. D.	Chicago, Ill.	1876	Yearly.		10
Luth. Kalender	W. Wackernagel, D. D.	Allentown, Pa.	1854	"		
Ev.-Luth. Kalender	Rev. D. Simon	Columbus, O.	1882	"		
Amerikanischer Kalender	Rev. W. G. H. Hauser	St. Louis, Mo.	1875	"		
Pilger Kalender	Rev. J. J. Kuendig	Reading, Pa.	1879	"		
Gemeindeblatt Kalender	Rev. A. L. Gruebner	Milwaukee, Wis.	1885	"		
Wartburg Kalender	Publishing Board	Waverly, Iowa.	1887	"	6,000	
Statisches Jahrbuch	M. C. Barthel, Agt	St. Louis, Mo.	1885	"		15

III. NORWEGIAN AND DANO-NORWEGIAN.

Ev.-Luthersk Kirkeblad	Prof. M. O. Baeckman, et al.	Minneapolis, Min	1890	Weekly.	9,500	1 00
Budbären	Rev. C. Lillethun	Red Wing, Minn.	1868	"	2,000	1 00
Lutheraneren †	Prof. G. Sverdrup, et al.	Minnenpolis, Min	1867	Monthly.		
Bornevennen	Rev. C. Lillethun	Red Wing, Minn	1877	"	4,000	35
Luthersk Börne-Blad †	Rev. O. Nilsen, et al.	Minneapolis, Min	1875	Semi-mo'thly		
Börne-Blad †	Rev. J. B. Frich	Minneapolis, Min	1875	"		
Börne-Budet †		Rushford, Minn.	1879			
Missions Vennen †	H. J. G. Krog	Baldwin, Wis.	1883	Monthly.		
Vort Blad †	Rev. N. C. Brun, et al	Chicago, Ill.		Weekly.		
Fredsbudet	Rev. J. H. Myhre	Rollag, Minn.	1880	Semi-mo'thly	6,000	50
Sondagsskole Blad	Rev. E. J. Homme	Wittenburg, Wis.	1857	"	8,000	35
For Gamuel og Ung	Rev. E. J. Homme	Wittenburg, Wis.	1880	Monthly.	4,500	1 00
Waisenhus-Kalender	Rev. E. J. Homme	Wittenburg, Wis.	1885	Yearly.		
Ev. Luth. Folke-Kalender		Decorah, Iowa	1886	"		
Ev. Luth. Kirketidende	Faculty of Seminary	Decorah, Iowa	1857	"	4,200	1 00

IV. SWEDISH.

Augustana	Rev. S. P. A. Lindahl	Rock Island, Ill.	1855	Weekly.	15,400	2 00
Missions Vännen	John Wenstrand	Chicago, Ill.	1872	"	over 12,500	1 50
Fosterlandet	Rev. C. A. Evald, et al.	Chicago, Ill.	1884	"	6,000	1 50
Veseusten		San Fran'co, Cal.		"	over 1,500	
Missionaren		Minneapolis, Min	1879	Monthly.		
Ungdoms Vännen †	Rev. C. A. Swensson	Moline, Ill	1874	Semi-mo'thly		
Barn-Vännen †	Rev. C. A. Evald, et al	Chicago, Ill.	1889	"		
Utah Missionaren	Rev. J. A. Krantz	Salt Lake City	1885	"	1,600	15
Barnens Tidning	Rev. H. P. Quist	Rock Island, Ill	1885	"	25,500	30
Kristlig-Skoltidning †	College Faculty	Lindsborg, Kan.	1876	Semi-weekly.	over 15,000	
Hemlandet	Hon. J. A. Enander	Chicago, Ill.	1876	"	10,000	2 00
Skaffaren	B. Anderson	St. Paul, Minn.	1880	Annually.		
Korsbaneret		Rock Island, Ill.				

V. DANISH.

Name.	Editor.	Where Published.	Began.	Appears.	Circulation.	Price.
Kirkelig-Samler	Rev. P. Kjoelhede	Cedar Falls, Io. Blair, Neb St. Paul	1872	Semi-mo'thly	1,200	1 25
Kirkebladet †			1878	"		
Boernevennen	M. Holst	Cedar Falls, Io	1881	"	1,200	75
Dannevirke	M. Holst	Cedar Falls, Io	1878	Weekly.	2,200	2 00

VI. FINNISH.

Name.	Editor.	Where Published.	Began.	Appears.	Circulation.	Price.
Unsi Kotiinaa	Aug. Nylund	N. Y. Mills, Minn	1881	Weekly.	1,500	2 00
Paimen Sanomia	Rev. J. G. Nikander	Hancock, Mich	1889	"	1,900	

VII. FRENCH.

Name.	Editor.	Where Published.	Began.	Appears.	Circulation.	Price.
Journal Lutherein	Rev. V. P. Goszweiler	Dexter, Iowa	1887	Monthly.		
Petite Feuille Religieusse						

VIII. ICELANDIC.

Name.	Editor.	Where Published.	Began.	Appears.	Circulation.	Price.
Sameiningin	Rev. J. Bjarnason	Winnipeg, Can	1886	Monthly.		

*.According to Rowell's Newspaper Directory, 1890. †.No report, and not quoted by Rowell. There are published in the United States 48 English periodicals, 56 German, 15 Norwegian, 13 Swedish, 4 Danish, 2 Finnish, 2 French and one Icelandic. The table explains more fully.

SYNODICAL CONTRIBUTIONS FOR BENEFICENCE.

Name of Synod.	Amount.	Name of Synod.	Amount.
Allegheny	$ 13,820	Northern Indiana	3,470
Augustana, Swedish	75,326	North Carolina	3,572
Augsburg, Ger	245	New York and New Jersey	9,069
Canada	2,900	Nebraska	5,227
Central Pennsylvania	6,183	Norwegian Ch. in America	59,133
Central Illinois	8,345	Ohio, Eng. Dist	3,585
East Ohio	5,711	Olive Branch	5,095
East Pennsylvania	27,817	Ohio, Joint Synod	50,000
Franckean	3,202	Pittsburg, G. S	9,292
Georgia	1,723	Pittsburg, G. C	61,405
Hartwick	4,940	Southern Illinois	1,540
Holston	ca. 325	Susquehanna	9,487
Iowa, Ger	27,360	South W. Virginia	16,433
Iowa, Eng	2,700	South Carolina	6,441
Indiana	645	Tennessee*	3,000
Kansas	5,540	United Norwegian* (Ed'n.	
Maryland	60,136	and H. Missions)	25,000
Miami	9,716	Virginia	5,185
Middle Tennessee	95	Wartburg, Ger	985
Ministerium of New York.	28,717	West Pennsylvania	29,118
Ministerium of Pennsylvania	64,775	Wisconsin	21,733
		Wittenberg	10,213
Missouri	155,465		
Northern Illinois	3,655		$848,324

MISSION CONGREGATIONS AND MISSION STATIONS MAINTAINED BY THE DIFFERENT SYNODS.

East Ohio Synod	3	Augsburg Synod	23
Ohio "District" Synod	14	Buffalo Synod	10
Southern Illinois Synod	4	Ministerium of New York	12
Iowa (Eng.) Synod	3	Danish E. L. Ch. Association	25
Iowa (Ger.) Synod	193	Maryland Synod	6
Olive Branch Synod	3	Holston Synod	2
Central Illinois Synod	3	Missouri Synod	675
Northern Illinois Synod	3	North Carolina Synod	4
Virginia Synod	12	South Carolina Synod	2
Middle Tennessee Synod	4	New York and New Jersey Synod	12
Pittsburg (G. S.) Synod	2	West Pennsylvania Synod	9
Susquehanna Synod	4	Franckean Synod	14
Hartwick Synod	11	Northern Illinois Synod	3
Canada Synod	ca. 25	Kansas Synod	19
Indiana Synod	5	Nebraska Synod	61
East Pennsylvania Synod	14	Pittsburg, G. C., (29 Missions)	55
Ministerium of Pennsylvania, (Missions)	42	Ohio (Joint) Synod, (45 men)	100
Wisconsin Synod	59	United Norwegian Synod	130
Allegheny Synod	9	Danish Church in America	59
Central Pennsylvania Synod	3	General Synod H. M. Board, (131 Missions)	200
Augustana (Swedish) Synod	150	English and Concordia Districts	23
Tennessee Synod	10	G. C. Home Mission Committees and Synods not reported above	66
S. W. Virginia Synod	45		
Georgia Synod	3		
Wittenberg Synod	6		
Icelandic Synod	22		
			2,162

* Reported in part.

WOMEN'S MISSION SOCIETIES.

Name of Synod.	Auxiliaries.	Remarks.	Members	Contributions.
East Ohio	16		436	$ 472
Ohio, Eng. Dist	21	Some are Aid Societies		
Iowa, Eng	19		309	525
Olive Branch	14		433	784
Central Illinois	11		240	691
Northern Illinois	18		404	611
Pittsburg, G. S.	39		1,059	943
Miami	19		566	1,350
Hartwick	18		614	611
Canada	9	No Particulars		
Indiana	7			107
East Pennsylvania	51		1,482	1,295
Ministerium of Penna		No Report		
Holston	2	Partial Report		35
Allegheny	38			1,356
Central Pennsylvania	29		537	810
S. W. Virginia	31		433	1,243
Georgia	10			
Wittenberg	23		434	
Ministm. of New York	75	Women's—generally miss.		
" "	16	Exclusively Mission		
" "	117	Others		
Maryland	37	Women's	2,213	4,101
	25	Young People's		
New York & New Jersey	19		493	658
Pittsburg, G. C.	50	Fifteen report, for year		1,355
South Carolina	29		515	732
Kansas	37			
Franckean	12		291	445
North Carolina	22		501	680

EXHIBIT OF THE CHURCH BY STATES IN THE UNITED STATES.

Parochial Schools marked *. Mission stations marked †.

State's	Synods.	Pastors.	Cong.	Communicants.	Value of Church Property.	Yearly Expenses.	For Benefi- cence.	S.& Par.Sch's Sch's	Pupils.
	Georgia,	1							
	Middle Tenn.	1	No charge.						
Alabama.			2†						
	Missouri,	2	5	534	$ 20,000	$ 3,000	?	4*	107
	Tennessee,	1	3	75	2,500	215		1	75
	Wartburg,	1	1	75					
	Total,	6	9	684	$ 22,500	$3,215			

Arizona,............ 1 No charge.

IN THE UNITED STATES.

State's	Synods.	Pastors.	Cong.	Communicants.	Value of Church Property.	Yearly Expenses.	For Benefi- cence.	S.&Par.Sch's Sch's	Pupils.
Arkansas.	Augsburg,	1	1	60					
	Missouri,	7	15† 14	1,347	$ 35,000	$ 9,800	$1,000	9*	375
	Other Synods,	3							
	Total,	11	15	1,407	$ 35,000	$ 9,800	$1,000		
California.	Augustana,	6	6	903	$ 61,800	$ 9,732	368	4	168
	Buffalo,	1	1	26					
	California,	Ger	man;	lately or	ganized.				
	California,	Eng	lish; l	ately or	ganized.				
	Danish, I,	3	6						
	Danish, II,	2	5	131					
	Missouri,	14	11	1,822	96,000	9,000		7*	404
	In new Synods and independ.	16	10	900	75,000	4,500	Estim'ated		
	Total,	42	39	3,782	$ 232,800				

An Immigrant Mission is maintained at San Francisco. The Missouri Synod has an Orphans' Home at the same place; and the Swedes are establishing one at Templeton. The California Synod, (English) organized May, 1891, with eight pastors, was admitted a member of the General Synod at Lebanon.

Colorado.	Augustana,	3	5	418	$ 67,400	$ 4,043	$2,083	2* 5	50 221
	Colorado,	Lat	ely or	ganized.					
	Missouri,	4	3	450					
	Norwegian Ch.	1	4	76	12,000	1,800		1*	10
	In new Synod and others.	7	9	200	?				
	Total,	15	21	1,144					

Twenty acres of land, in or near the Garden of the Gods have been given to establish a Home for Aged Ministers.

Connecticut.	Augustana,	8	13	2,028	$ 65,200	$ 19,241	$1,228	5* 7	248 435
	Danish Ch.,	1	4	204					
	Minis. of N. Y.,	6	6 1†	1,268				5	600
	Missouri,	5	9	1,559	40,000	6,300		3*	227
	N. Y. and N. J.	3	4	362	7,000	1,600		2	121
	Other,	1							
	Total,	24	36	5,421					

	Synods.	Pastors.	Cong.	Communicants.	Value of Church Property.	Yearly Expenses.	For Benefience.	S.& Par. Sch's Sch's	Pupils.
Stat's									
Dakota.	Augustana, Nor	12	22	Merged in Un. Syn.			1,175	15*	300
	" Swed	14	47	2,378	20,764	8,450	910	17	450
	Danish Ch in A.	2	10	242				15*	300
	Finnish............		1	100					
	G. C. Mission...	1	1	?	7,000			1	108
	Hauge	16	51	2,336					
	Icelandic.........	1	8	1,687					
	Iowa, Ger.......	30	101	2,802		11,582			
	Minnesota.......	3	11	330					
	Missouri	24	63 } 118† }	3,782	72,000			27*	528
	Nebraska	1	2	68					
	Norwegian Ch..	22	78	5,116					
	" United	58	194	15,000					
	Ohio, Joint Syn	4	4	700					
		188	593	34,631					

Institutions for higher education exist at Canton, Portland and Sioux Falls. They have property worth $55,000, fifteen professors and 282 students. A movement is on foot, headed by the Scandinavian Red River College Association, to establish a college in the Red River Valley, and Grand Forks, N. D., seems selected as its site.

Delaware—

Minis. of Penna...	3	2	296		2,430	675	6	756

Dist. of Columbia	Immanuel.......	1	1	450					
	Maryland.......	8	6	1,050	263,000	11,445	35,072	7	1,324
	Minis. of N. Y.	1	1	430					
	Missouri	1	1	420	50,000			1*	51
	W. Pennsyl'nia	1	3	94	6,000	1,000	200	2	109
	Others............	3							
	Total..	15	12	2,444					

A Free Infirmary was opened, about the beginning of 1890, in Washington City. in connection with the Memorial Lutheran Church; and a 27-acre tract of land, worth $1,100 the acre, has been donated to establish a Home for Aged and Infirm.

Florida.	Augustana, Sw.		1	17	1,000	147			
	Missouri	2	5	261	6,000	1,200		1*	39
	Georgia...........	2	2	153					
	S. Carolina......		1						
	Total............	4	9	431					

An Immigrant Mission is maintained at Pensacola.

IN THE UNITED STATES.

State	Synods	Pastors	Cong.	Communicants	Value of Church Property	Yearly Expenses	For Benefi-cence	S.& Par.Sch's Sch's	Pupils
Georgia	Georgia	6	16	1,302	105,849	6,000	1,523	12	950
	Minis. of Penna	1	1						
	S. Carolina	2	1	78					
	N. Carolina	1							
	Total	10	18	1,380					
Idaho	Augustana, Sw.	2	3	139	2,450	765	25	3	55
	" Nor.	1	1	57					
	Norwegian Ch.	1	1	50					
	Un. Norwegian		2						
	Joint Ohio	1	1						
	Total	5	8	246					
Illinois	Augustana	42	72	18,290	605,000	143,350	13,750	52* 62	989 7,784
	Augsburg	4	5	306				3*	68
	Buffalo	1	1	136				1	47
	Danish Assoc'n	1	2						
	" Church	4	11	709					
	Hauge	5	11	896					
	Immanuel	1	1	400					
	Illinois Central	28	25†	1,650	186,000	21,576	8,345	22	2,498
	" Northern	24	38†	2,560	170,850	27,419	3,517	37	3,542
	" Southern	6	15	781	20,650	4,068	1,505	11	696
	Indiana	6	5	773		2,305	268	4	672
	Iowa, Ger., includes part of Iowa	44	101	9,112		51,375		9*	
	Missouri	212	242	68,586	3,600,000	242,000		226*	18,460
	Un. Norwegian	12	16	2,900					
	Norwegian Ch.	6	14	1,703					
	Ohio, (Joint)	13	16	3,325					
	Pittsburg	2	2	165					
	Wartburg	24	22	1,962					
	Wisconsin	1	1	142					
	Total	431	600	114,456					
	Pastors other Synods	6							

At Addison there is a Parochial Teachers' Seminary; Carthage, Carthage College; Chicago, German Theological Seminary, Rock Island, Augustana College, Augustana Theological Seminary; Augustana Conservatory of Music; Springfield, Practical (Theological) Seminary, Pro-Seminary.

In all, eight institutions, with property worth $411,000; forty-nine professors and 882 students.

At Andover there is a Swedish Orphans' Home; Addison, German Orphans' Home; Chicago, Deaconess Emergency Hospital, Augustana Hospital,—Swedish;

Orphans' Home, Maplewood,—Danes; Jacksonville, Deaconess Hospital and Orphans' Home.

In all, seven institutions. They report property worth $188,000; three report nine teachers and helpers, and four have 222 inmates (orphans). The Swedes are opening an additional orphanage at Joliet.

Stat's	Synods.	Pastors.	Cong	Communicants.	Value of Church Property.	Yearly Expenses.	For Benefience.	S & Par.Sch's Sch's	Pupils.
Indiana.	Augustana, ...	6	10	1,464	$ 52,500	$ 7,405	980	8	539
	Augsburg, ...	1	1	40				1*	12
	Immanuel, ...	1	1	80					
	Indiana, ...	11	26	2,166		7,622	1,233	15	1,108
	Joint Ohio, ...	25	32	4,113					
	Michigan,.	2	1	200					
	Missouri,.........	83	95	24,575	1,320,000	95,000		86*	6,112
	Northern Ind...	31	63	3,736	156,000	24,950	2,374	60	4,536
	Norwegian Ch.		1	200					
	Olive Branch,..	13	28	2,037	95,200	10,980	2,782	26	2,600
	Other, ...	2							
	Total, ...	175	258	38,611					

At Fort Wayne there is a College of the Missouri Synod, with property worth $100,000; seven professors, and 225 students; Indianapolis, Orphanage; Richmond, Wernle Orphans' Home and Home for Aged. These institutions have property worth $28,000, and 131 inmates.

Iowa.	Joint Ohio,......	3	4	1,603				21*	1,487
	Augus., Swed...	25	58	7,621	$ 263,425	$ 74,057	7,252	50	3,414
	Augus., Nor. ...	5	13	804					
	Danish Asso.,..	2							
	Danish Ch.,.....	9	34	1,210					
	Iowa,...............	23	23	1,380	132,000	20,000	2,483	21	1,648
	Iowa, Ger.... }	83	90	10,340		72,458			
		Figures include report for S. Minn.							
	Missouri,.........	72	126	13,774	620,000	88,200		72	2,340
	Augsburg, ...	1	1	70					
	Hauge, ...	6	16	1,390					
	Norweg. Ch.,...	29	49	6,082					
	Un. Norweg, ...	32	84	8,500					
	Wartburg, ...	4	2	500					
	Total, ...	294	500	53,214					

At Bode there is Luther Academy; Decorah, Martin Luther College; Dubuque, Wartburg Seminary; Elk Horn, Danish High School; St. Ansgar, St. Ansgar High School; Stanton, Mamrelund Institute; Waverly, Wartburg College.

In all, seven institutions. Six of them report property worth $165,000; thirty-six professors, and 564 students.

At Andrew there is an Orphans' Home and Home for Aged; Beloit, College buildings to be used for Orphans' Home; Elk Horn, Danish Orphans' Home; Sioux Falls, Norwegian Hospital; Stanton, Orphans' Home.

IN THE UNITED STATES. 459

State's	Synods.	Pastors	Cong.	Communicants.	Value of Church Property.	Yearly Expenses.	For Benefi-cence.	S.&Par.Sch's Sch's	Pupils.
Kansas.	Augustana.......	18	41	3,037	$ 65,500	$ 16,171	2,837	25	1,041
	Danish Church.	2	8	128					
	Hauge............		1	16					
	Iowa, (Ger.)....	10	20	1,000					
	Kansas...........	45	43	2,441	234,000	36,000	4,660	35	3,500
	Missouri, (with Eng Conf.)...	44	69	6,195	304,000	41,000		42*	1,423
	Nebraska........	7	7	330					
	Norwegian Syn		3	418					
	Ohio, Joint......	1	5	400					
	Un. Norwegian	1	4	300					
	Other.............	5							
	Total...........	133	201	14,265					

Two educational institutions of the Church are in this State, one at Atchison and one at Lindsborg. They have property worth $193,000, 23 professors, and 392 students. The Orphanage at Mariedahl has a $10,000 property, two teachers and 20 orphans.

Kentucky.	Augustana, Sw		1	12	$	$			
	Iowa, Ger.......	2	?	?					
	Miami............	1	3	266	5,700	492	47	3	276
	Missouri.........	4	3 & † 1	492	10,000	2,100		3*	157
	Olive Branch...	5	7	1,226	31,800	9,572	1,594	5	1,824
	Joint Ohio......	1							
	Other Synods...	1							
	Total...........	14	16	1,996					

Louisiana—

Joint Ohio.........	1			$		$			
Missouri	9	12	2,511	60,000	12,000		11*	1,000
Total	10	12	2,511					

The Orphans' Home in New Orleans has property worth $6,000, two teachers and 20 orphans.

Maine.	Augustana, Sw		1	179	$ 2,570	$ 282	24	1	40
	Danish Church	1	2	115					
	Un. Norwegian	1	1	225					
	Total.	2	3	519					
Maryland.	Maryland........	61	87	15,058	$ 835,686	$138,452	25,064	103	17,651
	Missouri	10	13	3,057	320,000	14,300		9*	619
	Minis. of Penna	1	No charge						
	W. Pennsylv'ia	4	4	130					
	Joint Ohio	6	9	1,065					
	Total..........	82	113	19,310					

Two educational institutions and two for beneficence exist. At Baltimore is the Immigrant Mission of the Missouri Synod; at Frederick, the Loats' Orphan's Home for Girls; at Hagerstown and at Lutherville are Seminaries for young women. The latter have property worth $130,000, 27 professors and 193 students. The Immigrant Mission and the Orphan's Home have property worth $55,000, three teachers and helpers, and about 1,525 inmates during the year.

Stat's	Synods.	Pastors.	Cong.	Commu- nicants.	Value of Church Property.	Yearly Expenses.	For Benefi- cence.	S.& Par.Sch's Sch's	Pupils.
Massachusetts.	Augustana, Sw	5	6	1,139	$ 57,225	$ 10,726	2,315	3* 6	80 259
	Missouri	7	5† 6	1,768	80,000	6,000		4*	214
	Minis. of N. Y.	2	1	333				1	145
	N. Y. and N. J.	1	2	121	1,000	495		1	102
	Danish Church	1	3	63					
	Norwegian Ch.	1	2	345					
	Total	17	20	3,769					

In West Roxbury, the Missouri Synod maintains an Orphanage, with property worth $30,000, two teachers and helpers, and 27 orphans. It is on the celebrated "Brook Farm," on which Channing, Ripley, Curtis, Parker, Hawthorn, Dana, and others, found more poetry than they did potatoes in their transcendental philosophy combined with funny attempts at agriculture. Transcendentalism, Fourierism, Swedenborgianism,—collapse; and all in five years' time, despite the bright minds at the head of it! Christian love now uses it to give shelter to the fatherless. The Danes and the Swedes each maintain an Immigrant Mission in Boston.

	Augsburg	1	1	301	$	$		14*	168
	Augustana	19	38	4,050	111,035	30,110	4,277	32	1,902
	Buffalo	3	4	347					
	Danish Assoc'n								
	Danish Church	5	16	626					
	Finnish	4	11	2,300					
	Hauge	1	4	240				2	50
Michigan.	Immanuel	2	1	500					
	Indiana, North.	4	10	670					
	Iowa, Ger	17	30	4,200					
	Michigan	35	77	8,431					
	Missouri	78	117	25,977	1,278,000	936,000		96*	6,503
	Ohio, Joint	20							
	Wisconsin	4	7	1,940				4*	
	Norwegian Ch.	4	13	1,009					
	Un. Norwegian	7	13	2,500					
	Other	4							
	Total	208	342	53,091					

At Ashland there is a Danish High School; Albert Lee, Swedish High School; Adrian, Evangelical Lutheran Seminary; Saginaw, Classical and Theological Seminary; at Ishpeming the Finns are establishing an Academy.

At Norris there is an Institutute for Deaf and Dumb.

Three educational institutions report property worth $40,000, twelve professors

IN THE UNITED STATES. 461

and 198 students. The school for the Deaf and Dumb has property worth $25,000, three teachers and 45 pupils.

Stat's	Synods.	Pastors.	Cong.	Communicants.	Value of Church Property.	Yearly Expenses.	For Benefi- cence.	S.& Par.Sch's Sch's	Pupils.
Minnesota.	Augustana, ...	74	184	23,075	$ 583,650	$148,690	21,260	74* 114	4.452 7,922
	Buffalo,..........	2	2	282					
	Danish Asso....	6	6	250					
	Danish Ch.,.....	4	16	704					
	Hauge, ...	24	65	4,200					
	Icelandic, ...	1	4	394					
	Iowa, Ger., ...	16	30	3,000		24,000			
	Minnesota,......	58	86	15,660					
	Missouri,.........	77	147	16,880	945,000	132,300		92*	4,035
	Norweg. Ch. ...	53	148	18,367					
	Ohio, (Joint,)...	15	20	1,511					
	Un. Norweg....	88	246	30,000					
	Wisconsin,......	4	6	2,372				4* 3	
	Other,.............	3							
	Total,.........	425	960	116,695					

At Afton there is a Practical Seminary, Classical and Theological; Granite Falls, Norwegian Academy; Minneapolis, Augsburg College, and Theological Seminary; Luther Seminary, (Norwegian Synod), Emanuel Academy; Morehead, Hope Academy; Northfield, St. Olaf College; New Ulm, Martin Luther College, and Theological Seminary; Red Wing, Theological Seminary, and Preparatory Institute; St. Peter, Gustavus Adolphus College; Tyler, Danebod High School; Willmar, Luther Institute.

In all, sixteen institutions. Fourteen of them report property worth over $400,000, eighty professors, and 1,550 students.

At Minneapolis there is Bethesda Hospital; Norwegian Deaconess Home and Hospital; St. Paul, Hospital; St. Peter, Bethesda Hospital; Vasa, Orphans' Home.

| | Mississippi,..... | 9 | 10 | 600 | $ 5,000 | | 2.225 | 6 | 202 |

The Beth Eden Collegiate Institute has property worth $2,500; four teachers, and sixty-eighty students.

Missouri.	Augustana, ...	1	2	324	$ 60,000	$ 19,440	147	1* 1	20 104
	Cent. Illinois, ..	2	1	430	65,000	6.000	5,775	1	310
	Iowa, Ger.......	10	18	1,600					
	Kansas,...........	3	2	400					
	Missouri,.........	108	114	22,170	1,660,000	114,000	10,900	105*	6,254
	Mo., Eng. Syn.	5	5	160					
	Nebraska,.......	4	4	198					
	Norweg. Ch....	......	2						
	Un. Norweg....	......	1						
	Ohio, Joint,.....	1	8	600					
	South. Illinois,..	2	6	343	1,200	645	35	3	140
	Wartburg,......	1	1	100					
	Other,.............	4							
	Total,.........	141	159	26,325					

LUTHERANISM

At Concordia there is St. Paul's College; Gravelton, Concordia College; St. Joseph, Young Ladies' Institute; St. Louis, Concordia Seminary, Walther College. Five institutions, with property worth $282,000; twenty-five professors, and 579 students.

At Des Peres there is an Evangelical Lutheran Orphan Asylum; St. Louis, Evangelical Lutheran Hospital.

The two institutions have property worth $30,000; fifteen teachers and helpers, and 160 inmates.

State	Synods.	Pas-tors.	Cong	Communicants.	Value of Church Property.	Yearly Expenses.	For Benefi-cence.	S. & Par. sch's Sch's	rupis.
Montana.	August'a, Nor.		2	99	$	$			
			13†						
	Missouri,	3	4	160	$ 5,000	$ 600			
	Norweg. Ch.,	2							
	Un. Norweg.		1						
	Total,	5	7	259					
Nebraska.								24*	1,099
	Augustana	20	39	3,620	$ 165,100	$ 32,100	6,150	26	1,692
	Danish Assoc'n	8	4	260					
	Danish Church	6	27	736					
	Hauge	3	9	540	18,100			4	125
	Iowa, Ger.	30	{ Incl udes so me in Kan sas.	4,745	23,076 }			6*	
	Kansas		3	100					
	Missouri	88	133	11,600	568,000	93,100		83*	2,960
	Nebraska	57	63	3,274	283,500	50,000	4,000	50	3,500
	" Ger..	Lat ely org anized.							
	Norwegian Ch..	6	22	1,433					
	Ohio, Joint	6	9	485					
	Un. Norwegian	1	1	40					
	Wisconsin	8	11	2,381					
	Other	3							
	Total.	231	397	29,214					

The Church institutions are the Danish Classical and Theological Seminary at Blair, the Danish High School at Nysted, and the Swedish Academy at Wahoo. They have property valued at about $30,000, twelve professors, and 137 students. The Deaconess Home, the Orphans' Home, and the Hospital, in Omaha, have a $50,000 house, and are enlarging their work as the buildings are completed. The General Synod is working hard to establish a Theological Seminary in Omaha, and have $175,000 conditionally pledged for it.

New Hampshire—

							1*	40
Augustana	1	1	253	$ 9,000	$ 1,919	157	1	95
Un. Norwegian		1	?					

IN THE UNITED STATES. 463

State's	Synods.	Pastors.	Cong.	Communicants.	Value of Church Property.	Yearly Expenses.	For Benefi- cence.	S.&Par. Sch's Sch's	Pupils.
	Danish Church	1	4	189	$..........	$..........	......	......	......
	East Penna.....	3	3	568	30,000	4,248	1,330	3	600
	Immanuel.......	1	1	120					
New Jersey.	Minis. of Penna	12	15	3,234		14,642	3,328	13	2,418
	" of N. Y.	10	12	4,888				11	4,451
	Missouri	5	5	790	30,000	8,500		5*	259
	N. Y. and N. J.	11	10	1,265	104,500	11,878	1,590	11	1,584
	Norwegian Ch.	1	1	184					
	Total.	44	51	11,238					
	New Mexico— Nebraska	1	2	40	$	$ 262	28	1	20
								3*	92
	Augustana	6	9	2,767	164,000	22,324	1,951	6	851
	Augsburg........	1	1	750			30	1	120
	Buffalo............	9	12	2,260					
	Danish Church	1	12	419					
	Franckean......	23	34	2,379	125,000	13,819	,760	23	1,874
	Hartwick........	32	33	4,650	302,500	32,714	4,939	38	3,439
New York.	Immanuel.......	4	5	620					
	Minis. of Penna	3	3	1,774		19,233	5,406	4	1,883
								38*	2,854
	Minis. of N. Y.	93	96	35,125	2,005,000	277,723	28,717	98	19,964
	Missouri	63	72	22,172	1,530,000	864,000		48*	5,014
								1*	120
	N. Y. and N. J.	34	32	8,879	851,800	106,895	7,465	37	7,000
	Norwegian Ch.	4	4	693					
	Ohio, (Joint)....	1	2	200					
	Other	4							
	Total............	278	315	82,688					

At Brooklyn there is St. Luke's Academy; Buffalo, Martin Luther College and Theological Seminary; Hartwick Seminary, Classical and Theological Departments; New York City, Pro-Gymnasium, St. Matthew's Academy; Rochester, Wagner Memorial College.

In all, eight institutions, with property worth $225,000, 26 professors and 455 students.

At Brooklyn there is a Deaconess Hospital and Home, Finnish Immigrant Mission; Buffalo, Orphans' Home for Girls; College Point, L. I., Orphans' Home; Jamestown, Swedish Orphans' Home; Mt. Vernon, German Orphans' Home; New York City, Hospital, (Missouri Synod,) and Home for Aged, Immigrant Mission of the General Council, Immigrant Mission of the Missouri Synod, and of Swedes, Norwegians, Danes and Finns, Seamen's Temperance Home; Syracuse, Tabor Orphans' Home; Sulphur Springs, Orphans' Home for Boys; Ward's Island, Mission.

In all, seventeen institutions, with property worth $503,000. The five Orphans' Homes have 25 teachers and helpers, and 329 inmates.

State	Synods	Pastors	Cong.	Communicants	Value of Church Property	Yearly Expenses	For Benefi- cence	S.&Par.Sch's Sch's	Pupils
North Carolina	Alpha	3	5	200	$	$			
	North Carolina	30	54	6,162	156,600	15,083	3,577	44	3,097
	Ohio, Joint	4	5	300					
	Tennessee	17	59	5,491	69,440	3,265	1,840	28	989
	Others	1			—				
	Total	55	123	12,153					

At China Grove there is an Academy; Conover, Concordia College; Dallas, Gaston Female College; Enochville, High School; Hickory, Practical Seminary and Academy; Ilex, Holly Grove Academy; Mt. Pleasant, North Carolina College, Female Seminary.

Nine institutions, with 37 professors and 685 students. Eight institutions report property worth $63,000.

Ohio	Augsburg	1	1	1,685	$	$	88	1	450
	Augustana	3	5	313	15,500	8,115	126		
	East Ohio	35	74	5,760	441,500	31,500	5,711	68	7,140
	Immanuel	5	5	1,750					
	Iowa, (Ger.) { Including part of Michigan	18	63	8,032		32,354		11*	}
	Miami	27	40	3,716	260,000	27,780	7,382	45	4,886
	Missouri	43	54	16,027	820,000	54,000		45*	4,461
	Norwegian Ch.	1	6	250					
	Ohio, (District)	29	66	7,863	263,750	35,049	2,116	56	6,613
	Ohio, (Joint)	81	124	17,610					
	Pittsburg(G.C.)	12	27	1,830					
	Wartburg	3	1	90					
	Wittenberg	40	71	7,274	363,350	57,208	10,208	64	7,924
	Other	6							
	Total	304	537	72,200					

At Columbus there is Capital University, Theological Seminary; Springfield, Wittenberg College, Theological Seminary; Woodville, Teachers' Seminary; Lima, Co-Educational Institute being established.

In all, five institutions, with property worth $450,000; 32 professors and 600 students.

At Toledo there is a German Evangelical Lutheran Orphans' Home. Property worth $20,000, 2 teachers and 47 inmates.

Oklahoma,—Missouri, 1 congregation, 12 communicants.

Oregon	Augustana	2	6	436	$ 12,570	$ 1,870	172	1* 2	65
	Danish Ch.	1	2	40					
	G. C. Mission	1	1						
	Missouri	5	7	330	16,000	4,900		20*	
	Norweg. Ch.	1	1	50					
	Ohio, (Joint,)	1							
	Un. Norweg.	1	1						
	Other	2							
	Total	14	18	868					

IN THE UNITED STATES.

State	Synods.	Pastors.	Cong.	Communicants.	Value of Church Property.	Yearly Expenses.	For Beneficence.	S.&Par.Sch's Sch's	Pupils.
	Allegheny,......	59	132	12,162	$ 443,350	$ 70,259	13,802	133 16*	13,417 514
	Augustana,......	21	31	3,536	146,900	29,088	1,847	26	1,142
	Central Penn...	38	84	7,882	380,000	34,740	6,183	93	9,300
	East. Penn......	74	108	16,939	1,272,500	181,500	27,000	113	21,535
	Immanuel,......	4	4	1,500					
Pennsylvania.	Maryland,......	7	2	488	5,200	455	....	1 17*	84 1,398
	Minis. of Penn.	261	426	100,891	....	462,057	55,366	497	81,045
	Missouri,.........	17	26	6,552	430,000	31,200	....	17*	1,437
	Ohio, (Joint,)...	20	28	4,924					
	Pittsburg, G.C.	94	155	16,447	955,550	....	61,403	168	14,963
	Pittsburg, G. S.	40	75	7,425	273,785	46,482	8,038	64	6,445
	Susquehanna,..	43	68	9,273	449,950	57,096	9,487	71	11,324
	West. Penn.,...	81	126	21,633	902,900	97,951	27,934	135	20,538
	Other,............	8	1	40					
	Total,.........	767	1,266	209,692					

At Allentown there is Muhlenburg College; Gettysburg, Pennsylvania College, Theological Seminary of the General Synod; Greenville, Thiel College; Greensburg, Greensburg Academy; Mechanicsburg, Irving Female College; Philadelphia, West Green Street Institute, Theol. Seminary of the General Council, Deaconess School for Girls; Selinsgrove, Missionary Institute, Classical Institute.

In all, eleven institutions, with property and endowment amounting to $1,230,000; eighty-six professors, 1,070 students, and 70,000 volumes in their libraries.

At Delano there is Concordia Orphans' Home, and Home for Aged; Germantown, Orphans' Home and Home for Aged and Infirm; Loysville, Orphans' Home; Middletown, Emaus' Orphans' Home; Philadelphia, Drexel Deaconess Home, and Home for Aged, Children's Hospital, and care of German Hospital; Pittsburg, Deaconess Infirmary; Rochester, Orphans' Home for Girls; Zelienople, Orphans' Home for Boys.

In all, thirteen institutions, with property worth $742,000; ninety-five teachers and helpers, and over 700 inmates; or, if the patients cared for by the deaconesses in the German Hospital (1,900 yearly) be added, the number exceeds 2,600 each year.

State	Synods	Past.	Cong.	Commun.	Church Prop.	Yearly Exp.	Benef.	Sch's	Pupils
Rhode Isl.	August., Swed.	1	3	422	$ 6,200	$ 2,550	226	2* 1	50 46
	Missouri,.........				......			1*	
	Norweg. Ch....		1	120					
	Total,.........	1	4	542					

State	Synods	Pastors	Cong.	Communicants	Value of Church Property	Yearly Expenses	For Benefience	S. &Par.Sch's Sch's	Pupils
S. Carolina	S. Carolina,	33	58	6,572	$ 268,200	$ 30,530	$4,219	60	4,969
	Tennessee,	5	12	2,000	13,600	1,260	581	12	731
	Pastors of other Synods,	2	No charges.						
	Total,	40	70	8,572					

At Leesville there is an English and Classical Institute; Newberry, College, and Theological Seminary.

Four institutions, with property worth about $70,000; fourteen professors and 218 students. Funds are being gathered to establish a Hospital and a Home for the Aged, in Charleston.

Tennessee	Holston	10	1 † 28	2,152	$ 38,800	$ 2,615		12	217
	Missouri	3	3	269	12,000	1,800	59	2	69
	Middle Tenn...	10	11	930	29,750	2,411	93	8	586
	Past's oth'r syn	2	No charges.						
	Total	25	42	3,351					

Institutions for higher education exist at Mill Point and Mosheim, with property worth $3,500, seven professors and 200 students.

Texas	Augustana	3	4	592	$ 22,250	$ 5,136	630	4* 4	95 200
	Missouri	24	31	3,702	72,000	21,700		18*	844
	Norweg. Ch...	1	4	326					
	Texas	2?	55	7,711			2,018	6* 26	248 1,500
	Others	4							
	Total	59	94	12,831					

Utah	Augustana, Sw.	2	2	99	$ 35,000	$ 795		1* 2	24 38
	G. C. Mission...	1	1						
	Danish Church	1	2	22					
	Icelanders	1	2	40					
		5	7	161					

The Swedes have an academy in Salt Lake City, with three professors and 31 students.

Virginia	Maryland	1	3	375	$	$			
	Missouri	2	3	270	30,000	3,000		2*	47
	Ohio, (Joint)	1	3	159					
	Tennessee	11	34	3,000	55,350	1,600	425	11	501
	Virginia	21	54	3,668	155,900	16,904	2,556	54	3,987
	S. W. Virginia	34	56	3,907	105,685	12,400	4,133	54	3,908
	Other	3							
	Total	73	153	11,379					

At Graham there is Wartburg Seminary; Luray, Von Bora College; Marion, Marion Female College; Salem, Roanoke College; Staunton, Staunton Female Seminary; Wytheville, Trinity Hall.

Six institutions, with property worth $300,000, 50 professors and 519 students. The South View Orphans' Home, at Salem, has a $10,000 property, three teachers and helpers and twenty orphans.

State's	Synods.	Pastors.	Cong.	Communicants.	Value of Church Property.	Yearly Expenses.	For Beneficence.	S.&Par.Sch's Sch's	Pupils.
Washington	Augustana	5	7	406	$ 41,500	$ 2,660	182	2	60
	G. C. Mission	1	1						
	Hauge	1	?	?					
	Iowa, (Ger.,)	5							
	Missouri	1	1	48					
	Norweg. Ch	1	1	40					
	Ohio, (Joint,)	5	4	120					
	Un. Norwegian	6	8	425					
	Other	5							
	Total	25	22	1,039					

The Swedes have an Orphans' Home, with 40 acres of land attached, near Tacoma. The Norwegians are establishing the Pacific Lutheran University near the same place.

	Synods.	Pastors.	Cong.	Communicants.	Value of Church Property.	Yearly Expenses.	For Beneficence.	S.&Par.Sch's Sch's	Pupils.
West Virginia	Maryland	3	7	956	$ 42,000	$ 3,018	560	3	633
	Missouri Eng.	1	1	30					
	Ohio, (Joint,)	9	18	1,245					
	Pittsburg, G. C.	1	1	500					
	Pittsburg, G. S.	1	1	272	25,000	2,403	496	1	481
	Virginia	7	22	1,458	35,400	3,248	609	14	1,544
	Other	2							
	Total	24	50	4,461					
Wisconsin	Augustana	12	38	3,674	$ 48,125	$ 12,830	1,148	7* 19	272 809
	Augsburg	9	12	2,022			63	6* 7	625
	Buffalo	5	7	1,322					
	Danish Asso'n	2	4	200					
	Danish Church	7	38	1,384					
	Hauge	8	28	1,660					
	Iowa, (Ger.,)	28	62	7,380		32,427		6*	
	Missouri	109	190	39,315	1,860,000	171,000		108*	8,943
	Minnesota	1	2	110					
	Northern Ill	2	7	371	19,050	2,146	138	2	148
	Norweg. Ch	35	125	14,017					
	Ohio, (Joint,)	21	38	4,911					
	Wartburg	2	4	334					
	Wisconsin	135	223	66,494			21,003	162* 103	
	Un. Norwegian	46	121	19,000					
	Total	422	899	162,649					

At Milwaukee there is a Theological Seminary and Concordia College; West Denmark, Danish Seminary, Theological and Practical; Watertown, North-Western University; Wittenberg, Indian Mission School and Norwegian Normal School; Stoughton, Academy.

In all, seven institutions. Six of them report property worth $191,000; thirty-four professors, and 649 students.

At Madison there is a Norwegian Orphans' Home; Milwaukee, Deaconess Hospital; Wittenberg, Orphans' Home, Missouri Synod; Orphans' Home, United Norwegian Synod.

Three of these institutions report property worth $201,000, and have fourteen teachers and helpers. The four, last year, had 651 inmates. The Danes, also, have opened a Hospital in Racine, in charge of deaconesses; but, while some Lutherans are in the Board of Directors, the institution is not under control of the Church.

Wyoming,—Nebraska, 2 pastors, 3 congregations, 119 communicants.

Stat's	Synods.	Pastors.	Cong.	Communicants.	Value of Church Property.	Yearly Expenses.	For Benefi- cence.	S.& Par.Sch's Sch's	Pupils.
	Buffalo,	2	4	600				18*	
Canada.‡	Canada,	38	81	8,800		$ 27,095	$2,875	63	3,425
	Icelandic,	2	10	1,845				10	300
	Minist. of N.Y.	2	2	366				2	180
	Missouri,	19	40	5,155	$ 96,000			24*	1,063
	Norweg. Ch. ...		2	80					
	Pittsburg, G.C.	6	19	2,307					
	Pittsburg, G.S.	1	1	16					
	G. C. Missions,	4							
	Total,	74	159	19,169					

‡ Including Assiniboia, Manitoba, Nova Scotia, Quebec and Winnipeg.

IN OTHER LANDS.

Br. Guiana, East Pa.	1	1	195	$ 46,400	$ 1,420		2	222

Africa,..............Franckean,.. 1 pastor.
.................New York and New Jersey, ... 1 "
Denmark,...........Missouri,.. 1 "
India,................Different Synods,..................................... 6 "
Germany,..........Different Synods,.....................................20 "
Australia,...........Missouri,.. 1 "
Madagascar,.......United Norwegian,................................. 2 "

SUMMARY FOR UNITED STATES.

General Body.	District Synods.	Pastors.	Congresses.	Communicants.	Educational Institutions.	Institutions of Beneficence.
1891.						
General Synod................	16	1,000	1,436	157,845	15	7
General Council............	9	1,256	2,108	325,453	16	39
Syn. Conference.	4	1,367	1,991	396,134	15	18
Un. Synod......................	9	199	414	36,271	21	2
Independent Synods.........	13	1,004	2,399	254,201	42	22
Independent Pastors, &c		70	80	14,000		
We have for 1892..........ca.	61	5,028	8,400	1,188,854	109	88
To this, add.................ca.			1,500	preaching	places	

GROWTH OF LUTHERAN CHURCH IN THE UNITED STATES BY DECADES.

Year.	Pastors.	Congresses.	Communicants.	Increase per cent.
1820...	170	850	35,000	
1830...	300	1,000	55,000	57
1840...	400	1,200	120,000	118
1850...	757	1,624	143,543	19
1860...	1,134	2,017	235,000	62
1870...	1,933	3,417	387,746	64
1880...	3,092	5,388	694,426	75
1890...	4,830	8,200	1,153,212	66

Increase from 1820 to 1890, 3,200 per cent.

LUTHERANS IN THE WORLD.

I. EUROPE.

LAND.	Pastors.	Churches.	Members.
1. AUSTRO-HUNGARY: Hungary,	630	*630	1,125,000
Transylvania			211,000
Other Parts,	150	523	290,000
2. DENMARK:	1,960	2,000	2,150,000
Iceland,	180	299	72,400
Faroe Islands,	22	22	11,200
Danish West Indies,	(In N. A	merica.)	
3. GERMANY: Alsace-Lorraine,	254	222	254,000
Anhalt,			205,000
Baden,			450,000
Bavaria,			1,668,000
Brunswick,			360,000
Bremen,			110,000
Hamburg,			560,000
Heligoland,			2,000
Hesse,			470,000
Lippe,			5,000
Luebeck,	22	15	66,000
Mecklenburg-Sch.			575,000
Mecklenburg-Str.			110,000
Oldenburg,			260,000
Prussia,			17,367,000
Saxony,			3,100,000
Thuringia,			1,260,000
Waldeck,			55,000
Würtemberg,			1,395,000
Total in Germany,	15,550	20,450	28,272,000
France,	124	95	90,000
Great Britain,	24	27	24,000
Holland,	68	58	72,000
Italy,	11	11	6,000
Lapland,			17,500
Norway,	869	960	2,000,000
Rumania and Servia,	12	12	7,600
RUSSIA: Finland,	800	1,002	2,070,000
Poland,	72	104	300,000
Other Parts,	564	1,138	2,678,000
Sweden	2,550	2,500	4,770,000
Total in Europe,	23,586	30,051	44,165,000

* Also, 320 chapels.

II. ASIA.

LAND.	Pastors.	Churches.	Members.
Asiatic Russia,...	18	18	12,000
China,	61	20	5,500
India,	183	96	89,100
Palestine,	16	9	700
Black Sea and Orient,	12	12	5,700
Total in Asia,	290	155	113,000

III. AFRICA.

North—Egypt,	2	2	1,000
East,	12	6	100
South, Missions,	251	175	63,550
South, Colonists,	19	26	22,200
West Coast and Congo,	87	40 ?	10,126
Madagascar,	43	300	26,000
Total in Africa,	414	549	122,976

IV. AMERICA.

United States and Canada,	5,028	8,328	7,000,000
Greenland,	15	12	8,000
West Indies,	3	4	4,800
Argentine Republic, Brazil, Chili and Uruguay, S. A.	50	64	95,000
Total in America,	5,096	8,408	7,107,800

V. OCEANICA.

Australia, Colonists,	80	275	75,000
Australia, Missions,	14	8	290
New Zealand and Hawaii Islands,	14	14	13,100
Borneo, Sumatra, Nias,	27	22	14,950
New Guinea, Samoa and Fejee Islands,	6	3	360
Total in Oceanica,	141	322	103,700

SUMMARY.

Total in Europe,	23,586	30,051	44,165,000
Total in Asia,	290	155	113,000
Total in Africa,	414	549	122,976
Total in America,	5,096	8,408	7,107,800
Total in Oceanica,	141	322	103,700
Total in the World,	29,527	39,485	51,612,476

· ✢ · THE · ✢ ·
LUTHERAN EVANGELIST

16 PAGES.

Only $1.50 per Year, in Advance.

Vigorous,

Progressive,

Complete.

READ the *Evangelist* and you will keep abreast of the best thought and freshest news, not only of General Synod Lutheranism, but of all Christendom.

Send for free sample copy and premium supplement.

The Hosterman Publishing Co.,

SPRINGFIELD, O.

"The Envelope System"

OF GATHERING
CHURCH OFFERINGS.

For Envelopes, Record of Offerings, and all helps to the efficiency of the system, write to the

GOODENOUGH & WOGLOM COMPANY,
122 Nassau Street, NEW YORK.

HOOK & HASTINGS,
(F. H. HASTINGS.)

Church Organ Builders

ESTABLISHED 1827.
MAIN OFFICE AND WORKS AT KENDAL GREEN, MASS. (FITCHBURG RR.)
Boston Office, 10 Tremont St.
New York Office, 145 E. 23d St.

KENDAL GREEN, MASS.

YOUNG LUTHERAN CO.
UTICA, N. Y.

publishes The

"Hand-Book of Lutheranism,"
PRICE $1.50,
and

"THE YOUNG LUTHERAN,"

A sixteen page out-and-out Lutheran monthly, with a circulation exceeding that of all other English Lutheran Church papers combined. Samples free.

L. C. CHILDS & SON,

PRINTERS, BINDERS *MAKERS OF* FINE BLANK BOOKS,

33-35 CHARLOTTE STREET,

SPECIALTIES: (PRINTERS OF THIS BOOK.)
BOOKS, SERMONS,
ILLUSTRATED CATALOGUES,   (*Established* 1862.)   UTICA, N. Y.
SPECIAL RULED BOOKS.

J. & R. LAMB,

59 Carmine St., NEW YORK.

CHURCH FURNITURE.	STAINED GLASS.
CHURCH DECORATION.	MARBLE AND MOSAIC.

All questions in regard to the Church Interior answered. Illustrated Hand-books free.

The Lutheran Augustana Book Concern.

Owned and Controlled by the Augustana Synod.

Publishers, Book-Sellers, Importers, Job Printers.

PUBLISHERS OF

THE OLIVE LEAF. A CHRISTIAN MONTHLY PAPER for Sunday schools and families, specially adapted for children and young people. Attractively illustrated. Price 30 cents a year—$15 per hundred. Any number over 5 to one address at 100 rate.

THE LUTHERAN AUGUSTANA BOOK CONCERN,
Rock Island, Ill.

SPERRY & BEALE,

83 White Street, ... NEW YORK.

MANUFACTURERS OF

= ELASTIC FELT CHURCH CUSHIONS. =

IMPORTERS OF

Worsted Damasks

Write us for samples and prices.

THE VOCALION.

(Church Organ.) It is undistinguishable in tone from a pipe organ except that it has a sympathetic quality not obtained from pipes. It does not occupy one fourth the space or cost one-half the price of a pipe organ of equal capacity.

For full particulars write the Manufacturers,

MASON & RESCH,

10 E. 16th Street,	5-15 Summer Street,
NEW YORK.	WORCESTER, MASS.

THE
Lutheran Observer.

PUBLISHED WEEKLY
.. AT ..
524 Walnut Street, Philadelphia.

Rev. F. W. CONRAD, D. D., LL. D., Editor.

Prof. V. L. CONRAD, D. D., } Associate Editors.
Rev. SYLVANUS STALL, A. M., }

With a Large Number of Able and Popular Writers as Contributors.

The Lutheran Observer
.. is ..

The Oldest,
    The Largest,
        Most Widely Circulated, and
            Most Influential Weekly

OF THE LUTHERAN CHURCH IN THE UNITED STATES.

Terms Cash in Advance.

One Copy per annum, including Postage, - - - - - $2.00
One Copy six months, - - - - - - - - - 1.00
On Trial, for three months, - - - - - - .50

THE WAY OF
Salvation in the Lutheran Church

By REV. G. H. GERBERDING.

Written for the Common People. Eleventh Thousand.

"The most successful book ever issued by our Board."—*Report at General Synod.*

"It is not often that we have the privilege of examining so admirable a book as this one."—*Dr. Schmucker, in The Lutheran.*

"Thoroughly Scriptural, and presents the essential truths of the Gospel and the design and character of the means of Grace in systematic order."—*Lutheran Observer.*

"The Doctrine is sound as well as clear."—*Dr. Loy, in Lutheran Standard.*

"We wonder at the beauty and completeness of this way of salvation. So lucid in its arrangement, so strong in its teaching and withal so eminently fair in its positions."—*The Workman.*

"It unfolds, in plain language, how a sinner is made a saint, according to the teachings of the Lutheran Church."—*Lutheran Visitor.*

"One of the best, if not the best, work we have ever read on the subjects treated. We hail its appearance with joy."—*Our Church Paper.*

"Creditable both to the head and heart of the author."—*Foreign Missionary.*

"A precious book."—*Rev. C. Spielman.*

"Refreshing and popular."—*Rev. T. B. Roth.*

"It can be safely recommended for the widest distribution among the people. In its sphere, it can scarcely be surpassed."—*Dr. Jacobs, in Church Review.*

"There is a wide-spread need for just such a work"—*Lutheran Quarterly.*

Highly recommended by the most prominent ministers in all parts and languages of our Church. Pages 240. **Price $1.00.**

New Testament Conversions.

BY THE SAME AUTHOR.

"These plain, pungent sermons show great practical acquaintance with the human heart, under the operation of divine truth. An exceptionally good collection to be placed in the hands of young converts."—*The Independent.*

"We hope that this book may help to counteract the popular mistakes on this matter of conversion, and be instrumental in turning many from the error of their ways."—*The Living Church.*

"We find very much sound teaching on the nature and necessity of the new birth, while Christ is kept the central and foremost figure, and the work of the Holy Spirit is magnified above all."—*The Northwestern Congregationalist.*

"We judge from this book that the author is an eloquent and persuasive preacher, for these sermons are productions of real power."—*The Interior.*

"Our Church needs scores of just such works."—*Lutheran Standard.*

"It impresses a conviction that the Lutheran teaching on conversion is Scriptural. Very pointed in its applications. Not one sermon is dull or devoid of life"—*The Lutheran.*

"A valuable book to correct erroneous views on conversion."—*The Lutheran Observer.*

"A graphic picturing of facts, illustrating how the people of the first century got religion."—*The Workman.*

"A book for the people. The entire treatment is such as to reach the heart."—*The Church Review.*

Heartily commended by Drs. Rhodes, Loy, Jacobs, Stellhorn, Miller and a host of others from all parts of the Church. Pages 283. **Price $1.00.**

Discount to clergy. Agents wanted. Liberal terms.

Send orders to

REV. G. H. GERBERDING,
FARGO, NORTH DAKOTA.

Christian Art Institute.

R. GEISSLER,
52 and 54 LaFayette Place,   NEW YORK.

 FURNITURE,
DECORATION,
MARBLE WORK,
STAINED GLASS.
—— Send for Descriptive Circular. ——

Established 1862.

A. B. FELGEMAKER,
Church Organs,

ERIE, PA.

New Factory, 157, 159, 161, 163 W. 19th St.

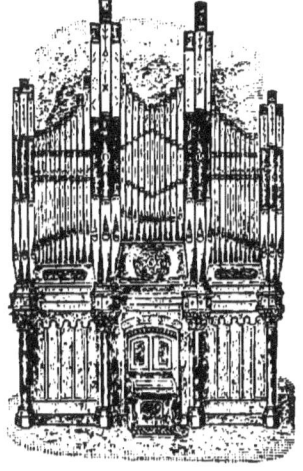

ALL Modern Improvements, Musical and Mechanical.

Correspondence INVITED from Clergymen, Organists, and Church Music Committees.

Descriptive Catalogues furnished on application.

WATER MOTORS,
for blowing Organs, furnished.

Wartburg Publishing House

of the Evangelical Lutheran Synod of Iowa and other States,

PAULUS LIST, Manager.   WAVERLY, IOWA.

——PUBLISHERS OF——

Kirchenblatt, circulation, ... 4,000
Blaetter aus den Waisenhaeusern, ... 6,000
Kirchliche Zeitschrift, ... 500
Wartburg Kalendar, ... 6,000

and books for church, school and family. Write for Catalogue.

Valuable Ecclesiological Manuals.

—BY—

EDWARD T. HORN, D. D.,

CHARLESTON, S. C.

Outlines of Liturgics.

Cloth, 150 pp.

CONTENTS: Definition of Liturgics; the Nature and Essence of Christian Worship; Relation of Worship to Art; Sacred Seasons and Places; The Sacramental and the Sacrificial Acts in Christian Worship; History of the Development of the Christian Liturgy; Matins and Vespers; History and Literature of Liturgics; Index.

Price, post-paid, 50c.

The Evangelical Pastor.

A Summary in English of Dr. Walther's Pastorale.

Cloth, 256 pp. **Price $1.00.**

CONTENTS: Preface (*on the Lutheran idea of Pastorale*); The Pastor's Conversation; The Call; The Beginning of the Pastorate; The Pastor's Preaching; Holy Baptism; Preparation for the Holy Sacrament; The Holy Supper; Marriage; Confirmation and Catechisation; Seelsorge; House Visitations; Visitation of the Sick, etc.; The Dying and the Dead; Discipline; Sunday Schools, Collections, etc.; In the Community and the Home; The End of the Pastorate; Indexes.

The Christian Year.

Cloth, 95 pp. **Price, $1.00.**

CONTENTS: The Origin of the Church Year; The Christian Year as a whole, and different conceptions of it (in the Greek, Roman, Lutheran and Anglican Church); The Advantages which some find in this Peculiar Division of Time.

Church Pews,

CUSHIONS, PULPITS,
PULPIT CHAIRS,
COMMUNION TABLES.

Altar Railings, Altars, Litany Desks, Confessionals.

And everything in the line of church furnishings.

NEW AND MATCHLESS

GLOBE DESKS.

Globes, Maps, Blackboards, Charts,
Dictionaries, Bells, Clocks, Crayons,
Erasers Numeral Frames,

And every article used in the school.

GLOBE FURNITURE COMPANY,
NORTHVILLE, MICH

MASON & HAMLIN ORGANS.

THE CABINET ORGAN was introduced by MASON & HAMLIN in 1861. Mason & Hamlin Organs have always maintained their supremacy over all others, having received Highest Honors at all the Great World's Exhibitions since 1867.

The Liszt Organs,

(Styles 501, 503, 514, 520, 901, etc.) As compared with the smaller sized pipe organs these instruments at least equal them in power and quality of tone, and greatly surpass them in variety, proportion, vivacity, and adaptedness to secular as well as sacred music; while they occupy but small space, and are furnished in plain or elegant cases, forming a chief ornament for any position, *at a fraction of the cost of pipe organs*. Also, Styles having **One, Two** or **Three Manuals**, and **Ten** to **Thirty-two Stops**, some with **Full Pedal Base**, at **$200** to **$900**. These Organs are adapted not only to popular, but especially to artistic use, so that it may be said that the more cultivated the musician the more certain is his appreciation of them.

"Matchless, unrivalled."—*Franz Liszt.*

LISZT ORGAN.   "Musicians generally regard them as unequalled."—*Theo. Thomas.*

Furnished with or without Pipe Top.

USED AND ENDORSED BY

DR. STAINER,   GEO. W. MORGAN,   DUDLEY BUCK,
FRED. ARCHER, GEO. W. WARREN, S. P. WARREN, S. B WHITNEY,

AND BEST ORGANISTS EVERYWHERE.

Other Styles, $22, $32.50, $60, $78, $96, $105 and up.

MASON & HAMLIN ORGAN AND PIANO CO.
BOSTON.   **NEW YORK.**   **CHICAGO.**

www.ingramcontent.com/pod-product-compliance
Lightning Source LLC
Chambersburg PA
CBHW051234300426
44114CB00011B/728